INSIDE REAL ESTATE

ALSO BY GRACE LICHTENSTEIN

Machisma: Women and Daring
Desperado
A Long Way, Baby

The INSIDE
Complete Guide
to Buying and Selling Your Home,
Co-op or Condominium

REAL ESTATE

by
H. I. Sonny Bloch and
Grace Lichtenstein

Grove Weidenfeld
New York

The comments, observations and recommendations in this book are the opinions of the authors, and are based on Sonny Bloch's twenty-five years in the real estate and development business. Any decisions made by the reader that could have any financial consequences should be reviewed and approved by the reader's attorney and accountant prior to the application of the principles stated here.

Copyright © 1987 by H. I. Sonny Bloch and Grace Lichtenstein

Published by Grove Weidenfeld
A division of Wheatland Corporation
841 Broadway
New York, NY 10003-4793

Library of Congress Cataloging-in-Publication Data

Bloch, H. I.
  Inside real estate.

  1. Real estate business. 2. House buying.
3. House selling. 4. Condominiums. 5. Apartment
houses, Cooperative. I. Lichtenstein, Grace.
II. Title.
HD1379.B515   1987   333.33'8   86-28303
ISBN 1-55584-320-4 (pbk.)

Manufactured in the United States of America

Printed on acid-free paper

Designed by Irving Perkins Associates

First Weidenfeld & Nicolson Edition 1987

First Evergreen Edition 1989

10 9 8 7 6 5 4 3 2 1

Acknowledgments

From Sonny Bloch:
A special thank you to Grace, who introduced me to the worlds of publishing and baseball.

I want to thank my radio and TV friends, the people who listen to me, watch me and ask the hard questions that are the substance of this book.

I am grateful to all the authors and seminar givers whose books and seminars I critiqued on the air. Here is your chance to do the same to mine.

I owe a major debt to my radio and TV producers, Gale B. Nemec and Michael Castello, who had to make impossible schedule changes to allow me the time to write this book.

In addition, my thanks to Professional Publishing, the National Association of Homebuilders, the National Association of Realtors, the American Institute of Mortgage Brokers, Housemaster, Cardinal Industries, the American Resort and Residential Development Association, the Land Development Institute, the National TimeSharing Council, and to Ron Taft, Howard Bloch, Pauline Bloch, Harriett Fuller, Ivan Bloch, Stuart Bloch, and Steve Kahn.

From Grace Lichtenstein:
Many thanks to my writers' group for its encouragement, to Judith Vladeck for lodging and especially to Janice Goodman. For continuing inspiration, I am indebted to Aretha, Jackson Browne, Lenny and the Mets.

Both authors wish to thank their agent, Charlotte Sheedy, for her untiring labors on their behalf; Constance Sayre and Betty Lee of Weidenfeld & Nicolson; Anna Jardine, the copy editor; and, above all, Dan Green, a splendidly attentive editor and publisher.

To my family, friends, business associates and colleagues who for the past ten years have said to me, "Why don't you write a book?"

—HISB

To Dorothy Degen Rosenthal and Tillie Fein

—GL

Contents

Part III. Selling 241

PART I

Introduction—How to Use This Book

This book is about one of your most important rights, something that touches your life every day. You live in it, ride on it, work on it, have fun on it, walk through the park on it. It is called real estate. Look around; real estate is everywhere. It touches you.

For most of you, real estate first and foremost means a home. That home probably is the most important, most expensive purchase you will ever make. Yet nearly everyone is an amateur when it comes to its purchase and sale.

As a professional, my role is to demystify buying and selling a home for you. That is the purpose of this book.

Today is as good a day as any to find the home you have been dreaming about. Maybe you have recently agreed to buy or sell and are concerned about the closing. Perhaps you are thinking about refinancing your current home or buying a recreation property. Is time sharing on your mind? Considering moving from the home you are in because people are making tremendous offers on it? Having problems getting equity out of your home? Wondering about how good modular housing is? This book answers your questions.

Many people do not wait for the best time to buy or sell their home. They do it when they *think* they have to—when they are about to move, or when their family is about to expand, or when they feel flush because of a raise. I can save you thousands of dollars by teaching you the virtue of waiting. I will show you how to track economic indicators so you will buy or sell at the *right* moment, not the expedient moment. And I can explain how the new tax law affects your situation.

I look forward to sharing my twenty-five years of experience as buyer, seller and real estate professional. I harp on things that may seem obvious but are not. For instance, I believe that whether you are buying or selling a home, condo, co-op, vacation place or time share, your best

3

barometer of a community is the people who live there. I teach you how to play "inquiring reporter" in every place you shop, to ask tough but fair questions.

To begin: Below you will find "road maps" to the information on buying and selling contained in the book. They show how to use these pages, and what your opposite number—the buyer or the seller—is doing as you follow the express route to your new home. The timetable will likewise give you step-by-step guidance along the way.

Now you are in the driver's seat. With this book's help, you are going to have a wonderful trip.

One final note: The comments, observations and recommendations in this book are the opinions of the authors, and are based on my twenty-five years in the real estate and development business. Any decisions made by the reader that could have any financial consequences should be reviewed and approved by the reader's attorney and accountant prior to the application of the principles stated here.

H. I. Sonny Bloch

ROAD MAP

Buyer	Chapter	Seller	Chapter
How to find a house that you like and can afford	1	Getting your house ready for the sale	18
How to find the best real estate agent for your purchase	2	Do you need a real estate broker to sell your house?	20, 21
How to choose a real estate attorney to help you buy	3	Can a real estate attorney help you sell your house?	22
Are you paying too much?	4	How much is your house worth?	19
When is the best time for you to buy?	5	Should you sell before or after you find a new house?	28
How to negotiate the deal successfully	6	Strategies for playing the negotiating game	24
Where to find the money to finance the purchase	7	Should you help your buyer with financing?	25
How to reach the finish line (the closing) without detours	9	Arriving safely at the closing	26

BACK ROADS

Buyer	*Chapter*	*Seller*	*Chapter*
How to benefit from the new tax reforms	28	How to benefit from the new tax reforms	28
Is the lease with option to purchase your best bet?	8	How you can use the lease with option to purchase as a selling tool	8
Buying a condominium, as either a first or a second home	13	Trading your home when you cannot sell it	27
Buying a co-op apartment	14		
Buying vacation property	15		
Choosing a time share	16		
Building your custom home	11		
Should you buy a modular home?	12		
Should you renovate a "fixer-upper"?	10		
How to buy home insurance	17		

BUYER AND SELLER TIMETABLE

When You Are the Buyer	*When You Are the Seller*

1. Make the decision: "I am going to buy a home"
    Who is involved: you
	1. Make the decision: "I am going to sell"
	    Who is involved: you

2. Assemble your team
    You and your real estate attorney
	2. Assemble your team
	    You and your real estate attorney

3. Find your Geographic Comfort Zone
    You
	3. Sign a listing agreement
	    You, attorney, licensed real estate broker

4. Find your Financial Comfort Zone
    You and your certified public accountant
	4. Review purchase offers
	    You, attorney, broker

5. Shop for a house, co-op, condominium
    You and a licensed real estate broker
	5. Accept one offer
	    You, attorney, broker

6. Make an offer on a property
    You and broker
	6. Set closing date
	    You, banker, attorney, broker

7. Get your offer accepted
    Broker and seller
	7. Close and move out
	    You, banker, attorney, broker, buyer

8. Proceed with inspections Professional home inspector	
9. Seek financing (at same time as 8) You and a banker	
10. Set closing date You, attorney, banker, broker	
11. Close and move in You, banker, broker, attorney, seller	

PART II

Buying Your Home, Condo, Co-op or Vacation Property

Chapter 1

Your Comfort Zone—How to Establish Your Profile as a Buyer

You want to buy a home. But where? In the heart of a city, in the suburbs or in a rural area? Do you want a log cabin or a sophisticated penthouse? Can you afford it?

In order to be an efficient house-hunter, you need to determine what I like to call your "Comfort Zone"—the range of homes, locales and costs that will allow you to sleep at night.

Finding your Comfort Zone is not unlike choosing the right outfit for a special occasion. Homes come in different styles, prices, colors. The key is pinpointing the appropriate home for your lifestyle. To do that, you need to put yourself through a quiz.

First, a general question for you to mull over: why do I want to leave the place I am living in now? Many of my listeners call with the thought of moving from their present home. By the time our conversation is over, they are convinced they should not move in the first place.

It is *not* a terrific idea to move just because you think you can make money on your current home. How are you going to replace your present level of comfort? How much will it cost? Is it worth the effort? If your home or apartment has increased in value, chances are the homes you will visit in search of a possible replacement have also gone up. Weigh the pros and cons of a move before you start house hunting.

The flip side is never, *never* buy a home just because you think it is a good deal. The primary search is for a place you like, not one on which mortgage payments are low.

On the other hand, if you have been renting an apartment for ten years, paying $1,000 a month, or $12,000 a year, in rent, you have spent $120,000. What have you got to show for it? Rent receipts. You could paper the walls with rent receipts if they were more attractive than they are, but other than that they do not do you much good. That is a pretty good reason to buy.

Now we come to a series of questions to define your Comfort Zone.

HOW COSTLY A HOUSE CAN YOU AFFORD?

The first question is this: what is my monthly *Financial* Comfort Zone?

Unless you are in financial trouble, you know you can spend at least as much as you are now paying for rent, maintenance or mortgage. Put that number in the appropriate blank on the Financial Comfort Zone Worksheet at the end of this chapter.

Next, *tally your monthly expenses:* food, clothing, utilities (heating, fuel, water, electricity, telephone), taxes (property, school) insurance (home, health, life), auto payments, savings, entertainment, laundry, credit card payments.

Deduct from this number your *total monthly take-home income.* Then deduct a minimum of 10 percent from your take-home pay as an additional safety cushion. If you are not now a homeowner, some of this money will be spent during the year on such items as lawn care, a home insurance policy that is likely to be higher than your renter's policy, repairs (electricity, plumbing, painting) and perhaps higher taxes.

If there is money left over, it can be added to your present monthly housing payment. That is how to determine how much you can afford each month on a mortgage.

The old rule of thumb, which held that you should not spend more than 20 percent of your income for housing, or not more than 28 percent of your take-home pay, is not applicable to present-day standards. Most families would rather cut back on other things in order to have better housing. My formula, which you can figure for yourself on the worksheet, will not put you in the poorhouse and is still within almost anyone's Comfort Zone. Glance at the chart on page 13, for a rough idea.

Here is an example. You are a couple, in your thirties, living in Denver. You both work and maintain separate apartments. You are

WHAT HOUSE CAN YOU AFFORD?

If yearly income is:	*You can get mortgage of:*	*With down payment of:*	*On house priced in this range:*
$30,000	$55,000– $65,000	$5,500– $6,500	$55,000– $65,000
$35,000	$75,000– $85,000	$7,500– $8,500	$75,000– $85,000
$40,000	$95,000–$105,000	$9,500–$10,500	$95,000–$105,000
$45,000	$110,000–$120,000	$11,000–$12,000	$110,000–$120,000
$50,000	$125,000–$150,000	$12,000–$15,000	$125,000–$150,000
$75,000	$210,000–$225,000	$21,000–$22,500	$210,000–$225,000
$100,000	$250,000–$275,000	$25,000–$27,500	$250,000–$275,000
$150,000 and over	$425,000–$450,000	$42,500–$45,000	$425,000–$450,000

about to start living together or about to get married, and you want to buy a home. The two of you pay rent to the tune of $500 a month each.

Your combined income is $80,000, meaning $50,000 in take-home pay. Your total monthly expenses amount to $500 a week, or about $2,000 a month, or roughly $26,000 a year. That leaves $24,000.

By subtracting 10 percent ($5,000) for safety from your take-home pay, leaving $19,000, you have roughly $1,500 a month left over to add to your current $1,000-a-month rent. That is $2,500 a month you can afford for mortgage payments.

Let us translate these monthly payments into the price of the house you can afford. It is done with an amortization schedule, which shows monthly payments in terms of different interest rates. There are amortization tables in the back of the book.

The basic rule is that for every $100,000 that you borrow at 12 percent, your monthly payment is 1 percent of $100,000. So if you have $1,000 a month to spend, you can afford a $100,000 mortgage. If you are like the Denver couple, you have $2,500 a month to spend at 12 percent, so you can afford a $250,000 mortgage.

Add to the size of the mortgage you can carry 10 to 20 percent for a down payment. That will give you the price range of your house. (We will talk later about financing both down payment and monthly payments.) Now you know roughly what your Financial Comfort Zone is in terms of home prices.

The Financial Comfort Zone for the couple we mentioned above is in the $250,000 range. There are beautiful places in that price range in Denver as well as Boulder.

Unless you are in a region with a single-industry economy (Detroit and autos, Houston and energy), you can assume your home will increase in value faster than inflation. This future value is not the major element in your buying profile.

Still, you are not just buying a place to live, you are making a sound investment. Even if you buy stocks, bonds, precious metals or pork-belly futures, a house is the only investment you can live in. And the house investment is the only one that cannot be manipulated, because of the wide base of ownership throughout the nation.

THINKING OF TRADING UP?

When do you make a decision to increase the size of your home—either by moving to a larger place or adding a room to your current home? Naturally, if you plan to have more children, you will need more space. Or you might want more room because you would like to spread out a bit.

In moving up, your Financial Comfort Zone must take into consideration not just the cost of a higher mortgage. You should recalculate your monthly expenses as well, because you will be paying more for taxes, electricity, repairs, insurance and everything else. There may be additional regular costs, such as pool maintenance and your contribution to the community private-security patrol. The bigger the home, the bigger the bills.

Can you afford to move up? My philosophy is that a few dollars a month more is okay—it is forced savings. More than a few dollars? Use the charts in this chapter to estimate how much your monthly outlay will be before you go mansion shopping.

WHAT LOCATION IS RIGHT FOR YOU?

The next question is: what is your *Geographic* Comfort Zone?

For the Denver couple, the choices seem endless. They could live in Aurora, close to the airport, since they both travel for business a great deal. But they also like Boulder, because they want to be closer to the mountains. Or they might look within the city limits, because they enjoy urban pleasures such as the symphony and regional theater.

If you are in a similar situation, you must put in hours at this point. Drive around a few neighborhoods or suburban towns you are interested in. I am not talking an hour, but a minimum of a full day.

Go into the shopping areas. Check out the movie theaters, the parks, the athletic and recreation facilities. Are there tennis courts nearby? Is there a Little League? If you have children, of course take a look at the schools. If you are a churchgoer, check into churches. If you are particularly concerned about security, talk to the local police about their crime statistics.

Chat with people in the area. Tell them you are thinking of buying. Do they know of problems you should be aware of? What do they like best about their region? Are they the kind of people you are likely to have as friends?

You will also want to check the taxes. Some small municipalities, because of home rule, have the ability to force taxation on you, taxes for roads, new sewers and schools, for instance. Find out what, if any, highways are going to be constructed in the near future. They might make the area more palatable, or less attractive.

Zoning is very important. If you want to be in a totally residential area, make sure the zoning is not changeable or that a change is not on the horizon. Go to the county courthouse and look up the general city plan. A good real estate agent will tell you about how an area is zoned, *if* you ask. But you cannot rely on the agent to let you know that an industrial park is planned for that empty space two blocks from a house you like.

Do *not* merely accept on faith the brochure from a developer that says "Churches, schools, shopping, recreation." You might have a rude awakening if you fall in love with a house but do not like the geographic area. A castle in a place you despise becomes a hut.

If you move from one city to another (one out of five families in the U.S. today moves because of a job transfer), my recommendation is to go in advance and spend a week living in a hotel, to get the sense of the place and to drive through possible neighborhoods. Or rent a house for a while before doing serious house-hunting.

A third choice is to *lease a house with an option to purchase.* I leased a condo with an option to purchase when I moved from Washington, D.C., to New York City. Why? You do not know whether you are going to be comfortable in an area until you spend time in it. The lease-with-option-to-purchase alternative is remarkably practical . . . yet not put into play often enough. Turn to chapter 8 on leasing with an option to purchase for all the details.

GET AN OVERVIEW OF THE REAL ESTATE ENVIRONMENT

Your first visit might be to one of the novel information centers springing up around the country known as *Housing Consumer Libraries* or *Home Buying Centers.*

A center brings together information on all the builders, real estate companies, condos, co-ops and single-family developments in the community under one roof. Typically, the center has a series of maps, buying brochures, videotapes and slides of houses in various districts.

These centers are run by local entrepreneurs, in many cases the same ones who publish free "houses for sale" magazines or newspapers that you can pick up in almost any real estate office.

Browsing through such a library gives you a handle on the status of your market. You can get a *quick, accurate overview,* learning what kind of homes are moving and what kind of lifestyles are available.

Theoretically you can walk into a Home Buying Center, pick the geographic area you like the best, and locate the schools, shopping and other details. You can then look in the brochures for a particular type of house, compare prices, and even get mortgage information.

WHAT WILL YOUR HOUSE LOOK LIKE?

Your Geographic Comfort Zone is based not on what is going to happen within the walls of your house but on what happens when you walk out the front door. The next questions relate to your *Esthetic* Comfort Zone.

The first question actually is whether you want a new home or a used one. You can look in the new home inventory list in your preferred area, which you can find at the local home builders' association. In most years, however, 80 percent of home buyers buy used, or preowned, homes.

Your Esthetic Comfort Zone is what strikes your eye as you drive up to a place. That is the first thing you are going to see as you arrive home every day. A house may be in the perfect neighborhood and the perfect price range, but if you cannot stand to look at the façade, you are going to be a very unhappy person. Purely subjective taste determines what suits you. Do not be afraid to take a stand by telling an agent, "I like modern ranch houses," or, "I love Victorians." And if an unusually scenic view can make a difference in feeling wonderful at the end of the day, let the agent know that too.

The *least* important consideration is the look of the inside of most homes. They are all the same, except for dimensions. Aside from decoration—superficial things such as furniture, lighting, paint, wallpaper, mirrors, floor coverings, window trimmings—a bedroom in one house is the same as a bedroom in the previous one you visited. It consists of four walls, a ceiling, a floor and windows. Close your eyes if you hate the Victorian decor in a house that otherwise suits you. You can change the inside of the house, the undergarments.

You have complete control over the space inside the four walls. It is the suit or dress—the outside of the house—where your Esthetic Comfort Zone counts.

If your Esthetic Comfort Zone calls for a home that was built at the turn of the century, take into account that you are likely to have proportionally more challenges than if you bought a 5-year-old ranch. The main question when considering a house more than 40 or 50 years old (pre–World War II) concerns what kind of upkeep the previous owners have done.

There *are* homes 50 years old or older in marvelous condition—sometimes as good as a 5-year-old ranch. But the only definite way to know this is to have the home *checked by a professional inspector.* In chapter 4, we tell you how to find a qualified inspector, as well as what to look for yourself by accompanying the inspector on his tour of the house you want to buy.

HOW MUCH UPKEEP DOES THE HOUSE NEED?

Chances are, your *Maintenance* Comfort Zone will clash with your Esthetic Comfort Zone on an older house. That is all right, as long as you do not mind spending money to please your esthetic taste. In this case, the question to ask is: what is the prognosis as far as maintenance is concerned?

What is your tolerance for maintenance? You know that with a new home, you have a one-year warranty. With a 10-year-old home, you know most of the bugs are out, provided it has been well maintained.

Nevertheless, there is no such thing as a 100-percent maintenance-free home. Wiring, plumbing, roofing, basement leaks and other problems can crop up, especially in a pre–World War II house that has not been kept in tip-top shape by the previous owners, but also in a newer house of shoddy construction. That is why a professional inspection is *essential.*

Once you have a home professionally inspected, you will have a reasonable idea of what repairs *you* will have to make, should you purchase it. You may come across a 1920 home, for example, that has been rewired, with a new roof and new air-conditioning and heating systems. It might need a few windows replaced, but might not need new plumbing.

However, there are upkeep problems that might not show up on inspectors' reports or engineering studies, because they concern the "life expectancy" of parts of a house that periodically need replacement.

In ANY house, whether 5, 50 or 100 years old, you can *always expect certain things to deteriorate.* For example, after 10 years or longer, the roof, heating and cooling systems and major appliances wear out, even with normal use. Doors, windows and floors will need refurbishing, at the minimum.

On an older home, be prepared. In the worst-case scenario, five days after you close, the electricity could go out. If you buy a wooden home in San Francisco, you will have to paint it every few years. In the Snow Belt, where you get a heavy load on the roof every winter, you will have to replace the roof probably every 10 to 15 years.

CAN YOU BUY AND SELL AT THE SAME TIME?

If you are buying a new home and selling your current one at the same time, assess your *Timing* Comfort Zone.

Many of us do a sale and purchase simultaneously. Adventurous souls do not mind selling their house first, regardless of whether or not they have glimpsed their new dream house yet. They worry afterward about where they will live once the current home is sold. The rest of us want to know where we are going.

Ask yourself how comfortable you will feel putting your house up for sale right away. Are you confident that you will be able to find the right next home—that bigger, better home—afterward? Are you willing to move into a rented house or apartment if you find a buyer for your home before you find another home for yourself? If you are moving to a new region, can you put up with a hotel room filled with suitcases for a few months?

You may have to consider the fact that you have children. To one radio listener who did, I suggested NOT taking the chance of selling his current house and having to move the family into a rental unit. He was in the process of building a custom home, but you would be amazed at how much time that can take.

Stay put for a while, I said. Once he had purchased a lot, he could go to a bank and use the equity position in his current home in order to raise money to get started on his new house. When there were 90 days left until completion of the new house, he should put his original house up for sale.

An alternative would be for him to sell his house immediately, contingent upon his paying rent to the person who bought it until he got his other house finished.

You can find a more complete discussion of how to buy and sell at the same time—without going crazy in the process—in chapter 28.

WHAT ABOUT AN APARTMENT OR TOWN HOME?

By the year 2000 half the American population will live in common-wall dwellings: apartments or town homes. There are doomsayers out there who believe condominium living is fading as a lifestyle; they are wrong. The cost of land is soaring so high that in many areas we will no longer be able to live in single-family detached residences. Right now there are more people moving from single-family homes to condominiums than vice versa.

For people looking at buying apartment or town home condos or co-ops, the Financial and Geographical Comfort Zones are the same as they are for single-family houses. The difference lies in the esthetics of living in a common-wall dwelling.

A condominium suits a person who does not want to be bothered by lawns, driveways, roofs or basements. Many of us are becoming accustomed to an easy-care apartment where we can lock the door and leave for a month.

You need to judge how comfortable you are not just with the façade but with the hallways, the entrance, the lobby, the elevator. Also, think about how you react to other people. Those of you who have lived in apartments or town homes before know whether you enjoy the closeness of other families.

If you have been living in a single-family detached residence all your life, you need to gauge whether common walls will make you feel restricted or inconvenienced. Have you ever heard footsteps on the ceiling or music seeping up from the floor? You would do well to lease before you buy, to see what your comfort level is in a shared situation.

It is time to draw your profile as a buyer. Fill out the Comfort Zone worksheets to see what you can afford and what geographic and esthetic considerations mean most to you. Then take these worksheets with you on your house tours.

Financial Comfort Zone Worksheet
(Fill in the blanks to see how much you can afford to pay for a mortgage.)

Monthly Expenses

a. Rent or current mortgage	$_____
b. Property taxes if homeowner*	+ $_____
c. Insurance (total of home, health, life, and auto)*	+ $_____
d. Utilities (water, fuel, electric, phone)*	+ $_____
e. Auto payments, upkeep, garage	+ $_____
f. Food & clothing	+ $_____
g. Household expenses (repairs, laundry, lawn)*	+ $_____
h. Credit Cards	+ $_____
j. Entertainment	+ $_____
k. Savings	+ $_____
l. TOTAL of above	= $_____

Monthly Income

m. Take-home pay	$_____
n. Minus 10-percent cushion	– $_____
o. Subtotal: Spendable income	= $_____
p. Minus total monthly expenses (line l)	– $_____
q. **Available** monthly income (line o minus line p)	= $_____
r. Plus current rent, mortgage, and property taxes (lines a + b)	+ $_____

Monthly Amount Available for Mortgage
(lines q + r)   = $_____

*You may not be paying for these items now, but If you move into a new house, they must be factored in to establish your Financial Comfort Zone.

Geographic Comfort Zone Worksheet
(Distance to important facilities and zoning notes)

Facility	Miles	Time
Work	_____	_____
School	_____	_____
Church	_____	_____
Recreation	_____	_____
Airport	_____	_____
Train	_____	_____
Hospital	_____	_____
Shopping (minor)	_____	_____
Shopping (major)	_____	_____

Zoning

Present zoning _____

Future area development _____

Esthetic Comfort Zone Worksheet
(Facilities you desire, and how you rank them)

Home Style in Order of Preference

1. _____

2. _____

3. _____

Amenities You Desire		**Available?**
(Rank in importance from 0 to 5)		(yes/no)
Pool	_____	_____
Tennis	_____	_____
Golf	_____	_____
Horses	_____	_____
Skiing	_____	_____
Fishing	_____	_____
Hot tub	_____	_____

Note: Complete one of these for each house you consider.

Single-Family Detached Home Worksheet

Neighborhood (Circle one)   Excellent   Very Good   Good   Fair

Rank in importance and quality (condition, size, layout, etc.) on scale from lowest,1, to highest,10.

Area	Importance	Quality	Comments
Bedrooms (how many?____)	_____	_____	_____
Baths (how many?____)	_____	_____	_____
Living room size	_____	_____	_____
Family room size	_____	_____	_____
Kitchen	_____	_____	_____
Dining room	_____	_____	_____
Study	_____	_____	_____
Porch	_____	_____	_____
Garage	_____	_____	_____
Backyard	_____	_____	_____
Front yard	_____	_____	_____
Closets	_____	_____	_____
Storage areas	_____	_____	_____
Workshop	_____	_____	_____

Condo/Co-op Apartment or Town Home Worksheet

Neighborhood (Circle one)   Excellent   Very Good   Good   Fair

Rank in importance and quality (condition, size, layout, etc.) on scale from lowest,1, to highest,10.

Area	Importance	Quality	Comments
Bedrooms (how many?____)	_____	_____	_____
Baths (how many?____)	_____	_____	_____
Living room size	_____	_____	_____
Family room size	_____	_____	_____
Kitchen	_____	_____	_____
Dining room	_____	_____	_____
Study	_____	_____	_____
Porch or terrace	_____	_____	_____
Garage or parking	_____	_____	_____
Backyard	_____	_____	_____
Front yard	_____	_____	_____
Closets	_____	_____	_____
Storage areas	_____	_____	_____
Workshop	_____	_____	_____
Lobby	_____	_____	_____
Security	_____	_____	_____
Service staff/concierge	_____	_____	_____
Rules and regulations	_____	_____	_____

Chapter 2

How to Choose an Ethical,
Competent Real Estate Broker

There are over 700,000 licensed real estate brokers in this country who are members of the National Association of Realtors, plus 400,000 more who are not members. My estimate is that 85 percent of these brokers are decent. But how to tell the good, the bad and the ugly?

Perhaps you already know a real estate professional. But what if you don't know any, or what if you don't like the ones you know? Then it is homework time. I do not mean talking to your Aunt Suzie. I mean finding a well-qualified agent with whom you can do business. (Yes, you can buy without using a broker at all, but it is a bit like driving a stickshift car. Unless they are experts at going it alone, most people prefer automatic shift and brokered home purchases.)

The biggest mistake buyers make, especially if they are from out of town, is accepting the very first real estate agent they visit. Interview three or four agents. I guarantee you will see differences in style and experience. You can always go back to the first one if he or she ranks first on your list after your search.

REALTORS, BROKERS, AGENTS

Let us get our terms straight first. A *broker* is a real estate person who is licensed to practice real estate by the state. A *sales associate* or *agent* must also have a license issued by the state, but the sales agent who is not a broker must work under the supervision and strict approval of a licensed broker. That broker is responsible to the public for the sales agent's activities.

Realtor is a title owned by the National Association of Realtors. A realtor is a real estate professional, usually a licensed broker, who belongs to the association and subscribes to its code of ethics. The organization is self-governing. Many members have taken special courses in various aspects of realty conducted by the association.

Your real estate person may use any of these terms, so you might want to ask if he or she has a license and/or a membership in the NAR.

Additional NAR designations next to a realtor's name include CRI (Certified in Residential Sales), CRS (Certified Residential Specialist) and GRI (Graduate, Realtors Institute). In addition, some realtors may be members of the national appraisers institute (see chapter 4 for more on appraisers). The various designations indicate that a realtor has taken the trouble to enroll in courses giving sophisticated information in a specialized part of the real estate market.

The realtors who have taken these courses are usually people who have been in the business for at least five years. Overall, they are the experts. It should be reassuring to deal with people who feel that good about their business. The flip side is that it is dangerous to deal with part-time salespeople for whom real estate is an extra income. They often do not do as good a job as the real professionals, and that might cost you money in the end.

WHICH SIDE ARE YOU ON?

Once you decide on a broker, always remember whose side he or she is on. There is a common misconception that brokers represent the buyer and the seller equally. Not so.

The broker has a financial, legal and moral responsibility to the seller, who pays his commission on the sale. In other words, the broker is *employed* by the seller, unless you arrange to hire a buyer-broker; this is an exciting new option we will discuss later in this chapter.

My broker friends are going to cringe, but recent legal decisions in Illinois and Pennsylvania have evened things up a little. According to these decisions, not only is the broker responsible to the seller, but brokers are also responsible to the buyer if they have *prior knowledge* of anything major that is wrong with a house. In some states, brokers must disclose "major defects" in houses.

The question is, what is major, what is minor? The law does keep brokers from being liable for "oral representations." If a broker tells you, "The plumbing is terrific," it does not mean anything, legally. I think broker claims occasionally push the limits of salesmanship. Before you accept a claim by a broker, tell the broker, "If it is worth saying, put it in writing."

Do not be misled by the fact that in many situations there are two brokers involved in a deal. Your broker will check the local multiple-listings book, in which most brokers in the area list the properties they are representing. The broker you have chosen shows you houses listed by another firm. You think to yourself, okay, the person I have been driving around with represents me, because another broker represents the seller.

Wrong. "Your" broker is a subagent of the seller. He or she has the same responsibility to the seller that the listing broker does. (The two of them will split the seller's paid fee when you buy the house.) It is crucial to keep this in mind.

Recently the National Association of Realtors voted to have its members give buyers a written disclosure notice, which announces in writing that they represent the seller in negotiations. That is a giant step toward better consumer relations. Remember, though, that the non-members do not have to follow the association's lead.

AUDITIONING BROKERS FOR THE JOB

As a prospective client, you might follow this scenario when you walk into a real estate office.

Consider whether the person you talk to is a broker or a sales associate. Check his or her professional credentials. Then request a list of business references. Note how long the person has been selling in this particular neighborhood.

Dealing with a complete stranger or someone about whom you have doubts? Ask the broker if there are any objections to pulling a credit report on the broker, in order to see if there are any outstanding judgments against the person or the business.

Be pleasant but firm. I always wind up by saying, "Could you give me the name of two or three clients with whom you have done business so I can talk to them?" Finally, how about some examples of some homes the broker listed and/or sold in the past two months?

Your agent should have a *local reputation.* If he or she does not give you references, run the other way. Anybody who is afraid to give you references is a bad bet. A broker lives on his or her reputation. As Alan

Yasky of Spring Valley, New York, president of the New York State Association of Realtors, pointed out on one of my programs, you, the consumer, are looking for service, and you must have confidence in the agent with whom you are dealing.

"When I co-broker with other brokers," he said, "I look for professional designations. I want to know that they have gone to school and taken courses and that they have been recognized to have an expertise in different phases of real estate. I look for personal references. I am not embarrassed to ask a broker if he can please give me the name of three or four people he has dealt with recently. We are talking about big dollars, and we do not want people to make mistakes.

"I call realtors out of the area," Yasky continued, "and ask them if they can refer me to someone in the area. It may sound silly, but if I were going to Long Island, I might call two or three brokers in Westchester—perhaps strangers—and say, 'Can you do me a favor by recommending brokers on Long Island?' What I'll get is brokers who have good reputations with other brokers who have dealt well with their clients and have satisfied another professional."

Real estate agents rarely are subjected to this kind of questioning. Find somebody who smiles at you and says, "Thanks for asking. Here are my references."

If you are a stranger in town, an extra question for your prospective agent is "What connections do you have with lending institutions?" Then call the lending institutions to see if the relationship exists. The connection might come in handy.

It is prudent to ask whether there is a relationship between the agent and the lender. Some agents are also licensed mortgage brokers, who get a commission for arranging your financing. That does not mean you must use a lender suggested by the agent. (See the chapter about comparison-shopping for money.) Most people recommend their friends, and by comparison-shopping you can tell if the friend offers the best deal around.

Do you shop for a single agent? Or do you go to several offices and let all of them know you are looking for a house? If your time is limited, I recommend hiring a broker for a set fee. (See "A New Wrinkle," below.)

If you have plenty of time, let everyone try to find a house for you, and start calling people who put "For Sale by Owner" ads in the paper as well. There is no law that says you must use one agent, although they all have access to the multiple listings. It is not your responsibility to disclose to a broker that you are using more than one.

There are two advantages in using more than one agent. They will all be calling to take you out on rides. And if a hot listing comes into one office on a Monday, the agent might show you that listing before it goes into the multiple listings on a Friday. (I will explain multiple listings in a moment.) Although it is not entirely cricket, many brokers stockpile extra-hot marketable houses for two to four weeks before they add them to the multiple listings. They know such houses are under-priced and will go fast.

What if two agents show you the same house and quote two different asking prices? You have the right to place an offer for that house through the agent who quoted you the lower price. Competing claims for the commission would have to be worked out afterward by the agents themselves. Unless a buyer-broker is involved, commissions are the seller's responsibility, not the buyer's.

Once you begin a relationship with a broker, you should be willing to answer many of his or her questions about you. The most important questions concern your finances—your current and near-future earnings, your ability to afford a mortgage, your debt structure and your current rent or mortgage payments.

It is common for people to be leery of real estate agents who ask for their annual income, the name of their banker, their credit status. The agents are not being nosy. They are trying to establish the buyer's "affordability zone."

This information aids a good real estate person in matching you with the right house (within your price range) and perhaps leading you to the right mortgage: a realistic mortgage based on your financial situation.

In addition, the agent has the right to know what kinds of homes you like, what your family needs are (how many bedrooms you need, for instance), whether you prefer two-story houses to one-story houses, and what neighborhoods you most want to live in. Another question the agent should ask: "How soon do you need the house?"

The more you tell your agent, the easier it is for the agent to show you precisely the type of house you desire, rather than waste your time on residences in the wrong financial, geographic or esthetic comfort zones.

Charlie Isaacs, a savvy author and real estate consultant, has some good tips on what to *avoid* in dealing with a broker.

First, there is the "just between us" error. Say you become friendly with a very nice broker who starts showing you houses. Then you see a house you like. It is priced at $100,000. You make an official offer of $85,000. But you tell the nice broker, "Look, I can go to $92,000 on this—just between us." Big mistake! That broker still represents the seller, not you, and he or she will tell the seller about your top price.

Then there is the "greedy buyer" error. You now know the broker gets a commission if he or she lands the sale. It might cross your mind, after a broker has shown you a nice house, to bypass the broker and cut a deal directly with the seller, saving both of you money by avoiding the commission. That is wrong. The broker deserves that commission and will demand it if he learns you have gone behind his back. If the problem is that you are short a couple of thousand dollars or a few percentage points, explain your problem to the broker. Sometimes the broker will reduce his fee or find another way to bring the price down. (See chapter 4 on how to avoid the "two-story" house.)

A NEW WRINKLE—THE BUYER-BROKER

Recently the biggest consumer-oriented bonus in residential buying involves *brokers who represent the buyer, rather than the seller.*

For anyone moving to a new state, or an unfamiliar area, I would recommend hiring one of these "buyer-brokers." It saves you time and guarantees you an agent working on your behalf. There are many brokers who are resisting this new idea, but I think it is great for you and great for the profession.

How do you hire a broker to find a house for you? What kind of documentation should you ask for? Naturally, start out by interviewing several buyer-brokers, so you can compare their services. Buyer-brokers are particularly helpful when someone needs a very special type of property that is not normally on the market—an estate with a separate guest cottage, say, or a penthouse with views of Central Park in a prewar Manhattan building.

You, the buyer, say, "Dig this thing out, go knock on doors, go use all your sources, and for your efforts I will pay you." Buyer-brokers, or procuring brokers, as they are sometimes called, also can save you many hours of shopping if you have limited time, if you are transferring to an unfamiliar area, or both.

What can you expect this "buyer-broker" to do for you? He or she should search the market for you, check the ads, conduct preliminary inspections of homes to see if they meet your requirements. The broker should accompany you to physical inspections of places he or she recommends and should research the future of the community. The broker should represent you as your agent in negotiations.

As a final option, you might want the broker to provide post-contract services—arrange mortgage financing, obtain professional inspections, supply legal services, and help you prepare for the closing.

How much money you pay this procuring broker depends on the services the broker performs. There is *no such thing* as a "STANDARD COMMISSION." You can work on a commission basis, or hire the person for a flat fee. Commissions and fees are *negotiated* by both the seller and the buyer.

Let us imagine that you tell the buyer-broker, "Find me a $500,000 estate with a pool and room for a vegetable garden within an hour's commute of San Francisco." The commission would ordinarily be around 6 percent of the purchase price, paid by the seller. It is negotiable, depending on the services performed by the broker.

How do you pay a buyer-broker if he or she does all the work for you? The trend is that if you ask the broker simply to find the property, you might agree that is worth 3 or 4 percent of the purchase price. If you also say, "I want you to do all the other services you normally do —see that the title is clear, make sure a survey is done, get me a mortgage," the fee may go up to 5 to 7 percent total.

I do not believe in having a procuring broker do anything beyond finding me a house. I think everyone needs to handle his or her own title insurance, lawyer, mortgage shopping, or else risk losing control of the situation. But if you are tied up in an international business deal and do not mind delegating those powers, go ahead.

The flat fee should be based on time spent. In an easy marketplace, I might pay a buyer-broker $500, whereas in a tough marketplace I might pay up to $2,000. Like everything we pay for, fees are market-driven. If you were buying in Houston in 1986, brokers might pay you to let them find a house for you!

A conflict of interest can arise if the buyer-broker sells you one of his or her own listings. The two of you had better discuss the possible conflict first. If, by coincidence, you decide to buy a house this same broker has listed, you should not have to pay a fee. The broker will get his commission from the seller. Your contract with the broker should specify that the fee you pay is refundable in this case.

A contract with a buyer-broker should include the following:

1. the names of the parties;
2. the date the contract begins and the date it should end, usually for a length of 3 to 6 months;
3. the services the broker will provide, as mentioned above;
4. the broker's fee, whether a retainer, an hourly fee, a percentage of the purchase price or any variation;
5. the right to terminate the agreement on 10 to 30 days' notice if you do not feel you are being served well enough;
6. a clause stating that if you do not buy, you do not pay.

Everything is negotiable. The services of a buyer-broker could wind up costing you nothing when there is no seller's broker involved. In that case, the price of the house you choose could be lowered to reflect the fact that the seller is not paying a commission. Or your buyer-broker can negotiate a reduced commission on the seller's end, if the house is listed with someone, to facilitate the deal.

On the following pages is an example of a typical buyer-broker contract.

HOW MANY HOUSES ARE ON THE MARKET?

Once you determine which broker to use, make certain you are shown *all* the houses that might be to your liking. If a broker lured you to his or her office with an ad for one house that reads as if it had your name on it, expect to see additional ones that have your middle initial as well. Here are insights about how a good broker can match your needs with the houses currently on the market.

In each area most of the real estate people belong to the local board of realtors. Each local board has a suborganization known as the *Multiple Listing Service (MLS)*. Each brokerage firm enters the listings it receives each week into a computer with all the pertinent information and each office receives the same printout.

As soon as you hire a good broker, he or she will pull out the multiple-listings book for the area you are interested in, flip through the pages with you to show you all the listings in your style and price range, and photocopy the listings you pick to visit.

In the best offices, brokers have a computer terminal on which to show the latest listings, rather than a book. You can order printouts, including photos, from the terminal with the push of a button. The Computerized Property Listing Service (CPLS) has a picture of houses

Sample Buyer-Broker Contract

Retainer Agreement: The undersigned, _____,
hereinafter designated as Client, hereby retains _____,
hereinafter designated as Broker, for the purpose of exclusively assisting
Client to locate property of a nature outlined below or other property acceptable to Client, and to negotiate terms and conditions acceptable to
Client for purchase, exchange, lease or option of or on such property. This
agreement shall commence this date and terminate at midnight of _____.

General Nature, Location, and Requirements of Property: _____
_____
_____
_____

Price Range, and Other Terms and Conditions: _____
_____
_____

Retainer Fee: Client agrees to pay, and Broker acknowledges receipt of a retainer of $_____, as compensation for initial professional counseling,
consultations and research. Said fee is nonrefundable, but shall be credited
against the Brokerage Fee under paragraph 4, below.

Brokerage Fee: Client agrees to pay Broker, as compensation for locating
property acceptable to Client and negotiating the purchase or exchange, a
fee of (check one) $_____, or _____% of the acquisition price.

Client agrees further to pay Broker as compensation for obtaining an option on a property acceptable to Client a fee of $ _____, and to pay
Broker the balance of a fee of _____% of the purchase price in the event
the option is exercised or assigned prior to expiration of the option.

Client agrees further to pay Broker as compensation for locating a property
acceptable to Client and negotiating a lease thereon a fee of $_____ If:

1. Client or any other person acting for Client or in Client's behalf, purchases, exchanges, obtains an option for, or leases any real property of the nature
described herein during the term hereof, through the services of Broker or
otherwise.

2. Client or any other person acting for Client or in Client's behalf, purchases, exchanges, obtains an option for, or leases any real property of the nature
described herein within one year after termination of this retainer, which

Sample Buyer-Broker Contract (continued)

property Broker, Broker's agent, or cooperating brokers presented or submitted to Client during the term hereof and the description of which Broker shall have submitted in writing to Client, either in person or by mail, *within ten (10) days after termination of this contract.*

In the event the Seller, optionor, or lessor pays a fee under a listing agreement, and Broker, with the consent of Client, is entitled and has agreed to receive any portion thereof, that portion shall be credited against the obligations of Client hereunder.

It is understood that Broker may cooperate with other brokers and their agents in an effort to locate a property or properties in accordance with this agreement, and may share fees with them.

In the event legal action is instituted to enforce the terms of this agreement or arising out of the execution of this agreement, or to collect fees, the prevailing party shall be entitled to receive from the other party a reasonable attorney fee to be determined by the court in which such action is brought.

Notice: The amount or rate of real estate commissions is not fixed by law. They are set by each Broker individually and may be negotiable between the buyer and the Broker.

Broker's Obligations: In consideration of Client's agreement set forth above, Broker agrees to use diligence in locating a property acceptable to Client and to negotiate terms and conditions for the purchase, exchange or lease of said property or for obtaining an option on said property, acceptable to Client.

Broker agrees that he will act for Client only and will not accept a fee from the Seller, optionor or lessor unless full disclosure thereof is made to Client prior to the execution of an offer to purchase, exchange, option or lease.

Receipt of a copy of this agreement is hereby acknowledged.

Date: _____   Time: _____

_____ Broker _____ Client

_____ Address _____ Address

_____ Phone _____ Phone

By: _____

[Adapted from Professional Publishing Corp. Form 100. Used with permission.]

on laser disks, and it can even produce Polaroid photos clearer than any you will see in the multiple-listings book.

HOT MARKETS, COOL CUSTOMERS

Now that your agent is showing you what is available, factor in one more number: shelf life, or the length of time a property is on the market.

In a good market a listing should be sold within 30 days. In an average market, 60 to 90 days. If the market is slow, the average house is listed for 3 months before it is sold. In a hot market, a listing might last only 1 to 10 days. Ask your broker how houses have been selling in the area. I have had radio friends tell me they have lost out because a seller in a hot market got four full-priced bids within 24 hours. It is useful to know whether you might have to make a quick choice.

THE REFUNDABLE BINDER

When you get ready to make an offer on a house, most brokers will ask for a "good-faith deposit," some money to show that this is a serious offer. This is a "binder." The amount usually is 1 percent of the sales price. It should always be REFUNDABLE if the deal does not work out. It is NOT a fee. When you write a check for this, you should write on the back of it that it is refundable in case there is no transaction completed. (A sample of a refundable binder can be found in chapter 6, page 77.)

The "good-faith deposit" is NOT the same thing as the larger deposit you make when you are ready to go to contract. At that point, you will probably be asked to put down 5 or 10 percent of the purchase price. That contract, if written properly, will let you out of the deal if certain conditions are not met—for example, if the house has termites, if you cannot get a mortgage, or if a major structural problem is discovered when you get your professional home inspection report (see chapter 4 for details.)

However, let us say a contract is made, and the seller meets all the terms. In the interim, you, the buyer, have a change of heart. Perhaps you have seen an even dreamier dream house or you are having second thoughts about the neighborhood. If you attempt to withdraw the deal, there is a question in my mind whether the deposit, or binder, should be kept by the broker as "liquidated damages," payment for the trouble he or she has gone through.

Be sure, in this case, that your contract limits your exposure to the amount of the deposit.

WHEN YOU ARE BUYING AND SELLING AT THE SAME TIME

What if you are selling your old house and looking for a new one in the same area? There is great value in using the same real estate agent for both transactions, provided you have used this person's services before and are satisfied with those services.

Normally, you would pay this agent around 6 percent for selling your house. But in this case the agent would be "double-dipping"—collecting on both ends. Therefore you can negotiate a lower commission on both your new house purchase and your old house sale. Or you can pay a flat fee for the agent's finding you the second place.

For instance, I might negotiate 25 to 40 percent off the commission rate on the sale. So if the agent lists as well as sells my house, I want to pay 3½ or 4 percent. If the same agent then sells me one of his or her other listings, I want a couple of percentage points off the price of the house I am buying, too.

These are issues that must be negotiated with your agent *in the beginning,* before you sign a listing agreement, the initial piece of paper. Dear readers, this peek behind the scenes will ruffle the feathers of some brokers, who would dearly like to collect as much as possible on every sale. But the law says that no fee is carved in stone. All commissions are negotiable. Do not let anyone tell you anything else.

CO-OP AND CONDO APARTMENT BROKERS

If you are looking for an apartment, use a specialist in apartments. Choosing a real estate agent is like choosing a physician. You would not go to an internist for a broken bone. The same goes for condos, co-ops, country homes or single-family homes—you want a person who understands the specific marketplace and the particular type of home. Just because a person is a friend who sold you your house does not mean the same person can help you find a good apartment. That is probably out of his or her area of expertise.

CHECKLIST:
13 Questions to Ask a Broker

1. Are you a licensed broker, an agent or a sales associate?
2. How long have you been licensed?
3. Are you a member of the National Association of Realtors?
4. Do you work full-time as a real estate professional?
5. Do you have special designations, credentials or expertise?
6. How long have you been involved in this town/neighborhood/county?
7. Can you give me three references of recent clients?
8. What houses have you sold in the past 60 days?
9. Can you give me banking and credit references?
10. (If buyer-broker) What fees will you charge me?
11. Are you showing me any properties that are your own listings?
12. Can we negotiate your commission if I choose one of your own?
13. Will you put that in writing?

Chapter 3

When Do You Need a Real Estate Attorney?

We are fortunate that lawyers now specialize in real estate law. You need to find the good ones, because if you have an incompetent one, you could end up in worse shape than before you went to see the attorney. A good divorce lawyer does not necessarily know a thing about real estate.

A real estate attorney is vital when you do not understand every single document that is being put in front of you. If a phrase or a word puzzles you in a contract or an offer, an attorney can interpret for you. The few hundred dollars you spent for attorney fees can save you a lifetime of aggravation and thousands of dollars.

On the other hand, do not let an overzealous attorney kill a deal if you think it is valid. Attorneys are trained to look for pitfalls rather than opportunities. Your attorney may be too cautious. One of my own rules is, never ask for an attorney's opinion of a real estate deal. Would you ask a plumber to evaluate an electrician's work? Ask for legal opinions, not business opinions.

You should shop for an attorney as carefully as you shop for a real estate agent. Your family lawyer or trusted friends can recommend one if you are buying a house in your current area. Look for the phrase "practice restricted to real estate" when you are shopping. Make sure he or she is an expert.

In many towns, a single law firm handles the vast majority of real estate work. You can find out which firm this is by checking deeds and mortgages at the courthouse, if you are moving to a new area.

POPPING THE QUESTION ON FEES

Do you walk into an attorney's office and immediately request to know the fees? You bet. But as Dennis Brouner, a Seattle attorney, said on one of my programs, make sure the attorney is not holding coffee, because he will be so surprised he might spill it.

I cannot emphasize enough times that, despite your trepidation, as a consumer you have a right and a duty to your pocketbook to ask questions like "Are you going to charge me by the hour? Will you charge me a contingency fee? Can you offer me a flat fee for everything related to this purchase?" (I prefer flat fees to hourly rates.) Otherwise, you might go into shock at a closing when, instead of paying what you expected to amount to a few hundred dollars, you are hit for a few thousand. The best attorneys understand that consumers are more aware now than ever before of the service relationship between client and lawyer.

The silver lining is that if, by asking, you demonstrate that you are sensitive to fees, there is a chance you will be charged a bit less than the average client.

The typical charge for a closing on a three-bedroom, two-bath house nationwide is $300 to $500. In Los Angeles you might pay more, in Des Moines less. Even $1,000 is not an exorbitant price to pay for the comfort in knowing everything is buttoned up. Most attorneys ask for a portion of their fee, between 15 and 20 percent, at the beginning, as a retainer.

LEARNING LAWYER MANAGEMENT

It is important that you manage your attorney, since he or she is managing your legal affairs. At the outset, get a letter from your lawyer that spells out not just the costs but the services to be performed. A nonthreatening way to phrase this: "Can you please state this in a letter so that I know I will not go over budget?"

As you proceed, call your attorney on a regular basis to keep up with a transaction. Have the attorney send you copies of all letters he sends or receives in connection with it. Be the squeaky wheel among your attorney's clients so you get the grease, the attention you deserve. Never give up your responsibility by saying, "Here's the deal; take care of it and call me when it's done."

"STANDARD" IS AN OIL, NOT A CONTRACT

You should never make an offer without an attorney unless you understand the language of the offer form backward and forward. Play it safe; operate without an attorney on a purchase only if you are an accomplished, sophisticated real estate pro. Actually, I am a pro and I still use a lawyer.

Real estate agents should never act in a legal capacity. Restrict them to introducing you to a property. Do not sign papers put in front of you by a real estate agent until your attorney looks at them. People are constantly getting into trouble by signing on-the-spot offer sheets or purchase agreements, or even a mortgage commitment, that do not include key clauses . . . pertaining to such matters as the furniture included, the date of closing, a guarantee of the interest rate on the mortgage and so on.

"This is a standard contract." Has a real estate agent said that to you yet? What makes it "standard" is nothing more than the phrase "standard contract" printed on the top of the page. There is no such thing as a standard contract. Even on the preprinted forms you purchase in a stationery store, there are many blanks to be filled in that customize each deal.

"USE OUR ATTORNEY" AND OTHER SCAMS

Do not let a bank or a real estate company talk you into using its attorney. There is no law anywhere demanding that you allow someone else's lawyer to represent you. If someone implies that you do not have a choice in the matter, that is a signal to insist that your own lawyer get involved. A recent scam perpetrated in several states illustrates why.

Joan and Jack Smith were moving from Elmira to Yonkers, New York. In Yonkers, seeing a "For Sale" sign on a beautiful house, they telephoned and were shown the house a half-hour later by a pleasant woman. Other houses in the area were selling for $250,000; she offered this one for $150,000. The price was good for 24 hours. The couple replied, "We'd better get an attorney."

The woman suggested her agency's attorney, at no charge. "What a deal! We're getting the house at $100,000 below market price plus a free attorney," thought the Elmira couple. At the attorney's office, the attorney wrote a contract, collecting a $25,000 deposit on the spot. The attorney later called to tell them the mortgage work was done, so they could move into the house. Three months later, after the Elmira folks were ensconced in their new home, there was a knock on the door. A Mr. Chapman strolled in. "I just wanted to meet my new tenants," he said.

The Smiths protested. A broker and an attorney had sold them the house! Unfortunately, those two turned out to be a pair of con artists who would go to a town and rent a house from someone who had moved out of state. Next they would print phony calling cards, rent an office for a month, put a "For Sale" sign in front of the rented house, and then wait for unsuspecting marks like the Smiths to fall for their deal. The con artists had walked away with the Smiths' $25,000.

This sad tale emphasizes several precautions. Never use someone else's attorney. If you choose one with whom you were not previously acquainted, check the diplomas on the wall and get local personal references. Most important, follow up the references by calling or visiting them personally.

WRITE-IN CANDIDATES

On the financing side, a lawyer can build some breathing room for you by writing "jump-out" clauses into the contract. For instance, if you are worried about getting back your deposit if you cannot get the mortgage at the rate you have been promised, or if you are not sure at the time of closing that you have the down payment, a clause may give you 30 extra days to find the money. (See chapter 6 on negotiating, page 83, for examples of buyer protection clauses.)

A lawyer also can help you obtain the best value in title coverage because most real estate lawyers belong to a consortium called Lawyers Title Guarantee Fund, which provides a discount. But you must ask for the discount. You can save 10 to 15 percent.

A good real estate attorney can easily prepare special papers for situations such as *zoning, co-ownership* and *equity sharing.*

Zoning laws can be tricky. If you buy what you think is a two-family home, your lawyer should make sure you are not in a residential area restricted to single-family residences. Thousands of properties are sold illegally as combined commercial and residential buildings, with professional offices on the first floor.

Certificates of occupancy, known as C.O.'s, can also be a roadblock. A New York man made a deposit on a loft condominium in Manhattan. It was sold in "as-is" condition, requiring further work before a certificate of occupancy was issued. He could get a commitment on a mortgage, but no lender would let him close until a C.O. was issued, for the buyer's own protection. Yet the contract stated he had to close before the seller fixed the place so he could get a C.O. He was stuck in condition stalemate.

In all these cases, an attorney can protect you from a needless run-in later on with local authorities. Similarly, your attorney will check any deed restrictions on the title.

You need a *co-ownership agreement* if you buy property with a relative, friend or business associate. In addition, as my friend Cecile Weich, a New York attorney, recommends, couples about to get married should consult a lawyer to draw up a *prenuptial agreement* to protect current or future real estate holdings of both bride and groom, should a divorce occur later.

It may sound strange to prepare for such an eventuality at the start of a relationship, but as Mrs. Weich says, "true love can survive a little practical thinking." Real estate is the major asset owned jointly or individually among middle-income couples; in many states, community property laws dictate that such assets are shared in a marriage, unless a prenuptial contract says otherwise.

A co-ownership agreement between husband and wife, siblings, parents and children, or nonrelated associates spells out the rules of the game and includes a buy-sell agreement in the event that one party wants to buy or sell his or her portion. Otherwise, it can be dangerous to family health.

An attorney can lay out the terms. Should, heaven forbid, one partner die, or have a change of heart, there has to be a statement of what will happen when one wants to sell and another does not, of who will get which property or money, and so forth.

Harry Frieland, an attorney and real estate consultant, cites several key pieces of paper you will need if you are buying a house under an *equity sharing* arrangement. With equity sharing, a parent or other investor contributes the down payment on a house that a child or other occupant will live in and contribute the monthly payments for. (For details on equity sharing, see chapter 7 on shopping for money, page 98.)

First, there is the *co-tenancy agreement.* This stipulates the responsibilities of each of the parties, sets terms of a buyout, establishes an appreciation schedule for buyout, states default provisions, specifies monthly payments, and provides protection for the investor.

With that Frieland includes an *integrated lease,* very important from the investor's standpoint. Unless the investor leases out his half interest, he will not be able to write the place off on his taxes. The integrated lease spells out the arrangement under which part of the money paid by the occupant to the investor is rent, making it a commercial agreement in the eyes of the IRS, and thus deductible.

The investor also needs a *subordinated mortgage,* which is a non-interest-bearing mortgage, plus a *deed in lieu of foreclosure,* which states that if the occupant defaults in payment to the investor, the investor can easily take over full ownership of the house.

WHEN YOU DO NOT NEED A LAWYER

An attorney is NOT essential every time you *close* a real estate deal. You can do it in trust with a bank, and in some states you can do it at the title company. "In trust" means that an officer of the bank or title company represents you at the closing and is liable if something goes wrong. You need to have an agreement in writing that you have designated such an institution to handle the closing for you. In California and Florida more closings take place at title companies than they do in lawyers' offices. (I will discuss this again in chapter 9, on the closing.)

For "quick-reference" guidelines on when a buyer needs an attorney, when a seller needs an attorney, and what the attorney does at each stage of the purchase of a house, see the introduction, "How to Use This Book."

GUIDELINES:
11 Questions to Ask an Attorney

1. May I have a written schedule of the fees you will charge me for this deal?
2. What does each charge cover?
3. Are there contingency fees?
4. Will you do this deal on a flat-fee basis? If so, how much?
5. Is your practice limited to real estate?
6. Do you have an attorney/client relationship with either the lender or the seller in my situation?
7. (If the attorney is a stranger) Can you give me a few references among your clients?
8. Can you get a discount on title insurance and pass it along to me?
9. Will you include jump-out clauses in this contract, giving me breathing room if I have trouble with the financing?
10. Have you double-checked zoning laws on this house?
11. (If you are doing an equity-sharing deal) Have you prepared shared-equity documents recently?

Chapter 4

Are You Paying Too Much?
Understanding Appraisals and
Inspections

There ARE ways to determine if the price of a house is fair.

First, there are appraisals. Second, there are inspections. An appraisal is an informed opinion of the market value of the house; the home inspection is an accounting of what is wrong with a house and how much it will cost to get it fixed.

I recommend strongly that you get an appraisal, but I hasten to add, make sure it is an honest one. People call me all the time and start out, "Sonny, my house is worth $150,000." "Who told you that?" I ask. "My broker," they say.

Forget it. That is not an appraisal.

Shop for an honest, licensed appraiser with the initials MAI or ASA next to his or her name. The first stands for "Member, Appraisal Institute," which is the American Institute of Real Estate Appraisers. Those who add the initials RM are "residential members," with at least five years of expertise in residential, rather than commercial, property. ASA indicates membership in the American Society of Appraisers.

Only a few thousand "appraisers" nationwide belong to either of these two top professional groups with excellent codes of ethics. About

90 percent of appraisers do *not* belong. Unfortunately, there are no industry-wide appraisal standards and few state regulations governing appraisers, a situation the good appraisers would like to correct. I have found that the MAI appraiser is the one called upon the most as an expert witness.

Banks depend on appraisers and, boy, do they get screwed! A story in *The Wall Street Journal* a while ago noted that bad appraisals "allegedly have contributed to the collapse of Beverly Hills Savings & Loan Association and San Marino Savings & Loan Association, two of the biggest thrift failures in history."

On the other hand, *Forbes* magazine declared the average appraiser "just a pawn" who is used by a thrift institution to put an inflated price tag on a property to justify a loan. Either way, you, the buyer, are not getting the help you need. The federal government, recognizing the crisis, is expected to impose regulations on appraisers.

"We all were going along through the late 1970s and early 1980s when we had a strong economy and high inflation. Everybody was happy," admitted Peter Bowes, president of the Appraisal Institute. Now that property is not increasing in value as fast, he told me, "realtors, developers and appraisers are taking a snapshot of the future from a point in time, and interpreting it in accordance with forecasting, as best they can."

WHAT AN APPRAISAL IS . . . AND IS NOT

An appraiser gives you an educated opinion on the value of your house. It takes time. Checking public records, the appraiser looks for sales of comparable houses, inspects a previously sold house to make the best comparison between it and the current house, conducts a detailed inspection of the house about to be bought, and writes a report. This work can delay closings, as happened in the spring of 1986, when lenders and appraisers were overwhelmed with loan requests, thanks to lower interest rates.

Another set of circumstances taken into account by an experienced appraiser is the state of the economy in the region. If you were buying a house in a region depressed by falling oil prices in 1986, the appraisal was likely to be lower than it might have been in 1980, when the oil boom was still going strong.

A lending organization usually orders the appraisal. If you want your own, rather than the bank's, consult a few appraisers and request in writing an estimate of the time and cost of the job, as you would any other professional service.

The cost of a full-fledged appraisal of a three-bedroom, two-bath house in a neighborhood without unusual problems should be somewhere between $175 and $500.

Here are a few tips on interpreting a full-fledged appraisal:

The "boilerplate," or repeated paragraphs, often declares that it is only an opinion. You can sue if you think that opinion is wrong, but your chances of winning are not great. Different appraisers sometimes offer widely disparate judgments. Declining markets are harder to deal with than hot markets.

There is a tendency to pay too much for another house on your own block. Such a move reinforces your decision about buying the first house, if you happen to have paid less than what the one next door is said to be worth. Watch out for your emotions.

Check the date on any appraisal you see. If it is more than a year old, get an update. Values change quickly. An UPDATE on an existing appraisal is inexpensive—about $100 to $200—and worth it.

DRIVE-BY: THE "QUICKIE" APPRAISAL

There is an excellent alternative to a full-fledged appraisal if you want confirmation of the bank's judgment or simply a quick fix—the "Drive-by" appraisal.

A drive-by appraisal is often your best—and cheapest—bet for a rough estimate of value . . . within a 10- to 15-percent margin. An expert, an appraiser or someone like a local broker who has been in the market for many years, eyeballs the property from the outside, then goes inside to make sure it is basically all in working order.

Additionally, he or she does a quick search of comparative property sales in the area. A drive-by runs between $100 and $150 for an ordinary residential property. If you are in a hurry, a drive-by is better than no appraisal at all.

DO-IT-YOURSELF APPRAISALS

Your final choice is to do the legwork yourself. The local market determines what the price of a house is in any area. And where is the market in real estate? In the classified section of the local paper, in the minds of landlords selling or renting on their own, and in brokers' multiple-listings books.

Go play reporter. Ask questions. Tour the neighborhood and ring the bell of anyone with a "For Rent" or "For Sale" sign. That's for starters.

Next, check the public records. Sales, mortgages and notes of recently sold houses are recorded by the local real estate records clerk. Tell the clerk what area you are researching; the clerk will direct you to Book Number 87, or whatever. Once you find out the recent mortgage on a comparable house, you can estimate that the mortgage equals 80 to 90 percent of the total value.

The feds have a system to help you even further. Deeds recorded with the mortgage have federal, and in some cases state or even county, documentary stamps on them. Ask the clerk how many thousands of dollars each stamp indicates.

GHOSTLY NEIGHBORS AND OTHER CONSIDERATIONS

Why do two houses that look alike differ in price? There is *no simple formula* that will show you how much an extra bedroom, bath, finished basement, terrace or swimming pool adds to the value of the house. However, if you look at two houses priced at $100,000, in the same condition, in the same neighborhood, on the same size lot and with the same square footage, and one has an extra bathroom, you can assume the extra bath makes that house a better buy.

It is hard to put a monetary value on individual amenity. An in-ground swimming pool in the Sunbelt adds about $10,000 or more to a house. An *above-ground* pool does NOT add nearly that much.

For further details on what amenities add—and do not add—to the value of a residence, read chapter 19, which tells sellers how to set the right price on a house.

More land makes a house worth more. The land is worth at least 25 percent of the cost of the house. So if you are thinking about a $100,000 house, the land is worth about $25,000. If you are offered a double lot, you can add $25,000 to the price.

What a house borders on can make a difference. A radio friend told me about the house she bought at what she thought was $10,000 to $15,000 below market value. Neighbors had paid more for look-alike houses. Now she was hoping to sell at a profit.

The kicker? The house was next to a cemetery!

That is one "amenity" that makes a house more difficult to sell. She simply had to find a buyer who, like herself, believed that the peace and quiet of the neighboring land outweighed any negative ghoulishness.

In another case, I helped a woman figure out whether a piece of property on a hill in Vermont, with a lovely view and only the foundations of a house, was worth the asking price. It was 3½ acres, with a price tag of $18,000.

The woman asked a logical question: "I like it. It's beautiful. But is it worth $18,000?" First, I noted that the foundation value was not that great—$20 a square foot for 600 square feet, or $12,000. There would be equal ownership in the right-of-way leading to the property with two other houses already built on the road.

The key here was to compare the price of other 3½-acre parcels in that area. The woman had seen another parcel that was only $4,000 for 3½ acres, although it had neither the foundation nor the great view. Nevertheless, it seemed to me that the parcel she liked might be a little overpriced.

It was a simple matter of driving around for a day to get a feel for land costs in the vicinity. With this knowledge, what about making an offer on the parcel she liked—$14,000, or the value of the land plus the foundation?

Suddenly, the woman added that there were electric poles on the property she liked. She did not know it, but she had just added from $1,200 to $2,000 to the value. I suggested she make an offer of $16,000. But if the seller was firm on $18,000, she should not lose the parcel over a measly $2,000.

HOME INSPECTIONS

"Check it before you buy it." That is a phrase no home buyer should forget. Why?

You buy a new house. You move in. The boiler breaks down. The refrigerator does not work. The door falls off. The air-conditioning makes the place feel like Death Valley in July. The roof leaks. Sound familiar?

Well, it happens. To avoid these all-too-common discoveries, you need to hire a <u>professional</u>—underline that word—home inspector to look at your prospective purchase and give you an analysis. If you are really smart, you purchase from the same company a warranty, just as you would on a car, for a year. This assures you that the inspector told you the truth and is willing to stand behind what he says, *in writing*.

Home inspection is *more valuable than an appraisal* if you are buying a house. It is the most underused, most needed part of the preliminary steps to be taken before a purchase.

Over the past two decades the pre-purchase inspection of a house has become a fact of life for home buyers—those fortunate enough to know about it. It is a logical extension of the consumer protection movement into the housing market. It is not to be confused with an appraisal. An

---

Fair-Price Scorecard
(Fill in the blanks to compare estimates.)

Original asking price of house: $_____

Range of like houses in classified ads: a. highest $_____

b. lowest $_____

Add a and b, divide by 2 for average $_____

Drive-by appraisal: $_____

Bank-ordered appraisal: $_____

Recent sales, from courthouse records: $_____   (date)_____

$_____   (date)_____

$_____   (date)_____

---

appraisal tells you how much the house is worth in dollars. An inspection tells you if it is sound.

The professional home inspection has gained near-unanimous acceptance as the best means for protecting the interests of all parties involved in a sale. Many smart lawyers and mortgage officers now require it as an integral part of the purchase procedure. The courts have ruled that brokers have to disclose not only what they know, but also what they *should* know, about the condition of a house when they sell it.

Still, only an estimated 25 to 30 percent of home buyers actually get professional inspections before they make a deal. And that is ridiculous.

My feeling is that you do not buy a home unless you put in the contract that it is subject to *your approval* of a professional inspection. The same goes for a condo or co-op. And consider hiring only an inspector who offers at least a one-year warranty. Some warranties are for longer periods.

LOCATING A RELIABLE INSPECTOR

How do you find a home inspector? On what basis do you select one over another? What does a home inspector do?

Let us say I am moving into a new town. The real estate person says, "Charlie's brother down the street looks at homes." How do I know that person really knows what he is doing? You have to be careful. Ask questions. Does Charlie have a company that offers a warranty to back up its inspections? How many years has it been in business? How many locations does it have?

Ken Austin, a charter member of the American Society of Home Inspectors, is an eminent professional whose company, Housemaster, has done some 50,000 home inspections. Austin's inspectors are engineers with degrees, who have gone through a specific instructional course before being turned loose on a house. This is the kind of professionalism a buyer should demand.

The first thing Ken warns is never to buy a "two-story" house. "That's a house where you get one story before you buy the house and another story after you move in." There are some real estate agents who are uptight about the idea of inspections. They may not grasp the fact that a professional inspection protects them as well as the buyer.

One realtor I talk to frequently puts it another way: "I'm not a plumber; I'm not an electrician; I'm not an engineer. I can't go up and inspect the roof. I'm in a small community. When I sell a house, my buyer becomes my neighbor. Not only do I want my buyer to bring an engineer, I want him or her to bring an engineer before they sign the formal contract."

Some buyers feel they do not have a need for an inspection. You are spending $100,000 and up on a house. Why balk at the $225 to $250 that a professional home inspector charges for an average house?

An inspection usually takes no more than three hours. It covers all the systems in the house—heating, cooling, plumbing, electrical connections. It includes the structure of the house—foundation, walls, ceilings, floors. And of course, an inspector checks the roof and its gutters and downspouts.

If it is a condo or co-op you are buying, a standard inspection does not cover the common elements of the building or development, But it will check the windows, doors, the appliances, the plumbing, the electrical system in the unit.

How do you tell major, chronic problems from easily fixable ones?

By insisting, at the time you hire an inspector, that the inspector's report contains certain information.

First, ask that the report be in understandable, lay person's English. Second, require that the report list the following:

- major problems . . . and what the cost will be to correct them;
- minor problems . . . and what the cost will be to repair them;
- the costs you might incur for maintenance during the expected life of such items as the roof, windows, furnace, electrical system and major appliances.

GO WITH THE DOCTOR TO THE CHECKUP

Why not accompany the professional home inspector who is examining the house? Wear old clothes. Crawl around with the inspector in the crawlspace. You can learn about the condition of the house, as well as how to maintain it in good repair.

Take along the Buyer's Home Inspection Kit (at the end of this chapter) to keep track of your findings.

Do not expect the home inspector to give you a flat "don't buy it." That decision still rests with you. The defects that turn up may give you a leg up in negotiating a better price.

WHAT IF THE HOUSE HAS A VIRUS?

Let us say you buy a house with a clause in the purchase agreement that says "subject to inspection by a professional home inspector." The inspector reports back that the house has a foundation problem. According to the report, it is more than a head cold but less than pneumonia.

Evidence indicates the house is sinking, perhaps because it is on unstable ground. The inspector does not even know if the house can be stabilized by such methods as shooting a special plastic/cement liquid piling underneath. (The material then hardens to form a solid base.) "We are talking $40,000 to $50,000 of possible exposure," says the inspector.

Whose responsibility is it to stop the sinking? In this case, with such a major defect, probably the seller's. For lesser defects—air-conditioning problems, a few thousand dollars' worth of roofing—many times the seller and buyer work out a compromise. The rule of thumb is a fifty-fifty split on the cost of repairs. The purchase price of the house is lowered by the amount of the buyer's 50 percent for repairs.

Of course, if you had not had the house inspected as part of the sale, you as the buyer would wind up paying 100 percent for roof repairs after the first rainstorm at your new address.

Although an inspection is critical in evaluating a resale house, many people do not think it is needed on a brand-new house. You never can tell.

New modular homes built by quality firms receive high ratings from professional inspectors. (See chapter 12, on modular housing, for more on the subject.) But critics of more common custom-built new housing contend that new houses cannot hold a candle to older ones in terms of solid craftsmanship. A friend who was in the process of buying a new home in a southern state happened to hear a show I did on inspections. He drove immediately to the developer's office, saying he wanted to hire an inspector. The developer got very upset.

Guess what? There were some structural problems with the brand-new house. My friend saved himself thousands of dollars by having that brand-new home professionally checked.

In another case, a woman came to a home inspection service because she had seen water in the basement of a brand-new house. When she inquired, the builder insisted that it was necessary to keep the concrete wet in order for it to cure! "Don't buy *that* story," the inspection firm warned. "It's amazing what people are told, and what they will believe," says Ken.

Even if you are buying a home or apartment that is not finished yet, there is no reason to forget about an inspection. Just insist that the developer or seller allow you to put the phrase "subject to buyer's approval of a professional inspection upon completion" in the contract.

A NOTE ON RADON

Radon, a radioactive gas, has been discovered in homes in certain parts of the country. It comes from the natural breakdown of uranium. You cannot see it, smell it, or taste it.

You might want to have a radon gas report done on a house before you buy it. To get a radon-measuring kit, write to the U.S. Environmental Protection Agency, Office of Radiation Programs, Washington, DC 20460. The agency will send a report on how to check for radon gas and which local agency and company to consult.

AFTER THE CHECKUP, BUY HEALTH INSURANCE

Okay, the house is healthy and you have bought it. The next step is to buy a health insurance policy . . . a warranty for a year from the date of closing. A national firm like Housemaster charges $150 or one-tenth of 1 percent of the sale price. Anything found in structural or sound condition during the inspection should be covered by the warranty.

In a standard warranty, there is a $100 deductible, just as there would be on the health insurance you bought after a physical. So if your roof starts to leak a few months later, the warranty will pay most of the roofer's charges.

Buyer's Home Inspection Kit

Date Inspected _____
Residence _____ Year Built _____

Item	Excellent	Good	Needs Repair	Estimated Repair Cost
Structural Elements				
Roof	_____	_____	_____	$_____
Siding	_____	_____	_____	$_____
Foundation	_____	_____	_____	$_____
Walls/ceilings	_____	_____	_____	$_____
Insulation	_____	_____	_____	$_____
Floors	_____	_____	_____	$_____

Notes: _____

_____

Heat and Air				
Furnace	_____	_____	_____	$_____
Water heater	_____	_____	_____	$_____
Air-conditioning	_____	_____	_____	$_____

Notes: _____

_____

Plumbing				
Kitchen	_____	_____	_____	$_____
Master bathroom	_____	_____	_____	$_____
Other bathrooms	_____	_____	_____	$_____
Laundry	_____	_____	_____	$_____

Buyer's Home Inspection Kit (continued)

Item	Excellent	Good	Needs Repair	Estimated Repair Cost
Plumbing (continued)				
Water pressure	___	___	___	$___
Sprinklers	___	___	___	$___
Septic tank, sewers	___	___	___	$___
Well storage tank and pump	___	___	___	$___
Notes: _____				
Wiring				
Interior lighting	___	___	___	$___
Exterior lighting	___	___	___	$___
Electrical outlets	___	___	___	$___
220-volt-appliance wiring	___	___	___	$___
Phone jacks	___	___	___	$___
Other	___	___	___	$___
Notes: _____				
Appliances and Related Equipment				
Refrigerator	___	___	___	$___
Stove	___	___	___	$___
Ovens	___	___	___	$___
Microwave	___	___	___	$___
Dishwasher	___	___	___	$___
Disposal	___	___	___	$___
Washer/dryer	___	___	___	$___

Buyer's Home Inspection Kit (continued)

Item	Excellent	Good	Needs Repair	Estimated Repair Cost
Appliances and Related Equipment (continued)				
Intercom/security system	_____	_____	_____	$_____
Smoke detectors	_____	_____	_____	$_____
Garage-door opener	_____	_____	_____	$_____
Exhaust fans	_____	_____	_____	$_____
Other	_____	_____	_____	$_____

Notes: _____

_____

Glass and Other Interior Elements				
Windows	_____	_____	_____	$_____
Glass doors	_____	_____	_____	$_____
Storm windows	_____	_____	_____	$_____
Enclosed shower	_____	_____	_____	$_____
Enclosed tub	_____	_____	_____	$_____
Mirrors	_____	_____	_____	$_____
Carpeting	_____	_____	_____	$_____
Drapes/window treatments	_____	_____	_____	$_____

Notes: _____

_____

Exterior				
Landscaping	_____	_____	_____	$_____
Patio-porch	_____	_____	_____	$_____
Deck	_____	_____	_____	$_____
Swimming pool	_____	_____	_____	$_____
Other	_____	_____	_____	$_____
Total repairs				$_____

Notes: _____

_____

Chapter 5

Timing—Buy Now or Later?

When is the right time to invest in a house? The easy answer is, when you have the money to make the monthly mortgage payments. As a start, you have learned how to figure out your Financial Comfort Zone in chapter 1.

That is only one aspect, however. For a majority of buyers, the tax and investment advantages of home ownership are the keys to a family's decision about when to buy a house, according to a survey by the National Association of Realtors.

Once you reach the decision that the time is right in your life for home ownership, you cannot just jump into the pool. You need to wait until the weather is right. Smart consumers buy property while the economic sky is still clouded but sunshine is in the forecast. In market terms, they buy in a bear real estate market that is about to become a bull market.

"Okay, wise guy," you are saying to yourself. "I'm neither a weatherman nor an economist. How can I figure out that timing?"

The same way I do: by analyzing news and key government statistics issued regularly to the public.

There is no hocus-pocus involved. Your first tool for analysis is the classified real estate advertising section of a local newspaper. This is a tremendous source of intelligence data.

If you know you are going to move to an area in three to five months, order the Sunday paper from the region each week prior to moving. Look at the real estate classified ads, and see how the market shapes up. How many offerings are there? Do the same places show up week after week?

For general real estate news, there are the financial pages of your local paper, plus "The Ground Floor" section of *Barron's* and the real estate columns in each Wednesday's *Wall Street Journal.*

Economic indicators are your most important forecasting tools. Indicators such as the money supply in the U.S., the movement of foreign capital into the U.S. and the actions of the Federal Reserve Board are covered daily in the business pages of your local paper as well as in *The Wall Street Journal, Barron's* and other business publications.

The trick is to know which indicators predict real estate *trends,* versus those that simply announce what already has taken place.

You do not need a master's degree in economics to anticipate trends. All you need in order to time a home purchase is a good "thermometer."

TAKING THE TEMPERATURE OF THE MONEY MARKETPLACE

Certain economic figures can tell you when mortgage rates are about to climb up or inch downward to a healthy lower level. The most important THERMOMETER is located at the Federal Reserve Board. The most important TEMPERATURE READING I look at there is the Fed's report on the nation's *money supply.*

The Federal Reserve Board keeps track of several categories of money. In terms of housing, the most reliable is M1—the amount of cash, traveler's checks, checking-account funds and similar deposits held by the U.S. public.

When the Federal Reserve Board announces that the M1 money supply is expanding, you can expect the prime lending rate and the discount rate to decline, and interest rates to decline as well within a few months.

Why? Because the Fed is telling us there will be more money available, so naturally it will cost home buyers less. If there is a bumper crop of corn, the price of corn that year will be less than the year before when there was a drought. It is the same market supply-and-demand theory.

For example, in July 1985, the Fed broadened the target range for the nation's money supply, thus expanding that supply. Economists quoted in an article in *The Wall Street Journal* immediately predicted lower interest rates. They were right. By expanding the money supply, the Fed pushed interest rates lower several months later.

This is the kind of article to watch for. A smart buyer, reading it, would have begun shopping for a house, knowing that by the time he or she found one, the interest rate on almost any mortgage would be reduced.

In 1986 the Fed, with great fanfare, told the world not to pay too much attention anymore to M1, because the government was not able to control the expansion to its satisfaction. No matter. The growth or shrinkage of M1 still predicts what is going to happen to lending rates within a few weeks.

I take the temperature of the money marketplace by keeping an eye on other indicators in conjunction with M1. A second reading that I note is the Federal Reserve Board's national *discount rate.* This, too, is listed on the financial page of your local paper. The *discount rate* is the rate at which banks themselves may borrow.

A reduction in the discount rate is not an immediate advantage to you as a consumer. But in a typical market it eventually filters down. If a half-percent reduction in the discount rate is passed down to the banks in your geographical area, those banks pay less for their money. If they feel comfortable that it is going to be in effect for some time, the banks reduce their own *prime rate,* the interest rate they charge their best customers. When the prime rate drops, the *mortgage rate,* in a delayed reaction, drops too—usually 30 to 40 days afterward.

The entire chain reaction is like a row of dominoes falling. To sum up: if the *basic money supply (M1)* goes up, that is an indication of an *easier credit policy,* which often leads to the lowering of the Fed *discount rate.* If the *prime rate* then goes down, you can tell *mortgage rates* are going to come down. The more money there is, the less it costs for you to rent it.

On the other hand, if you see the money supply shortening, the prime rate inching up, and the discount rate inching up, then it is time—if you are getting ready to buy a house—to get a commitment on a mortgage at a current mortgage rate *immediately,* because you can be sure that mortgage rates will soon creep up.

Won't the lenders hold off making loans if the money market temperature cools off? Odd as this may sound, lenders are not as smart as you think they are. It might be hard to believe, but 99 percent of the people do not look at these signals. Before the lender, through the bureaucratic system he or she deals with, can change the interest rates, you can go in and lock in the currently advertised rate.

This one tip—to track the money supply and the prime rate—might be worth the price of this book.

Another reading you will want to watch is *government spending* on money. Pay attention when a story in the financial pages says foreigners are buying fewer U.S. government securities, such as treasury bills. This means our government will have to gobble up the money that is sitting there—money that you need to buy your house.

If the newspapers report that the foreign capital buying government-backed securities is drying out, as happened in periods during the 1950s, 1960s and 1970s, you can expect interest rates to start rising drastically within 60 days.

So keep tabs on treasury bills and notes. A big yellow caution flag goes up when the U.S. government starts paying more for money (interest rates on T-bills and U.S. bonds). Money is more in demand, and that is what drives mortgage interest rates. If T-bill interest rates start inching up—from 6 percent one week to 6¼ the next . . . until suddenly the rates have increased 2 or 3 points in five to six months—you know that pretty soon the country will be back to 12-, perhaps 15-, or even 16-percent interest rates on mortgages.

Conversely, watch for steady decreases in interest on T-bills and notes. From the fall of 1985 to the spring and summer of 1986, we saw the opposite. Interest rates shrank month by month. Mortgage rates were cut back to single digits as a result.

Another way of saying this: the more money available that is not being competed for by the U.S. government, the less money it will cost you to rent that money. Which means interest rates go down, or will stabilize.

DO NOT WAIT FOR THE VERY TOP OR BOTTOM IN INTEREST RATES

How could anyone know that within six months of an article on declining mortgage rates, interest rates would go still lower and continue downward for a total of nine months? That is what happened in 1985–1986. The question drove people up a wall.

Callers would say to me, "I just got a loan for 10¼ percent, Sonny. Do you think the rates are going to go up or down, and when?" At such a juncture, I rely on a gut feeling. If you are experienced, you try to handicap the money market as you would handicap horse races. I advised my listeners to jump in at 10¼. In some places, interest rates dropped another one-quarter to three-quarters of a point because of government manipulation.

Still, my listeners came out winners. If mortgage rates went down 3 or 4 points from when you first looked at a house, you had to say, "Okay, I made a good deal." If rates dropped a point or a half a point after you secured your mortgage, it was nothing to cry about. Interest rates rarely "crash" to the 5- or 6-percent level. If they did, you could refinance your mortgage at a lower rate anyway. (See the seller's financing chapter for a step-by-step guide to refinancing.)

A FEW "INDICATORS" YOU CAN IGNORE

Remember that I said the trick is to know the thermometer readings that predict trends from those readings that tell you what has already happened?

Let me show you an example of a misleading "economic indicator." We regularly see headlines about the housing market in this vein: "The Median Price of a Home in the U.S. is $100,000." Sounds inflationary, right? And the number is always inching upward, suggesting that homes are creeping out of the reach of middle-income families.

However, what the headline really means is that half the houses for sale cost *less* than $100,000. Still, unsophisticated consumers often assume they are being priced out of the market.

If such consumers were to run a finger down the columns of my favorite business page—the real estate classifieds in a local paper—they would be apt to come across numerous homes priced at $35,000 to $99,000.

Another signal you can safely ignore? The monthly reports of new housing starts and new housing sales. The majority of homes bought and sold are RESALE homes. Therefore, reports of new home sales mean absolutely NOTHING, unless there is a huge oversupply, in which case you can buy at a great discount. This is another instance of learning what already HAS happened, not what is going to happen.

Besides, when you have a complete industry go down the tubes like the oil industry recently, the new home sales figures nationwide are going to be totally lopsided and tainted, because of the terrible lack of sales in one particular area.

New home sales mean something to you only if you are in the building business or building-supply business, or if you are an investor in building-industry stocks.

The one time the new home sales figures do mean something is when sales are going down and you are looking to buy a new home in an area where they are down. An oversupply offers you the chance to get a heck of a good deal with a builder who needs to cut down inventory.

Some experts think a key to lower interest rates is the "weakening of the economy." This is usually measured by looking at economic indicators like the gross national output, the wholesale price index and so on. There are economists who believe that a weak economy brings mortgage rates down.

It is my opinion that *this is not the case.* If you look at a 50-year mortgage table you will find that a weakening economy could actually bring mortgage rates up. Concluding that a weakening economy is a source for driving down interest rates really has to be tied to the supply and demand of homes in the marketplace, as well as to the availability of mortgage money.

If there is a weakening economy that drives foreign capital out of the nation, then interest rates will go *up,* because our government has to borrow money that you then borrow to build and buy homes.

The final signal that will *not* do you much good for forecasting may come as a surprise. It is the weekly or monthly *charts of mortgage rate increases and/or decreases.* By the time current rates are published in your local paper, or a chart of the lowest mortgage rates in the nation appears in *Money* magazine, you *already know* you can apply for that mortgage rate.

A SEASON TO BUY, A SEASON TO SELL

What is the best time of year to buy a home? Or the worst time to sell a home?

In the southern part of the U.S., the best time to buy is summer. In the north, the best time to buy is winter. In other words, the best time for a deal is out of season, when people are *not* buying homes.

So . . . you are a buyer moving to Phoenix? Get on a plane and go to Phoenix in August. Suffer in 106 degrees, avoid heatstroke, and you are apt to get a better deal. Moving to Cleveland? Go in the middle of a winter storm. Sellers are motivated; they are spending a fortune to heat their homes and they are dreaming of a move to Phoenix.

UP, UP, AND AWAY

How do you determine the appreciation factor on a house? Geography counts. You have to look at the marketplace, at housing supply and demand and at the local business climate. If you are in an area where appreciation is 15 to 20 percent a year, and builders come in and overbuild, then the appreciation will drop until the new homes have been absorbed—purchased by new people moving in.

There is a myth in the real estate world that real estate appreciation is driven by inflation. *Let us not be misguided by this myth.* Inflation is only one of the factors that drives up the market value of homes. The major factor in appreciation is the demand for housing in that specific geographic area.

Assume for a moment that the national inflation rate was 3 percent last year. In Houston, a depressed area, houses did NOT go up 3 percent. But in Bergen County, New Jersey, where there was 3-percent inflation, houses went up as much as 30 percent, *ten times* the inflation rate.

As a professional, I look at real estate industry figures to get a handle on supply and demand. Among the national figures, I look at those from the U.S. Department of Commerce, which you too can obtain free of charge, as well as those of the National Association of Realtors and the National Association of Homebuilders.

In a specific geographic area, I ask local real estate brokers and local chambers of commerce for information. What new industry, new plants or new employment opportunities are available in the area that will supply growth? As for new homes, the local building department can tell me the number of housing permits that have been issued for new houses. All I do is gather this material, grind it up, put it together in commonsense words, and talk about it to the public on radio and television. You can do the same research as I do.

If you are worried about whether an area has an oversupply of housing, do a bit of detective work. First, thumb through the multiple-listings book. You will see the date each house was listed and sold. Next, go into a neighborhood, talk to people on the block, and ask, "How long has your house been listed?" If they say 6 months, 9 months, 10 months all up and down the street, you know that it is a troubled area . . . or an area of great opportunity, if you are a buyer. It is also a way of avoiding getting stuck with a house that you do not intend to occupy for a great length of time.

TIMING AND COMPARISON-SHOPPING—MY OWN EXPERIENCE

I spent several weeks hunting for a condo apartment in New York City recently. This description of my own shopping tour might help you time —and plan—your own search, regardless of what type of house you need or where in the country you are buying.

The first thing I did when I arrived was to read the Sunday *New York Times* classified and display ads for the previous three weeks. My homework thus told me which condos were spending the most money to advertise, as well as which "for-sale-by-owner" condos were still on the market after three weeks.

I was relatively new to New York, so I hired a car and driver, for $20 an hour. I wanted to see which sections appealed most to my Geographic Comfort Zone. When I narrowed my choices down to a few areas in Manhattan, I picked certain blocks that had attractive-sounding condos. All this took about two and a half days.

Next, I made appointments to visit apartments that were for sale by individuals. The prices were fairly predictable. Obviously, in Manhattan, everyone paid attention to what everyone else was doing.

I was hoping to find that rare New York breed, the "motivated seller," who either needed to sell quickly or had held on to an apartment for too long. A few ads said "moving to a new location" or "divorce." Those condos were 15 to 25 percent cheaper than the rest. At new condo sales offices, I looked at specific units, but made no offers.

I continued buying the Sunday *Times.* By my next trip, four weeks later, I knew which condos had been on the market for more than 60 days.

I revisited the new condo sales offices, paying no attention to the sales charts on the walls. Agents tend to put "Sold" stickers up there to make their sales record look good. Instead, I asked to see the specific units I had inspected a month earlier. Sure enough, they were still available, indicating to me the market for them was soft.

Another month went by and I repeated the process. By that time I had been studying the market for 90 days. My reading of the "soft" market proved correct; some developers of the new condos began discounting the prices on unsold units. One reason was that a host of new condo buildings were all coming up at the same time, creating a temporary higher-priced apartment glut.

My decision was to find an investor who had bought a unit already and offer to lease it with an option to purchase. That way, I could control the property for nothing down over 24 months.

At that point, I got what I wanted—a new, luxurious condo, with a relatively low price (considering it is centrally located on Manhattan's East Side) at a reasonable monthly payment, in a neighborhood that made me comfortable.

Please note: I gave myself *a full three months* to learn both the city and its real estate situation. Most people do not begin to shop *early enough* to know whether or not they are getting the best price.

The attitude of real estate sales agents changed drastically over the 90 days. When I first arrived, their position was: "Take it or leave it, because it will be gone tomorrow." On my return trips, I let them know that I could see the units were not moving, *and* that I was comparison-shopping. I was not shy about flashing the classifieds, with my big red circles all over them.

Real estate professionals, like any other salespeople, behave differently toward "price-sensitive," aggressive, challenging shoppers like myself. The condo salespeople started trying harder, quoting lower prices.

My technique would NOT have worked in suburban Bergen County, New Jersey, where, during the same time frame, houses were selling like umbrellas in a monsoon. However, had I gone to Bergen County, my first trip would have taught me that houses were being snapped up within days, or even hours, after being listed. Subsequently, I would have made my move immediately.

Sonny Bloch's Real Estate Thermometer
(Use these steps to gauge the range of market "temperatures" in an area.)

1. How long have houses here stayed on the market?

    Less than 1 month   (15 points)

    1 to 2 months   (10 points)

    3 to 5 months   (5 points)

    6 months or more   (0 points)   1. Points ____

2. What was the price of a home in your style and size 1 year ago? $_____

    Current price up more than 30 percent   (30 points)

    11–29 percent   (15 points)

    0–10 percent   (8 points)   2. Points ____

3. By how much has the population grown in the area in the last 5 years?

    Increased more than 20 percent (+10 points)

    Increased 11–20 percent   (+8 points)

    Increased 5–10 percent   (+4 points)

    Increased less than 5 percent   (0 points)

    Decreased   (–5 points)   3. Points ____

4. Have any major industries left the area or are any ready to leave?

    No (+5 points)

    Yes (–5 points for each)   4. Points ____

5. Are any major industries moving in?

    Yes (+5 points for each)

    No (0 points)   5. Points ____

Sonny's Real Estate Thermometer (continued)

6. How does the local chamber of commerce rate the general business climate?

      Excellent   (+10 points)

      Good   (+5 points)

      Fair   (0 points)

      Poor   (–5 points)   6. Points ____

7. Does a check of courthouse records show

      An unusually high number of real estate transactions? (+3 points)

      A reasonable number of real estate transactions?   (+1 point)

      An unusual number of foreclosures?   (–7 points)

                                   7. Points____

8. In shopping and commercial areas, are the number of vacancies

      Proportionally low? (+3 points)

      Moderate?   (+1 point)

      High?   (0 point)   8. Points____

                                  Total _____

If your total adds up to

      80 or higher: chances are it is a hot market

      60–79: comfortably warm

      40–59: cloudy skies, so-so market

      Under 40: chilly conditions; buy with care

Chapter **6**

Negotiating—The Difference Between a Good Buy and a Great Buy

Negotiations in buying a house are serious. But like a good drama, they can be fun to play out. This chapter introduces you to the elements in the drama: counteroffers, backup offers, contingency offers and especially the jump-out clause.

You begin negotiations to buy a house the minute you say hello to a broker and/or a prospective seller. Your opening move is to try to get them to *answer questions* rather than to throw offers on the table. You want them to talk about what their needs and ultimate goals are.

THE OVERTURE

Let's set the scene. There you are, strolling through the rooms of a lovely home in the neighborhood you have targeted. Chatting with the agent or the owner, you try to find out what the owner of the property is going to do with the down payment. Does the owner have another house already purchased? How much does he or she need for the down payment? Is the owner just going to put the money in the bank?

Let us say the owner is asking for $50,000 down. But it turns out that this person needs only $20,000 *cash,* because he or she is about to make a $20,000 down payment on another new house, and the remaining

$30,000 would go into a money market fund. You could negotiate to give him the remaining $30,000 in the form of a note or some other non-cash form that pays him or her *more* than the money market.

However, if the owner is moving to another town and needs most of the money right away, this negotiating point is out the window.

You can look at this last example yet another way. If someone needs the cash badly, then the purchase price of that person's house becomes a flexible item. You might want to offer more of a down payment on a lower overall price.

ACT ONE: YOUR FIRST OFFER

Now let us set the stage for making a formal offer. You have looked at the house, you have talked to the broker, and you probably have met the owner. Sitting at the kitchen table or in the living room, you make that offer.

At this point, both the seller and you, the buyer, ought to understand as much about each other as possible. You know whether or not the owner needs all the cash for or from a down payment, whether that person is in the middle of negotiations on another house, whether the family is moving because of a job transfer, and so on.

The offer can be written as a *binder* on the property. (An example of a binder is on page 77 of this chapter. When you hand it over, you also need to know as much as you can about the property itself, as well as about this particular deal.

If you are going to make the offer subject to your attorney's approval; if you are going to make the offer subject to a pest control inspection for termites; if your purchase is subject to financing; if you have not yet had an appraisal but feel you must—each of these items should be *in writing* and on the table.

All of the "subject to's" mentioned above are important. These are *contingency clauses* that define a deal and always protect you. You will find a list of buyer protection clauses at the end of this chapter.

Even pros, when buying a business or rental property, forget contingency clauses such as one that makes the offer subject to the buyer's inspection and approval of the books, records, leases, personal management contracts, underlying encumbrances and/or preliminary title report; one that requires physical inspection of a residence; or one that gives the seller 14 days to to remove such contingencies in writing.

The hardest time to change any item is *after* the offer is made. Leaving out a "subject to" is the biggest mistake that most people make.

In some parts of the country, such as New York City, it is a common practice to make verbal offers on a home or apartment, even over the phone. To me, that is meaningless hot air.

It is *real estate suicide,* I feel, to have verbal offers going back and forth! So many people have told me, "Gee, I made an offer over the phone, but somebody else bought the place the very next day." That does *not* happen if you make offers in writing. When I make an offer, I want to be able to see the offer to purchase or good-faith binder and then write a check.

Any real offer you make should be in writing. If it's worth saying aloud, and the parties agree, then write it, *now!*

INTERMISSION: CONTACTING A LENDER

In some cases, you already may have had preliminary discussions with a bank or mortgage company before putting your offer on the table, especially in a hot real estate market where you think somebody could grab the house before the end of the day.

If you have not contacted a lender yet, go ahead and make your offer, subject to a lender's approval. But remember, a smart buyer checks potential trouble spots such as zoning and the availability of money. The more you check these things before making an offer, the less "subject to's" you have to put into the contract.

ACT TWO: COUNTEROFFERS, BACKUP OFFERS, LOWERED OFFERS

The house you like was listed at $175,000. You offer $150,000. The seller balks. "No way," he or she declares. "I was originally asking $175,000, and I want at least $160,000."

That is known as the *counteroffer.* The seller writes out a counteroffer, or simply crosses out the $150,000 figure that you put on your offer sheet, writes in the $160,000 amount, initials it, and gives or sends it back to you. A sample counteroffer is included on page 76 of this chapter.

Now it is your turn to accept or reject the counteroffer. If you have decided you can afford to go up to $155,000, which is halfway between $150,000 and $160,000, then you come back with what is known as a counter-counteroffer. There are no rules about how much over or under —this is bargaining, a game that undoubtedly began when some caveman saw a nicer cave down the road and offered to pay his neighbor a handful of flints for it.

You go back and forth as many times as you need to in order to arrive at an agreement. Offers can be countered (it is always best to do so in writing) until one party says, "That's it, no deal, good-bye."

Not comfortable with bargaining? You automatically set yourself up for a higher price. You are the type good bargainers such as myself love doing business with.

If you are not comfortable haggling, you would be well advised to hire a procuring broker (see chapter 2 for a discussion of buyer-brokers) to do it for you. I do not recommend letting your attorney bargain for you: this is not a legal procedure, it is a marketing one.

On the house we have used as an example, there may be a *backup offer* lurking in the shadows. You have offered $150,000. A smart seller might already be holding an offer sheet from another person for $160,-000. That backup offer gives the seller a powerful bargaining tool in reply to you.

In a different scenario, your $150,000 offer could be the backup offer. The seller might hold you off a bit just in case the first serious buyer who looked at the house comes in with an offer of only $140,000.

Even if you have put a binder, or good-faith money, on a house, you *can* change your mind and make a *lowered offer*—rather than withdraw entirely. As long as there are "subject to's" in your offer, you have every right to lower it, should you discover something amiss.

One woman from a northeastern state who telephoned me had located a handsome house through a broker who told her it was worth $125,000. The broker said she could grab it for $120,000 if she put a $100 binder on it right then and there. Later, to her dismay, the woman learned that houses in that area were only in the $95,000 range.

I agreed that the woman should return to the broker and explain that research indicated the house was not worth $120,000. She should make a lowered offer. If the broker said, "You can't," she could demand her money back. If the broker refused, she could threaten to report the broker to that state's real estate licensing agency. No broker in his right mind would risk a complaint like that just to keep a $100 binder.

EXITING BEFORE THE FINAL CURTAIN

This brief dramatic framework does not force you to stay in your seat if you do not like the show. That is what a *jump-out,* or *buyer protection, clause* is for. Jump-out clauses are safety valves—legitimate, special contingency clauses, written into your offer subject to your accomplishing something before making the sale.

A typical jump-out gives you the right to accompany the real estate agent when he or she presents the contract to the seller, so you make sure the agent does not make an inadvertent mistake that blows the deal. Still another jump-out allows you to cancel if you do not get the correct fixtures, shrubbery, TV antenna, heating unit and other major items originally promised.

Are you an impulsive person? A jump-out clause protects you from the kind of error that broker Charlie Isaacs calls the "careless autograph." This mistake crops up when you finally discover a house that seems perfect for you. You are sitting in the kitchen with the seller and the broker. Everyone has agreed to what appear to be all the major points.

Then the broker reaches into an attaché case, pulls out a form, and hands you a pen. "This is where you sign, this is where the seller signs," the broker says. Whoa! The form he is holding could be a binding contract. It probably leaves out 90 percent of the terms you want to put into an offer. But if your excitement gets the better of you and you sign it, you are bound to the terms you have signed. You are guilty of a "careless autograph."

Relax. You can correct the error without an eraser. In fact, you do not even have to read the form. Find some blank space above your signature and write, "Notwithstanding anything contained in this document, this agreement is contingent upon the buyer's consultation with counsel and signing of formal contract by both parties no later than ——— [a certain date]."

That is a mouthful of Charlie's multisyllabic language, but it will do the job. In plain English, friends, it is the *all-inclusive jump-out clause.* A shorter way to put it is: "subject to my attorney's approval." It is a built-in excuse to get out of the deal.

BEHIND THE SCENES IN THE NEGOTIATION DRAMA

Many people know how to root out a good bargain. They know how to find the right neighborhood. But when they get face to face or on the telephone with people, they blow it.

I love looking for deals and bargains, whether in real estate or at flea markets and garage sales. My first rule is: always *be prepared to walk away.* If you cannot get your terms, back out.

As Roger Dawson, a negotiations consultant, told my radio audience, "The other side can sense when you really want that property. The minute you say to yourself, 'I want this property,' or, 'I'm going to get this,' you've lost as a negotiator."

There is nothing worse than an overenthusiastic buyer. Learn to play the reluctant suitor. Practice phrases like these: "I'm not really interested, this is not exactly what we're looking for, but I appreciate your taking the time to show me the property."

After what writers like to call a pregnant pause, you can add, "Look . . . just to be fair to you, since you were nice enough, what is the very lowest price you would take?" It is strange, says Dawson, how that squeezes people's negotiating range before negotiations even start.

Everybody has a mental negotiating range—a high figure that he or she hopes to get . . . an acceptable midpoint . . . and a bottom line. You need to find those numbers. If a seller starts to wriggle out of a deal, find out what it takes to keep it together. Maybe it is a matter of upping the price $5,000, or increasing the down payment.

Perhaps you always prefer to buy with the least amount of money down. You had better be able to "read" other people. If you listen, they will tell you, whether or not the least amount down is good for them too.

Be flexible. Settle in your own mind, in advance, those things you might compromise on.

Body language will give you a lot of clues about the other party. If that person is a smoker, chances are he or she will not smoke when tense. You can lighten things up to the point at which the seller lights up—thus signaling that you have eased some of the tension.

Another symptom of tension, Roger Dawson tells me, is the buttoned jacket. The moment a stiff, formal banker reaches down and opens up his jacket, you know he has relaxed enough to listen in earnest to your negotiating points.

STOCK CHARACTERS IN REAL ESTATE DRAMA

Every deal reveals typical personalities at work on either side. Experienced negotiators like Roger Dawson learn to recognize them and use them. So can you.

For example, Roger once bought a duplex on which two other investors were also bidding. He made the *lowest* offer of the three, yet he still got the seller to accept it. Why? "Because I recognized the particular personality style of the seller," he explains. "The *amiable* personality." This character is extremely concerned with the attitude of the buyer who will own the property next. The amiable personality, in Roger's deal, needed to know that the tenants would be well taken care of. Roger was careful to make it evident during negotiations that he would be a caring landlord.

The opposite style belongs to the *pragmatic* personality. This type could care less what the new owner of the property is going to do or whether the rents will be raised.

Negotiating conversations may contain hidden meanings, which you can learn to pick up. There are certain phrases Roger calls "preparers." If you want to convey something to a seller that might be a bit touchy, you prepare the seller first. One example is the much-used sentence beginning, "I don't mean to put pressure on you." In fact, you are saying that you are indeed about to apply pressure.

Next are the "legitimizers." When a person starts off with "frankly speaking," you can expect that person will try to justify something that he or she does not really believe in. When Rhett Butler told Scarlett O'Hara, "Frankly, my dear, I don't give a damn," he probably did!

You become a good negotiator by learning to be a good listener . . . and that includes listening intently to the "little" words that mean a lot. According to Roger Dawson, phrases like "as you are aware" or "incidentally" or "before I forget" usually precede something that is pretty important.

Why not practice negotiating before you actually speak with a seller, broker or lender? We show-business folks talk to the mirror all the time. So can you. You can also rehearse with a friend, practice an upcoming conversation with a tape recorder, or write out a few sentences that you can read back during a telephone conversation.

What constitutes "winning" a negotiation? I don't mean trying to put something over on the seller. The ideal negotiation culminates in two winners, the "win-win" solution.

A classic win-win deal—one every buyer should know about—is the lease with option to purchase. If you are unsettled, or you do not have enough money for a down payment, this could be the best solution for you. (See chapter 8 on this option for details.)

One final suggestion in negotiating for the best buy: look at the situation from your counterpart's point of view too. Read the seller's chapter on negotiating, in which I suggest how a seller should act during negotiations.

Sample Counteroffer

(Use this form to make counteroffers in writing, as either buyer or seller.)

Date: _____

In response to the **Offer_____ To Purchase, _____ To Exchange, ____ To Lease** the property commonly known as . _____

_____

made by _____ on (date) _____,
the following Counteroffer is submitted:

_____

_____

_____

_____

_____

_____

All other terms remain the same.

If this is Seller's Counteroffer, Seller reserves right to accept any other offer prior to Purchaser's written acceptance of this Counteroffer. Acceptance shall not be effective until personally received by Seller or Seller's agent.

This Counteroffer expires unless a copy with Seller's (Purchaser's) written acceptance is delivered to Purchaser (Seller) or agent on or before _____ (time) on _____ (date).

Signed _____ Purchaser (Seller)

Date: _____

The undersigned Seller (Purchaser) accepts the above Counteroffer.
Signed _____

Receipt of acceptance acknowledged on _____ (date)
by _____ Purchaser (Seller)

[Adapted from Professional Publishing Corp. Form 101-A. Used with permission.]

Sample Binder

Memorandum of Agreement

The Seller of a house located at

_____

acknowledges receipt of $ _____ as a good-faith deposit

on the above-described house from _____ (Buyer),

hereinafter known as Buyer. The total price of the house is $_____,

and a formal agreement will be executed on or before _____ (date).

If Buyer does not execute the agreement on or before abovementioned

date, then Seller shall keep the deposit as liquidated damages. If Seller fails

to execute an agreement on or before the abovementioned date, Seller

shall return to Buyer the deposit as described above.

If an offer has been made subject to any conditions, those conditions shall

be signed by both parties, attached to and made part of this agreement.

Accepted this ____ day of _____ (month), 19____ by

_____   _____
(Seller)   (Buyer)

_____   _____
(Seller)   (Buyer)

[*Note:* The binder money should be paid by check, made out to the "trust account" of the seller's attorney.]

Sample Purchase Agreement and Deposit Receipt

Received from _____ hereinafter designated as Purchaser, the sum of $_____, evidenced by ____ cash, ____ personal check, ____ cashier's check, ____ other, _____, to be deposited upon acceptance with _____ _____on account of the **Purchase Price** of $_____ for the real property situated in the City of _____, County of _____ State of _____, described as:_____, upon the following terms and conditions:

1. **Deposit Increase:** The deposit shall be increased to $_____ within _____ days from acceptance, evidenced by cash.

2. **Prorations:** Rents, taxes, interest and other expenses of the property to be prorated as of the date of recordation of the deed. Security deposits, advance rentals or considerations involving future lease credits shall be credited to Purchaser.

3. **Closing:** On or before _____ or within _____ days from acceptance, whichever is later, both parties shall deposit with an authorized escrow holder all funds and instruments necessary to complete the sale in accordance with the terms hereof. Thereafter any party, including Agent, may disclose the terms of sale. The representations and warranties herein shall not be terminated by conveyance of the property. Escrow fee to be paid by

_____.

4. **Physical Possession:** Physical possession, with all keys and garage door openers, shall be delivered to Purchaser either
   ____a. Upon recordation of the deed.
   ____b. After recordation, but not later than midnight of _____
_____. Unless Seller has vacated the premises prior to recordation, Seller shall pay Purchaser _____ per day from the recordation to date of possession and leave in escrow a sum equal to the above per diem amount multiplied by the number of days from date of closing to date allowed for delivery of possession. Said sum to be disbursed to the persons entitled thereto on the date possession is delivered.

5. **Evidence of Title** in the form of ____ a policy of title insurance, ____ other _____, to be paid for by _____ .

Sample Purchase Agreement and Deposit Receipt (continued)

6. **Examination of Title:** Fifteen (15) days from date of acceptance hereof are allowed Purchaser to examine the title to the property and to report in writing any valid objections thereto. Any exceptions to the title which would be disclosed by examination of the records shall be deemed to have been accepted unless reported in writing within said 15 days. If Purchaser objects to any exceptions to the title, Seller shall use due diligence to remove such exceptions at his own expense before close of escrow. But if such exceptions cannot be removed before close of escrow, all rights and obligations hereunder may, at the election of Purchaser, terminate and end, and the deposit shall be returned to Purchaser, unless he elects to purchase the property subject to such exceptions.

7. **Encumbrances:** In addition to any encumbrances referred to herein, Purchaser shall take title to the property subject to (a) real estate taxes not yet due and (b) covenants, conditions, restrictions, rights-of-way and easements of record, if any, which do not materially affect the value or intended use of the property. The amount of any bond or assessment which is a lien shall be ____ paid, ____ assumed by _____.

8. **Fixtures:** All items permanently attached to the property including attached floor coverings, draperies with hardware, shades, blinds, window and door screens, storm sashes, combination doors, awnings, light fixtures, TV antennas, electric garage door openers, outdoor plants and trees, are included free of liens.

9. **Personal Property:** The following personal property, on the premises when inspected by Purchaser, is included in the purchase price and shall be transferred to Purchaser by a Warranty Bill of Sale at close of escrow. No warranty is implied as to the condition of said property: _____

_____

_____

10. **Maintenance:** Seller covenants that the heating, air-conditioning (if any), electrical, sewer, drainage, sprinkler (if any) and plumbing systems including the water heater, as well as built-in appliances and other mechanical apparatuses shall be in normal working order on the date physical possession is delivered. Seller shall replace any cracked or broken glass including windows, mirrors, shower and tub enclosures. Until physical possession is delivered, Seller shall maintain existing landscaping, grounds and pool (if any). The fol-

Sample Purchase Agreement and Deposit Receipt (continued)

lowing items are specifically excluded from the above: _____
_____.

11. **Notices:** By acceptance hereof, Seller warrants that he has no notice of violations relating to the property, from City, County or State agencies.

12. **Provisions:** The provisions checked below are included in this agreement on the reverse side [of an actual purchase agreement].

_____ A. Pest control inspection, paid by ____ Purchaser ____ Seller
_____ B. Existing pest control report dated _____, by _____
_____ C. As is, but subject to Purchaser's approval
_____ D. Waiver of pest control inspection
_____ E. Roof inspection within ____ days of acceptance
_____ F. City and County inspections
_____ G. Condominium disclosure
_____ H. Home protection contract for $_____, paid by _____
_____ I. Maintenance reserve of $_____
_____ J. Inspection of property condition, pool, septic tank and energy efficiency
_____ K. VA appraisal clause
_____ L. FHA appraisal clause
_____ M. Smoke detectors, provided by _____
_____ N. Flood hazard zone
_____ O. Contingent upon the sale of _____

13. **Access To Property:** Seller agrees to provide reasonable access to the property to Purchaser, inspectors and appraisers representing Purchaser.

14. **Liquidated Damages:** By initialing this provision Purchaser _____ and Seller _____ agree that in the event Purchaser defaults in the performance of this agreement, Seller shall retain the amount of the deposit, or 3 percent of the purchase price, whichever is less, as liquidated damages for such default. The remainder of the deposit, if any, shall be refunded to Purchaser. The parties agree to confirm this provision upon making the additional deposit with the escrow holder.

15. **Default:** In the event that Purchaser shall default in the performance of this agreement, unless the parties have agreed to a provision for liquidated damages, Seller may, subject to any rights of the Agent herein, retain Pur-

Sample Purchase Agreement and Deposit Receipt (continued)

chaser's deposit on account of damages sustained and may take such action as he deems appropriate to recover such portion of the deposit as may be allowed by law. In the event that Purchaser shall so default, unless Purchaser and Seller have agreed to liquidated damages, Purchaser agrees to pay the brokers entitled thereto such commissions as would be payable by seller in the absence of such default. Purchaser's obligation to said brokers shall be in addition to any rights which said brokers may have against Seller in the event of default. In the event legal action is instituted by the broker or any party to this agreement to enforce the terms of this agreement, or arising out of the execution of this agreement or the sale, or to collect commissions, the prevailing party shall be entitled to receive from the other party a reasonable attorney fee to be determined by the court in which such action is brought.

16. **Expiration:** This offer shall expire unless a copy hereof with Seller's written acceptance is delivered to Purchaser or his/her Agent within _____ days.

17. **Time:** Time is of the essence of this agreement.

18. **Additional Terms And Conditions:** _____

_____

_____

_____

The undersigned Purchaser has read both sides of this agreement and acknowledges receipt of a copy hereof. Purchaser acknowledges further that he/she has not received or relied upon any statements or representations by the undersigned Agent which are not herein expressed.

_____ Real Estate Company

By: _____ Agent

Dated: _____ Time: _____

Broker's initials: _____ Dated: _____

_____ Signature of Purchaser

_____ Name of Purchaser

Acceptance

Seller accepts the foregoing offer and agrees to sell the herein described property for the price and on the terms and conditions herein specified.

Sample Purchase Agreement and Deposit Receipt (continued)

Commission: Seller hereby agrees to pay to _____,
Broker in this transaction, in cash from proceeds at close of escrow, for services rendered: _____ (dollars).
In the event that Purchaser defaults and fails to complete the sale, Broker shall be entitled to receive one-half of Purchaser's deposit, but not more than the commission earned, without prejudice to Broker's rights to recover the balance of the commission from Purchaser. The mutual rescission of this agreement by Purchaser and Seller shall not relieve said parties of their obligations to Broker hereunder. This agreement shall not limit the rights of Broker provided in any listing or other agreement which may be in effect between Seller and Broker, except that the amount of the commission shall be as specified herein.

Dated: _____ Time: _____

The undersigned Seller hereby acknowledges receipt of a copy hereof.

_____ Signature of Seller

_____ Name of Seller

_____ Real Estate Company

By: _____

[*Note:* In actual Purchase agreements, details of provisions listed under section 12 above would be spelled out and appropriate ones indicated by check mark on additional pages.]

[Adapted from Professional Publishing Corp. Form 101-CAL. Used with permission.]

BUYER PROTECTION CLAUSES
("Subject-to" clauses that can be included in a purchase agreement)

1. This offer is subject to buyer getting adequate financing.
2. This offer is subject to buyer's approval of title insurance policy, to be obtained at seller's expense.
3. This offer is subject to buyer's attorney's approval.
4. This offer is subject to buyer's written approval of an itemized list of all personal property items that remain with the property.
5. This offer is contingent upon written approval from buyer's spouse.
6. This offer is contingent on buyer's approval of an engineer's report, to be paid for by seller.
7. This offer is contingent on buyer's final inspection of the property prior to closing.
8. The liability for seller's note shall be limited to the property and shall not extend beyond this. [Known as the "Exculpatory" clause]
9. Should buyer refuse to complete the transaction, then seller can keep buyer's earnest money as *total* liquidated damages. [Known as the "Liquidated Damages" clause]
10. The note payable to seller shall be amortized over _____ years with a balloon payment in _____ years from date of execution.
11. Seller agrees that his second mortgage shall be junior to and inferior to an extension renewal or replacement of the existing first.
12. In the event that buyer cannot obtain financing at a rate not to exceed _____ percent per year when balloon payment comes due, then the loan shall be extended for one year.
13. All dates and times shall be automatically extended 30 days if necessary for lender approval.

Chapter 7

Shopping for Money

Just a few years ago, you would go to your local bank, get a rate, fill out a form, and a few weeks later you would have a mortgage for 25 or 30 years, at a fixed rate of interest.

Now, everything has changed. Adjustable rates were introduced, confusing many people. Interest rates zoomed sky-high as money got tight. Then, when rates went down, an even more insidious process began. Bankers began to make great promises that they could not keep.

Today, too many of us accept a handshake from a banker, only to get the back of his hand later on. Early 1986, to use a recent case, seemed like an ideal time to get cheap mortgages. How many people accepted a handshake promise from their friendly banker for a new mortgage of 9½ percent? A lot.

And how many people found out, when they returned two weeks later, that the rate had jumped to 10 or 11 percent with 2 points on closing, because they had never obtained the original promise on the right piece of paper? A lot.

It will not happen to you after you read this chapter. Later, on pages 96 through 101, you also will learn about *nontraditional* ways to find money from the growing ranks of reputable *mortgage brokers.* And you will discover that you can get *creative loans from other sources,* such as private investors, your family or the seller of the house you want, when you do not have enough for a down payment.

First, let us take a look at what most mortgages offer, how they differ, and how you get one. A helpful hint: think of a mortgage as simply another appliance or "thing" that you are buying. It is an expensive item—perhaps the most expensive you will ever purchase. Even so, you would not buy a car, a fur coat or a computer without shopping around for a good deal, would you?

These days you have to shop for money every bit as carefully as you shop for the house itself. Just ¼ percent less for a $100,000 mortgage could save you more than $125,000 over the life of a 30-year fixed-rate loan.

WHERE TO BEGIN YOUR COMPARISON-SHOPPING

Most people begin by telephoning the bank where they have their savings or checking account. Make an appointment, and lay out your needs. Take the comparison-shopping chart at the end of this chapter and jot down the numbers your bank offers.

But do not sign anything. Get recommendations for other mortgage sources from friends or the sales agent on the house. If you have plenty of time, shop by phone for several weeks. Compare offers. If you make two calls a day for a month, you will have talked to sixty lenders. I can guarantee you will come up with an offer after those sixty calls that is better than the first one you received.

Lenders include mutual savings banks, savings and loans, commercial banks, credit unions, mortgage brokers and private investors. Since the major business of savings and loans is lending mortgage money, you might find they offer the best rates. But that changes from market to market.

The best rates are not necessarily available from a lender with the best service. Shop for service as well as rates. There are many mortgage companies that give you lower rates . . . and lousy service. Sometimes companies disappear, often taking your initial application fee with them. Check your potential loan company's references.

Your company's bank or credit union might be an excellent place to get a mortgage, if it passes the comparison-shopping test by offering the least amount of points, the best interest rate and the greatest period of time. (I know, for instance, that teachers' credit unions lend mortgage money at good rates.)

Ask your company's chief financial officer or a staff member for the name of an individual whom you can talk to personally. A company bank is expected to perform for corporate customers.

MORTGAGE MANIA

As interest rates have gone down, mortgages have become cheaper; but *shopping* for one can be like wandering through an Asian bazaar. One of my radio listeners, Mike, asked a while back, "With everyone on the bandwagon, how does one choose a type of mortgage? Between ARMs, GEMs, conventional loans and balloon mortgages," he moaned, "I don't know which way to turn."

To evaluate what kind of mortgage was best for him, I asked how old he was, whether he had a family, what tax bracket he was in, and what monthly payments he felt he could afford. From there, he could work his way backward to the alphabet soup at the bank, or to another, nontraditional but perhaps more comfortable financing arrangement, such as equity sharing.

THE OLD STANDBY: A FIXED-RATE MORTGAGE

The best deal for many Americans today is the *fixed-rate mortgage,* with a clause in it that there is no penalty for prepayment. You will understand why as you read through this chapter.

"Fixed rate" means that the interest rate remains the same for the life of the mortgage, whether interest rates rise or fall. You write a check each month for the same amount—this year, next year, 10 years from now.

Fixed-rate mortgages are usually for a period of 15 or 30 years. In general, the longer the better, since you pay less per month on the longer mortgage.

The reason you want *no penalty for prepayment* is to cover yourself. If you do end up with a windfall, or an increase in salary, you can decide to pay more money each month toward principal, provided the bank agrees, with no extra charges.

A young couple I knew, on the verge of buying a first home in Suffolk County, the tip of New York's Long Island, present a textbook example of people who would benefit most from a *conventional fixed-rate mortgage.*

The couple had a combined income of $55,000, fairly stable jobs and a decent credit record. They had savings of $45,000 to use toward a down payment on a house priced at $145,000.

They would need $100,000, plus $5,000 in closing costs. Because they were young, I felt they would be best off with a 30-year term. For prime candidates like these, there are many lenders who will offer competitively priced fixed-rate loans.

Who should look for a 15-year versus a 30-year fixed-rate mortgage? A person who does not have good self-control. A 15-year mortgage forces you to pay up earlier than you normally would; it carries larger payments, so you have to have more income.

If you are close to retirement, you might be better off with a 15-year term because you will pay off your house more quickly. Then, when you are retired on a reduced income, you will not be stuck with big payments. My recommendation for retired people is to have a house free and clear of any payments whatsoever by the time they retire. You can get money out of a debt-free house instead of putting money in.

For a comparison of a 15-year versus a 30-year fixed-rate mortgage, see page 105.

BE CAREFUL OF THE CALL TO ARMS

ARM stands for adjustable-rate mortgage. This mortgage has in it a clause stating that each year, or each six months, the bank has the right to raise the mortgage a certain number of points, usually no more than 2.

Most ARMs will have a *cap,* a lid on how much the rate can be raised. If you buy an 8½-percent ARM, it usually has a cap on it of 13½ or 14 percent. At least you are forewarned. Should mortgage rates nationally go up to 13 percent or higher, you are going to pay the full amount of that ARM cap, which is 13½ to 14 percent.

The bank cannot raise your ARM rate if mortgage rates decline in general. Your rate changes yearly according to the marketplace. It is usually tied to some index, such as that of T-bills or Ginnie Maes or money market funds. If the index falls, an ARM might be adjusted downward.

In general, I am opposed to bankers who want your ARMs. You might as well throw in a leg, too. With mortgage rates as low as 10 to 11 percent recently, for instance, there was no reason for consumers to take the risk of having their mortgage rates go up.

Listen closely, friends. *ARMs are very dangerous.* They are recommended only to a purchaser who is going to be in the house less than 5 years, because it is you, the borrower, and not the bank, who is taking the risk on the rise and fall of mortgage rates.

Sure, the big bank ads look tempting in the newspaper. You may begin to borrow on an ARM in the first year at 7½ percent, a lower rate than you would get on a conventional mortgage. But then you get a thing called "Payment Shock" 2, 3 and 5 years down the line. If you are going to bail out at that time, fine. Otherwise, hold out for a fixed rate. I would have said the same thing to anyone buying a house in 1981, when rates were at 15 percent. You can always refinance.

The bankers did a heck of a marketing job on ARMs. They shoved them down the consumers' throats. But by July 1986, less than 15 percent of mortgages were ARMs, whereas in November 1985, when rates were much higher, ARMs accounted for 60 percent of mortgages. The consumer is becoming more educated.

GOOD AND BAD POINTS

When you shop for a mortgage, you may be quoted a rate of, say, 11 percent "plus 2 points." The *points are a one-time fee* that you pay the bank at the time you take out the mortgage. One point equals one percent of the loan.

If a lender does not mention points, ask. Almost every lender charges points these days. A point is a "kicker" that you pay someone for the privilege of borrowing his money. Sometimes so many points are tacked on that a good rate is actually mediocre. By "doing the numbers" at the end of this chapter, you can see how the points affect the proposed deal.

You may also be asked to pay a separate *origination fee,* quoted in points. This is another one-time charge you pay solely for paperwork.

NEGOTIATING WITH A BANKER

You might think a lesson in talking to a banker is so elementary that everyone knows it by heart. Not true—especially first-time home buyers. So let us follow Mr. and Mrs. Buyer, who are hot on the trail of a three-bedroom, two-bath house near the apartment they now rent, as they shop for a loan.

They know that it will speed things up if they bring with them as much financial material as possible. Once they shake hands with a bank employee in the mortgage loan department, the banker does, in fact, ask them to fill out a form.

This application asks for their combined income, credit card payment debt, current rental payments or mortgage payment, car payment and any other debts. It may also require a copy of their latest tax return. In addition, the bank wants to know: Do they have any outside income from stocks or bonds? What about their savings? Do they own any securities? Have they inherited any money? Are they the beneficiaries of any insurance policies or trusts?

After the Buyers fill out the form, the banker could request a copy of the offer-to-purchase contract. When they explain that they are still shopping for the right house, the banker will want to know what their price range is and how much of a down payment they can make. The Buyers are looking for a house costing about $150,000. They are prepared to put down as much as 20 to 25 percent.

The banker might then agree to "process" their application and to make sure they "qualify" for a 75-percent mortgage, on the basis of the data the Buyers have provided. Thus the bank can have a standby mortgage available when the Buyers get ready to purchase the house.

Being good shoppers, the Buyers want to get an idea of what the terms would be. More than likely, the banker will not want to "lock in" a rate until they settle on a specific house. But the banker can give a rough estimate of the rate, as well as the points.

As suggested by the phrase "mortgage mania," interest rates fluctuate weekly. "As soon as you bring me the purchase contract, I can give you a rate that I will *lock in* for sixty days, which is the industry standard," the banker says. "We will order the appraisal and the survey then, to get things rolling."

The Buyers have heard horror stories from friends whose banks could not get all the paperwork done in 60 days. By the time the paperwork was done, the rate those friends had "locked in" was gone. The new rate was half a percent higher!

An honest banker will admit that times are not normal right now. Then it is the Buyers' turn to request from the banker the names and phone numbers of the appraiser, the credit reporting firm and the surveyor, so they can push those people to get the paperwork done on time. This is an excellent suggestion. However, if someone drags his feet, a logjam would occur for the Buyers, just as it has for millions of others.

Nevertheless, the Buyers have made considerable progress. Their next move would be to ask the same questions of a second savings bank, then a nearby commercial bank, then a savings and loan, then a mortgage broker.

What happens once you (or Mr. and Mrs. Buyer) have received at least four good offers?

The next step is reviewing the charts at the end of this chapter to calculate which lender has offered you the best interest rate over the period of the loan, and which charges the least amount of points and closing costs.

Finally, go back to the banker and negotiate for the best deal. That means getting the assurance that there will be no penalty for prepayment of the loan, and that it will be *assumable* for a qualified buyer of the house further down the road.

IS THE LOAN ASSUMABLE?

An assumable loan means that the person to whom you sell your house 5, 10 or 20 years after buying it can take over, or assume payments on, your loan. It is a very attractive selling point for your house, since the financing is already in place.

Lately it has been fairly easy to get an assumable clause on ARMs, but it is more difficult on conventional mortgages. Your bargaining capability comes into play here. Do not be afraid to ask. Fight for an assumable clause. It is worth it—and it costs you nothing to ask. Personally, I would not take a mortgage without an assumable clause. A nonassumable mortgage is a stumbling block should you need to resell your house.

As mentioned earlier, if you happen to come into some extra money, or if you want to refinance your mortgage when rates go down, you will want to be able to pay on the principal of your mortgage *without penalty*. It is not difficult to get a "no-prepayment penalty" clause. However, it is not automatic. *You have to ask for it.*

LOCK THAT RATE!

I cannot begin to tell you how many angry people have telephoned me to complain about promises broken by bankers on a good interest rate. When "mortgage mania" hit consumers and banks in 1986, even those people who thought they had iron-clad guarantees watched helplessly as the 60-day period expired without the lender finishing the paperwork. When a loan was finally approved, the good rate was no longer in effect.

Here are some steps to take to "lock into" a good rate:

First, ask your banker to guarantee the rate he quotes you *in writing.* A verbal guarantee is a bunch of empty words.

Second, get the rate guaranteed from *date of application,* not the date of approval. Let us say that a lender quotes you a 10⅝-percent mortgage, but adds, "That is our present rate. When you are approved thirty days from now, whatever the market rate is, we will guarantee it then." That is very different from the lender who says, "I will guarantee the following rate in writing from today through the next sixty days."

Third, be careful of how the interest rate on the mortgage is stated. Many lenders solicit customers with ads stating that the "contract rate" for a mortgage is 10 percent. Sounds great, huh? But the next line in the ads states: "APR: 10.141 percent."

What is APR? Annual, or actual, percentage rate—the *real* rate. "Contract rate" is nothing but an advertising ploy—it is the rate without all the costs factored in. The use of "contract rate" and "APR" listings is a big scandal in the lending industry.

Fourth, ask as well for a guarantee that if the rate goes down in the interim, you will get the lower rate.

Fifth, get the points guaranteed, in writing. Unfortunately, many people think they have a written guarantee, when all they have is a piece of paper. Here is why:

After you get a *verbal mortgage commitment* on the size and interest rate, the lender often follows by sending a statement of the terms of the offer, under the federal "truth-in-lending" law. The statement looks as though you have a written commitment now. Unfortunately, it is not —*unless an officer of the bank or lender has signed it.* Even if someone has signed it, these statements can have their own jump-out clauses, allowing the lender to *change the terms.*

Read the "commitment" carefully. Does it *specifically state* that the lender will loan you X number of dollars on or before such and such a date, at X percent of interest, over X number of years? If not, go back and demand a *real* commitment in writing, signed by an officer who has authority to issue it. Otherwise, you do not have a mortgage commitment. Period.

In a "mortgage mania" market, it may not be realistic to expect a real, in-writing commitment locking in a rate until all the paperwork is done. Do the best you can.

SECURE THE DEAL WITH CASH WHILE YOU WAIT FOR THE MORTGAGE

Suppose the Buyers found a great house but the lender said, "Sorry, we have a line of people ahead of you. You have to wait ninety days for the mortgage to be processed."

Meanwhile, the owner said, "You have thirty days to close the deal. Otherwise, forget it."

The Buyers are afraid they might lose the house. They are in one of the hottest real estate pockets in the country. Other lenders are just as swamped. What can the Buyers do?

Here is a solution suggested by one knowledgeable broker, Alan Yasky. "Most transactions do not close in thirty days," he points out. What people *really* want is *a firm commitment in 30 days,* so they can take their house off the market without worrying whether it will have to be relisted.

Make that seller comfortable, he suggests, by giving the seller the *down payment in cash.* As long as you put 25 to 40 percent of the selling price in cash and you can convince people—by displaying a recently conducted credit check—that you are credit-worthy, most sellers will be reasonable about waiting for the mortgage to come through within a few months.

Once the seller has agreed to a temporary all-cash deal, that seller does not have to worry about the house being pulled off the market. In addition, you, the buyer, have plenty of time between the contract and the closing to secure a mortgage. The actual closing date can be flexible. Some people take as long as six months to close such a deal.

If a seller refuses to budge on this cash down payment scenario, ask your bank for a 90- to 120-day *bridge loan,* which will pay the seller in full. You can pay off the bridge loan when you close on your mortgage. (See page 95 in this chapter for more on bridge loans.)

This may be the first time you are buying a house, but chances are it will not be your last. If you are "trading up" to a bigger home, or simply buying a new house while you sell your former one, read chapter 28, which explains how to handle both deals without getting ulcers.

Also, let me repeat what I said in the chapter on attorneys: have your own real estate attorney review the legal (but not business) aspects of all mortgage documents that are presented to you.

OTHER KINDS OF MORTGAGES

Conventional fixed-rate and adjustable-rate mortgages are the instruments the majority of Americans use to finance their homes. But there are others that might be right for you.

The *graduated-payment mortgage,* or GPM, literally could be just what the doctor ordered. This is a fixed-rate mortgage with accelerated payments each year as your income goes up. A GEM, or *growth equity mortgage,* is almost the same thing. In both, you might make payments of $400 a month the first year, $600 the second year, $700 the third year. Thus, instead of paying off your loan in 30 years, you may pay it off in 18 years or less.

Typically, this benefits a young physician who is just beginning his or her practice, and who knows his or her income is going to increase dramatically in coming years. It is also great for a new MBA who is entering a field like investment banking. It is not much good for teachers or other people on nongrowth salaries.

A RAM, or *reverse annuity mortgage,* is helpful to the senior citizen or anyone whose house is paid for in full. You go to a non-bank lender and sell the house to that lender. The seller now gets regular payment *from* the lender. You still live in the house. A RAM, sometimes known as a Grannie Mae, is good for seniors on fixed incomes, without a life expectancy of more than thirty years. It gives extra bucks to live on.

A *buy-down* is a situation in which you buy from a builder, and the builder pays some money toward your mortgage. This reduces your mortgage payments over the first 3 to 5 years of a loan. It is a sales inducement.

A quick comparison chart of the most popular loans can be found on pages 105–6.

MAKING THE SELLER YOUR LENDER

In certain cases a buyer is better off financing a house without ever visiting a bank or mortgage broker. The alternative is for the buyer to ask the seller of the house to finance the sale.

In a poor marketplace, *seller financing* is common. That is understandable. A seller eager to get rid of a house, knowing that sales in his or her area are slow, often jumps at the chance to take a note for the down payment and have a buyer take over an assumable mortgage.

Seller financing makes sense to you, the buyer, not just when the seller has an assumable mortgage. It is quick—you do not wait weeks to qualify for a mortgage. It is a handy way to buy a house that has no mortgage on it. It also clears a major hurdle when you want to buy but do not have enough money for the down payment and the seller does not need the down payment in cash. You start working with notes, instead of dollars.

Seller financing increases as interest rates go up. From 1980 to 1983, that awful period when interest rates were over 15 percent, seller financing was involved in over half the sales made in the country.

On the other hand, you might do better in lower-interest times with a mortgage. Before deciding if seller financing would benefit you, compare it with the conventional loans that you have found in your comparison-shopping.

Also, read chapter 25 for a discussion of seller financing from the seller's point of view.

WRAPAROUND MORTGAGES

The *wraparound* is a combined mortgage or contract that sometimes comes into play in conjunction with seller financing.

Let us say that someone wants to sell you a house for $150,000. You are willing to pay $10,000 down. The seller is willing to take it. Let us assume further that the house has an existing $90,000 mortgage, which is assumable. That leaves $50,000 to be covered by additional financing.

You can ask the seller to take back a second mortgage for this $50,000. You then enter into a contract, under which you pay the seller X number of dollars a month. The seller uses this monthly payment to pay off the two mortgages. You, the buyer, wind up making a single regular payment that covers the financing by the seller and the existing mortgage.

The contract for this arrangement is known as a wraparound. One payment by the seller goes toward both the first mortgage and the second mortgage. The seller, who holds both, makes the actual payments on the mortgages and gets a profit.

It is not as complicated as it sounds.

Imagine a box. Inside is the existing $90,000 first mortgage and the $50,000 second mortgage. You put the top on the box and wrap the whole thing up with a ribbon. The ribbon is the document that ties things together. That document is what we call a wraparound mortgage.

No points or origination fees need to be paid. Best of all, there is no waiting for the loan to be processed.

BLENDED MORTGAGES

A *blended mortgage* combines two interest rates. Let us say you want to buy a house on which the seller has a first and a second mortgage, both assumable. If the first and second mortgages are with the same bank, and the two mortgages have an interest rate spread of 3 points or more, you will want to ask the bank how much interest it would charge you on a new mortgage blending the two rates.

FHA AND VA LOANS

Veterans qualify for Veterans Administration (VA) mortgages. This kind of financing is useful if you have a veteran's certificate and want to buy a house for 5 percent or less, even nothing, down. There is a cap on the size of VA loan you can get—perhaps $110,000. Such a loan is ideal for a vet who is buying a lower-priced home, under $90,000. Veterans should apply to their VA offices for a certificate and advise their lenders that they are veterans and can qualify.

FHA, or Federal Housing Administration, loans are valuable for Americans without a huge income who are buying modest-priced houses. Look for properties that are offered as "FHA-approved." These houses have met strict requirements set by the FHA.

BRIDGE LOANS

What if you do not get mortgage papers processed fast enough on a house you really like and you are afraid of losing the deal? One solution, mentioned earlier, is to make a temporary cash payment. And what if you do not have the cash?

A second solution is a *bridge loan.* In this arrangement, you get money to tide you over, usually in the form of a short-term note from your bank, secured by your second home or other collateral. Because it is a temporary measure, a bridge loan commonly is for quite a short term—30, 60 or 90 days. Such loans are provided both by banks and by private mortgage brokers.

I know of one radio friend who was buying a major property for $1.5 million. She needed $500,000 while waiting for her financing, which was already in the works. I sent her a list of private mortgage brokers (see page 96), who had sources of funds *outside her state.* Many of them are happy to provide a bridge loan for such a person.

There *is* a catch: you pay a hefty price for a bridge loan—in this woman's case, perhaps $5,000 or even $10,000. But if you have a deadline on a contract, a 12-percent bridge loan might be an excellent investment.

EQUITY LOANS FOR VACATION HOMES

An *equity loan,* as the name implies, is a loan for which you use the equity in your house as collateral.

You can make excellent use of your money by taking out an equity loan to purchase a vacation property. You will get the same rates on an equity loan as you will on a fresh mortgage, or even lower rates. An equity loan, however, is a much quicker loan.

Beware, though, of equity loans with adjustable rates. In some cases, a bank gets the right to adjust the rate *quarterly.* You could wind up paying 15 percent very quickly on a loan that you believed carried a 10-percent rate. Go to your own bank first, then compare its rates with those of other lenders. For details on vacation home buying, see chapter 15. For more on equity loans, see chapter 25, page 325.

CREATIVE FINANCING

There are other ways to finance a house that probably have never entered your mind.

When you want a personally tailored suit or dress, you might start at a department store, then discover you have better luck at a specialized clothing boutique.

The same holds true for money. In recent years, there has been a revolution in the finance industry. Experts have developed creative financing for individual clients. Now, when you cannot find a mortgage tailored to your needs at a bank, you go to a reputable mortgage broker. And equity participation is yet another kind of creative financing that involves neither banks nor mortgage brokers.

WHEN TO USE A MORTGAGE BROKER

What happens when you ask the people at your friendly savings and loan for some money and they get hysterical with laughter? Fifteen years ago, you would have gone to another bank, hoping for a better greeting.

Now I urge people, especially angry, frustrated home buyers who call my radio show night after night complaining about banks, to go to a licensed, sophisticated *mortgage broker.*

A mortgage broker operates somewhat the same way a travel agent does. He or she is a middleman who does your mortgage shopping for you, at little or no cost to you. Instead of walking into a cold bank, you walk into the broker's personal office. The broker's service is geared to you.

When a mortgage broker arranges financing, the lender pays the broker a commission for bringing in the client, just as an airline pays a travel agent a commission. There is little or no extra charge to you.

In an era in which loan rates, closing costs and other costs vary tremendously, a middleman can simplify things. The variety of mortgages now available has created the need for a professional who represents the home buyer to the lenders.

My experience indicates that mortgage brokers sometimes—though not always—provide better deals and better service than banks do. I have received two or three calls from mortgage brokers who would say, "I have one lender who will give you a mortgage for X percent, and another who will give it to you for a lower percent and X points." I love that level of personal service. Mortgage brokers can usually arrange financing faster than banks, too.

Not every shopper has as happy a relationship with mortgage brokers as I have had. There are people who receive equally good service from a bank. But my comfort zone is with a mortgage broker. Actually, I am a little lazy. The mortgage broker takes all the pressure off me.

Some bankers disparage mortgage brokers, which I find ridiculous. The idea is to find a licensed person with a good reputation, the same way you find yourself a good travel agent, lawyer or real estate broker.

To begin, is the mortgage broker a member of either the Mortgage Bankers Association or the American Institute of Mortgage Brokers? The latter is a new organization. Of course, ask for references, just as you would with any professional.

Earlier I spoke about shopping for service as well as for money. Because there have been fly-by-night outfits in business to collect mortgage application fees and run off with them, it is extremely important to deal with a reputable lender. Some people, thinking they were getting a low-priced mortgage, lost $350 to $1,000, plus plenty of precious time, when con artists shut their doors and disappeared.

So pay close attention to the last column on the comparison-shopping chart on page 103. Ask the mortgage broker how long his company has been in business. If it is a new company, be very wary.

SERVICE FOR THE OUT-OF-THE-ORDINARY BUYER

Who should consider skipping the banks entirely and go directly to a mortgage broker?

You should, if

- you are a person who likes to shop and take a little more time to get a better deal;
- you have an erratic income, as might those of you who work on commission or own your own business;
- you have had some credit problems in the past but you have straightened them out.

A good mortgage broker will ask much of the same questions that the banker asked Mr. and Mrs. Buyer—income level, debt structure, type of mortgage sought, amount of down payment. Then the broker typically will offer you a choice of mortgages from a "menu" of adjustable- and fixed-rate loans. Some may be from national savings and loans, giving you a wider choice of loans beyond your home town.

Here is one guideline used by mortgage brokers to gauge how much of a loan you can afford: 28 percent of your gross monthly income should equal your mortgage payment (principal and interest) plus taxes. Banks are willing to look at the nature of your debt, so you could go as high as 38 percent of your gross monthly income.

If you have a very good credit history, good employment history and good past mortgage history, these ratios could be stretched from 30 to 38 percent.

Who should *not* go to a mortgage broker? The same person who prefers to shop airlines directly for the cheapest airfare, rather than go to a travel agent. Also, you might not need a mortgage broker if you have a good relationship with an individual banker.

EQUITY SHARING: NOT JUST A WEDDING PRESENT

A story some time ago in *The New York Times,* headlined "Helping the Kids Get Started," was illustrated with a cartoon showing parents popping out of their newlywed children's wedding cake, holding a house and a sack of money. The article told of using *equity sharing,* or *equity participation,* as it is sometimes called, to help a young couple buy a first home.

Equity sharing is one of the most exciting new ways to finance a mortgage. It is also a super way for parents to help a young couple who do not have the money for a down payment. But it need not be limited to just parents and newlyweds. Anyone, a relative or a stranger, can be your partner in an equity participation arrangement.

Equity sharing is good for parents of not-so-young couples who have not saved anything and for grown children with money who want to help their parents, and it is also good for the investor, for uncles and aunts, for the dentist who has a client and wants to own a piece of the action.

Most of all, it is good for you, the buyer. It means you do not own 100 percent of your house, at the beginning. But isn't it better for you to own 50 percent of something than to collect rent receipts?

For example, if you were to purchase a house that required a $10,000 down payment, you could get an investor to make the down payment for you. You would make the monthly payments on the mortgage and live in the house. Then, when you sold the house, you and the investor would share fifty-fifty in the profits derived.

DOING WELL BY DOING GOOD

The nice part of equity participation is that someone helps you get a house, and that person gets a part of the action in return. Both buyer and investor need to set up the arrangement with the help of a knowledgeable attorney. The best plan is outlined in chapter 3. Incidentally, shared equity can be a legal, safe tax shelter for the person who lends the money.

Here is a standard case of equity sharing. Parents (or a friend or investor) give Mr. and Mrs. Buyer the money for a down payment and closing costs. In return, the parents receive half the equity in the home. From that point on, the young couple pays all the carrying charges— principal, interest, taxes, insurance. They have the security of knowing that, unlike rent, their payments cannot be raised by an arbitrary landlord, although their property taxes may go up.

Suppose Mr. and Mrs. Buyer purchase a $100,000 home. Their parents put in $20,000 for the down payment and closing costs. Both parties sign a contract, usually running a shorter term than a mortgage —5 to 7 years. The contract says that anytime within that period, the occupants, the young Buyers, can buy out the parents.

After five years, the house is worth $150,000. The couple sells it. The parents get their $20,000 back, plus a percentage of the appreciation. On a fifty-fifty deal, the parents make a profit of $25,000.

If the couple does not want to sell, or if they are not able to buy the investor out, they all go to the bank and refinance the place for $150,000. As in the buyout, the parents get the $20,000 back first. They then split the remainder equally. The profit? $5,000 a year, plus tax write-offs.

A key benefit is that rather than have a landlord-tenant relationship, which might strain family or other ties, the lender and borrower are partners. Even if you do not live nearby, even if you are purely an investor and do not know the occupants personally, the downside risk is small.

Sounds great, doesn't it? One problem everyone should know about is that the occupants—the children or the borrower—must *qualify* for the loan along with the investor. If the son or daughter or occupant/partner has a small income or none at all, he or she might get turned down by a bank, unless the investor/partner has a strong credit rating.

FINDING AN INVESTING "ANGEL"

Broadway producers often try to mount shows by finding "angels" who will invest in them. You, too, can find an "angel" to help you buy a house.

It is amazing how few people know about private investors and how simple it is to find them. All you have to do is advertise in the classified section of a newspaper.

A man from a southeastern U.S. city who called me was a good candidate to join with a private investor.

This fellow already had a house, but he had not made mortgage payments in three years because of money troubles. He wanted to refinance. His house was worth $160,000. He owed over $50,000 in loan and interest. So he had a $110,000 equity. He would have trouble getting money from a lending institution because of his past credit problems.

"You need a private investor," I told him. "Put a classified ad in your local paper with the headline 'Money Wanted.' The ad would then read: 'Have $110,000 equity in my house. Will give you a first mortgage on my house if you will loan me $50,000 or $60,000.' There are lots of people out there who will take a first mortgage on your house and lend you the money," I said.

The man would arrange with an investor who answered the ad to give the investor a 50-percent security position in the house. He would also pay his investor 1 or 2 points *above* going mortgage rates.

Then an attorney would set up a deed in lieu of foreclosure. That investor would stand to make double his money, if he were forced to take the man's house away. "But you're not going to let him have the house," I continued. "Like other people in your position, you just need a new start." It was another "win-win" shared equity arrangement.

More on Creative Financing

Write to these sources for names and addresses of companies offering unconventional financing at low rates, and say Sonny Bloch referred you:

American Institute of Mortgage Brokers, 1265 K Street, N.W., Washington, DC 20005

Mortgage Bankers Association, 1125 15 Street, N.W., Washington, DC 20005

U.S. League of Savings Institutions, 111 East Wacker Drive, Chicago, IL 60601

I also recommend these magazines: *Financial Freedom Report* and *Creative Real Estate;* and these books: *Nothing Down* and *Creating Wealth* by Robert Allen; *Smart Investor's Guide to Real Estate* by Robert Bruss; and *Government Loans* by Wayne Phillips.

Comparison-Shopping Scorecard

	A Date Called	B Banker or Company	C Person Contacted	D Interest in $ over Term of Loan*	E Length of Loan	F Cost of Survey, Credit Report and Appraisal
1						
2						
3						
4						
5						
6						
7						
8						
9						
10						
11						
12						
13						
14						
15						

*The bank or lender is required by law to give you this information in writing. If you do not want to wait, simply use this example on a $100,000 house, financed at 12 percent for 30 years. You are paying $370,000, plus your initial closing costs. Your total *interest* will be $270,440 for that $100,000 house!

for Mortgages

G Origination Fee	H Application Fee	I Total of Additional Costs: F + G + H†	J Prepayment Penalty? Yes/No	K Assumable? Yes/No	L Lender's Reputation and Years in Business	
						1
						2
						3
						4
						5
						6
						7
						8
						9
						10
						11
						12
						13
						14
						15

†Use Column I for a quick-scan comparison of closing costs. A more detailed worksheet is in chapter 9, page 121.

Formula for Analyzing the Best Deal
(Complete this chart for each lender you are comparison-shopping.)

Total amount of points $ _____

Plus total fees   + $ _____ (Application, Origination, Credit
                                   Report Survey, Appraisal)

Equals total costs   = $ _____

Divided by months of loan + _____ months (Example: 15 years* = 180
                                   months)

Gives **Total** of   = $ _____ extra per month that you pay for
                                   fees over life of loan

Add monthly mortgage
payment   + $ _____

Actual monthly
cost of mortgage to you   = $ _____

Example

Using a $100,000 fixed-rate mortgage for 30 years at 12 percent, with 3
points plus additional fees of $600:

Total amount of points: $ 3,000

Plus total fees: + $ 600

Equals total of: = $ 3,600

Divided by months of loan +   36 (will stay in house 3 years)

Gives **Total** of   = $ 100 extra per month for initial fees†

Add monthly mortgage
payment   + $ 1,029 (on $100,000 loan at 12
                                   percent)

Actual monthly
cost of mortgage to you   = $ 1,129 (plus insurance, state, local
                                   taxes)‡

*Use the number of years you really expect to stay in the house before selling.
†If your closing costs were $7,200 and you planned to stay in the house 3 years, you would
pay $200 per month over the 3-year period to cover those up-front closing costs.
‡This example helps you determine only which mortgage source is best. To analyze your
total Financial Comfort Zone, see chapter 1.

MORTGAGES AT A GLANCE

Type of Loan	*Benefits*	*Drawbacks*
Fixed Rate, Fixed Payment		
1. Conventional 30-year	Fixed monthly payments 30-year payout No surprises	Higher initial rates than ARM Perhaps not assumable
2. Conventional 15-year	Lower rate than 30-year Faster equity buildup Quicker payoff of loan	Higher monthly payments
3. FHA/VA 30- and 15-year fixed	Low down payment Fully assumable No prepayment penalty	May mean heavy points Possible red tape and delay in application
4. Balloon loans (3- to 10-year terms)	Possible discount rates Other favorable terms Possible seller financing	At end of 3 or 10 years entire balance due in lump sum
Adjustable Rate, Variable Payment		
1. ARM, adjustable-rate mortgage; payment changes on 1-, 3-, 5-year schedule	Lower initial rate especially in first year Often assumable Possible future rate decreases Caps may protect you against huge increases May be convertible to fixed after 3 years	Greater rate risk for borrower If no cap, monthly payments could soar

MORTGAGES AT A GLANCE (*Continued*)

Type of Loan	Benefits	Drawbacks
2. GPM, graduated payment mortgage; payments go up during first 5–7 years, then level off	Buyers with marginal incomes may qualify Good for those certain income will increase May be combined with ARM to lower initial rate further	May have higher annual percentage rate (APR) than fixed or ARM May have negative amortization—increasing debt owed by lender
3. GEM, growing equity mortgage; Increasing portion of monthly payment pays off principal; typically pays off in 15–18 years, not 30	Lower up-front payments Quicker loan payoff than fixed or ARM	May have higher rates and down payment than other loans Tax deduction for interest decreases over time

15-YEAR VERSUS 30-YEAR FIXED-RATE MORTGAGE COMPARISON

15-year fixed mortgage after 15 years:		*30-year fixed mortgage after 15 years:*	
Mortgage amount	$50,000	Mortgage amount	$50,000
Interest rate	11½ percent	Interest rate	12 percent
Monthly payment	$584.09	Monthly payment	$514.31
Total amount paid	$105,138.76	Total amount paid	$92,575.80
Total interest paid	$55,138.76	Total interest paid	$85,426.82
Total principal paid	$50,000	Total principal paid	$7,148.98
Mortgage balance	0	Mortgage balance	$42,851.02

Chapter **8**

Unsettled? Think About a Lease with Option to Purchase

When you do not have a down payment, or you are not really sure you are going to like a place, you can negotiate *not to buy it immediately,* but to *lease* it, with an option to purchase it eventually. This is an excellent plan for anyone moving to a new town. It allows you to try out a home without the major commitment involved in an immediate purchase.

When I moved to Manhattan, I was not sure whether I would be there on a permanent basis, so I sought a builder who, in the overbuilt condominium market, needed to fill some empty units. I offered to move in on a lease with option to purchase for 24 months. A portion of my monthly payment goes toward the purchase price. I actually did move into the unit for nothing down.

If I decide I do not want to exercise my option, I simply leave. The builder gets the condo back, and I have had a chance to test the waters. I will have paid some extra money over the years, but it is worth it.

A lease with option to purchase is better than a straight lease because you are in a position to purchase the unit or house for a set price in 2 to 5 years.

THE "NOTHING-DOWN" SOLUTION FOR YOUNG FAMILIES

What about young families who would be happy with the bare four walls but have no money left for a custom home? Few realize they can get a new home under the "lease with option to purchase" alternative.

Many builders of new subdivisions are hungry for families to occupy these houses because they are at the end of a development or they need to cut down on their inventory of empty homes.

Explain to the builder that you have a job in the area, and that you would like to lease the model or new home with an option to purchase. Perhaps the builder will be amenable to a deal. You simply sign an agreement to pay the builder's monthly payments on his existing mortgage and pay extra, for example, $100 a month. After 3 years, you would have paid $3,600 toward the down payment on the purchase.

One night I got a call from the perfect candidate for a lease with option to purchase. He was twenty-eight years old, single, living at home. His salary as an employee of a New England state was $19,600 and he had only $7,500 in savings, but he wanted to have his own place. He was not a carpenter by trade but he was willing to get dirt under his fingernails on weekends.

"You're going to have to find a place where someone is willing to take very little money down—maybe $4,000 or $5,000," I said, "and a lease with option to purchase." The idea is to find someone with a house for sale at, say, $75,000, who needs to leave it soon, because of a job transfer or a divorce or for another reason.

He would explain to the seller that he could not go to a bank immediately to get the 20-percent down payment—$15,000 on a $75,000 house. Instead, he would like to give the seller $4,000 or $5,000 as a down payment, with an option to purchase in 24 or 36 months. Meanwhile, he would move into the seller's house and make the mortgage payments.

"You give me the benefit of the mortgage going down," the young man would tell the seller. In other words, a certain amount of that monthly payment would go toward the buyer's option to purchase.

What did this do for the seller? It would solve his problem of getting rid of the house. At the same time it would resolve the problem of the buyer's lack of a down payment. The buyer would be able to occupy the house—perhaps even fix it up on weekends—without having to worry about qualifying for a mortgage. He would be building up his credit by making the monthly payments.

Two years down the road, the young man could be in an excellent financial position to buy the house. The seller would not have lost money. Everybody benefits under a lease with option to purchase.

TRYING OUT YOUR RETIREMENT HOME

Or how about my seventy-four-year-old friend in Titusville, Florida? He dreamed of selling the house he paid $20,000 for a decade earlier because he felt he could get $50,000 for it. Then he and his wife could live their final years in a dream location like Boca Raton: "I could go out in style," he said.

He wanted to know if I thought he should sell his old house or keep it. He knew he could rent it out for more than the $190 a month he was paying on his mortgage.

This man already had a $40,000 equity in the house. He had more than doubled his money in 10 years. Go drive south, I suggested, from the central coastal area of Florida where he was located, through towns like Vero Beach, Stuart, Boca Raton. Shop for a condo in those places. The condominium market in southern Florida was overbuilt, so he might find a steal.

At that point, if he was *really* sure he wanted to move, I advised him not to keep the house in Titusville. "Use the money from the sale of that house to buy the new condominium," I said. Then he would have small or no monthly payments in his new condo.

But what if he got to southern Florida and started missing Titusville? I felt he should stick his toe in the pool without diving in. Keep the house in Titusville and rent it out, I told him. Meanwhile, *lease* a place in south Florida for one year with an option to purchase. After he was truly comfortable in there, he could sell his Titusville place without worrying.

Sample Residential Lease with Option to Purchase

Received from _____
_____, hereinafter referred to as
Tenant, the sum of $_____ (_____dollars),
evidenced by_____as a deposit
which, upon acceptance of this Lease, the Owner of the premises, hereinafter referred to as Owner, shall apply said deposit as follows:

	Deposit Received	Balance Owing Prior to Occupancy
Nonrefundable option consideration	$_____	$_____
Rent for the period from		
_____ to _____	$_____	$_____
Security Deposit	$_____	$_____
Other	$_____	$_____
Total	$_____	$_____

In the event that this agreement is not accepted by the Owner or his/her
authorized agent within _____ days, the total deposit received shall be refunded.

Tenant hereby offers to lease from the Owner the premises situated in the
City of _____, State of _____, described
as _____
_____ ,
and consisting of _____
upon the following terms and conditions:

1. **Term:** The term hereof shall commence on _____ 19____, and
continue for a period of _____ months thereafter.

2. **Rent:** Rent shall be $_____ per month, payable in advance, upon
the _____ day of each calendar month to Owner or his/her authorized agent, at the following address: _____
_____, or at such other
places as may be designated by Owner from time to time. In the event rent is
not paid within five (5) days after due date, Tenant agrees to pay a late charge
of $_____ plus interest at _____ percent per year on the delin-
quent amount. Tenant further agrees to pay $_____ for each dishon-
ored bank check.

Sample Residential Lease with Option to Purchase (continued)

3. **Utilites:** Tenant shall be responsible for the payment of all utilities and services, except _____ , which shall be paid by Owner.

4. **Use:** The premises shall be used as a residence with no more than_____
adults and _____ children, and for no other purpose, without the written
prior consent of Owner.

5. **Pets:** No pets shall be brought on the premises without the prior consent
of Owner.

6. **Ordinances and Statutes:** Tenant shall comply with all statutes, ordinances
and requirements of all municipal, state and federal authorities now in force,
or which may hereafter be in force, pertaining to the use of the premises.

7. **Assignment and Subletting:** Tenant shall not assign this agreement or sublet any portion of the premises without prior written consent of the Owner
which may not be unreasonably withheld.

8. **Maintenance, Repairs, or Alterations:** Tenant acknowledges that the premises are in good order and repair, unless otherwise indicated herein. Owner
may at any time give Tenant a written inventory of furniture and furnishings
on the premises and Tenant shall be deemed to have possession of all said
furniture and furnishings in good condition and repair, unless he/she objects
thereto in writing within five (5) days after receipt of such inventory. Tenant
shall, at his/her own expense, and at all times, maintain the premises in a
clean and sanitary manner, including all equipment, appliances, furniture
and furnishings therein, and shall surrender the same, at termination hereof,
in as good condition as received, normal wear and tear excepted. Tenant
shall be responsible for damages caused by his/her negligence and that of his/
her family or invitees and guests. Tenant shall not paint, paper or otherwise
decorate or make alterations to the premises without the prior written consent of Owner. Tenant shall irrigate and maintain any surrounding grounds,
including lawns and shrubbery, and keep the same clear of rubbish or weeds,
if such grounds are a part of the premises and are exclusively for the use of
Tenant.

9. **Entry and Inspection:** Tenant shall permit Owner or Owner's agents to enter the premises at reasonable times and upon reasonable notice for the purpose of making necessary or convenient repairs, or to show the premises to
prospective tenants, purchasers, or mortgagees.

Sample Residential Lease with Option to Purchase (continued)

10. **Indemnification:** Owner shall not be liable for any damage or injury to Tenant, or any other person, or to any property, occurring on the premises or any part thereof, or in common areas thereof, unless such damage is the proximate result of the negligence or unlawful act of Owner, his/her agents or his/her employees. Tenant agrees to hold Owner harmless from any claims for damages, no matter how caused, except for injury or damages for which Owner is legally responsible.

11. **Physical Possession:** If Owner is unable to deliver possession of the premises at the commencement hereof, Owner shall not be liable for any damage caused thereby, nor shall this agreement be void or voidable, but Tenant shall not be liable for any rent until possession is delivered. Tenant may terminate this agreement if possession is not delivered within _____ days of the commencement of the term hereof.

12. **Default:** If Tenant shall fail to pay rent when due, or perform any term hereof, after not less than three (3) days' written notice of such default given in the manner required by law, Owner, at his/her option, may terminate all rights of Tenant hereunder, unless Tenant, within said time, shall cure such default. If Tenant abandons or vacates the property, while in default of the payment of rent, Owner may consider any property left on the premises to be abandoned and may dispose of the same in any manner allowed by law. In the event Owner reasonably believes that such abandoned property has no value, it may be discarded. All property on the premises is hereby subject to a lien in favor of Owner for the payment of all sums due hereunder, to the maximum extent allowed by law.

In the event of a default by Tenant, Owner may elect to (a) continue the lease in effect and enforce all his/her rights and remedies hereunder, including the right to recover the rent as it becomes due, or (b) at any time, terminate all of Tenant's rights hereunder and recover from Tenant all damages he/she may incur by reason of the breach of the lease, including the cost of recovering the premises, and including the worth at the time of such termination, or at the time of an award if suit be instituted to enforce this provision, of the amount by which the unpaid rent for the balance of the term exceeds the amount of such rental loss which the Tenant proves could be reasonably avoided.

13. **Security:** The security deposit set forth above, if any, shall secure the per-

---

Sample Residential Lease with Option to Purchase (continued)

formance of Tenant's obligations hereunder. Owner may, but shall not be obligated to, apply all portions of said deposit on account of Tenant's obligations hereunder. Any balance remaining upon termination shall be returned to Tenant.

14. **Deposit Refunds:** The balance of all deposits shall be refunded within two weeks from date possession is delivered to Owner or his/her authorized agent, together with a statement showing any charges made against such deposits by Owner.

15. **Attorney's Fees:** In any legal action brought by either party to enforce the terms hereof or relating to the demised premises, the prevailing party shall be entitled to all costs incurred in connection with such action, including a reasonable attorney's fee.

16. **Waivers:** No failure of Owner to enforce any term hereof shall be deemed a waiver, nor shall any acceptance of a partial payment of rent be deemed a waiver of Owner's right to the full amount thereof.

17. **Notices:** Any notice that either party may give or is required to give, may be given by mailing the same, postage prepaid, to Tenant at the premises or to Owner at the address shown below or at such other places as may be designated by the parties from time to time.

18. **Heirs, Assigns, Successors:** This lease is binding upon and inures to the benefit of the heirs, assigns and successors in interest to the parties.

19. **Time:** Time is of the essence of this agreement.

20. **Holding Over:** Any holding-over after expiration hereof, with the consent of Owner, shall be construed as a month-to-month tenancy in accordance with the terms hereof, as applicable. No such holding-over or extension of this lease shall extend the time for the exercise of the option unless agreed upon in writing by Owner.

21. **Pest Control Inspection:** The main building and all attached structures are to be inspected by a licensed structural pest control operator prior to delivery of physical possession, Owner is to pay (1) for elimination of infestation and/or infection of wood-destroying pests or organisms; (2) for repair of damage caused by such infestation and/or infection or by excessive moisture; (3) for correction of conditions which caused said damage; and (4) for repair

Sample Residential Lease with Option to Purchase (continued)

of plumbing and other leaks affecting wood members, including repair of leaking stall showers , in accordance with said structural pest control operator's report.

Owner shall not be responsible for any work recommended to correct conditions usually deemed likely to lead to infestation or infection of wood-destroying pests or organisms, but where no evidence of active infestation is found with respect to such conditions.

If the inspecting structural pest control operator shall recommend further inspection of inaccessible areas, Tenant may require that said areas be inspected. If any infestation or infection shall be discovered by such inspection, the additional required work shall be paid by Owner. If no such infestation or infection is discovered, the additional cost of inspection of such inaccessible areas shall be paid by Tenant.

As soon as the same are available, copies of the report and any certification or other proof of completion of the work shall be delivered to the agents of Tenant and Owner who are authorized to receive the same on behalf of their principals.

Funds for work to be done at Owner's expense shall be held in escrow and disbursed by escrow holder to a licensed structural pest control operator upon receipt of Notice of Work Completed, certifying that the property is free of infestation or infection.

22. **Option:** So long as Tenant is not in substantial default in the performance of any term of this lease, Tenant shall have the option to purchase the real property described herein for a **Purchase Price** of $_____
(_____ dollars), upon the following **Terms and Conditions:** _____
_____
_____
_____
_____.

23. **Disclaimer:** The parties acknowledge that speculation of availability of financing, purchase costs and lender's prepayment penalties is impossible. Therefore, the parties agree that these items shall not be conditions of performance of this agreement and the parties agree they have not relied upon any other representations or warranties by brokers, sellers or other parties.

24. **Fixtures:** All improvements, fixtures, attached floor coverings, draperies

Sample Residential Lease with Option to Purchase (continued)

including hardware, shades, blinds, window and door screens, storm sashes, combination doors, awnings, outdoor plants, potted or otherwise, trees, and items permanently attached to the real property shall be included, free of liens, unless specifically excluded.

25. **Personal Property:** The following personal property, on the premises when inspected by Tenant, shall be included in the purchase price and shall be transferred by a Warranty Bill of Sale at close of escrow.

26. **Encumbrances:** In addition to any encumbrances referred to above, Tenant shall take title to the property subject to (1) real estate taxes not yet due and (2) covenants, conditions, restrictions, reservations, rights, rights of way and easements of record, if any, that do not materially affect the value or intended use of the property.

The amount of any bond or assessment which is a lien shall be _____ paid, _____ assumed by _____.

27. **Examination of Title:** Fifteen (15) days from date of exercise of this option are allowed the Tenant to examine the title to the property and to report in writing any valid objections thereto. Any exceptions to the title which would be disclosed by examination of the records shall be deemed to have been accepted unless reported in writing within said 15 days. If Tenant objects to any exceptions to the title, Owner shall use all due diligence to remove such exceptions at his own expense within 60 days thereafter. But if such exceptions cannot be removed within 60 days allowed, all rights and obligations hereunder may, at the election of Tenant, terminate and end, unless he/she elects to purchase the property subject to such exceptions.

28. **Evidence of Title:** Evidence of Title shall be in the form of _____ a policy of _____ title insurance, _____ other: _____ _____, be paid for by _____.

29. **Closing Costs:** Escrow fees, if any, and other closing costs shall be paid in accordance with local custom, except as otherwise provided herein.

30. **Close of Escrow:** Within _____ days from exercise of the option, or upon removal of any exceptions to the title by Owner, as provided above, whichever is later, both parties shall deposit with an authorized escrow holder, to be selected by Tenant, all funds and instruments necessary to complete the sale in accordance with the terms and conditions hereof. The representa-

---

Sample Residential Lease with Option to Purchase (continued)

---

tions and warranties herein shall not be terminated by conveyance of the property.

31. **Prorations:** Rent taxes, premiums on insurance acceptable to Tenant, interest and other expenses of the property are to be prorated as of recordation of deed. Security deposits, advance rentals or considerations involving future lease credits shall be credited to Tenant.

32. **Expiration of Option:**   This option may be exercised at any time after _____, 19____, and shall expire at midnight, _____,19____, unless exercised prior thereto. Upon expiration Owner shall be released from all obligations hereunder and all of Tenant's rights hereunder, legal or equitable, shall cease.

33. **Exercise of Option:** The option shall be exercised by mailing or delivering written notice to Owner prior to the expiration of this option and by an additional payment, on account of the purchase price, in the amount of $_____ (_____ dollars) for account of Owner to the authorized escrow holder referred to above, prior to the expiration of this option.

   Notice, if mailed, shall be by certified mail, postage prepaid, to Owner at the address set forth below, and shall be deemed to have been given upon the day following the day shown on the postmark of the envelope in which such notice is mailed.

   In the event the option is exercised, the consideration paid for the option and _____ percent from the rent paid hereunder prior to the exercise of the option shall be credited upon the purchase price.

The undersigned Tenant hereby acknowledges receipt of a copy hereof.

Dated: _____ Time: _____

_____ Tenant's Broker

By: _____ Agent

Broker's Initials _____ Dated: _____

_____ Address and Phone

_____ Name of Tenant

_____ Signature of Tenant

_____ Address and Phone

Sample Residential Lease with Option to Purchase (continued)

Acceptance

The undersigned Owner accepts the foregoing offer.

Brokerage Fee: Upon execution hereof the Owner agrees to pay to _____ , the Agent in this transaction, _____ percent of the option consideration for securing said option plus the sum of $_____ (_____ dollars) for securing said option plus the sum of $_____ (_____ dollars) for leasing services rendered and authorizes Agent to deduct said sum from deposit received from Tenant. In the event the option is exercised, the Owner agrees to pay Agent the additional sum of $_____ (_____ dollars). This agreement shall not limit the rights of Agent provided for in any listing or other agreement which may be in effect between Owner and Agent. In the event legal action is instituted to collect this fee, or any portion thereof, the Owner agrees to pay the Agent a reasonable attorney's fee and all costs in connection with such action.

The undersigned Owner hereby acknowledges receipt of a copy hereof.

Dated: _____ Time: _____

_____ Owner's Broker

By: _____ Agent

_____ Name of Owner

_____ Signature of Owner

[Adapted from Professional Publishing Corp. Form 105. Used with permission.]

Chapter 9

The Closing—How to Avoid Nasty Surprises and Know What You Can Expect to Pay

The house is almost yours. The negotiations are done, the terms agreed on, the mortgage arranged for. The last major hurdle you face before you move into your new home is the closing.

Technically, *closing* is the word for exchanging papers that make you the official owner and for clearing up other details. But if you ask friends what the closing on a residence is, four out of five will reply, with a pained look, "the moment when suddenly you have to write a big fat check in order to really buy the place." But closing costs should not be the nasty surprises they often are.

The closing is simply a meeting, involving buyer, seller, their respective lawyers, real estate agents and lender. The approximate date is decided by you and the seller when you sign the contract to buy a house.

In today's world a typical closing should not take place any more than 45 days from the time you sign a contract, unless you cannot obtain a mortgage commitment. Then you both agree to extend the time period. If this is the case, there should be a provision in the contract that if that period does run longer you can extend the date without paying a penalty. The definite date is set when the mortgage company is ready to close the loan.

To make the closing as palatable as possible, why not think of it in terms of a big dinner party? I will give you the list of guests, and the menu is fairly standard for a residence. It is up to you to get the ingredients and cook the meal. What makes things easier is that you can prepare some of the "dishes" in advance—as early as *the day after you receive a mortgage commitment* from a lender. What's more, you can clear up many nagging details ahead of time with a few phone calls.

The federal government offers you a hand, believe it or not. Since 1974, everything at closing is governed by RESPA—the Real Estate Settlement and Procedures Act. The lenders must let you know prior to the closing exactly what costs are going to be paid by each party.

THE ESTIMATE: A LIST OF INGREDIENTS

Under RESPA, the lender is required by law to give you a *good-faith estimate* of settlement costs and a copy of the Housing and Urban Development booklet entitled *Settlement Costs* within three business days *after* the written loan application. The lender also is required to inform you which documents and services must be presented or completed before the closing.

If the lender designates that you must use specific settlement-service providers (lawyers, title company, etc.), you must be given the name and address of each.

Thus the estimate is your basic list of ingredients. These are items listed under section L on the Settlement Statement on pages 121–22. The seller pays the *sales commission* to the real estate agent, unless other arrangements have been made. The following fees are paid by you, the buyer:

Loan origination fee
Appraisal fee
Credit report
Lender's inspection fee
Mortgage insurance application fee
Assumption fee (if you are taking over someone else's mortgage)
First interest payment
Mortgage insurance premium
Hazard insurance premium

Reserves for hazard insurance, mortgage insurance, property taxes, assessments

Prepaid property taxes, utilities (such as heating oil remaining in tank, homeowner's insurance)

Pest inspection fee

Government recording and transfer charges

Title insurance

Survey fee

A quick note on the final two items in the list: you might save some money on title insurance if the seller's policy is less than three years old. Ask the company for an update, rather than a new policy. The same goes for the survey; save money by asking the surveyor to update the current one.

Shocked by how many fees you need to pay? So is everyone who buys property. But at least you are told in advance. You can assume that closing costs will range from 4 to 7 percent of the total cost of your new home. Yes, friends, that's from $4,000 to $7,000 on a $100,000 house.

THE PAPER TRAIL

Sometimes estimates are inaccurate, so do your best to keep tabs on any estimate that might go higher. If someone tells you that a number in the closing cost estimate might be changed, or go higher, protect yourself with a "paper trail."

Send a letter, certified, return receipt requested, confirming your understanding. This provides you with documentation. It puts you in a very strong position for negotiating and suing for breach of contract and nonperformance.

YOUR TIMETABLE FOR COPING WITH THE DINNER

Presumably you set a realistic date for closing with the lender and the attorney. Attorneys have a tendency to want to stretch it out because they have so much work to do.

There is nothing more infuriating than asking your banker or your lawyer, a few days before closing, how things are coming, only to hear, "Oh, we didn't get the appraisal yet," or "We didn't get the termite inspection yet." The time to act is *immediately on signing the contract.*

As soon as you sign the loan application, ask, "When are you going get the appraisal done? Who is doing it? Who is the person in charge?

A. Settlement Statement
U.S. Department of Housing and Urban Development

B. Type of Loan

1. ☐ FHA 2. ☐ FmHA 3. ☐ Conv. Unins.	6. File Number	7. Loan Number	8. Mortgage Insurance Case Number
4. ☐ VA 5. ☐ Conv. Ins.			

C. Note: This form is furnished to give you a statement of actual settlement costs. Amounts paid to and by the settlement agent are shown. Items marked "(p.o.c.)" were paid outside the closing; they are shown here for informational purposes and are not included in the totals.

D. Name and Address of Borrower	E. Name and Address of Seller	F. Name and Address of Lender

G. Property Location	H. Settlement Agent
	Place of Settlement

I. Settlement Date

J. Summary of Borrower's Transaction		K. Summary of Sellers' Transaction	
100. Gross Amount Due From Borrower		**400. Gross Amount Due To Seller**	
101. Contract sales price		401. Contract sales price	
102. Personal property		402. Personal property	
103. Settlement charges to borrower (line 1400)		403.	
104.		404.	
105.		405.	
Adjustments for items paid by seller in advance		**Adjustments for items paid by seller in advance**	
106. City/town taxes to		406. City/town taxes to	
107. County taxes to		407. County taxes to	
108. Assessments to		408. Assessments to	
109.		409.	
110.		410.	
111.		411.	
112.		412.	
120. Gross Amount Due From Borrower		**420. Gross Amount Due To Seller**	
200. Amounts Paid By Or In Behalf Of Borrower		**500. Reductions In Amount Due To Seller**	
201. Deposit or earnest money		501. Excess deposit (see instructions)	
202. Principal amount of new loan(s)		502. Settlement charges to seller (line 1400)	
203. Existing loan(s) taken subject to		503. Existing loan(s) taken subject to	
204.		504. Payoff of first mortgage loan	
205.		505. Payoff of second mortgage loan	
206.		506.	
207.		507.	
208.		508.	
209.		509.	
Adjustments for items unpaid by seller		**Adjustments for items unpaid by seller**	
210. City/town taxes to		510. City/town taxes to	
211. County taxes to		511. County taxes to	
212. Assessments to		512. Assessments to	
213.		513.	
214.		514.	
215.		515.	
216.		516.	
217.		517.	
218.		518.	
219.		519.	
220. Total Paid By/For Borrower		**520. Total Reduction Amount Due Seller**	
300. Cash At Settlement From/To Borrower		**600. Cash At Settlement To/From Seller**	
301. Gross amount due from borrower (line 120)		601. Gross amount due to seller (line 420)	
302. Less amounts paid by/for borrower (line 220)	( )	602. Less reductions in amt. due seller (line 520)	( )
303. Cash ☐ From ☐ To Borrower		**603. Cash** ☐ To ☐ From Seller	

L. Settlement Charges		paid from borrower's funds at settlement	paid from seller's funds at settlement
700. Total sales/Broker's Commission based on price $ @ % =			
Division of Commission (line 700) as follows:			
701. $ to			
702. $ to			
703. Commission paid at Settlement			
704.			
800. Items Payable In Connection With Loan			
801. Loan Origination Fee %			
802 Loan Discount %			
803. Appraisal Fee to			
804. Credit Report to			
805. Lender's Inspection Fee			
806. Mortgage Insurance Application Fee to			
807. Assumption Fee			
808.			
809.			
810.			
811.			
900. Items Required By Lender To Be Paid In Advance			
901. Interest from to @$ /day			
902. Mortgage Insurance Premium for months to			
903. Hazard Insurance Premium for years to			
904. years to			
905.			
1000. Reserves Deposited With Lender			
1001. Hazard insurance months @$ per month			
1002. Mortgage insurance months @$ per month			
1003. City property taxes months @$ per month			
1004. County property taxes months @$ per month			
1005. Annual assessments months @$ per month			
1006. months @$ per month			
1007. months @$ per month			
1008. months @$ per month			
1100. Title Charges			
1101. Settlement or closing fee to			
1102. Abstract or title search to			
1103. Title examination to			
1104. Title insurance binder to			
1105. Document preparation to			
1106. Notary fees to			
1107. Attorney's fees to			
(includes above items numbers:)			
1108. Title insurance to			
(includes above items numbers :)			
1109. Lender's coverage $			
1110. Owner's coverage $			
1111.			
1112.			
1113.			
1200. Government Recording and Transfer Charges			
1201. Recording fees: Deed $; Mortgage $; Releases $			
1202. City/county tax/stamps: Deed $; Mortgage $			
1203. State tax /stamps: Deed $; Mortgage $			
1204.			
1205.			
1300. Additional Settlement Charges			
1301. Survey to			
1302 Pest inspection to			
1303.			
1304.			
1305.			
1400. Total Settlement Charges (enter on lines 103, Section J and 502, Section K)			

When is this person expected to deliver it? From whom are you going to get the credit report? Who is doing the survey?"

Make a list of names and phone numbers and follow through in the weeks to come. You need to manage every item, because it's your house. *Manage* is spelled P-U-S-H.

If you have read the negotiation chapter, you know to obtain dates for appraisals and such in writing. Now, a week after you have received the mortgage commitment, call your banker and say, "We now have fifty-three days left before closing. What's been done?"

If the banker answers, "The file has been sitting on my desk for the last seven days," make it clear that this does not satisfy you. A good comeback is, "If you don't close in time, I am going to suffer damages." You have to push it. Otherwise you get put on a stack of files, like everybody else.

MAKE TITLE INSURANCE A MAIN DISH

Title insurance is a one-time premium paid to a company to guarantee that you own a particular piece of land and that no one else has a claim to it. A title search is *not* automatically conducted when you buy a house. *Insist on it.*

Obviously, title insurance is a crucial part of owning a house or condo. Yet most of us neglect to learn about it—until disaster strikes, often at the closing.

It happened to me a few years ago. I purchased a condo. I immediately asked for the title policy. The woman who handled it was a friend of mine. "Betsy," I said, "do you realize you sold me the wrong condo?" She turned chalk-white. It was as simple as making sure the number on the door was the same number that is on the title policy.

A title policy is taken care of by your attorney. You should obtain it at least five days before the closing. In 90 percent of the cases, you, the buyer, pay for it. The cost: about ½ to 1 percent of the first $50,000 and ¼ to 1 percent of everything after that. It fluctuates like the stock market. You can shop for title insurance, but you need to make only two or three calls; there is not that great a savings.

Here are some tips on how to read your title policy:

Make sure the legal description on the title insurance policy is *exactly* the same as the legal description on the deed. (You can request a copy of the unsigned deed in advance of the closing.) The best way is to have one person read the title policy to the person holding the deed, at or before the closing.

Next, look on the policy under "Exceptions." This will list all the items needed to clear the title on that specific piece of property in order for you to take possession. Exceptions could include such things as past due tax statements, liens from creditors such as Sears, in the event a previous owner failed to pay bills, or assessments for a road or sewer that has not been built yet.

If these exceptions have not been paid, and you were not told you had to pay them, that is a negotiating point for just before closing. Knock these costs off the seller's price. Or put this money in an escrow account to be held until the owner removes the exceptions from the title.

TASKS DONE THE DAY BEFORE OR THE MORNING OF CLOSING

If you request it, *one* business day before settlement, the person conducting the settlement *must* allow you the opportunity to see the HUD-designed Uniform Settlement Statement. This tells you precisely how much each closing charge will cost. (If there is no actual closing in your part of the country, or if you are out of town, this completed form must be mailed to you.)

Take advantage of this provision so you can bring a certified check made out to *you* for *your* portion of the known closing costs. If the closing does not go through, you can endorse the check and re-deposit it. If the closing does go through, you merely endorse your check and hand it over.

You might be surprised that at the closing your lender will give you a check for less than you expected. A sum of $50,000 discounted 3 points appears in the form of a check for $48,500.

Another step the day before the closing: verify the provisions of your contract by checking one final time that all "subject to" issues have been cleared up and that such things as surveys have been done. (Your earlier phone calls should have taken care of these things.)

Have you ever planned a party and then realized the day before that you forgot to open your freezer to make sure the steaks are there? The most common closing item people forget is to *inspect* for one last time the house they are buying. Your last-minute inspection of the property should cover its condition and any personal property you were led to believe you were getting with the house.

Your contract should have stated that the house is to be turned over to you broom-clean. The debris of moving, like trash and paper, is not to be left inside. Cleaning could cost you time and money. Besides, you do not want to bring your clean things into a dirty place. The bathroom, the kitchen, the oven, the refrigerator and other appliances should all be clean, and that fact should be stated in the contract.

Grace, the coauthor, forgot to check the condition of the dishwasher and other appliances included in her co-op apartment contract. A week after she moved in, she turned on the dishwasher—and water gushed all over the kitchen because the machine had been broken for twenty years!

Did *you* check the model numbers on the appliances in your newly purchased home, to make sure they are the ones you thought you were getting, rather than smaller or older ones substituted in the final hours before you moved in?

If the carpet is to be removed, make sure the floors have no cracks or major problems. Try all light switches. If it is winter, turn off the heat and turn on the air-conditioning. Summer? Vice versa.

If personal property is included, you should either have the lock changed once you get the key at the closing or make a list, to be signed by the seller, of items remaining, to be certain no one moves anything out.

After your final inspection, your last stop should be the county clerk's office or wherever the deeds or other documents are recorded. It is very important for you or your lawyer to make sure that no liens have been registered against the property at the last minute. The best time to check is the day of the closing.

GUESS WHO'S COMING TO DINNER

Now it's time for your closing "party." It can take place at the office of your attorney, the seller's attorney, the real estate agent or the title company or at the bank. In most cases, if a mortgage is involved, you will be in the mortgage broker's or the bank's office.

The "guests"—the people who will be there—include the real estate agent, who receives the commission check at the closing, the seller, the seller's attorney, your attorney and the closing agent or attorney for the company that is putting the mortgage on the property.

The get-together is for the purpose of signing the deed, signing the mortgage, inspecting the title, paying the closing costs and passing the keys to the property to you, the new owner. Business is normally conducted by the lender's agent or lawyer.

You are expected to bring with you a certified check for closing costs.

If you are in a new town, bring some identification, such as a passport or birth certificate.

SOME OF THE MOST IMPORTANT HOURS OF YOUR LIFE

The first thing that happens at the closing meeting is that the person in charge hands you, your attorney, the seller and the seller's attorney a copy of the settlement statement, a sample of which you have already seen on page 121. It is then read and discussed if there are any problems. If any changes are necessary, they are made right there. Then the statement is signed by both buyer and seller.

At this point the title insurance policy is handed to all parties. Your attorney will look at the exceptions. You have what is known as a title binder. The binder would say, for example, "in order to pass this property, you must have a warranty deed signed from the seller to the buyer." Your attorney will then ask for the warranty deed.

The bank representative then puts on the table the *mortgage* and the *note,* which will show the terms and the conditions of both. Your attorney reads them. If there have been taxes paid which do not show up on the title binder, your attorney will ask the seller's attorney for a copy of the paid tax bills.

As you discovered when you got the settlement estimate, items payable at the closing in connection with the loan include the origination fee, points, loan discount fee, appraisal fee, credit report fee, lender's inspection fee, mortgage application fee and assumption fee, *plus* interest on the loan for the period between the closing and the first scheduled payment due.

Also due are the *mortgage insurance premium* and *hazard insurance payment* (most lenders require payment of the first year's premium at closing).

Sometimes you will deposit with the lender your fee for the next insurance premium, as well as the fee for mortgage insurance the second year. A new insurance being offered by some lenders, at no added cost, is called Morgard. Under this policy your payments are made if you lose your job.

Taxes are paid too, although you can negotiate these with the lender. *If the lender holds some tax money, try to get the lender to pay you interest on money held for taxes.* When you have a $5,000 or $6,000 tax bill, that can be a nice piece of change.

*　*　*

Other documents that will be on the table:

• *a report from the pest control company,* saying that the place is free of termites;

• if you're going to prorate home insurance, the *home insurance policy* that you are assuming is handed to you with a statement from the insurance company showing that you are taking it over as of that date;

• a copy of your *loan commitment letter,* and the *contract to purchase* (these don't have to be laid out. But they should be in your attorney's file);

• if you are not taking over your seller's fire and home insurance policy, the lender will require that you bring with you a copy of a *brand-new* insurance policy on the house, showing the lender as loss payee; the lender, before giving you the mortgage check, wants to make sure there is coverage in case the house burns down;

• the *check from the mortgage company,* usually made out to you, which you will endorse to the seller;

• your *check for the down payment* (certified, and made out to you, which you also will endorse to the seller);

• if this is an all-cash deal, a certified check from you for the full amount, less any deposits or down payments made prior to the closing.

At this point you endorse the check for the house along with your check for the down payment and hand them to your attorney, who hands them to the seller's attorney. The seller then passes the deed to you, which gives you the property.

If there is an existing mortgage that is going to be paid off, there is a satisfaction of the existing mortgage, which is then handed to your attorney. He or she has to record that in the courthouse, to show that the previous mortgage has been satisfied.

There may be a few additional items for which you must pay. For example, if you have an oil-heated house, there may be $30 worth of oil left in the tank. (Or, if you have bought a house in northern Minnesota, there could be $900 to $2,000 worth of heating oil in the tank!)

The seller may have paid the water bill in advance. You may end up negotiating a prorated price on that. The seller may have put a deposit on the electricity; instead of getting it back, the seller assigns it to you and you owe a few extra dollars. There could also be prepaid lawn service. Property taxes that are due need to be paid at the closing.

Sometimes sellers have paid in advance. You could owe a few hundred dollars on this.

You can write a check from your personal checkbook for the extras. It is good to have at least $1,500 in your checking account, at the closing, just in case.

Congratulations, my friend, now you are officially the proud new owner of that home!

HOW LONG DOES THIS PARTY GO ON?

A good closing can take place in about 30 minutes; if there are many problems, a couple of hours. Here are a few items that could crop up at the closing:

You want to make sure the survey and credit report costs have been paid. These are bills incurred for services to get you to the point of closing. Sometimes the lender requires a survey. You want to make sure the pest control inspection has been paid. Finally, you should know whether the commission to the broker is being paid at closing. If not, you could have a broker barking at your door.

You can designate a bank or title company to close *in trust* for you. Closings at the title company are common in California and Florida, among other states. You might want to delay the transaction, or you might be out of town at the time of closing. You can close the deal in trust by giving someone else power of attorney, so you do not have to be physically present.

A closing in trust is the same as what is known as an *escrow closing*. It can be compared to what happens when two teams get ready to play pick-up softball for money. Both teams give money to someone sitting on the sidelines. He is an escrow agent.

When a buyer or seller cannot be there in person, or when there is something missing, the title insurance policy, for instance, you close in escrow. That is, you appoint an agent like a banker or trust officer.

Everything is held in escrow (in trust) by that person, in an escrow account, until the closing is finished. (If you are going to have a six-month closing, you might want to put the escrow money in an interest-bearing account held by your attorney.) Then you go ahead and close in reality and take possession.

Sonny Bloch's "No-Surprises" Closing Test

Section A. **Pre-Closing Reminders:**

1. Have you contacted seller, bank, real estate agents and your attorney to make sure everyone has the same closing date of _____ at _____ o'clock in office of _____ at (address) _____ .

2. Your good-faith estimate of closing costs, due 3 business days after the written loan application, according to federal law, was received on _____ .

3. Have you notified the seller's security agency (or, in case of co-op or condo, the person in charge of security at the building) that you are the new owner as of the closing date, so you can gain entrance to the property and change the code on a house security system? The security contact is _____, notified on _____ . The new security code is _____ .

4. Utility companies (electric—name and phone) _____ _____ , (water) _____, (gas) _____ , have been notified on _____ of the change of ownership.

5. Telephone company _____ (name of contact) has been notified and the new phone number is _____ .

6. The post office was told to forward mail and was given the change of address on _____ .

Section B. **Closing-Day Details**

1. Did you receive a federally mandated (RESPA) copy of the final settlement costs at least one day before closing?

2. Has your attorney or title company checked court records on closing day for last-minute liens?

3. Is there oil remaining in the tank for heat?

4. Has the electric and/or gas meter been read for final charges?

Sonny Bloch's "No-Surprises" Closing Test (continued)

5. Has the water meter been read?

6. Have you made your closing-day inspection of the new home?

7. Do you have your certified check for closing costs?

8. Is there additional money in your checking account for last-minute expenses?

9. Do you have a copy of the loan commitment letter in your closing folder?

10. Do you have a copy of your contract to purchase?

11. Have you received a copy of your new home insurance policy or a statement of ownership change from the seller's insurance agency?

12. Do you have personal identification?

13. Has the seller or real estate person been reminded to bring the keys to your new residence?

Chapter **10**

Renovating Older Residences—Don't Let a Fixer-Upper Be a Downer

"Fixer-upper" is a term used by real estate professionals to describe any house that needs more than cosmetic work such as a paint job, carpeting and minor repairs. A house that requires major work such as a new roof, new wiring or new plumbing gets the fixer-upper moniker. Some people buy $500,000 homes and are not concerned with $100,000 improvement bills. However, the real estate industry still labels such homes fixer-uppers.

It is imperative that you inspect a fixer-upper for both cosmetic and more serious problems before you make any decisions. You can make the first inspection yourself, following my "13 Steps." After that, have professionals give you their opinion.

Then, and only then, do the math to see if the place is really as cheap as it seems.

Fixer-uppers can be the *worst* real estate investment you can make. You are almost guaranteed to lose your shirt unless you do a lot of the renovation with your own hands.

When someone tells me about a fabulous house he or she is going to buy that "needs some work," I barrage the person with questions. Is it just a paint job? If more work is involved, how much will it cost? How do you obtain realistic estimates on repairs? Is your sweat equity going to pay off when you are ready to sell the house?

The truth is, most of the time you should not buy a fixer-upper. You will always end up paying more money than it is worth. The only reason to buy one, in fact, is if your love affair has no economic bounds, and you *accept* the idea that you will pay more per square foot than you would for a house that does not need work.

Of course, there are exceptions to the rule that fixer-uppers are really "fixer-downers." Some older homes—even those 50 or 100 years old—are kept in mint condition. They are prize-winners, not fixer-uppers.

Nevertheless, as I cautioned earlier, if you move into *even a well-kept home built before World War II,* you can expect to replace windows, doors and eventually the roof. A good home inspector or engineer will estimate how much such repairs will cost.

These professionals will tell you that they can go *only so far* in dealing with pre–World War II buildings. Such items as wiring might have been partially replaced but will need work within a few years. Be prepared for the surprises that lurk underneath basements, behind walls, inside heating and cooling systems and between layers of shingles.

WHAT IS A FIXER-UPPER?

Fixer-uppers can include brownstones and town houses in older cities, such as the famous Victorians in San Francisco, row houses in areas such as Gramercy Park and Chelsea in Manhattan, Park Slope and Brooklyn Heights in Brooklyn, and throughout cities such as Hoboken, Philadelphia and Washington.

Fixer-uppers can be found anywhere in suburban and rural areas as well. They are not necessarily old, pre–World War II homes. They are simply houses that have not been taken care of properly, or have been abandoned because of death, divorce or neglect.

HOW TO FIND A FIXER-UPPER

Drive through a neighborhood once you have discovered your Geographic Comfort Zone and look for abandoned houses. In newspaper classified ads, fixer-uppers will be listed as "handyman specials," "ready for renovation," "needs work." Look for words such as "quaint."

There are also tax sales by local government authorities as well as by the Federal Housing Administration (FHA), the Veterans Administration (VA) and the IRS (by auction). Banks regularly list of REOs (Real Estate Owned by bank). Public agencies are required by law to advertise in newspapers that they are selling such properties.

Let us assume that you have already done your homework in chapter 1 to find your Geographic and Financial Comfort Zones. Within those zones, you have located a property that has been confiscated by a taxing authority, a bank or a federal agency because a former owner failed to make payments on it. These properties are then sold at tax sales or auctioned in "as is" condition. There might be open or sealed bidding.

You have a right to inspect a property in these cases *before* you make a bid. Follow the steps outlined in this chapter, including having a professional inspection. Once you know what is wrong and you decide that fixing up the property is feasible, make a bid.

How do you bid? Add the *market value* for similar houses in renovated condition for that neighborhood *plus* renovation costs. Then *deduct* 50 percent from the *market value alone.* That is the amount you bid. For example, if the market value of a house is $100,000, and it will cost $25,000 to put it in perfect condition, you should pay no more than $50,000 for it. You would then have a $25,000 cushion in the purchase.

At an open auction, have your top price printed in big numbers on a card in your hand. Do not permit yourself to raise your hand once the price goes past that figure.

WHY YOU *SHOULD* BUY A FIXER-UPPER

Some reasons for buying an old house include the following:

• There is more space than in newer houses. In the old days it cost less per square foot to build.

• The house is within short commuting distance of a downtown. Sometimes older houses are the only ones available.

• The lot is already landscaped. Landscaping is a big expense in a new house. Besides, longtime neighborhoods frequently have parks and huge shade trees that make them esthetically pleasing, especially within the confines of an urban environment.

• An established neighborhood has sewers and water already in place. It is not likely to have unforeseen taxes levied on property owners, such as those for sewers, water or sidewalk construction.

• Charming details decorate houses from a bygone era. Some of the features you can get in an old house that you cannot find in a new one: old stone walls, thick plank flooring, hand-carved staircases. These romantic items sell old houses, despite their flaws.

CAUTION! DANGEROUS FIXER-UPPERS AHEAD

"It's potentially beautiful; all it seems to need is a bright coat of paint." If you hear these words, be very skeptical. The houses that look good on the surface are the ones that wind up surprising and even hurting people.

Watch out for the *sucker* house. This is the house you are buying from someone who has not been transferred. After only two or three years of living there, the owner is buying another house, pretty much the same size, in the same neighborhood. That person usually gives you a false reason for buying a new house. You can bet your last nail and hammer something is wrong with the house. Check it out. Do detective work.

Watch out for the *all-in-the-family* home, the house that has been in the same family for many years. The children have left and the old folks, who are now moving into a retirement home or condo, have not spent the money to bring the house up to date, nor have they modernized the kitchen or bathrooms. Although charming, such houses should always bring to mind a red flag; they need a very thorough check.

Watch out for the *irreplaceable but seedy* house. This is the house that has all the earmarks of a landmark but is decaying within. Years ago I bought a lovely French-style house in Bloomfield Hills, Michigan; it had been the summer home of the Henry Ford family in the 1920s.

I thought it was a bargain when I paid 20 cents on the dollar for it, because it would cost five times as much as I had paid to build the same house again from the ground up at current prices. But every time I pulled apart a wall to make one repair, I found five new things that needed fixing—rotted beams, poor wiring, the works. Some bargain!

OLDER DOES NOT MEAN BETTER

There is a belief in some quarters that they do not build houses the way they used to. That is true. They build the houses today *better* than they used to, because of new building technology that is available. Most of the items custom-built years ago in houses that create the biggest problems—such as windows, doors, cabinets—are now built in factories under close supervision on an assembly line.

What's more, you cannot beat central air-conditioning and some of the energy-saving items that are built into newer homes. Over a five-year period, you can save thousands of dollars in fuel alone with an energy-efficient new house, compared to an old house, not to mention maintenance in replacement of furnaces and air-conditioning units that usually need to be replaced in older homes. In many cases, a newer house built under recent energy codes will be a better investment if you plan to spend any longer than three years in it.

You cannot judge a book or a fixer-upper by its cover. A brick house is not necessarily better than an old wooden house. The outside material becomes a key factor only if, for example, bricks on a brick house are solid. If the bricks are falling apart, the renovation ends up costing more than fixing up a wood house.

One final factor to take into account: time. *Are you in a hurry to move?* If so, *stay away* from the fixer-upper.

Contractors are optimists. They will tell you it takes six months to renovate one, starting from the time you make your first visit until the day you are able to move in. I will tell you it inevitably takes from a year to a year and a half.

13 STEPS IN EVALUATING A FIXER-UPPER

My basic approach to a fixer-upper is probably the opposite of what most people think. When you see a home that needs a paint job, has ugly fixtures and cries out for new carpets, these are the *cosmetic flaws* I referred to earlier. They are *not* the things that should have you concerned.

What *should* have you concerned is what is behind the walls—wiring; what is underneath the floor—plumbing and drainage; and what is above the walls—the roof.

Here are the things I look at and the tests I conduct the first time I walk into a fixer-upper, even before I even have the plumbers, electricians and roofing people make their own inspections:

1. I look for *recently painted spots on the ceiling,* which would indicate a leak.

2. I *turn on and off all the electric switches* in the house.

3. I locate *warm spots* around light switches, by putting my hand on the wall around switches with lights that are on. This suggests faulty wiring.

4. I *flush the toilets,* look for stains around the pipes and listen for noises that sound unusual.

5. I *turn on all the faucets,* listening for rumbling. I look for dirt coming out of the faucet, which indicates some problems with rusty or old pipes that need to be replaced.

6. I always try to inspect a house during a rainstorm or shortly thereafter if possible, when *damp spots on the ceilings or the walls* may show up. If there is a leak in the roof, that water will travel through the ceiling and down to the sides of the walls. I also check the basement for leaks.

7. I look carefully to see if there are *any bubbles or soft spots in the walls* where the paint is coming off. This would indicate a leaking problem.

8. When walking into a frame house I *feel for soft spots that give under my feet,* which indicate a sag or poor flooring.

9. If it is winter, I *turn off the heat and turn on the air conditioner.* It's a sad day in July when you discover that the house you bought the previous winter has an air-conditioning system that does not work. It could cost thousands of dollars to fix.

10. A related technique for inspection goes on in the summer, when *I turn off the air conditioner and turn on the furnace* to make sure that it is in fact working. (In addition, you must have a professional inspect both the heating and the cooling systems, which are discussed in a moment.)

11. I make certain not to forget to *check the water heater.* I look for rust and cracks at the bottom of the tank and water running onto the floor. All you need is a flashlight. Figure on replacing the water heater before purchasing the home and adding it to the actual price that you will pay. That is part of the cost.

12. I check the *floor around the bathroom tub and shower and in the kitchen below the sink* and at the base of the cabinets. If those rooms are over other existing rooms, I look at the ceiling underneath the bathroom tub and the shower and the ceiling below a kitchen sink. Those are chronic leaking areas. Leaking causes wood rot and deterioration—and replacing the wood inside ceilings and walls is very expensive.

13. I check *outside foundation walls.* Are there any cracks, any holes? Cracks and holes are inevitable in most houses. If you see them, bring them to the attention of an expert hired to inspect the house for you.

BRING IN YOUR PRO TEAM

Once you have made your own tour of a fixer-upper, do not stop there. It's time to bring in the pros.

On your return trip, have a professional inspector go through the building. Check the yellow pages under "Home Inspection Services" or "Building Inspection Services." Some companies have offices nationwide, such as Arthur Tauscher, AMC Home Inspection Service, Universal Home Inspections and Housemasters of America.

If you have trouble finding a qualified engineer or home inspector, call your nearest FHA or VA office and ask the chief architect there to recommend one. Ask whom that office uses for termite inspections and septic tank checks (mandatory for government-insured homes). You also might want to check with a local builder or architect or search out a real estate appraiser. These people usually have names of home inspectors. Some of the appraisers are themselves qualified as inspectors too.

Be sure to specify that you want a *full structural check,* not just a surface check. You may have to hire separate people to check separate items. It is worth it.

You can expect to pay $225 to $350 for each full structural inspection.

GETTING THE GO-AHEAD FROM THE LOCAL BUILDING DEPARTMENT

When you are looking at a home that is fairly dilapidated, one of the first things you want to do is have your professional inspector go to the local building department. This office can tell you what will be needed to bring the house up to code. You may not be able to live in the house until work is done to bring items like plumbing and electricity up to local standards.

So you may not have a choice. You *may be forced* to make certain repairs simply because you will *not* get the certificate of occupancy which allows you to live in the house.

What if you do not check beforehand? How will the local board know you are working on the house? Once you bring in contractors to do work, they must obtain permits from the local board. At that point the building inspector comes to visit.

If you have already closed on the house and are beginning work, you may be told that rather than get by with spending $1,000 to repair a roof, you are required to put in a whole new roof and supporting rafters. That turns a $1,000 job into a $10,000 job.

The next step after getting the professional and local building department inspections is to obtain repair estimates. Hire an electrician, a plumber, a carpenter, a heating and air-conditioning appliance expert. Make sure they all have local licenses. Get three separate estimates, in writing. Major repairs done by good craftsmen vary widely in costs. Here is a rundown on the types and costs of repairs a typical fixer-upper needs.

8 MAJOR FIXER-UPPER JOBS AND HOW MUCH THEY COST

Whether you should buy a house depends, in large measure, on the renovation cost. The biggies in terms of repairs are:

1. *Heating and cooling systems.* Heating systems in older homes were not built to last longer than 10 or 15 years. If you need a new one, the best would be a forced warm-air heating system, in which a blower sends heated air through ducts to various rooms. The cost of a system for a 1,500-square-foot house with ducts already installed ranges from $2,500 to $5,500, depending on the length of the warranty. It is always better to get a furnace with a 10-year warranty that has a pulley-driven blower. You can tell if the current furnace is pulley-driven by taking off the front panel and checking if the blower is driven by the motor from a rubber pulley just like the fan belt in your car.

If you have to remove walls and drop ceilings to install ducts in your fixer-upper, figure on spending anywhere from $2,000 to $10,000, depending on the extent of the duct work.

Even if you do not need to replace the heating and cooling systems, there is the *energy trap.* Most of us have forgotten about those $500-per-month heating and air-conditioning bills that jumped up during the energy crisis, but they could reappear. Older houses almost always have higher fuel bills; heating and air-conditioning bills can wind up costing more per month than your monthly mortgage payments.

I always insist on seeing at least one year's electric and fuel bills before purchasing the house. These bills will tell you if this home has a real heating and air-conditioning problem.

2. *Replacing the roof.* On an older home, this can run anywhere from $500 to $40,000 (that's right—forty thousand dollars!), depending on size.

You can check the roof visually. Maximum roof life is 15 to 20 years. So be on the alert if your house still has its original roof. Look for worn-out rain gutters, as well as broken, cracked or missing shingles.

One of the *first* places a house starts to leak is the *flashing,* which is the material around the chimney. If there are any spaces between the chimney and the material around it, there usually is a leak.

If the house has been roofed since the present owners have been there, have them show you a copy of the bill. See how old it is. In some parts of the country, the deep South for instance, roofs wear out faster because of sun damage. You can bet that unless a house in the South has a tile roof, it will not last longer than 10 years.

Top-grade roofing for an old house runs approximately $100 per 100 square feet of roof area. New gutters are a must when replacing the roof. Add approximately $1,000 to $2,500 for new gutters.

3. *Septic tank problems.* If the waste matter in your house does not empty into a sewer line, that means you are working with a septic tank, sometimes known as a cesspool. Septic tank problems are extremely expensive. Minor repairs can run $500 to $1,000; replacement, $5,000 to $15,000.

If sewers are coming to your area, be sure to check on how much it will cost to hook up to that system. This does not include the cost of the line in front of your house, which will be assessed to the property. (We mentioned this assessment in chapter 9, when we discussed exceptions in the title policy.)

There are health hazards if you do not take care of septic tank problems—sewage backing up into the house, for example. It is difficult to determine if a septic tank is in bad condition. A good *soil engineer* or *civil engineer* can do spot-checking ("percolation" tests) on the type of soil that surrounds your septic tank. You can check with neighbors to find out if they have septic tank problems.

When an area becomes overbuilt and septic tanks are in use, you can usually expect to replace drain fields—the pipes that lead from the septic tank into the soil for absorption. You can definitely figure on having your septic tank pumped out at least three times a year, at a cost of usually $50 to $100 per visit.

4. *Insufficient well.* If you are looking at a house with a well, have the water checked to see if it is potable (safe for human consumption). This will also tell you if the well is deep or shallow. The local health department will test a sample of the water free of charge to see if it has any contaminants.

You can also talk with a local well driller to learn at what level the water in your well is. Ask neighbors if they have any trouble with drinking water. Finally, smell and drink some water from the tap.

5. *Wet basement.* This condition usually results from poor drainage around the house and wet soil. When water seeps into soil and has no place to go, it comes into your house through the foundation walls. Ordinary waterproofing material from a hardware store may keep the water out of a basement temporarily. When inspecting an old house, check the walls for signs of black asphalt waterproofing (purchased at a hardware store), intermittently painted over. This will indicate there has been a water seepage problem in the basement.

If the house is located in a valley, pay particular attention to water marks in the basement. These marks are less likely for a house on a bluff or in a mountain area. You could double-check for water marks by visiting after a heavy rain or during a snow-melting period in the spring.

6. *Obsolete electrical wiring.* The older a house is, unless it has been recently rewired, the more likely it is that you are going to have to rewire the house. Unless you are planning to have a very high fire-insurance policy, do not delay rewiring.

In 1940 you needed only a 30-amp electric service to power a house, including the lights. Today, with all the devices used, you need at least a 100-amp capacity. Common sense will tell you that if you put a 100-amp load on a 30-amp electric service, you are creating an instant matchbox.

If the home is going to have an electric washer and dryer, an electric range, electric heat and air-conditioning, you will need a 150- to 200-amp capacity. New electric services at the main electric board cost anywhere from $300 to $1,000. Figure on $15 to $30 for each new switch and double outlet. Heavy appliance outlets run from $75 to $125 each. Depending upon the accessibility of wiring, a seven-room home will cost from $2,500 to $6,000 to be rewired.

7. *Bad plumbing.* Before World War II, corrosion-resistant copper and bronze plumbing was not available. Most houses built before 1940, therefore, will have choked-up pipes. Over the years rust and corrosion tend to clog the pipes, just as cholesterol builds up and chokes off the blood flow in human arteries.

Some homes built after World War II also have iron or steel plumbing pipes. Since you cannot see most of the plumbing behind the walls, *get a magnet and run it along the walls* in the kitchen, and on pipes underneath the sink and in bathrooms. If the magnet grips the wall or the pipes, it means the pipes are not copper, bronze or plastic; the magnet will be drawn only to iron and steel.

If water is trickling out of faucets, you know you have a problem. Turn all the faucets in the house on at the same time. Then flush the toilet. If the water slows down to a trickle, it indicates a problem.

New plumbing can run anywhere from $3,000 to $10,000, depending on the extent and the size of the house. But do not jump to conclusions: sometimes low water pressure is caused by insufficient pressure from the street. In that case, the water supply line to the house needs to be replaced. That remedy costs less—from $300 to $1,200, depending on how much digging is needed.

8. *Floor sag.* Most of the time you can see this problem with the naked eye. However, a carpenter's level can tell you if your eyes are deceiving you.

Check windows and doors to make sure they are lining up squarely with each other and the frame. Make sure windows and doors open and close easily, without binding. If a carpenter or contractor has to replace supporting posts, this can be done. If a house is going to require work on the foundation, be sure to get an estimate. This work can run into the thousands of dollars.

WHICH BIG REPAIRS ARE NOT WORTH IT?

A *chronic wet basement* is a symptom of something far more serious —bad drainage in the vicinity of the house, or perhaps deterioration of the support walls. The remedy for the illness might be prohibitively expensive.

What if you must dig out the basement and put the house up on blocks to rebuild that basement? You are staring a $20,000 repair bill in the face. On the other hand, it could be just a $300 to $500 job involving redirecting water that is draining on the property.

Either way, you cannot ignore a chronic wet basement; it causes wood rot and spreads mildew around the house. Eventually basement blocks themselves have to be replaced.

The best way to cure a wet basement is to change the drainage around the house. It can be done inexpensively; but you need an engineer to do a topographical survey to determine where the water is going. The typical price for a good engineer and a wet-basement solution: $2,000 to $3,500.

In some areas, you may want to invest in a sump pump to pump out water that floods the basement quickly. Cost: $500 to $2,000.

Wood rot from termites and carpenter ants can sometimes be repaired, sometimes not. Do not panic. It depends upon how much damage the insects have done. If they have been in the house for more than three years, there could be structural damage.

Termites live in every state in the continental United States. They usually come in from the ground; therefore a termite expert should be brought in before the closing. Correcting minor termite damage can run a few hundred dollars. Major damage? It makes the house worthless, or it can cost thousands.

It is hardly surprising that sellers try to disguise termite damage. Recently, the executive producer of my shows, Gale Nemec, asked me to look at a house offered at $160,000 that she was considering buying in Washington, D.C. Dressed in jeans and armed with a flashlight, a screwdriver and a hammer, I went through the basement, where I found a crawl space full of old boxes.

I became suspicious when the owner said, "That's just a storage area. You don't have to go in there." I pulled the boxes away, went into the space, and noticed fresh paint on a two-by-four that was smaller than the others in the area. It had been eaten away.

With my hammer I pounded a bit. As the wood fell off, I saw the tellale tiny holes where carpenter ants and termites had eaten into the wood. When I asked the owner for the current termite inspection certificate, she reddened and answered, "I'm not sure where it is."

Thus alerted, I checked the rafters and noted more wood eaten away. My conclusion was that necessary repair work would make Gale's investment a disaster.

Another cause of wood rot is fungus, which can do just as much damage as termites. Be sure to have the termite inspector check for fungus wood rot as well.

MODERNIZING AN OLD FIXER-UPPER

Just about every fixer-upper I have seen requires some remodeling. The price tag can be high if you prefer Sub-Zero refrigerators or bathtubs with Jacuzzi water jets. Nevertheless, these are jobs you need to price, in order to figure how much your "bargain" ultimately costs you.

First, a disclaimer on remodeling costs: prices vary greatly from market to market. The figures quoted here are based on average figures nationwide.

1. Modernization of an old-fashioned or obsolete kitchen: from $7,500 to $20,000, depending upon how many goodies you wish to have.

2. A new half bathroom: from $3,000 to $8,000, depending on how fancy the fixtures are.

3. Remodeling of a full, old bathroom: from $4,000 to $9,000, depending on luxury.

4. Thermal insulation, including insulating window glass: you need proper exposure to the sun and new highly efficient heating equipment that can cut winter heating bills 40 to 50 percent. Local gas and electric companies will do a survey of the cost of caulking windows and other insulation measures to eliminate those drafts that make you cold even when your thermostat is set at 75 degrees. Cost: from $2,000 to $7,000, depending on how far you want to go.

A report on how to superinsulate a house is available from the University of Illinois Small Home Council, 1 East St. Mary's Road, Champaign, IL 61820. Send 75 cents for "Report C2-3 Illinois Lo Cal House."

If you have a choice between gas and oil to heat a home, always choose gas. It is cheaper to buy, operate and install, it is cleaner and simpler, and it requires less service and maintenance.

5. New windows: If you have to replace one window, you can bet that sooner or later the rest of the windows will have to be replaced as well. If one window replacement costs $500, and there are 20 windows, figure you will ultimately be spending $10,000 on windows.

CALCULATING THE TOTAL COST OF A FIXER-UPPER

Most people feel that if they are getting a bargain by buying a $100,000 house for $75,000, they are saving 25 percent because the house needs some work. If, after bringing in professionals, getting a list of problems and paying for fixing them, your *extra outlay* is $50,000, then you bought a $100,000 house for $125,000.

Is it worth paying $25,000 more for the privilege of having workmen in and out of your property for a long period of time? Ask yourself that question. If your answer is yes, then go ahead and pay $25,000 more.

Most people do not understand that the renovation costs must be added to the price they pay for a fixer-upper that they consider a "bargain." They brag afterward that they are living in a $50,000 house, when they have spent an additional $25,000 to make it habitable.

That is like someone's saying that the vintage Morgan roadster he is driving cost a mere $5,000—without mentioning that the auto mechanic who rebuilt it for him charged him another $10,000. The fixer-upper *actually* cost $75,000, just as the Morgan is a $15,000 sports car!

Here is how to do the numbers on a fixer-upper:

Determine your *total investment* in the fixer-upper by taking the purchase price and adding to it the cost of renovation and remodeling. Let us say you buy a $50,000 house and spend $25,000 fixing it up; your total investment is $75,000.

Now, find out the *market value* of similar homes in the area. Here is where the neighborhood that the house is in becomes very important. If, for example, you are buying a fixer-upper for $50,000 and you have to put another $50,000 in it to make it livable, and the houses in the area are selling for only $75,000, that means you are overbuilt for the neighborhood. You will not be able to get more money for a house that is overbuilt in a neighborhood.

Some "bargain" houses offered in newspaper ads or by government agencies are in terrible neighborhoods. War zones, rehab specialist John Coe calls them. "If I felt I had to get off a bus and fix bayonets to go home, it's not going to be a decent place. But that's not the case everywhere," he said.

A house is a good buy if, after adding purchase price plus renovation costs, your total investment is still within the market value of homes in the area.

My rule of thumb is this: your *total investment* in a fixer-upper should be *75 percent of the market value* of the house in perfect condition. To put it another way: take the purchase price plus the renovation costs, and add one-third of that to the total. The number you come up with should equal the market value.

Thus, if you buy a house for $50,000, and it costs you $25,000 to fix up, your total investment was $75,000. That house must have a market value of at least $100,000, or one-third more than your total investment. Your time and effort and the cost of tying up your money in this particular example are worth at least $25,000.

Another example, using a fixer-upper at a low price in the same neighborhood that has truly hefty repair costs: you buy a house for only $25,000 but spend $50,000 to renovate it. The market value must be, once again, $100,000.

One final example, in an even higher-priced community: the house costs $75,000. It will need $50,000 in renovations and remodeling. To be economic, it must ultimately have a market value of at least $166,-000. If similar homes in move-in condition in the area are going for $140,000, you are not doing your bank balance a favor.

Even John Coe, a rehab expert in the metropolitan New York area, knew some houses would be unprofitable, no matter how cheap the asking price. I asked what he would do if he saw a house in a great neighborhood, at a low price, but with lawns ruined, staircases gone, windows in disrepair, the side of the building a mess, the roof caving in. "I wouldn't suggest that to anyone without the experience," Coe replied honestly. "It's going to take a little too much time and expertise."

FINANCING THE PURCHASE AND RENOVATIONS

Banks require higher down payments on older homes than on new ones. However, there are low down payments available on FHA and VA home loans and repossessions. But in general it is just as easy to get financing for a fixer-upper as for any other house. It depends on how you present your case to the banker.

I will be frank: you have to do a selling job. Go to a bank, loan company or mortgage broker and show how much you are paying for the house, how much you are paying to fix it up, and what you are doing with the money to fix it up.

If you demonstrate that you are buying a $100,000 house fixed up for a total cost of $75,000 after expenses, you can get the money. But you need to bring the numbers to them. The numbers must be backed up with written estimates and appraisals showing the value of the house after the work is completed. The preceding chart will serve as a guide for your lender.

Put all the material in a neat binder with the chart in front, followed by the written estimates, which you should tab and number. Make several copies, since you probably will talk to more than one lender.

Once you have made up your mind to buy a fixer-upper, be sure the contract has plenty of those contingency clauses and "subject-tos" in the initial good-faith binder, and/or the contract to purchase, so that you go through with the deal *only* if you can get the financing for the rehab job, and *only* if it passes certain inspections. (See the examples of buyer protection clauses in chapter 6.)

I highly recommend the purchase of major warranty policies on used homes. Even the best engineers in the country can miss something in checking a house. Most of the national home inspection services offer used-home insurance.

Can This Fixer-Upper Be Saved Economically?

Estimate of Renovation, Repair Costs

Roof:	$_____
Heating/Cooling:	$_____
Wiring:	$_____
Plumbing:	$_____
Waste removal:	$_____
Sag:	$_____
Drainage:	$_____
Water heater:	$_____
Landscaping:	$_____
Other:	$_____

A. Subtotal—major repairs $_____

Estimate of Remodeling and Other Cosmetic Costs

Remodeling bathrooms:	$_____
Remodeling kitchen:	$_____
Additional fixtures:	$_____
Painting:	$_____
Window replacement:	$_____
Floor covering:	$_____
Other (doorknobs, window hardware, etc.):	$_____

B. Subtotal—remodeling and minor repairs   + $_____

C. **Add** A and B for total renovation costs   = $_____

D. **Plus** purchase price of house   + $_____

E. **Add** C and D for **Total Investment**   = $_____

F. **Multiply** by 1/3 for "sweat equity" or profit   X   .33

G. This is the **Market Cost** of house after renovation $_____

H. **Market Value** of comparable house in perfect condition,
     in same neighborhood $_____ *

* This figure should be the same or more than figure G. If it is less, you are paying a premium for your fixer-upper.

DOING IT YOURSELF

If you fall in love with a house, and you are confident you can do the renovation work with your own hands, you are a good candidate to buy a fixer-upper. If you can do much of the work yourself, you will save thousands of dollars on labor. You will use what is called *sweat equity.* Obviously, when you work hard you perspire, and in the case of working hard on a house, that sweat becomes dollars in the bank.

How much should you be prepared to do yourself? It depends on your time, expertise and desire. Some people like to paint rooms. The more you do, the more equity you put into the house with sweat instead of dollars. The people who make the most money on fixer-uppers are the handymen and handywomen in this country who make their money through sweat equity.

A worried woman from Columbia, South Carolina, called me recently because her handyman husband was eager to get a fixer-upper. She wondered if he might get in over his head. "The fact that your husband has the ability to fix things, to make sure the plumbing is good, to know how much it costs to paint something, to understand the cost of electrical repairs—all this will save you thousands of dollars over the person who must hire someone to get that work done," I told her.

DON'T FALL INTO THESE FIXER-*DOWNER* TRAPS

The Infatuation Trap. Do you have doubts about the house? Don't try to rationalize them out out of your mind because the house is so charming you cannot resist it.

Take a deep breath. Then sit down with a pencil and use the preceding detailed chart to learn what it will cost you to make this rakish charmer a habitable residence.

The $5,000 Roof Trap. Some people do not mind leaks or sparks coming out of the wall. But if you are one who does, you must factor in the cost of these repairs. Perhaps you need to negotiate a *lower purchase price.*

In other chapters, we talk about using the repairs needed as a negotiating item. In other words, once you find out the place needs a new roof costing $5,000, see if the seller will lower the asking price by that amount.

* * *

The Mansion-in-a-Slum Trap. Let me state my warning on costs once again. Will the fixing-up be done by someone else? Prepare yourself with at least three estimates on each job that is going to be done. Add up the cost. Does your total investment *after* renovation equal more than the market value of similar homes in the area? If so, you are overbuilding. This is *not* a good economic decision.

The Step-into-My-Bedroom Trap. One thing people fail to check when they purchase a home with rooms that have been added is the floor plan. When you come into the front door, what is the first thing you see? If you walk straight into your living room, with no hallway or foyer, you may want to consider another house.

Some older houses with rooms added on after the initial construction have poor traffic patterns. Imagine you have a guest arriving at your new abode. The front room is a sleeping porch. Is this what you want your guest to see?

How are the bedrooms laid out? Are the children's bedrooms right next to yours? Do you like this idea? Walk through the house as if it were a typical day. You are cooking dinner, your spouse is coming home, your children are bouncing in from school. Guests are coming. How does the traffic flow work? Will you have to add additional walls inside to change the flow? What will the walls cost?

The Beautiful-Fireplace Trap. Do not be dazzled by gimmicks. Are you buying a house because it has a gorgeous old fireplace and mantel? That is fine, as long as inspectors tell you the major elements—plumbing, heating, wiring, roof, and so on—are sound.

But if the charming old wreck's wiring has been jury-rigged, smoke could be coming out of the wires three months later. At that moment, the fireplace will be of small comfort.

I would like to end this chapter on an upbeat note, so here is the true story of one man's best bargain—one that you could be savvy enough to duplicate.

John Coe, the rehab specialist I mentioned earlier, ferreted out an apparently dilapidated old corner brick house recently in Jersey City, an up-and-coming rehab community. The place was just four minutes from Journal Square, a commuter train gateway to New York City. Asking price: $25,000.

No question about it; the inside needed work. But John's carefully ordered inspections told him the repairs were only cosmetic—a kitchen that needed a new floor, cabinets and a paint job. The fix-up cost estimates totaled a minuscule $4,000.

"I thought it was so gorgeous," John said, "that I called up my FHA-approved lender and asked him to please send out an appraiser." The lender warned him, "If you don't get the bid, you're going to have to pay the appraisal fee."

"I said, okay, I'll go for the $160," John said, laughing. After the appraisal, the bank felt that house was worth about $44,000. It gave him a loan of $33,600 to buy and renovate it. Right off the bat, he had an additional $8,600 in his overalls.

Eventually, John sold the Jersey City fixer-upper for a whopping $75,000. I hope every handyman and wise shopper reading this chapter makes out that well!

Chapter **11**

New Construction—The Ins and Outs of Dealing with a Builder or Developer

Buying a new custom-built or off-the-rack ("tract") home is a little like buying a new car. The sticker price on a car is really for a stripped-down model, and you pay extra for "frills" like a radio and power steering. The initial price of a house can mislead you, *unless you look beyond the base price.*

What precisely is "new construction"? Usually it is what builders refer to as a "stick-built" residence constructed at the site on which it sits.

It could be a model home, or one that has been built within the last couple of years, or a home that has never been lived in. Also in this category are custom-built homes, which you design and have built for yourself.

A modular house is a new *manufactured* home in a special category. You will learn about them in detail in the next chapter.

PUTTING MEAT ON THE BARE BONES

Let me start by cautioning you to assume that *nothing* comes with a new house *except* the walls, the windows, the roof, the floors and the front and back doors.

This would not be a habitable house until you add appliances and "standard" items. Among many builders, however, every other element in a house could come under the term "loading," in the same way cars have "optional extras."

Many times you are lured to a location by a beautiful ad in a newspaper promising a "three-bedroom, two-bath house, $59,500 in Luscious Lake, Minnesota, subdivision." Upon arriving, you discover there is an additional charge of $20,000 for the lot!

What about such items as a refrigerator, a stove and all the other things that make living comfortable, that you take for granted? That is where loading comes in.

Loading is a selling tactic. For example, a builder will ask, "Would you like a refrigerator? Would you like a lawn?" Those tend to be extras. *There is no such thing as a "standard" package.*

When you visit a model home, *go with a questioning attitude,* and take along the Guide to the Parts of a House on pages 160–61 and the New Home Wish List, pages 163–68. The best approach is to ask the builder or the sales agent, "Are these closet doors included in the actual home that I'm purchasing? Is this bathtub included?" and similar questions.

In short, ask if what you see is what you get. I will bet even money that the answer is no. Every deluxe item you see in the furnished model is extra.

There you are, strolling through a model in a development of homes advertised at $80,000, for instance. The bare bones that I just enumerated—walls, a ceiling, windows, doors, floors, roof—are considered basic, part of a builder's sticker price.

But the brand-name oversize refrigerator and ice maker that you see, plus the sophisticated alarm system, the whirlpool bath, the super-plush carpeting, the brass knocker on the front door, the paneling in the finished basement—all those and anything else are probably extra.

You need to know how much the extras will cost in order to transform the skeleton into a real home. In a typical situation, they are offered in terms of a "basic builder package."

For the $80,000 bare-bones home mentioned above, the basic package might add an additional $10,000. For that price, you would get such items as double stainless steel kitchen sinks, an oversize refrigerator and freezer, a dishwasher, a garbage compactor, a microwave oven, a deluxe regular oven, a whirlpool bath, glass shower doors and a few other amenities.

Still more add-ons might include better-than-average doorknobs and fixtures, carpeting, thermal windows, extra insulation and even items you would ordinarily think of as standard, such as as doors on your closets.

The options and packages vary from builder to builder. Often the cost of the standard feature is taken into account. So if you change single sliding doors to double sliding doors, you might get an *allowance* for the existing "standard" doors. The allowance is then deducted from the cost of the additional doors.

Does your builder make such allowances? You can discover the answers only by asking. If you are upgrading an item, make a note on the Wish List whether there is a dollar amount allowed for the "standard" item that you are *not* getting. *Do not* say, "Do you give upgrades?" The *foolproof* method of asking for a trade-in allowance on an upgrade from "standard" to "deluxe" is "How much is my upgrade trade-in allowance?"

A decorating package might be priced individually, item by item, or expressed as a total figure. On a $100,000 house, such packages range anywhere from $5,000 (5 percent) to $20,000 (20 percent).

Here is a typical, real-life example of a builder's package. The house in question costs $200,000. The *upgrade deluxe package* costs another $32,000. The package gives you the following:

- Landscaping—complete sodded lawn with five oversize trees and a fountain in the backyard
- Double stainless steel sink for kitchen, Maytag deluxe dishwasher, microwave oven, self-cleaning double gas oven, oversize refrigerator with ice maker and freezer, Amana garbage compactor
- Glass shower doors for bathrooms, whirlpool bath and bidet for master bath
- All-wool double-pile carpeting throughout
- Chandelier in dining room
- All-brass doorknobs and switch plates throughout
- Thermal windows
- Maximum energy-saving insulation
- Automatic garage door openers
- Deluxe ADT security system with intercom

There is nothing wrong with the *idea* of a decorating package in addition to the bare-bones home price. But keep in mind that when you add a $10,000 deluxe hardware/decorator package to a typical mortgage (30-year fixed, at 12 percent), you will pay a hefty $36,720 *just in interest* on the equipment over the life of the loan. You pay a lot more on the $32,000 package cited above.

It is better to get the pared-down house by itself. Then add the optional extras later, as you can afford them.

Even if you buy appliances on time, you will pay less in interest because the installment loan will be much shorter than the mortgage.

Whatever options you decide to have the builder add on should be listed in writing, item by item, including brand name, model number and price on the final agreement you sign.

In certain circumstances, you can negotiate for extras at no additional cost, or at a discount. There is a profit of 25 to 40 percent on the house calculated into costs by the builder or developer. If the company has been stuck with the house over a long period of time, the sales representative is more likely to accept less of a profit and throw in more goodies.

WHAT ARE HOUSES MADE OF?

The ideal woods for any exterior include oak, cedar and maple. Pine, if it is treated properly, is a good substitute in most parts of the country for all other woods.

You want wood that wears best in your part of the country. Native wood usually works best, just as native plants make the most appropriate landscaping, because they are accustomed to the local climate.

Pine is a good building material in the Midwest, if it has been seasoned, aged and prepared properly. If you are in southern Florida, it makes more sense to use cypress for the exterior because it adapts well to the heat and moisture.

If you are in a northern climate, you are better off with oak or a similar wood. Oak does not do well in the South. In a place like West Texas, you would use wood that is heat-resistant, rather than a wood that requires cold weather for it to be efficient.

I do not recommend wood for southwestern desert climates. I would rather have stucco or adobe, both of which make wonderful insulation and keep interiors cool despite blistering sun.

Watch out for a builder who is trucking in wood from other areas, where he can buy it more cheaply. If you are buying a wood house that is painted, be aware that you will have to repaint it every three or four years, depending on your section of the country.

Interestingly, wood is *not* the most exciting exterior in the eyes of the nation's most influential upscale new home buyers.

According to the trade magazine *Builder,* the most desirable material among shoppers for new homes with a median price of $145,000 is by a wide margin brick, followed by stone and then wood. One reason is that neither brick nor stone needs repainting every few years.

GRASS IS THE SAME COLOR AS MONEY

One of biggest optional items that can end up costing you a fortune is *landscaping.*

Is the builder putting in sod—strips of turf—for your lawn? Or will the lawn be seeded? Both front yard and back? Are you putting in shrubbery? Depending on the extent of the shrubbery and whether the lawn is sodded or seeded, landscaping can cost anywhere from $600 to $10,000. A $600 package would include seeding your front lawn and putting new shrubs in the front. Laying down sod is a more expensive landscaping procedure. You can spend really big bucks if you go in for formal gardens with flowing fountains.

In certain parts of the country, such as the Southwest, landscaping costs less. A home in Arizona might be decorated with a huge cactus and some rocks out front, as opposed to a sod lawn. Shrubs and trees native to an area work best. In Florida, palms and palmettos would be typical for outside decorations.

By now, you probably have memorized my number-one general rule, but I will repeat it. Be sure to get *written estimates* from your builder or landscaper.

PLAYING IT COOL ON INSULATION

The elements in a new home that a builder is most likely to skimp on are the insulation and the heating and the air-conditioning systems. (As a general rule, with current building codes you do not have to worry about bathroom and kitchen plumbing in a new house.)

The first thing you need to know is how the house will be heated. Most new houses today come with electric, gas or oil furnace heating systems, not boilers.

The difference between a furnace and a boiler is that a furnace creates heat within the furnace itself and blows that heat with fans through ducts to the rest of the house. A boiler heats water, which is fed through pipes in the house. The pipes give off heat that warms the house.

If you have a choice between gas and oil to heat a home, *always choose gas.* It is cheaper to buy, operate and install, it is cleaner and simpler, and it requires less service and maintenance.

For cooling, you are better off with *central air-conditioning.* Individual room air conditioners are not economical.

Sometimes an inexpensive heating or cooling unit with a low capacity will have to overwork to cool or heat a house. If you buy a large furnace that has to work only 80 percent of the time to heat a 2,000-square-foot home (as opposed to a furnace that must work full-time) you will save 25 to 30 percent on your fuel bill. It is the same principle as that of an automobile with a four-cylinder engine working at total capacity to go up a hill versus an eight-cylinder engine working at 40 to 50 percent of capacity to get up the same hill.

Regardless of whether you are buying in northern Wisconsin or the Florida Keys, on the Montana high plains or in the Nevada desert, get as much *insulation* as possible. The best heating and air-conditioning systems will not save you a dime, or make you feel more comfortable, if your home is poorly insulated.

You want double-paned insulated glass windows. If these are not available, are storm windows included? What about window shades and curtains? What about ceiling fans? Yes, you will spend more for these items when you buy a new home than you will on a resale house. But they are worth it.

In new construction, superinsulating a house (which brings energy bills down 35 to 50 percent) costs 4 to 6 percent on the total cost of the home.

Let us assume you pay $4,000 for superinsulation on a $100,000 home. You live there for the next 10 years. During the course of your stay, the cost of superinsulation will be less than $40 a month, and your savings on heating and air-conditioning will be closer to $100 a month. Makes sense, doesn't it?

The quality of insulation is expressed in terms of an *R factor.* R stands for resistance to heat flow. The R factor is used by the heating and air-conditioning industry to rate various grades of insulation, just as the auto industry uses horsepower to indicate the power of an engine. All builders and insulation salesmen are required by law to tell you the R values in all parts of the home and the type of insulation you are getting.

The optimal R factor for the floor of a house built on a basement is around R-19. For a floor on a slab, R-11 is optimal. For walls, the optimum is around R-30, and for an attic, about R-38 is optimal.

Homebuyer's Checklist: Shopping for an Energy-Efficient Home

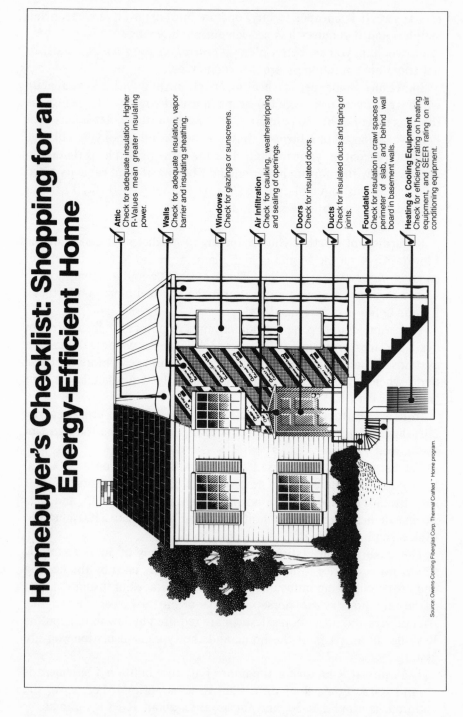

Attic
Check for adequate insulation. Higher R-Values mean greater insulating power.

Walls
Check for adequate insulation, vapor barrier and insulating sheathing.

Windows
Check for glazings or sunscreens.

Air Infiltration
Check for caulking, weatherstripping and sealing of openings.

Doors
Check for insulated doors.

Ducts
Check for insulated ducts and taping of joints.

Foundation
Check for insulation in crawl spaces or perimeter of slab, and behind wall board in basement walls.

Heating & Cooling Equipment
Check for efficiency rating on heating equipment, and SEER rating on air conditioning equipment.

Source: Owens-Corning Fiberglas Corp. Thermal Crafted℠ Home program.

Anything less than R-10 means the insulation is inefficient. So show off your newly acquired knowledge when you question a builder—do not ask for adjectives like *thermal* but for BTUs and R factors.

A report on how to superinsulate a house is available from the University of Illinois Small Home Council, 1 East St. Mary's Road, Champaign, IL 61820. Send 75 cents for "Report C2-3 Illinois Lo Cal House."

HAVE A PRO INSPECT IT

How do you judge the quality of workmanship on a new home? Here are a few things to look for as you make your initial tour:

- Are the floor and the molding around the bottom of the floor flush?
- Are there spaces between the walls and the floor?
- Are the walls square and even?
- Are the floors flat?
- Are there nails sticking out from areas where items have been fastened to each other?

Normally, *a model home looks better than the finished product.* Always ask the builder to show you a home *other than the model home.*

Another way I judge quality is to talk to people who have actually purchased homes from this builder. Try to look at the oldest homes each developer has built, to determine if he or she has cut corners by using substandard materials.

Just because a house is new does *not* mean it is a quality home for the geographical area you are in. That is why you need a *professional inspector* to examine a new house, even if it looks rock solid to you. The local building inspector and local building code will also specify what materials can and cannot be used.

The inspector you hire may have special expertise. For instance, your pro may be able to tell you whether the wood products in the house will wear well in that part of the country.

One radio listener told me about a developer in Pennsylvania who cut corners by using a very low-grade material for insulating some new homes. The material had a tendency to degenerate after one year. Its ability to insulate the home began to diminish rapidly after that.

Luckily a professional inspector checked the house before the listener bought it. The inspector was able to recognize the material. He warned the would-be buyer. The buyer took the issue to the builder, who agreed to put in the highest-grade insulation material instead.

If you are getting a home that is not yet built, you *must* have in the contract that this home is subject to your inspection and that of a professional prior to the closing.

"SIX MONTHS LATER, THE HOUSES BEGAN CAVING IN"

Recently, an inspector called my program with a classic horror story. A couple from Detroit wanted him to inspect a new home they were considering in central Florida.

When he arrived in the subdivision, he noticed the ground level in certain parts of the development was extremely low. He also found that this particular subdivision was in an area susceptible to sinkholes.

After checking the house that the couple had chosen, plus several of the homes other than the model home, the inspector found that many of the slabs of concrete that had been poured on the ground had cracks in them. This inspector advised the couple not to purchase *any* house in this specific geographic area, because of the possibility of sinkholes.

Six months later, the developer was sued by new homeowners, because, just as the inspector had predicted, the ground was not stable and many of the homes were sinking beyond the point of repair.

HOW: PROTECTION FOR NEW HOMES

A pair of radio friends in Tulsa called not long ago to thank me for urging them to buy a HOW—a Home Owners Warranty.

Seven months after moving into their new two-story house, they noticed cracks in the family room ceiling, which was under the upstairs bathroom. They repeatedly called the builder, whom they discovered had moved out of town.

They solved the problem temporarily by putting a large pot under the drip that started in the family room every time someone took a shower in the bathroom. But one day their entire first floor was flooded. An entire wall and the ceiling had caved in! They shut off the main water line and called in their insurance adjuster. They were told their home insurance did *not* protect them against faulty construction.

But their Home Owners Warranty rode to the rescue. A HOW representative said the plumbing throughout the place was below standard. Still, the plumbing in the upstairs bathroom, which had ruined the ceiling and everything else below it, was covered by the HOW warranty.

Every new home buyer should have the same protection, but sadly, a few do not. You can get an excellent one-year Home Owners Warranty that covers workmanship and materials, plus an additional ten-year warranty for major structural defects that affect plumbing, wiring, heating and air-conditioning. In most cases the one-time insurance premium for HOW is *paid by the builder.* It remains in effect even when the house is sold to another owner. A total of 12,000 home builders belong to the HOW program.

If the builder goes out of business, the warranty corporation will repair the major items. You also can get warranties on your appliances. Most builders will not come back to fix things that go wrong more than six months after you have moved in.

No one should buy a new home without a HOW policy, not even (or perhaps especially!) if it is a house built by your favorite nephew, your oldest friend or the most famous home building company in the country.

THE EASY PART: FINANCING A NEW HOME

Financing the cost of a new home is different from—and in some respects easier than—financing a resale.

Most new home builders have arrangements already preset with a bank. This makes it quicker for you. You might want to shop around to see if you can get a better deal on a conventional mortgage, because you can be sure that the builder is *getting a kickback* on the actual financing. Even with the builder's kickback, however, you sometimes wind up with a savings. Why? The builder works in a wholesale manner, getting what is known as "end financing" on several million dollars' worth of homes.

THE CASE OF THE VANISHING BUILDER

The biggest problem Americans face in buying a new house is not bad insulation or expensive sod or leaky basements.

It is the *vanishing builder.*

This is the guy who strikes you as someone you can trust. He shows you a beautiful, new, solidly constructed house (which might even be an FHA or VA home). But things invariably go wrong in the new home: perhaps a door that will not shut, sticky windows or broken faucets, or

Guide to the Parts of a House

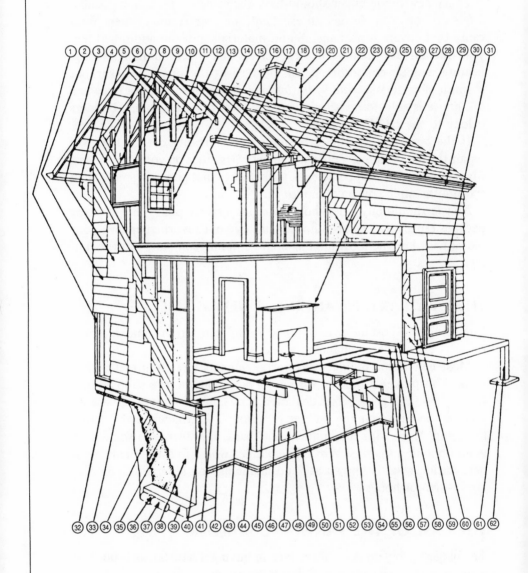

1. Double corner stud
2. Siding
3. Building paper
4. Downspout
5. Eave (roof projection)
6. Gable end of roof
7. Wall stud
8. Window jamb trim
9. Double window header
10. Ridge board
11. Collar beam
12. Mullion
13. Muntin
14. Window sash
15. Sheetrock
16. Double plate
17. Rafters or trusses
18. Chimney pots
19. Chimney cap
20. Chimney
21. Chimney flashing
22. Wall sheathing
23. Roof boards
24. Laths
25. Roof vent
26. Mantel
27. Roofing tar paper
28. Stud
29. Eave trough or gutter
30. Frieze board
31. Door trim
32. Sill
33. Termite shield
34. Backfill
35. Dampproofing or weatherproofing
36. Felt joint cover
37. Foundation drain tile
38. Foundation wall
39. Footing
40. Anchor bolt
41. Band or box sill
42. Plate
43. Girder
44. Building paper
45. Subflooring
46. Floor joist
47. Cleanout door
48. Concrete basement floor
49. Cinder fill
50. Ash dump
51. Finish flooring
52. Bridging
53. Tread
54. Riser
55. Stringer
56. Shoe moulding
57. Baseboard
58. Base top moulding
59. Insulation
60. Vapor barrier
61. Footing
62. Pier

something serious, like the flooding of the basement or a defective furnace.

Then, when you try to call the builder, he is nowhere to be found. There is no phone number listed or the phone has been disconnected. It is therefore prudent to do business with someone who has been in the community for a while. I like a builder who has no qualms about giving you his home phone number.

You might also run into a builder who says, to paraphrase that great country-western lyric, "Take your house and shove it." He insists, "I don't work here anymore," leaving you high and dry, or low and wet. Even if you take a vanishing builder to court, chances are 90 percent that you will *not* be able to collect. These are good reasons to take time to check a builder's reputation.

Most builders have high principles, do a great job, and are anxious to please their customers. Those are reasonable practices, since so much of their business comes from referrals.

Nevertheless, it is also sensible for you, the buyer, to check a developer's or builder's credentials so you do not accidentally buy from a crook.

First, call your local home builders' association. Another place to call is the National Association of Homebuilders in Washington, D.C. Yes, this is a lobbying group, but its members do not like crooks, either. Also check the local building and zoning departments. Ask the builder's banker. Talk to people living in homes built by the same builder. Find out if the builder is local or from out of town. Check the courthouse to see if any suits have been filed against the builder. In the case of a large developer, you might want to check with the American Association of Resort and Residential Developers in Washington, D.C.

If you purchase a house with an FHA mortgage, and the builder refuses to make repairs, you can have the Federal Housing Administration exercise its four-year major-defect guarantee. An FHA office will give you details.

A small but helpful point: most reputable builders use their *own name* as the company name.

When your builder talks about "jambs" and "trusses," you should be aware that he is referring to parts of your house, not your undergarments. To help you, the guide on pages 160–61 introduces terms used by contractors.

NOTES ABOUT THE NEW HOME WISH LIST

Siding. Although aluminum siding is a great way to avoid painting year after year, resale prices show that aluminum siding diminishes the value of a home. Brick is the most expensive and most salable siding.

Roofing. Asphalt is the least expensive material, but it costs the most to maintain and must be replaced most frequently. Slate is the most expensive material, but it lasts the longest and gives a house a very high resale value.

Entry doors. Decorative wood doors, higher-priced than others, help sell a home, but make sure they are solid wood, not hollow-core.

Garage. The larger the garage you have, the higher the resale value. A portion of a three-car garage can be used as a storage or work room. An automatic garage door is a valuable feature.

Outside amenities. A covered porch adds an additional room and increases the resale value. Hot tubs and saunas are now considered passing fancies.

Flooring. Hardwood floors are costly but most desired for resale value. Carpeting is useful in daily living. Asphalt tile, stick-on or rolled, is the least desirable flooring.

Windows, doors, walls. The greenhouse has come into its own. Skylights open up rooms with natural light. Real wood paneling is an exceptional selling feature in pre–World War II homes.

Security. Burglars can foil even deadbolt locks. Security systems, though costly, are considered best for protection.

Other indoor amenities. Central vacuum cleaners are very difficult to repair. A home with varied levels is desirable because of the illusion that the house has more than one story. Vaulted ceilings are extremely expensive and add cubic feet, not living space.

Kitchen items. Most new home buyers prefer stainless steel double sinks. Wood cabinets need the most maintenance. Ceramic tile counters help sell a house. Wood floors in kitchens are hard to maintain. Barbecue cooktops are the rage now, and island work areas are the hottest item of the past 20 years.

Bedrooms. Lack of closet space is a big complaint among new home buyers.

Bathrooms. Separate shower enclosures are particularly popular among men.

New Home Wish List
(Check boxes and fill in amounts to determine total cost;
$ = most expensive   # = most desirable   x = least desirable.
See previous comments on why items are expensive or desirable.)

Features	Included	Optional	Extra Cost
Siding			
x Aluminum	___	___	$ _____
$# Brick	___	___	$ _____
Cement block	___	___	$ _____
Hardwood	___	___	$ _____
Plywood	___	___	$ _____
Stone	___	___	$ _____
Stucco	___	___	$ _____
Vinyl	___	___	$ _____
Wood	___	___	$ _____
Wood shingles	___	___	$ _____
Other _____	___	___	$ _____
Roofing			
x Asphalt composition	___	___	$ _____
Clay or concrete	___	___	$ _____
Wood shake	___	___	$ _____
$# Slate	___	___	$ _____
Other (metal, etc.)	___	___	$ _____
Entry Doors			
Plain wood	___	___	$ _____
$# Decorative wood	___	___	$ _____
x Plain steel	___	___	$ _____
Decorative steel	___	___	$ _____
Windows			
$# Aluminum	___	___	$ _____
Vinyl-clad wood	___	___	$ _____
x Wood	___	___	$ _____

New Home Wish List (continued)

Features	Included	Optional	Extra Cost
Garage			
x Carport	____	____	$ _____
One-car garage	____	____	$ _____
Two-car garage	____	____	$ _____
$ # Three-car garage	____	____	$ _____
$ # Automatic garage door	____	____	$ _____
Outside Amenities			
$ # Covered porch	____	____	$ _____
x Hot tub or sauna	____	____	$ _____
Patio slab	____	____	$ _____
Security lighting	____	____	$ _____
Wood deck	____	____	$ _____
Indoor Flooring			
$ Hardwood	____	____	$ _____
x Tile	____	____	$ _____
# Carpeting	____	____	$ _____
Windows and Doors			
French doors	____	____	$ _____
$ Greenhouse or sunroom	____	____	$ _____
x Greenhouse window	____	____	$ _____
Sliding doors	____	____	$ _____
# Skylight	____	____	$ _____
Window seat	____	____	$ _____
Walls and Trim			
Built-in shelving	____	____	$ _____
x Decorative molding	____	____	$ _____
Mirrored walls	____	____	$ _____
$ # Real wood paneling	____	____	$ _____

New Home Wish List (continued)

Features	Included	Optional	Extra Cost
Security			
x Deadbolt locks	____	____	$ _____
$ # Security system	____	____	$ _____
Other Room Amenities			
Ceiling fan	____	____	$ _____
x Central vacuum	____	____	$ _____
Fireplace	____	____	$ _____
Recessed/Track lighting	____	____	$ _____
# Step-up or step-down rooms	____	____	$ _____
$ Vaulted ceilings	____	____	$ _____
Wet bar	____	____	$ _____
Kitchen Sinks			
x Single-bowl	____	____	$ _____
Double-bowl	____	____	$ _____
$ Porcelain	____	____	$ _____
# Stainless steel	____	____	$ _____
Kitchen Cabinets			
x Wood finish	____	____	$ _____
$ # European-style laminate	____	____	$ _____
Kitchen Counter Tops			
x Laminate	____	____	$ _____
# Ceramic tile	____	____	$ _____
$ Cultured marble	____	____	$ _____
Kitchen Flooring			
Resilient vinyl	____	____	$ _____
x Wood	____	____	$ _____
$ # Ceramic tile	____	____	$ _____

New Home Wish List (continued)

Features	Included	Optional	Extra Cost
Kitchen Appliances			
Microwave oven	____	____	$ _____
Single regular oven	____	____	$ _____
$ Double regular oven	____	____	$ _____
# Barbecue cooktop	____	____	$ _____
Trash compactor	____	____	$ _____
x Built-in food processor	____	____	$ _____
Other Kitchen Amenities			
x Intercom	____	____	$ _____
$ Walk-in pantry	____	____	$ _____
Eating area	____	____	$ _____
Snack bar	____	____	$ _____
Greenhouse window	____	____	$ _____
# Island work area	____	____	$ _____
Master Bedroom Features			
$ # Balcony or patio	____	____	$ _____
Fireplace	____	____	$ _____
x Sitting area	____	____	$ _____
# Walk-in closet	____	____	$ _____
Master Bath Features			
Bay window	____	____	$ _____
Upgraded fittings	____	____	$ _____
x Colored fixtures	____	____	$ _____
Water-saving fixtures	____	____	$ _____
Ceramic tile flooring	____	____	$ _____
Linen closet	____	____	$ _____
Mirrors	____	____	$ _____
$ # Separate shower enclosure	____	____	$ _____
Two sinks	____	____	$ _____

New Home Wish List (continued)

Features	Included	Optional	Extra Cost
Master Bath Features (continued)			
Vanity storage	____	____	$ _____
Ceramic tile walls	____	____	$ _____
Whirlpool tub	____	____	$ _____
Second Bedroom Features			
$ Balcony or patio	____	____	$ _____
Fireplace	____	____	$ _____
x Sitting area	____	____	$ _____
# Walk-in closet	____	____	$ _____
Second Bath Features			
Upgraded fittings	____	____	$ _____
x Colored fixtures	____	____	$ _____
Water-saving fixtures	____	____	$ _____
Ceramic tile flooring	____	____	$ _____
Linen closet	____	____	$ _____
Mirrors	____	____	$ _____
$# Separate shower enclosure	____	____	$ _____
Other _____	____	____	$ _____

Total Price of Desired Optional Features $ _____

[Adapted from *Builder* magazine Home Buyer Survey, 1986.]

13 Questions: How Reliable Is Your Builder?

1. How long has the builder been established in business?
2. Has the builder always operated under the present company name?
3. Do previous customers say the builder comes back to finished homes to fix things that go wrong?
4. What does the local bank say about the builder?
5. What kind of credit rating does the builder have with a local credit bureau?
6. Is the builder willing to show you houses already built?
7. Will the builder supply the names of at least six previous buyers of the builder's homes?
8. Do local building-material suppliers and subcontractors give the builder a good rating?
9. Does the builder belong to the local chapter of the National Association of Homebuilders?
10. What does the Association say about this builder?
11. Is the builder a member of the Home Owners Warranty program?
12. What do the Better Business Bureau, chamber of commerce and especially the local consumer protection agency say about the builder?
13. Does the builder have a listed telephone number?

Chapter 12

Going Modular—Today's Best-Made, Lowest-Cost Quality Homes

Did you know that new technology has transformed what used to be called the the prefab home? That term has a bad connotation and it is outmoded. Drop it from your vocabulary.

Instead, learn the new term "modular housing"—the biggest new force in single-family residences in the country today.

A modular home, once it is in place, is exactly like a custom-built, or stick-built home, except that when bought from a reliable company it is *sturdier* and *cheaper.* Modular homes are built on an assembly line like high-tech cars. They are more solid than conventional homes because the engineering is better.

As the words suggest, a modular home is constructed room by room in a factory, then transported to your site and assembled in an amazingly short time. In this chapter I will try to convince you that these are the best-made, lowest-cost quality homes in today's market.

Consider this: a custom home, built piece by piece by carpenters, electricians and roofing people, is a home "manufactured" on the site. The raw materials are delivered directly to the homesite. A modular home is built room by room by the same (or by more skilled) carpenters, electricians and roofing people, with the exception that they are inside a factory, in a climate-controlled, quality-controlled environment, using exactly the same (or better) raw materials.

There is no such thing in a modular home as a door being a sixteenth of an inch too narrow to close properly. I have inspected modular homes that are so insulated, so energy-efficient, that when you close a door your ears pop!

The true test of a modular home is that you can walk up to one and not be able to distinguish it from a far more costly, conventional stick-built home.

FROM MODEST TO DELUXE

Modular homes have made personal single-family residences affordable to millions of middle-income Americans—but they are not the only ones. The coming of age of modular homes now gives even the purchaser of a high-priced home the chance to get more bang for a buck —more house for less money.

I have seen modular homes two stories high, with swimming pools and cathedral ceilings. You can have amenities in a modular home that are as good as those in any luxury home.

Modular is not synonymous with "cookie cutter" or "four walls and a roof"—just the opposite.

Modular homes come, in some cases, with more features included in the basic price than stick-built tract homes have. Moreover, these homes can be customized at the factory, complete with wallpaper and carpeting. The quality-controlled assembly line and quantity purchases of raw materials bring down the cost of those extras, and usually they are part of the basic package.

In the moderate price range, for instance, one leading manufacturer offers its top-of-the-line 1,176-square-foot, two-bedroom, two-bath home at prices beginning at $47,450 (not including land). That is less than $41 per square foot. The same home, custom-built, would cost $70,000 to $90,000.

This home comes equipped with first-rate insulation; heat and air-conditioning; carpeting in the living room, dining room and bedrooms; a kitchen sink, range and garbage disposal; and bathrooms with toilet, tub and sink, all included in the basic price. Also included in that price is site preparation: a 28-inch concrete block foundation, back fill foundation and fine-grade, and even a six-by-six-foot front stoop. Want a two-car garage? That's an option for $6,500 more.

Here is an example of modular living on a grander scale. In Suffolk

County, a suburb of New York City where land prices have soared in recent years, one developer in 1986 was offering three- and four-bedroom homes ranging in area from 1,836 to 2,592 square feet, priced at $165,000 to $220,000. The same homes, stick-built, would cost at least $210,000 to $286,000 and more.

Modular homes can be found made of wood, metal, even brick or stucco. Just as you would customize any house, you can choose sliding glass doors rather than standard windows, as well as built-in bookshelves, extra closets and so on.

Depending on the modular home company you deal with, you can order such amenities as wood siding, vinyl siding, pitched roofs, shingled roofs, Roman tubs, Jacuzzis, fireplaces, sun rooms and laundry rooms for a modular home for less money than the same feature would cost in a custom home. *You can also add rooms after you move in.*

Zoning was once of greater concern to the modular home owner than it is now. Laws have changed in the past five years. Local governments are beginning to understand that in the next decade more homes will be built in factories than will be custom-built on lots across the nation.

Therefore, in most states, local zoning codes allow modular housing in single-family stick-built home neighborhoods. The same codes for wiring, construction and plumbing apply to homes built in a factory.

The major modular home companies guarantee buyers that the homes they deliver conform to state codes. While some areas prohibit mobile homes, they do not ban modular homes except in unusual instances.

FORGET DRAFTS OR HOT SPOTS

The energy efficiency of a modular home is generally better than that of a regular stick-built home, because controls and tolerances are closely monitored in the factory. The spaces between the floor and the wall and between the ceiling and the wall are much smaller in modular homes, preventing air from escaping or seeping in. I repeat, your ears practically pop when you close a door in one of these houses. They are this airtight because they must be strong enough to be lifted by a crane for transport to a site without falling apart.

The best modular home builders are proud of the energy savings. One large company offers a package that includes double-wall construction with seven inches of Owens-Corning Fiberglas insulation, a controlled attic ventilation system, a three-foot-wide roof overhang to screen out high summer sun but let in low winter sun, double-paned windows, a foam-core insulated front door with magnetic weather stripping and adjustable threshold, as well as other items.

Since these homes meet the performance standards set by Owens-Corning, the builder can actually *estimate each home's annual heating and cooling costs before you buy it.* The builder gives you an energy rating, similar to the miles-per-gallon estimate you would get for a car.

PLAYING HOUSE—FOR REAL

How do you shop for a modular home? Typically, a company has a display lot showing all the different options. The company also has a planning table, where you can move a miniature model bedroom from one side of the house to the other, or put the garage next to the kitchen, or change anything else.

You put the house together with pieces like building blocks. You are playing house, for real.

Then the house is built in the factory, brought to your lot, and assembled either on the basement that has been dug or on the pad that has been laid out.

The cost of grading the site and other preparation work may be partially included as part of a package from some modular home builders. For the $47,450 home mentioned earlier, the site is staked out, the company scrapes and cuts the pad, a concrete block foundation is laid, and the home is put together with a walkway, front stoop and steps. The whole place is cleaned up after the installation is finished.

The owner does have to pay for sidewalks, driveways and some additional outside work.

All the plumbing is put in the house before it arrives at the site. The bathroom arrives with a sink, bathtub and toilet. The rooms are assembled at the factory with plumbing and electricity.

Let us say your lot in a region near a modular home factory has been made ready and graded. Sewer hookups have been installed and electric poles erected. You can be living in your modular home within *three days after the parts leave the factory,* or even less. After all, the "house" has been constructed already. The pieces simply have to be glued or hammered together.

Once the modules are installed at your site, the electricity and plumbing are hooked up *in one day.*

The pricing of a modular house is done per square foot. The most important fact for consumers is that a stick-built house that costs $50 per square foot will cost in the area of $30 to $35 per square foot for the comparable modular house.

Before deciding whether to custom-build a house or buy a modular one, you should look into *panelized homes.* These are hybrids that cost more than a total modular home but still about 15 percent less than a custom home.

A panelized house is delivered in pieces. The walls, roof and floors are delivered to your lot by truck, after being built in the factory. They are then assembled at the site.

YOUR LOT OR THEIRS?

There are two ways to make an actual purchase of a modular house. You can buy from a developer who has already built a modular home on a lot. Numerous builders develop modular home communities, where the houses are assembled within a subdivision.

The second method is to buy a modular home for a lot you already have chosen. Wherever you are, the cost of the lot is the same for a modular as for a stick-built home. The difference is how the home is then constructed on the lot.

Some companies offer you their own warranty, financing, home insurance, site selection counseling and other services. In general, you finance a new modular home the same way you would finance a stick-built home.

Property taxes? You pay the same rates your neighbor in a custom home pays.

YOU WILL APPRECIATE THIS FINAL POINT

There is one further argument in favor of buying a modular home. It appreciates *more quickly in the beginning* than a stick-built home on the same site.

Few people realize this. Even though it is a little-known fact, the appreciation potential is a big plus for modular construction, and it stands to reason. Let us say you place a $70,000 modular home in a community where custom homes with the same square footage are selling for $100,000. As soon as you move in, your home increases in value to $100,000, provided you have bought from a first-rate company and opted for the same amenities as neighboring residences.

My prediction is that by the year 2000, three-quarters of the homes built in this country will be built in factories, not stick-built on the site.

We cannot ignore that fact. And now that you have read about the quality of modular homes, you should be delighted by them.

The Best Modular Home Companies

Cardinal Industries, 10 Plumosa Avenue, Casselberry, FL 32707 (also with offices in Columbus, OH; Atlanta; Baltimore)

Champion Homes, 5573 East North Street, Dryden, MI 48428

National Enterprises Corporation, Earl Avenue and Wallace Street, Lafayette, IN 47904

Ryan Homes, 100 Ryan Court, Pittsburgh, PA 15205

U.S. Home Corporation, 1800 West Loop South, Houston, TX 77252

Chapter 13

Condos—Buying into the Fastest-Growing Segment of the Residential Market

Condominiums, whether they are clusters of town homes, apartments, vacation homes or offices, are part of a different real estate ball game with rules you may not know about. They also constitute the fastest-growing segment of the American residential market.

This chapter introduces you to the rules of the condo game. It also spells out such issues as associations, maintenance fees and restrictions.

By the year 2000 over *half* of the residential ownership in this country will be condominiums (common-wall residences), either apartments or town homes. Furthermore, I predict that condos will appreciate at a *faster* rate than single-family residences, because of the appeal of carefree living, combined with the fact that condos offer more for the money.

After all, if you were to purchase a single-family residence and own, for instance, a game room, a park, a swimming pool and tennis courts, you would pay much more than if you purchased a condo and shared those amenities with other people.

But condos are not to everyone's taste. Nor do they fit every family's needs. I can help you understand the game; it is up to you to decide if you want to play.

WHAT DOES *CONDO* REALLY MEAN?

The best way to describe a condominium is to imagine your building as a pie in a pie dish. If there are ten condo units in the building, the pie would be cut into ten pieces. Each individual would own a single piece of the pie, and then all of you together own the dish in which the pie sits.

When you purchase a condominium, you own a *specific portion of a development,* whether it is an apartment in a high-rise or low-rise building, a town home, a resort home or a hotel. *Common areas*— hallways, parks, lobbies, amenities such as golf courses, tennis courts, swimming pools and riding trails—*are owned by everyone* who lives there. Common areas are paid for and maintained through the *condominium association,* to which every owner belongs.

You pay a monthly fee to the association for the maintenance of the common areas; maintenance includes keeping the hallways clean, the lawn and shrubbery mowed and clipped, and the swimming pools in working order.

No one owns a specific portion of the common areas. Everyone owns an undivided share not only of the land the building is on and the facilities, but of the outside walls, the plumbing and wiring, and the parking lots as well.

Usually you do *not* own your patio or your balcony—those areas are called *limited common areas.* The condo association owns them. However, only the individual owners of one particular unit have the use of a limited common area. Another limited common area can be a garage or parking space. You do not own it, but only you can use it.

You receive an actual deed to a piece of real estate when you buy a condo. In the case of an apartment, the deed would be for the walls that surround the space you are living in, plus an equal share, known as an undivided share, of the common areas.

Thus, owning a condo is exactly like owning any other piece of real estate except for the common ownership element. You pay real estate tax on a condo just as you would on a single-family residence or vacant piece of property. You also enjoy all of the tax deductions available to single-family real estate owners.

* * *

Condos are usually built by developers in a resort area, or in a community where the real estate land prices are so high that the condos, which take up less land than single-family homes, make economic sense. The developer runs a new condo community until the majority of units are sold, then turns control over to the condo association.

Nationwide, 75 percent of condos are apartment buildings. Town homes make up almost all the remaining 25 percent. A town home is a general term to describe a condo that is usually two or more floors with a common wall joining one home with the one next door.

Another example of a condo would be the "extended-care" (nursing home) condominium, where you own a room in a nursing facility. The common areas include everything you would have in a normal condo, plus an infirmary with a full-time doctor, nurses and a restaurant.

In a few special cases there are single-family detached homes that are condos. These are built very close together and on what is known as a "zero lot line" basis, which means that little or no property goes with the residence. These homes usually include a community tennis court, swimming pool and other amenities.

WHAT IT COSTS TO OWN AND LIVE IN A CONDO

As a condo owner, you pay your own monthly mortgage payments and property taxes, *plus* the condo maintenance fee.

Each owner is charged a fee based on the overall monthly cost of maintaining the public areas. In a 100-unit development, if all the units are the same size, and if the cost to maintain the common areas amounts to $10,000 per month, each owner would pay a maintenance fee of $100 per month.

However, the size of your condo determines what you pay for maintenance. If you own a larger unit, the more votes you have in the condo association, and the more you pay in maintenance fees.

The monthly maintenance fee, incidentally, is *not* deductible from income taxes. However, it is often smaller than the maintenance fee in cooperative buildings, which are discussed in the next chapter. Also, the common elements of a condo *cannot* have a mortgage on them. (Co-ops, in contrast, can have mortgages on everything.)

Condos are priced according to the marketplace. However, there are certain *extra added attractions* that make one unit in a condo almost automatically higher in purchase price than another that may at first glance seem very similar.

Expect to pay more for

- additional square footage
- an attractive view, whether of a city skyline, a park, a lake or simply a pleasant landscape
- a higher floor in an apartment building
- a terrace or balcony
- a lakefront residence
- an oceanfront residence or view
- a unit close to a golf or tennis clubhouse

THE JOYS OF CONDO LIVING . . .

For many people, happiness is owning their own home without having to mow the lawn. That is one attraction of a condo. You do have equity, but you do not have the responsibility of maintaining the exterior of the building or the common areas. Condos at their best are *hassle-free* homes.

Another plus is the *security* of condo living. You can leave home, lock the door, and not worry about your furnace, your mail, your front yard, or any of the other things a single-family resident worries about.

Condos are a great way for dedicated urbanites to *build equity.* In the heart of many older cities, such as Boston, Chicago and New York, where there simply are *no* single-family homes except million-dollar mansions, condos provide the answer.

Condos (and co-ops, as discussed in the next chapter) allow nonmillionaires to *own, rather than rent,* a residence they could not otherwise afford. Some luxury condos are indeed the equivalent of a piece of a mansion.

One giant selling point in many condos is the *recreational opportunities.* Some condo communities make you feel as though you are living at a country club: playgrounds, rec rooms, pools, golf course with clubhouse, tennis courts, health club—all those facilities we associate with the "good life."

As an owner, you have access to all these amenities. The condo association does have the right, however, to raise monthly maintenance fees if the cost of running the amenities rises (more about this later).

. . . VERSUS THE DRAWBACKS

Certain pitfalls in condo living cannot be taken lightly.

LESS PRIVACY. If you are looking for wide open spaces and seclusion from neighbors, a condo clearly is not the place for you.

Perhaps you like to have neighbors close by. You enjoy living in an environment filled with people to talk to and have fun with. Nevertheless, an obnoxious neighbor might temporarily spoil that community feeling. You might be forced to complain to the condominium association and have to go through unpleasant procedures—including calling the police—to make your home more peaceful.

HIGHER UPKEEP COSTS. When it comes to maintenance *inside* your condo apartment or town home, living in a condo is *not* like living in a rented residence. A developer offers you a paint job in the beginning, but after you own the place, you pay for internal jobs.

The same rule holds true for a leaky faucet in your kitchen. As the owner, it is your responsibility to fix it unless the leak is coming from a common area pipe in the wall. The general rule is that if it is happening *within* your walls, it is your problem.

For example, if a main line breaks and causes damage to your carpet, the association must repair the pipes and the plaster ruined because workmen had to go through your wall to fix it. But the association is *not* responsible for replacing the wallpaper or the carpet in your home.

Your homeowner's insurance policy should include a contingency clause for redecorating and replacing items ruined by a leak or a break from the common area.

The very benefits that make some condos so attractive can also become pitfalls.

RISING ASSESSMENTS. A condo association may have to raise maintenance fees if the cost of amenities, such as maintaining a swimming pool, goes up. Or the association can start to charge for features that once were free, such as the use of the tennis courts or health club. (On the other hand, a condo association can lower maintenance fees if costs go down.)

This is a sticky issue. One of my radio listeners called about a 50-percent increase that was assessed at his place by the condo association for rebuilding the pool and increasing security.

Sometimes a developer uses an amenity—free membership in the health club, for example—as a sales tool. Then, before turning the community over to the association, the developer starts charging a fee for what was originally a freebie.

In southern Florida, one developer built an entire community around a golf course. In sales pitches the developer trumpeted free use of the golf course as part of the overall package. When the community association took over the common areas, the developer sold the golf course to a third party. Suddenly those same owners had to pay greens fees.

There were howls of protest. It turned out that tiny print in the sales contract did give the developer the option of selling the golf course to a third party.

The lesson here is that if a salesperson promises that a major amenity, such as a free golf course, goes with the condo, do not accept that person's word alone. Make the sales agent show you, in the documents that are registered with the state, that this amenity will in fact be turned over to the association when the developer relinquishes control.

On occasion, a developer charges low membership fees but, as the condo project becomes established, relinquishes control of the recreational facilities by selling them *to the local residents themselves,* at very hefty prices.

This happened in Florida, at Boca West, a posh community built with four golf courses, thirty-four tennis courts and a clubhouse.

The Boca West amenities were owned for years by the developer, who charged fees to those who wanted to join. When the developer decided that the recreational facilities were no longer profitable, homeowners were asked to *buy* the entire amenity package. Under an "equity-conversion offering," members who wanted to continue to play golf on Boca West courses would have to buy shares for $10,000 and up in a new corporation set up to own and run the facilities, and pay membership fees on top of that.

The result? Lawsuits that are still in the courts.

Your maintenance fees can, and often do, increase—even if you do not benefit personally. Condo associations in "singles" and "yuppie" havens might vote to resurface the development's tennis courts each year. You might never play even one set of tennis, but still you will be assessed your proportional share of the cost.

NO CHILDREN, PREGNANCIES OR DOGS ALLOWED

Every condo development imposes restrictions on residents that single-family homeowners do not have to take into account.

ADULTS ONLY. There *are* adult condos that have *age requirements*

—residents must be at least thirty years old, or fifty, or whatever. Some of these and others prohibit *children,* and not just infants. (A Texas condo development forbade "children" under sixteen.)

Several cases have been fought in the courts in an attempt to break such rules, but it pays to examine the condo association restrictions thoroughly before you buy. In the past, some associations in adult condos have won the right to tell a couple to move if the wife gets pregnant!

PET RESTRICTIONS. Another rule might prohibit pets or limit their numbers. If you adore your Fido, you need to weigh your attachment to him against the benefits of a condo that will force you to send him to boarding school.

Generally, subleasing is unrestricted. However, if you sublet your two-bedroom condo to a family of ten, the association could demand that they be removed. If tenants use the condo for illegal purposes, the association could protest. Of course, those are extreme examples.

LIMITS ON REMODELING A CONDO

Let us say you purchase a lovely two-story, three-bedroom town home. Since you do not need the extra bedroom on the first floor, you want to knock out the wall separating it from the living room, creating a marvelously spacious layout.

That is okay, as long as you play by the rules. All condos have *restrictive covenants* that regulate how much you can do. Universally, you need permission to move any supporting walls. Nonsupporting walls in a condo can usually be changed.

What about turning the master bedroom windows and door into one sweeping floor-to-ceiling sliding glass door leading to the balcony? Check first with the association. You cannot change windows unless you receive permission.

What if you want to enclose the balcony in Plexiglass or screen it into a porch? Almost everywhere, you must obtain approval for changes in those "limited common areas." Most places will not let you cut down trees without permission.

Each condo development might have additional restrictions. They are based on the lifestyle that the developer initially perceives is best for that particular market.

I know of one cluster of town homes where no campers, trailers or buses are allowed in owner driveways. In another, you cannot put in a pool. Elsewhere, only in-ground pools may be permitted in backyards, or you may have to use only certain materials in above-ground pools.

Some fancy condo developments require you to put your garbage out for collection only in a certain location. One condo association forced a homeowner to remove a satellite-dish antenna on the grounds that it did not harmonize with the landscaping.

At a place in Marina Del Rey, California, a much-decorated World War II veteran was taken to court by his condo association in an effort to force him to remove a twelve-foot flagpole from his back patio, where he flew Old Glory around the clock.

My favorite condo covenant tale involves a suburban Philadelphia development where the town house exteriors could not be anything but wood, stone or brick. An owner preferred vinyl siding, but his request was denied. Guess what the owner did in protest? He painted the entire wooden exterior of the house a deep, eye-catching purple!

No condo owner wants to get embroiled in such disputes, so read those covenants carefully *before you buy,* should you have remodeling or flagwaving in mind for the future.

SIZING UP A CONDO ON YOUR FIRST VISIT

Once you have determined that a condo will fit both your pocketbook and your lifestyle, take your first tour. Inspect the facility closely to get an overall impression of how well it is maintained. For instance:

- Are the walkways clean?
- Are the hallways free of debris?
- Are the walls painted?
- Is the carpeting in the hallways clean and well kept?
- Are the elevators in good working condition?
- Are the shrubbery and lawn well kept?
- Is the security as protective as you would like?
- Do the service people you meet (doorman, security guards, maintenance employees, etc.) seem attentive?
- Is the swimming pool area clean?
- If there are commercial shops or professional offices within the complex, are they fully occupied?

The best way to size up a condo is to talk to at least five people who live there already.

How long have the people in the apartment or town home next door to the one you are contemplating lived there? Would they recommend this as a place for a person with your interests? Has the monthly maintenance fee gone up since they moved there? By how much? Do these residents like their neighbors? Do they have a good relationship with the condo association?

Does the place have a good manager? That is crucial to a condo's well-being. A condo manager operates the same way a building superintendent does. He is responsible for making sure the common areas function properly. In addition, the manager is the person you call when there is a structural problem, a failure of the electrical system or any other matter involving your unit and the rest of the building or development.

Finally, what improvements do your potential neighbors think should be made to make this a better place to live? What are the chances those improvements will become a reality?

CONDO CONVERSIONS: EQUITY AT A DISCOUNT

In cities like New York, condo and co-op apartment buildings exist side by side. Many erstwhile rental buildings have in recent years been converted to condos, as well as to co-ops.

A developer converts a rental building to condo status by improving the facilities and then applying to state and local authorities for the right to sell the apartments. The application papers include a legal description of each unit. These units are then sold after an extensive, and expensive, registration process designed to protect you, the buyer. The procedure requires the developer to have financial depth and responsibility. A developer must post certain *performance bonds* as insurance that the company will follow through on its plans.

In addition, a converter usually gives the current renters the *right of first refusal.* They can choose to purchase the unit in which they live, at a price that is less than an outsider would pay; this is known as an insider discount.

In New York City, most condos today are converted under a noneviction plan. Those who prefer not to buy continue paying rent. However, it is considered a bit risky for an outsider to buy an apartment in a building converted under a noneviction plan. Remaining renters are likely to battle to keep rents low, voting against improvements that will add to the building's worth.

Elsewhere, there are conversions in which tenants not covered by rent control can be evicted if they do not want to buy their apartments.

A CONSUMER-PROTECTED PURCHASE

Consumer protection laws are stronger for condo buyers than they are for single-family residents. Most states have very strict laws governing the sale of condos.

A full statement must be presented to you, the buyer, before the closing. It lists rules and regulations and describes the common areas.

If you have questions about the financial stability of a condo community, it is not difficult to conduct your own investigation. All documents must be filed with the state government.

These documents give you the name of the financial institutions involved in the condo. A few telephone calls will tell you whether or not the condo is in good fiscal health.

In particular, look in condo documents for a *contingency fund* for emergency expenses and a *reserve fund* for future improvements. A portion of your maintenance fee should be contributing to these funds.

When you read the financial statement and when you interview the various owners, ask if there have been any *recent special assessments* and what they have been.

You may also want to ask the board and the management company if any major repairs are being considered, and how much they will cost. Is there money being held in reserve for them? How much will they assess each owner for this new expense?

In some parts of the country, condo apartment buildings have been used as tax shelters, as investment opportunities for wealthy foreigners or as corporate alternatives to hotel suites. Before buying in a new condo building, find out *how many units* are being purchased by *investors.*

Why? Owners are the best neighbors. If the building has more than 50 percent investor ownership, that means half your neighbors will not be owners. Investors are not as caring as owners.

Finally, make sure before closing, if you are buying a preowned condo, that you are not assuming a seller's *unpaid assessment.* That is like renting a hotel room and inheriting the previous occupant's towels.

WHO'S IN CHARGE?

The condo association—you and your neighbors—does not take over the management of the condo until the developer has sold a majority of the units within the building, usually 70 percent or more. (This percentage varies from state to state.)

Thus, *you have no say* in how the community is run *until the condo association takes over.* In that respect, it is a bit like renting rather than owning.

Once the condo association takes charge, the size of your condo determines the number of votes you have in the association. You and your fellow residents elect officers from among yourselves to sit on the association's board of directors. The board is entrusted to enforce the rules that, at least in theory, have been created to make your life in the condo more pleasant. The board can also set new rules.

Be familiar with the members of your board of directors or board of managers. Many decisions that affect you will be made by the board. One way to become part of the decision-making process is to seek actively election to the board of directors.

THERE WAS A HOUSE IN NEW ORLEANS . . .

If you are unhappy with your board of directors, you can, by petition, have members removed and have some of the bylaws changed. Consider yourself a voter in what amounts to a very small town.

Politics plays a very big role. There was a political upheaval some time ago in a condo development in Virginia that served as a bedroom community for the bureaucrats in Washington.

The owners discovered that the board of directors had given contracts to friends for the common area's coin-operated washing machines and soft-drink machines. One board member even owned an interest in one of the concessioner companies. A group of angry owners banded together, put an end to the kickbacks, and had the entire board removed.

A New Orleans case indicates how common referendums and petitions are in condos. The condo association of a downtown community began receiving complaints about people coming in and out of a particular unit at all hours of the day and night.

The visitors were men; the resident, a woman, was a well-known socialite. The unit was being run as a "house in New Orleans," just as in the famous song. The other owners did not like the tune. They circulated a petition to have the socialite ousted. When she received notice about it, she promptly sold her unit. Had she refused to sell, the condo association would have sought a court judgment forcing her to sell, on the grounds that she operated an illegal business.

THE PECKING ORDER

Perhaps the most important role the condo association's board of directors plays is hiring the management company that handles actual day-to-day operations. (In some smaller condo buildings, the association's board does its own managing.)

The management company hires your doorman, superintendent and maintenance crews. The management company also collects the maintenance fees and prepares and submits all accounting to the board. The management company can make the difference between a wonderful living experience and an awful one. That is a good reason to question your potential neighbors on management efficiency.

A bad company can push fees through the proverbial roof. They can hire poor or overpriced subcontractors to make major repairs, or collect up-front fees from your condo association in addition to regular fees.

In the very worst situation, especially where there is a soft real estate market, a sleazy management company can declare bankruptcy, run off with your fees, then open for business elsewhere under a new name and rook other communities.

Happily, there is an excellent community association of co-op and condo owners, in which you can sharpen your knowledge of condo management. The Community Associations Institute (CAI) is a national nonprofit organization created in 1973 to help officers in condo and co-op associations. Members include homeowners who are officers of their condo associations, homeowner associations or co-op boards; builders of such developments; managers; public officials and others.

The Institute performs a tremendous service through meetings and newsletters. It offers seminars to help association board members understand their roles and deal more effectively with their management companies, insurance companies and fellow residents.

If you are interested, write the CAI at 1423 Powhatan Street, Suite 7, Alexandria, VA 22314, or call (703) 548–8600.

FINANCING AND INSURING A CONDO

Getting a mortgage for a condo is no different from getting financing for a single-family home. Read through chapter 7 and do the math to compare the down payment, mortgage costs and closing costs on each condo.

Insurance becomes a bit more complicated in a condo. To use a liability case that has occurred, let us say that your cleaning person slips, falls, and ends up with a permanent disability. Who pays for it?

If the person slips inside your apartment, your insurance must cover it. If the fall occurs in the lobby or hallway, the association insurance must cover it, or you will be sued.

Condo associations may also be held liable for *criminal acts by strangers* against residents or nonresidents. In a Hawaii case, guests of a condo owner were attacked inside the owner's unit. A court held that since the assailants had to use the condo's "common areas," either elevators or stairs, to gain entrance to the unit, the association was responsible. The association and its management company had a duty to keep the premises well protected.

Laws regarding condos, co-ops and homeowner associations change constantly. *The Law Reporter,* a newsletter put out by the Community Associations Institute, can keep you posted.

SHOULD YOU BUY IT BEFORE IT IS FINISHED?

Buying a unit in an existing condo is like buying a resale house; you know you can occupy it on closing day. Buying in an unfinished building is like betting on a horse. You are *pretty sure* the horse will finish the race, but you are *gambling* that your pony will come in first.

Condos under construction are a gamble. If the commitment from the builder is for January 1, you can hope for that date. But plan on moving in six months *after* that. Condos rarely are finished on time!

The good news about buying in a new or unfinished building or development? While the units are being sold, there are *no* maintenance fees. Usually no fees are paid until the amenities and recreational facilities are completed.

However, you will *not* know how much the fees will be when the maintenance is turned over to the condo association. You take the chance they will not be prohibitive, although the developer will give you an estimate.

You will also be inconvenienced. If you are queasy about stepping through muddy roads and having workmen wake you up early in the morning, you may want to reconsider moving into a new or unfinished building.

Nevertheless, if you are a bargain hunter, the best time to buy a condo is *before* it is built. Prices start very low to attract buyers and raise money. You can be the beneficiary, provided you shop carefully.

I recommend that you follow the same procedures in checking out your condo builder as those discussed in chapter 11 on new construction.

For instance, did you check your builder's reputation? Has he or she ever been bankrupt? Have you run a credit check on the builder? Visit another condo built by the the same firm, and talk to the people who live there. Was maintenance done well while construction was under way? Was access easy? How much are fees now in the finished buildings?

Most builders will give you an estimated monthly maintenance fee. Compare the estimate with that for similar buildings. If it is much lower, become suspicious. Demand to know why there is such a discrepancy.

CONDOS VERSUS CO-OPS—WHICH COST MORE?

Within five to ten years, fewer and fewer co-ops will be available because more buildings will be converted to condos instead. (One reason is that co-ops have proved to be cumbersome for lending institutions.) The bottom-line profit for developers is higher on condos, and buyers seem to prefer the flexibility of condos. Soon the condo concept will be held by a majority.

But what about now? What if you have a choice of two buildings in the same neighborhood, one a condo and the other a co-op?

In comparing expenses, the size, age or location of a building means almost nothing. The determining factor is the building's condition. The main exception is that you will pay more money for an apartment in an older building, in a city such as New York or Chicago, because of its unique charm or character.

Might the time come when you want to move elsewhere but keep your condo? What if your company transfers you to another locale? It is generally much easier to rent or lease your condominium to a tenant than to lease or rent out a co-op.

Take the time to understand the portions of condo documents about leasing your apartment. If you do not understand them, hire an attorney to explain what your rights are.

When all is said and done, in my opinion, *you will pay less to live in a condo* than you will in a co-op.

Initially, condo purchase prices may appear higher. A New York real estate broker quoted in a 1986 *New York Times* story reported that one-bedroom luxury Manhattan condos were priced $24,000 per room *higher* than equivalent co-ops.

The question marks are *maintenance fees, monthly mortgage payments, down payment, closing costs* and *tax deductions.*

Condo closing costs tend to be *higher* than those for co-ops, because condos are treated like actual real estate while co-op sales are transfers of shares in a corporation. Condo down payments generally are *higher* than those for co-ops, except in exceptionally restrictive co-op buildings that might require from 50 to 100 percent of the purchase price up front.

But condo monthly maintenance fees tend to be *lower* than those in co-ops. The latter add an owner's share of underlying mortgages and real estate taxes to the cost of upkeep. Condos, in contrast, do not have mortgages. According to one Westchester County, New York, expert quoted by *The New York Times,* "the *total monthly outlay* turns out to be around *30 percent less"* in a condominium.

The following chapter tells you more about co-ops. If you are comparing a condo with a co-op, use the chart on page 203 to compare various costs.

Recommended Reading on Condos

"Questions About Condos," a free booklet from the U.S. Department of Housing and Urban Development, Washington, DC 20410

"Tax Information on Condominium and Cooperative Apartments," IRS Booklet 588, free from a local Internal Revenue Service office

Checklist: Doing the Numbers on a Condo

Expenses	Condo #1	Condo #2	Condo #3
A. Purchase price	$ _____	$ _____	$ _____
B. Down payment	$ _____	$ _____	$ _____
C. Total closing costs	$ _____	$ _____	$ _____
D. **Initial** outlay (B + C)	= $ _____	$ _____	$ _____
E. Monthly mortgage payments	$ _____	$ _____	$ _____
F. Annual property taxes (12 months)	$ _____	$ _____	$ _____
G. Monthly maintenance fees	$ _____	$ _____	$ _____
H. Special assessments (if any)	$ _____	$ _____	$ _____
I. Extra fees for parking, club membership, etc.	$ _____	$ _____	$ _____
J. **Total** monthly outlay (add E through I)	= $ _____	$ _____	$ _____

Chapter **14**

Co-ops: An Old Way of Life—and Different Rules—for City Dwellers

Living in a co-op is a special experience. With the gentrification (renovation and upscaling) of the nation's cities, cooperative apartments are becoming a way of life for many who have never been exposed to them before. Co-ops include some of the finest apartment buildings in the U.S., located in the heart of the most desirable urban communities.

This chapter talks about the advantages and pitfalls of co-ops in both the Northeast, where they have existed for a long while, and in other parts of the country, where they are not as prevalent.

A CORPORATION, NOT JUST A BUILDING

Although it looks like real estate, wears like real estate, and is used like real estate, *a co-op is not real estate* in the legal sense of the term.

If you own a co-op, you do not actually own the apartment, you own stock in a corporation that owns the building in which the co-op you live in is located. You have the right to occupy that apartment and the right to use the common areas, guaranteed by a legal document known as a proprietary lease, or certificate of beneficial interest.

To maintain your rights, you must pay a certain portion of the upkeep and the expenses. The standard procedure is to assign such costs according to the number of shares you own. You pay in the form of a monthly maintenance charge.

Unlike condo expenses, the expenses of a co-op usually include a mortgage on the building for the common areas, and real estate taxes (you pay a portion of the taxes rather than individual taxes on your unit). Your monthly maintenance fee also covers your share of repair and renovation costs.

Why does the "corporation" status of a co-op matter? Because the unusual nature of a co-op might cost you money.

You might wind up paying *more* for a co-op since monthly maintenance fees tend to be higher than those of equivalent condos. Also, it might be harder to obtain financing at the same rate as that for a condo. Owning a co-op is *almost* like owning real estate, in the eyes of some lenders. However, the loan to you is a personal loan, and the loan, instead of being secured by real estate, is secured by stock in the corporation that owns the building.

GREAT BUILDINGS—AND SNOB APPEAL

According to historian Christopher Gray, the first cooperative apartment house was built over 100 years ago on West 57th Street in Manhattan. Its name set the tone for co-ops to come: it was christened The Rembrandt.

Although there were and continue to be plenty of middle-income co-ops, many of the famous ones, such as The Dakota and River House in New York City, are deluxe habitats with prices to match. Superluxurious, landmark-status co-ops line New York's most prestigious streets.

In fact, it is almost impossible to live on Park Avenue, Fifth Avenue, Central Park West or Central Park South in Manhattan without buying a co-op, since almost every building on the most elegant parts of those streets are structured as co-ops, rather than rentals or condos.

When you buy a co-op, you commit yourself to a particular lifestyle. For one thing, you and your family must be approved by the building's shareholders.

No one buys in a co-op unless members of its board of directors (tenant shareholders who are elected by their peers) agree to accept the prospective new resident. You might think you have "the right stuff" —a high income, a stable family, a good occupation, the best references —and still be turned away. New York co-ops have refused to allow world-renowned show business entertainers and even a former president, Richard Nixon, to buy into their buildings.

Actually, the most common reason people are turned away is that co-op boards are afraid that certain prospective owners will not be able to afford the maintenance fees. Since a default by one owner affects all shareholders, it is understandable that boards are quite exhaustive in delving into an applicant's finances.

A less common reason, though the more publicized one, is that co-op boards fear certain people might throw noisy parties or change the reputation of their building.

The advantages of buying a co-op include the opportunity to be neighbors with people who are likely to be in a similar income bracket. You can feel a bit closer to them because of mutual interest in the building, and this feeling is often missing in some condos and most rental buildings.

Buying a co-op is like being admitted to the best college or country club. And you will not see frequently changing neighbors, thanks to the strict subletting and noninvestor ownership policies.

In the best co-ops, boards are scrupulous about hiring the finest management companies and providing tremendous personal service. Tight security, 24-hour doormen, elevator operators, handymen on call round the clock, package rooms, bicycle rooms, maid's quarters and concierges are available in superluxury co-ops.

However, at tax time, co-op owners do *not* get the same tax deductions available to single-family and condo home owners.

Are you the type of person who would enjoy co-op living? Test yourself with our Co-op Candidate Quiz at the end of this chapter.

CO-OPS HAVE PITFALLS, TOO

The biggest drawback of a co-op is that you *do not have the freedom to share, sell, sublease, remodel or utilize your property* as you do in a condo, or in a standard single-family home. The rules concerning children and dogs can be stricter in a co-op.

What if you are a single person, who at some point might invite a roommate or lover to share your co-op permanently? The co-op board could say, "Get married or get out." A New York law generally gives you the right to share a residence with a roommate. However, a recent court decision held that certain co-ops do *not* come under that section of the real property law, so a board could demand that your roommate leave. Furthermore, co-ops have the right to restrict the subletting of apartments and often exercise those rights strenuously.

You cannot remodel, make internal wall changes, window changes or even, in some cases, add air conditioners without co-op board approval. Potential buyers who envision extensively remodeling an apartment are strongly advised to test the board's feelings first.

Your ability to sell a co-op is restricted by the necessity of board approval of buyers. Your deal could fall through because your board does not like your buyer. You may think you have a sale sewn up, only to see it come apart because your buyer is rejected. You have to start listing and showing your apartment all over.

One radio listener experienced several of these co-op roadblocks. This working woman held on to her co-op in a small building when she made a job transfer to another city. She sublet the place to friends. At the time, her co-op board's policy was to allow subleasing for 18 months. When the 18 months on this sublease expired, the board of directors refused to allow her a second long-term sublease.

The woman had to continue to pay maintenance and mortgage charges while the apartment was empty.

Finally, she decided it was wise to sell. But to make matters worse, the board rejected several prospective buyers. It was a catch-22 situation. She could not sublet, she could not sell, and she could not live in the apartment. She spent a sizable amount of money before she could locate a buyer who was approved by her board.

You can wind up paying for expensive renovations in a co-op building with structural, wiring, waterproofing or plumbing problems. Numerous buildings have to take out heavy new mortgages to pay for major repairs. The mortgage charges are passed on to shareholders in the form of increased monthly maintenance charges.

In certain superluxury co-op buildings, there are restrictions on how much of the purchase you can finance. Some co-op boards require that apartments be bought for anywhere from 50 to 100 percent cash. That is a heck of a lot of loot—$1 million is not unheard of for a three-bedroom Park Avenue apartment—out of your bank account.

Finally, there could be a problem with mortgage tax deductions regarding the 80/20 rule. More about that later in this chapter.

HOW TO INSPECT A CO-OP

Shopping for a co-op is much like shopping for any other residence, except that *you are investigated as much by the co-op board,* in some instances, as the co-op is investigated by you!

To save time and embarrassment, use the questionnaire on page 202 on your real estate agent when you take your initial tour. It will help you root out trouble spots—such as the size of down payments required by the building and the type of buyer the board is apt to approve.

Satisfy yourself that the building is well run. As with condos, politics plays a large role among board members in a co-op. Talk to residents about possible maintenance increases, large repair jobs, level of service, and about friction within the board on what changes should or should not be made.

Make an effort to *meet those in charge of day-to-day care.* The resident manager and/or superintendent is usually hired by and works closely with the management company. Not all co-ops have a resident manager, although most do have superintendents.

As in the case of condos, some co-op boards are plagued by disputes with management companies over fees, repairs and personnel. Play investigative reporter. Learn about the management company as well as the co-op board.

CUTTING THROUGH THE JARGON OF ANNUAL REPORTS

How can you learn if the co-op is about to take out a second mortgage, or if it needs to replace its boiler and therefore monthly maintenance is about to skyrocket? Make sure you or an advisor *scours the co-op board's minutes and financial statements for hints of trouble* down the road.

If you are contemplating a very expensive co-op, or if you have doubts about the building, play it extra-safe. Unless you have a degree in accounting, you would be smart to hire an accountant to interpret the good and bad points in the financial statement.

The items most likely to cost a co-op a bundle are heating and air-conditioning systems, and structural work and roofs. Nevertheless, it can be very difficult, even for a CPA, to tell if a particular co-op will face such a major expense.

Most semiannual reports are written in very careful legalese to make sure the board of directors does not put itself in a position in which it can be reprimanded or sued. The language is boilerplated—it protects the people who write it from actions against them more than it protects the shareholders.

As an example, the past three annual reports of a large, well-known Manhattan co-op basically say, "Hey, it was a tough year, but we made it through. Yea, team!"

A microscopic inspection of every part of the minutes and annual report, however, would disclose that at one time the building did not have excess cash, and yet major structural renovations had to be done. During that period, monthly fees did go up sharply.

YOU CAN HELP NAVIGATE THE SHIP

A lesson to be learned from annual reports is that once you buy a unit in a co-op, the way to find out what is going on is to seek office on the board actively. Some people would rather sail along as passengers on the ship and enjoy the cruise. Others like to chart the course and help navigate.

One warning to would-be navigators: being a board member takes up a huge chunk of your spare time (and some of the time you would normally spend on your actual profession)!

How do you get on a board? By meeting your fellow board members and shareholders in the elevators and lobby and sending postcards or letters, you can let them know who you are and what your qualifications are, and that you are interested in becoming active.

A big problem in the past is that people who have run co-op boards do not do it professionally. "Outside professionals"—usually management companies—really run the building. When co-op boards fail to do their homework, they may be hurt by hiring an inefficient or inattentive management company.

The fact that a company manages many buildings or has a recognizable name is no guarantee that it is the best, quality-wise or price-wise. What I said about condo management applies to co-op management as well. A bad company can fail to make repairs or can hire unnecessarily costly repair companies.

If you are about to buy a co-op for which there has been a recent change in the management company, it pays to visit other buildings handled by that company. Get in touch with board members and residents. These contacts will give you an inkling of the level of service *you* are about to get.

When disreputable management companies have problems collecting management fees, it's not unusual for them to go out of business all of a sudden as ABC Management Company, file for bankruptcy, and open up the next day as XYZ Company. There have been such cases.

As a last resort, a co-op board, especially one with fewer than fifty tenant shareholders, can manage the building itself. This has been done in numerous New York City buildings, many of whose boards hire a full-time, on-site manager.

Other buildings thrive without a full-time manager, dividing the chores among board committee members. If you are thinking of buying into such a building, it is probably wise to question residents even more closely about the financial and day-to-day living comfort zone of the apartment house.

There are several associations of co-op owners, from which you can obtain advice and training in co-op management, especially if you are buying into a building that is about to "go co-op" or has recently converted to a co-op.

In New York City, the Council of New York Cooperatives (167 West 72nd Street, New York, NY 10023; telephone, (212) 496-7400) runs a yearly conference, puts out a newsletter, and keeps co-ops informed of important legal and tax matters. This organization is affiliated with the National Association of Housing Cooperatives, 2501 M Street, N.W., Washington, DC 20037, which also offers educational material, workshops and courses.

The Community Associations Institute, mentioned in the last chapter, is a national nonprofit membership organization for officers in co-op and condo associations. If you are interested in membership, write CAI, 1423 Powhatan Street, Suite 7, Alexandria, VA 22314; or call (703) 548-8600.

FINANCING A CO-OP PURCHASE

The banking industry has special institutions that are comfortable with financing co-ops. These financial institutions are, however, dwindling in number, because of concerns over underlying mortgages that the co-op corporations hold. Thus, most co-op loans are between one-quarter and 1 interest point *higher than loans for condos* or conventional residences.

A word about tax deductions. Under the terms of Section 216 of the IRS code, you may deduct your proportionate share of the municipal taxes and the mortgage interest paid by the co-op corporation. In addition, you can deduct the interest that you pay on your purchase loan by using the stock as collateral as well.

For tax purposes, it is important *not* to get caught in the 80/20 rule. If you are living in a building that has commercial space on the ground floor and more than 20 percent of the corporation's income is derived from sources such as renting commercial space, the tenants lose all of the homeowner deductions. This makes a co-op's tax situation different from that of homes and condos.

THIS RED HERRING IS NO FISH STORY

In the world of apartment houses, a "red herring" is a notice from the landlord telling tenants that a building is being converted into a co-op. It states the terms and conditions of the conversion and gives tenants an opportunity to purchase at an insider price—a lower price—the unit in which they live, before it is offered to the outside world.

There are two types of co-op conversions: eviction and noneviction plans.

In New York City, since 1983, a landlord must have pledges to buy from 51 percent of the tenants, excluding certain elderly or handicapped ones, before an eviction plan can be accepted for filing.

Under such a plan, the sponsors—the owner or syndicate converting the building to a co-op—can take back the apartments of nonbuying tenants once three years have elapsed after the plan is accepted.

Because of the 51-percent rule, most conversions today are noneviction; tenants who do not wish to buy are allowed to remain as tenants as long as they like. A noneviction plan needs the approval of just 15 percent of the tenants before it can be filed.

Why are rental buildings converted to co-ops rather than condos? In part, so that the landlord and/or sponsor can realize a profit.

Furthermore, some rental buildings will not meet the specifications of the condo rules and regulations imposed by a state. It is less expensive and quicker to make such buildings co-ops.

The conversion of a rental building to a co-op takes anywhere from 1 to 4 years after a red herring is distributed, depending on the expertise of the developer and the extent of renovation that needs to be done.

Why the delay? The plan must be approved by the local municipality as well as by the state. The approving departments vary from state to state. In most states it is the department that regulates securities and corporations that must approve the co-op conversion plan.

The state's responsibility is to make sure the sponsor meets the needs of the current tenants by offering them a fair shake on the purchase of their units. The state also requires that local building codes are met and inspects the financial stability and expertise of the sponsors.

Incidentally, it is estimated that Americans pay from 15 to 20 percent of the total purchase price of a converted apartment for government regulations. You do not see these added costs, because they are factored into the sales price.

During the red-herring period, you can expect conversion plans to change in minor ways as the result of negotiations between sponsors, tenants and state authorities. For the most part, the basic conversion plan will not change unless there are blatant building-code violations.

TO BUY OR NOT? TO FLIP OR NOT?

In previous years, you could make a bundle of money by just being in a building when it was converted to a co-op, then *buying at the low insider price* and shortly thereafter "flipping"—selling the apartment— for a 100-percent profit or more to an outsider. (The outsider would pay the "fair market" rate.)

However, many buildings now reduce that profit by imposing a *flip tax*—a resale fee, either a percentage of the sales price or a percentage of the profit—on the sale by an insider to an outsider. (Some longtime co-ops have changed their rules and impose a flip tax on *any* sale.)

The flip tax is a controversial matter that has been the subject of court cases and legislation. Before you buy, ask whether there is a flip-tax provision in your building and if it has been tested in court.

New York City, with its large number of co-ops, has used co-op conversions as a measure of the condition of a neighborhood. In a community that might formerly have been considered marginal, the conversion of buildings one by one, from rentals to co-ops and condos has often been an accurate sign that the neighborhood is improving.

Viewed in this light, the purchase of a co-op by a tenant could be a terrific deal, in terms of building equity, the potential growth in appreciation of the apartment and the comfort and security of the shareholder's family.

If you are happy with the building and you can afford to buy, do so. The disadvantage of not buying at conversion time is that you are most likely going to pay a higher price by waiting.

CO-OP CANDIDATE QUIZ
(13 questions to ask yourself *before* buying any co-op)

1. Do I like the neighborhood?
2. Have I talked to the people in the building to ask them how they feel about living there?
3. Do I like the people I have met in the building?
4. Am I willing to be cross-examined by strangers on the board in order to live here?
5. Have I examined the outside of the building and the common areas and hallways and elevators for visual signs of good housekeeping?
6. Have I checked to see if financing is available and if in fact I can finance my co-op?
7. Have I checked to see if banks are loaning money on this particular building? Where are those banks located?
8. Can I obtain a second loan in case I am not able to come up with the cash to pay for a large assessment?
9. Do I like the level of personal service the building offers?
10. Will I be content with the restrictions on guests, subleases, children, pets and so on?
11. Am I getting as much for my money in this co-op as I would buying into a similarly located condo?
12. Have I learned who my immediate common-wall neighbors are and whether they share a similar lifestyle to mine, in terms of noise, comings and goings, parties?
13. Does the apartment have good appreciation potential, should I plan to sell within a few years?

CO-OP BOARD QUESTIONNAIRE
(17 questions to ask your real estate person *before* you meet a co-op board)

1. How old is the building?
2. What was the most recent major capital improvement?
3. What other improvements are being discussed?
4. How is the board of directors selected?
5. How often do directors rotate or change?
6. May we see some annual or semiannual reports?
7. How often does the board meet?
8. What income is required of prospective shareholders?
9. What are other considerations?
10. How much of the purchase price can I finance?
11. Are there restrictions on refinancing?
12. Has the board rejected anyone recently? Why?
13. How many (or what percentage of) apartments are investor-owned?
14. Are washers/dryers permitted in apartments?
15. Can a Jacuzzi or whirlpool be added?
16. What are the subleasing restrictions?
17. Who manages the building's day-to-day operations?

SCORECARD: FINANCIAL BENEFITS OF A CO-OP VERSUS A CONDO

Benefit	Co-op	Condo
Sales price	$_____	$_____
Down payment needed	_____ percent	_____ percent
Mortgage available?	yes/no	yes/no
Monthly mortgage payment will be	$_____	$_____
Board approval of me is considered	excellent/good/fair	(automatic)
Current occupant satisfaction?	excellent/good/fair	excellent/good/fair
Resale possibility?	excellent/good/fair	excellent/good/fair
Added assessments within 2 years are	certain/possible/unlikely	certain/possible/unlikely

Chapter **15**

How to Buy Recreational Property Despite Your Neighbor's Horror Stories

A vacation home can be a wonderful retreat or an albatross. I am sure you have friends who have had very pretty pictures painted for them in their favorite resort area—pictures that then have been smashed by the reality of burdensome mortgages, changes in tax laws, high vacancy rates.

It does not have to be that way.

The first rule of vacation homes is this: buy one because you plan to enjoy it, not as a tax shelter. The second rule: buy one you can afford, or else look into time sharing. The third rule: buy your acre of paradise in a market where you can *offset many of your costs* by renting your home while you are not using it.

In a moment, I will show you how to shop, as well as how to choose the best management company to rent, clean and protect your vacation home. And you will have a handy list of tough questions to ask realtors and management companies.

FUN LOVERS, THIS IS YOUR CHANCE

If you do not yet have a vacation home, and if you *can* afford one, you are apt to find bargains galore. Since pure investors can no longer take advantage of major tax breaks, real vacationers can jump into a buyer's market.

How do you know if you are a "real vacationer"? Easy.

Do you reserve time every year to play golf at Hilton Head, in Florida, in Palm Springs, on Long Island, or anywhere else? Do you head for the Colorado ski slopes (as coauthor Grace does) as soon as the lifts open every winter? Are you first in line for a hunting or fishing license in your favorite neck of the woods each season? Do you leave your city residence every weekend in search of a place to recharge your batteries?

If your answer to any of these recreation questions is yes, it is time to figure out what that annual, semiannual or every-weekend trip adds up to in U.S. currency.

Using the formula on page 206, figure what it will cost you *over the next 10 years.* You have to increase the amount each year to cover inflation. I use a conservative rate of 4 percent a year.

Let us assume your two golf holidays (or July by the shore) ran $4,000 a year in lodging last year. That equals $40,000 for vacations for the next 10 years. Add 4 percent a year for inflation, and you can end up spending $60,000 to $70,000 for those lovely holidays.

In many parts of the country, $60,000 to $70,000 will allow you to buy a splendid recreational home. The exceptions are areas a few hours from New York City, Boston, Chicago, San Francisco and other metropolitan areas where affluent city dwellers do not blink an eye at paying $100,000, $200,000 or more for a weekend country home.

In any case, you would probably put 10 to 20 percent down and take out a mortgage for the rest. This is *money you would have paid for a vacation in any event,* and you can *build equity* at the same time.

Here is another way to analyze it. If you pay $4,000 a year for vacation lodging, and you make an allowance for inflation, by the end of the decade you have spent $50,000 but *earned nothing.* However, if you spend that money each year paying for a $50,000 vacation condo or cottage, by the end of the decade you have *earned an equity position* in a $70,000 second home.

Should your vacation home be in a major destination resort such as the Disney World area of Florida, or Vermont or Colorado ski country, or a popular beach community, this second home probably will *grow in value* to $84,000 by the end of 10 years. If the home costs $100,000 to begin with, you can bet it will be worth $150,000 by the end of the decade.

The 10-Year Vacation Kitty

Last year I spent the following for recreation lodging:

Trip to:	Number of Days	Cost
1. _____	_____	$ _____
2. _____	_____	$ _____
3. _____	_____	$ _____
4. _____	_____	$ _____
5. _____	_____	$ _____

A.   **Total** annual cost of vacation lodging
    last year (1 through 5)   = $ _____
    multiplied by 4 percent inflation   x   .04

B.   annual cost in 2nd year   = $ _____
    4 percent inflation   x   .04

C.   annual cost in 3rd year   = $ _____
    4 percent inflation   x   .04

D.   annual cost in 4th year   = $ _____
    4 percent inflation   x   .04

E.   annual cost in 5th year   = $ _____
    4 percent inflation   x   .04

F.   annual cost in 6th year   = $ _____
    4 percent inflation   x   .04

G.   annual cost in 7th year   = $ _____
    4 percent inflation   x   .04

H.   annual cost in 8th year   = $ _____
    4 percent inflation   x   .04

I.   annual cost in 9th year   = $ _____
    4 percent inflation   x   .04

J.   annual cost in 10th year   = $ _____

K.   **Add** A through J for

10-year Vacation Kitty $ _____

Note: If you buy a $50,000 vacation home with 10 percent of the amount in K as down payment, your mortgage is $45,000. In the new top tax bracket of 28 percent, your net payment after taxes will be about $300 per month (actual cash out of pocket).

WHAT IS YOUR PREFERENCE IN PARADISE?

In the United States alone, scores of places fit someone's idea of paradise. A few of us have clear notions of the ideal spot. For one family, it is a cabin in Minnesota. For another, it is a condo in Snowmass, a tennis town home in Arizona or a saltbox on Cape Cod.

The funny thing is, most people do *not* start out with a clear picture of their ideal vacation home. They pick a vacation from a brochure, or through a television show, or after hearing about a place through a friend.

No wonder so many people at resorts say, "This is not really what I thought it was. Now that I'm here, I'm thinking of going someplace else."

Going someplace else is the appropriate move for such a vacationer. My advice to everyone but the diehard is, have an engagement period by renting, prior to the marriage of owning. Sometimes the vacations we take in our heads do not equal the reality of the trip itself.

Realize, too, that there are two versions of the second home—an individual residence not related to a resort, or a home that is within a planned vacation community.

If you are considering an individual home that is *not* part of a resort community, you should approach this purchase the same way you would deal with the purchase of a primary residence. Especially if you are shopping for a second home in the $100,000-and-up range, follow the steps outlined in chapters 1 through 10.

In addition, pay special attention to these elements:

Security. Do you plan to leave your second home vacant for periods of time, such as Monday through Friday in the case of a weekend home? Make sure there is an adequate security system.

Winterizing. Will temperatures dip below freezing in winter? You must decide whether to drain all pipes and put antifreeze in toilets, or keep the home heated at about 55 degrees, which is an added fuel cost. You should have someone periodically check the home if you do not visit in winter, to be certain the power does not go off and the fuel does not run out, causing pipes to freeze and crack.

Insurance. Your policy should cover all personal items in your second as well as first homes. Most people underinsure second homes.

COURT A RESORT BEFORE YOU MARRY ONE

Most developers of planned resorts have a generous plan for people who want to "get engaged" to a resort, to test it out. These developers rent cottages, apartment units, town homes or even hotel suites to potential buyers *at a discount.*

In some cases, they give *stays free of charge,* with one tiny string attached—you might have to listen to a brief sales pitch and take home an offering brochure.

Others might offer you a "refundable" discounted stay, with the money you pay plus the cost of your airline tickets deductible from the purchase price of a property, should you decide to buy.

About 95 percent of resort developers will give you *some form of a deal,* if you request it. For example, The Landings, a resort in Beaufort, South Carolina, normally charges $250 a night for a family on its golfing/boating/fishing package. But if you are a potential buyer, the first night is free, and the next six nights cost $100 a night for a family.

Travel agents are good sources for the names of developers, as are vacation properties advertising sections of newspapers and magazines.

How can you be sure the developer is not a fast-buck artist with three condos on a swamp that he swears will be a golf course by next April, when you arrive for your "vacation"? First, ask to see the offering statement filed with the state and federal governments. Then, ask those offices if the developer has posted a *cash bond* guaranteeing construction of amenities.

What a fabulous way to plan your next vacation! Instead of returning to the same old place, shop for a developer eager for a trial run. For the next year, or two, or five, you can take vacations in different places, *at a lower price* than you would pay for a straight package deal.

THE WEEKEND GETAWAY HOME

One quandary that many second-home buyers face is whether to shop for a weekend retreat, which they could use often, in season and out of season, or a place farther away, where they could go less often but for longer periods and where they would perhaps eventually retire.

To resolve the problem, you have to be realistic about how much time you have.

If you are worn out after long hours Monday through Friday, you may prefer the weekend getaway. If you are self-employed, you can make appointments with yourself to go near or far, often or rarely. If you work on weekends, or if your company may transfer you to another part of the country or world, you need to take that into consideration. I will return to the retirement issue later in this chapter.

Because "paradise" is a very subjective judgment, even those of you who hope to find the perfect weekend house within a few hours' drive of home should *try places on a rental basis* before committing yourself to ownership.

A man who described himself as "a single yuppie stockbroker" called my program one day for help in locating a weekend "hideaway." He already knew the rolling countryside two hours from Chicago that he liked. What he did not know was how to begin his search.

"This will be one of the most fascinating shopping trips you have ever taken," I promised him. I suggested he introduce himself to sales agents in the area, telling them he wanted to visit. In some cases they would surely offer a place to stay either gratis or at a discount. And what better way to find out about the other single people who spent time in his dream vacation haunt than by being there himself?

WHAT KIND OF RECREATION ARE YOU AFTER?

The stockbroker's question prompted a Baltimore woman to call with a different but common vacation predicament. "My husband likes weekends at the beach and playing tennis. I prefer gardening, and maybe occasional golf, in the country. How do we satisfy both of us?" she asked.

Scores of places satisfy all the needs of both the woman and her husband, I replied. There are some beautiful condo resorts in Michigan and North Carolina, for example, that give you a country atmosphere as well as the resort activities—tennis, golf, water sports—all in the same area.

"You need to make some visits as a prospective purchaser to a variety of developments. You'll get an idea of what life has to offer you in the vacation lane," I told the woman.

That goes for you, too. For a list of planned developments in a specific area, write the American Resort and Residential Developers Association, 1220 L Street, N.W., Washington, DC 20005.

Once you honestly know what your personal vacation preferences are, you can start to shop seriously. But do not buy on your first date.

Certain cost factors apply anywhere. In choosing between a town home and an apartment at the same price, you are better off with the town home. In the long run, *your investment return on a town home will be greater.* The same size two-bedroom detached house is apt to carry a higher price tag than the town home, because such houses are in even greater demand. In a beach area, you will pay more for an oceanside residence.

TIMING A VACATION HOME PURCHASE

Back in the chapter on timing, I made a big point of how cyclical the real estate market is, and how important it is to *buy when mortgage rates are down and the market is ripe for buyers.*

You cannot always time your primary home purchase. But you have more leeway when you shop for a second home.

At various times, vacation areas from the Poconos to Palm Springs, from Sun Valley, Idaho, to Vero Beach, Florida, have been under-developed, stable, frenetic or overbuilt. How does a lay person recognize what cycle a place is in?

Local and nearby newspapers are always a prime source of information for me. For example, if you are shopping in Vero Beach, you should look at the Miami and Palm Beach papers as well as the Vero Beach paper.

Find out if many properties are available. Then drive around the area. How many "For Sale" signs are there? How many listings do brokers have?

If there are pages and pages of properties for resale and the prices are extremely negotiable, you know you are in an overbuilt area. That happens to be a good time—a bargain hunter's time—to buy, provided it is a major destination resort.

But if there are very few properties, the region may be in the doldrums temporarily or not yet in the big leagues, or it may be a hot market with sizzling prices. Take care not to get burned.

IS YOUR PARADISE WITHIN YOUR BUDGET?

To avoid disappointment or debt you cannot handle, have a realistic idea of how expensive a property you can afford. One measure is the chart on page 206, which gives your 10-year vacation kitty. That is your projected recreational rent.

In order to buy, of course, you must be able to meet a down payment and monthly payments. To learn what those numbers are, do the math for your Financial Comfort Zone in chapter 1.

The spendable extra income you have remaining after you cover your monthly costs is money you can earmark for investment in your vacation home.

INSPECT THE HOME, NOT JUST THE VIEW

Whether you plan to buy a $60,000 vacation condo or a $300,000 country estate, you should use almost the *same approach* shopping for a vacation home as you would for a primary residence. Unfortunately, many people are in too romantic a frame of mind when they are in a resort or weekend area. They fail to ask the basic questions.

Those questions deal with the same matters involved when they are buying primary real estate. For instance, title problems, credit checks, down payments, professional inspections, access to property 365 days a year, and safety are all major issues with second homes.

Since you will undoubtedly deal with a broker, an attorney, an appraiser, a lender and a seller in purchasing your recreation home, review chapters 1 through 9.

NEW VERSUS RESALE VACATION HOMES

In vacation areas, the rules of purchasing brand-new homes versus resales are about the same as for primary residences. However, if the market is soft in a vacation area, you will *find better bargains in resales* than you might in a residential home area.

Use the same techniques I discussed earlier. Train yourself to notice "For Sale" signs. Look for abandoned places. You will be amazed at the bargains on homes in the 5- to 10-year age group. This was certainly true in the Southwest in 1986. When the oil industry dropped, prices for vacation properties fell 20 to 50 percent. In the 1970s, prices of second homes in the automobile manufacturing region of the Midwest dropped as much as 60 percent.

Keep cycles in mind, however. The Midwest has bounced back since the 1970s. And the Southwest will rebound even more strongly because of its pleasant weather.

If a developer in a planned resort is having problems, or a bank has taken over a resort, you might be in a strong position to buy a newly built home or condo at a reduced price.

In this scenario, do business directly with the developer or the bank. Banks do *not* want real estate. They are very motivated sellers. But even in a foreclosure or distress sale, you should be in love with the place as a vacation home, *not* as an investment.

Vacation home shoppers run into trouble when they start believing the honey-coated promises made by salespeople for planned resorts *not yet built or still under construction.*

The typical horror story usually takes place in an out-of-the-way location, one that is not near major destination resort areas. A developer buys the land very cheaply, intending to create a self-contained resort.

Hungry sales agents assure you that The Nowheresville Chateau Complex soon will rival Lake Tahoe as a major area. Slick brochures show the place in full flower, with fifty-year-old trees, a hubbub of activity around the swimming pool, homes full of luxurious interiors.

A handful of people buy, on the basis of these sales pitches. But they are not enough to keep the developer from going bankrupt. The bank that ends up with the half-finished resort does not know how to run it. But the bank *does* know how to collect monthly mortgage payments. The unlucky buyers end up with a home in the middle of nowhere, with nothing to do.

The moral of this story is this: unless you know the developer, and it is a major company like Westin Hotels or Marriott, be very cautious. It is always better to buy a resale. If you are dealing with a major developer backed by a huge corporation and a long track record, you could end up getting a slightly better deal buying at predevelopment prices.

An unfortunate part of the vacation property business is the hard sell. This is true of good resorts as well as "horror stories." You become so caught up in the promotional selling procedure that you forget why you are there.

Once you have heard a sales pitch, *walk away.*

Do *not* make a decision until you sleep on it for at least four or five nights. My friends in the industry will be upset with that advice. But it is the only way to prevent poor decisions.

Just as the detached single-family home is the first choice for a primary residence, detached single-family cottages are number one on the vacation home hit parade. But *condo* apartments and town homes are coming on strong. Condos will top the charts with about 55 to 60 percent of the vacation home market by the year 2000.

As a cautionary note, I would steer clear of second home fixer-uppers. In a normal market, they are not good buys. Even if you are a handyman or handywoman, chances are you will not spend enough time there to do the work. If you leave the work to others, you probably will not be on the site to supervise your contractors properly.

I would also be leery of hotel rooms that are sold as condominiums. *Forbes* magazine called them "terrible investments," and I agree. They are highly overpriced with little or no market for resale. Furthermore, buying a hotel condo room was said to be a good tax shelter with good return on investment after taxes. The projections put forward on these investments have *not* been true. I predict there will be many lawsuits and fraud investigations involving condo hotels.

WHAT IF YOUR TASTE OR YOUR VACATION COMMUNITY CHANGES?

You should examine *resale value* closely in any vacation area. What if your taste in vacations changes? How long do you really expect to keep your second home?

If you are not buying for eventual retirement, make sure there is a secure resale market for your second home. Otherwise, you may end up with something that will become an extremely difficult burden.

Sometimes the region itself can change. Isn't it interesting that some of you purchased *vacation properties that are now becoming suburbs?* In the New York City metropolitan area, for instance, many people are saying, "I think we need to get a little farther out." The suburbanites who move to towns with commuting times of two hours and more are occupying your vacation areas.

Take the Poconos, a well-known resort area in eastern Pennsylvania. An hour's drive away is central New Jersey, an area to which a number of major business corporations have relocated. Thus the Poconos have become an ideal residential area for commuting employees of these companies.

Houses in the Poconos sell for $100,000 *less* than an equivalent home a buyer would get on a lot the size of a postage stamp in central New Jersey. Primary home buyers are coming to scout what used to be vacation homes. As a result, the resale value of second homes in the Poconos has risen.

WHO MOWS THE LAWN AND CLEARS THE SNOW?

There are certain homeowning *responsibilities* particularly applicable to recreational property. You need to inquire about them.

For instance, is snow removal available in winter in a resort that is primarily a summer vacation area? In a winter resort, are the stores open in the summer? Who watches the place in the off season?

If you are buying a place where winter does blow in every November, what do you do to winterize the residence in case the heating system fails? Do you still pay for heat? If you have a telephone during the season, will the phone company give you a special rate so you do not lose your phone number in a "vacation cutoff" situation?

Appliances, among other "frills," may or may not be important, depending upon your family. A Sub-Zero refrigerator or elaborate bathroom fixtures tend to be less significant in a vacation property, because you usually spend more time out of the unit than in it. On the other hand, a fireplace may be the one "frill" you have always coveted.

In any case, you want *good, sturdy, name-brand sinks and toilets and kitchen appliances.*

RENTALS HELP PAY YOUR MORTGAGE

Before you buy your dream vacation home, take into account its rental possibilities. Regardless of how wealthy you are, you should always consider renting the place when you are not there. Rentals bring you income and a steady return on your investment.

The pitfalls of renting are mismanagement by those people you have entrusted to care for your home and the possibility of getting ripped off by bad tenants. You avoid both by hiring a professional management company.

In major destination resorts, solid management companies abound. How do you recognize one?

First, find out how long the company has been in business. Poor resort management firms do not last long. Second, ask for references, and talk to other owners about their experience with the company. Third—and this is a key test—phone the management company *as if you were a prospective renter.* Do not tell the person on the line that you are a potential owner-client.

How many questions does the company ask you about yourself? What kinds of forms need to be filled out? How much work is done to follow through on *your* references? Does the company quote the same prices you were led to expect when you approached the company with your owner's hat on? At the end of the phone call you should have an accurate picture of the firm's renting procedures.

HOW TO CHOOSE A MANAGEMENT COMPANY

Naturally, you want your second home kept neat and orderly. Minor repairs should be done by the management firm. Advance deposits and rents should be collected promptly and you should receive a monthly statement.

A good management operation makes sure tenants do not walk off with your coffee pot—or your coffee table. Some firms will ask owners each year whether or not they are willing to have their places rented by such tenants as college students, discount tour group members or people with pets.

If your recreational property is a single-family home, it can be rented independently of others handled by the same firm. However, if it is part of a condo development or multiunit resort, income might go into a *rental pool.* In every case, the management firm takes a percentage of the rental as its management fee.

It is a good idea to explore different rental options, especially under the new tax reform guidelines. (See chapter 29 on the new tax law for details.)

Under the rental pool arrangement, all money is shared by all owners. For example, if 80 out of 100 units are rented, the rental from the 80 is distributed among the 100 units. This may work for you in a popular resort where rentals are much in demand. But it may hurt you if rentals are sporadic, or if the resort has a poor year.

Under an alternative plan, resort units are rated according to how attractively they are furnished. The best units are rented first. Rents are not pooled, but allocated to owners according to the actual rentals of each unit. The drawback is that if there are many gorgeous units in your resort, you must spend money to upgrade your own, or risk losing rentals to the higher-rated ones.

Yet another option: manage the place yourself. This is feasible when your second home is close enough to your primary residence, so you can visit it regularly. Do you want to be a landlord? Do not take on the management tasks unless you can answer with an enthusiastic yes.

FIND YOURSELF A CARETAKER

Here is another alternative in second home rentals. You can hire an *individual caretaker* to do the renting, maintenance and managing.

Some of the best caretakers are retired people. Check the classified ads in the local newspaper in your resort area. I look for retired people who have backgrounds as carpenters or building trade people. Those are the kinds of people who watch things for you, and they are handymen as well.

Retired people love to manage second homes. It gives them something to do, and they do not usually charge as much as people who do this for a living. Nevertheless, ask for references and check them. A retiree can be an excellent solution for you if you become dissatisfied with your professional management company.

Last winter, a distraught radio caller asked for my advice on a ski chalet he owned but rented out most of the ski season. The first year he signed up with a management firm, it was eager for his business and took 30 percent of the rental fees, leaving him with a comfortable 70 percent.

But the next season the company charged an exorbitant 43 percent of the rental fees. Worse, the owner was charged a fortune every time a light bulb needed to be changed or a minor repair made.

I urged him to dismiss his management company as soon as his contract permitted. Then he could advertise in the local paper for a retiree to manage the property. The ad would read: "Help wanted. Desire retired person looking for extra income to take care of my condo. Out-of-town owner seeks someone with time on his hands and honesty in his heart. Call this number. . . ."

RETIRING TO YOUR VACATION HOME

It is hardly surprising to find plenty of retired people in a resort environment. They might have bought their places as second homes. But as they got older and became empty-nesters, they began spending off-season time, as well as the high season, in their vacation retreats. Eventually, they moved permanently to "vacation" homes, usually smaller and easier to maintain than their original homes.

A phenomenon today is that people are retiring not just to warm-weather areas, but to resort communities in spots like Massachusetts, Maine, upper Michigan and Minnesota.

Keep retirement potential in mind. If you love a place, it may be just the spot for you to spend the moonlight years of your life. Location becomes paramount when you shop for a vacation home that might become your retirement home.

I pointed this out to one radio friend from Cleveland who had his sights set on warm, sunny Yuma, Arizona. He and his wife loved Yuma, but the rest of their family remained in Ohio.

"Do you really want to be that far away from your children and grandchildren?" I wondered. When you turn recreational property into retirement property, *it is a mistake to be too far away from your family.* "One thing a vacation can't bring to you is your loved ones," I told the Cleveland man.

The size of the mortgage on your second home can also be a hindrance if the place might become your retirement home. As a retiree, you will be on a fixed income, so that recreational property should have a *very short-term mortgage.* You should be in a position at the time of retirement to pay for it in full, so you will have a rent-free, mortgage-free roof over your head.

DO'S AND DON'TS: HOW TO SHOP FOR RECREATIONAL PROPERTY

DO:

- Buy a vacation property for enjoyment, not for investment.
- "Test drive" your vacation locale by renting there before buying.
- Ask if a developer is offering an inexpensive "try-out" vacation at a resort.
- Ask yourself if you might like to retire eventually to this place.
- Inspect your vacation home choice as carefully as you would inspect a primary residence you are purchasing.
- Shop in the off season to find better deals.
- Ask at least five owners in the same resort area if they are happy with their choice.
- Give yourself a "cooling-off" period after hearing a sales pitch, before you sign any papers.
- Get all the details about renting out your second home when you are not using it.
- Check a developer's credentials with the local resort association, Better Business Bureau and/or American Resort and Residential Developers Association.
- Get references from at least three current clients of a management company before signing a management contract.

DON'T:

- Buy in an area you are visiting for the first time, no matter how wonderful it seems.

- Be tempted by recreation property in an area you visit rarely or never at all, no matter how much of a bargain it is.
- Buy on the spur of the moment.
- Expect good rental income unless the property is in a major destination resort.
- Assume that any services such as lawn mowing or snow removal are provided by a resort or management company unless they are specified in a written contract.
- Disappoint yourself by shopping in a resort that you cannot yet afford.
- Purchase a fixer-upper as a vacation property if you are not going to be there most of the time to supervise contractors.
- Succumb to sales pitches for condo hotel rooms, since most are bad investments.

14 Questions for Resort Management Companies

1. How do you find customers for your rental units?
2. May I see the rental records for the past three years for the unit I expect to purchase?
3. May I have the names and phone numbers of clients who have used your service for the past three years?
4. What is your annual management fee?
5. What percentage or dollar amount of each rental fee do you take each season?
6. Does this cover daily, semiweekly or weekly linen changes and maid service?
7. If the answer to 6 is no, what is the charge for these services?
8. How much of a reduction in the fee do I get if I refer a rental customer to you?
9. Is rental income distributed to owners via a pool, or unit by unit?
10. How do you decide which unit to rent first?
11. Will I get a preferred place in the rental pool if I add such items as new furniture or new kitchen appliances to my property?
12. If you rent units on the basis of a rating system, who does the rating?
13. If there is such a rating system, how high a position would my unit hold as of right now?
14. May I have a list of your charges for minor maintenance, such as fixing leaky faucets and changing light bulbs?

Chapter **16**

Can Time Sharing Be a Terrific Vacation Investment Instead of a Rip-off?

A few years ago, time sharing was almost a dirty word. Now ITT, Westin Hotels, the Marriott Corporation and Disney are entering the time-share business for the first time.

The reason? Profit. I personally have bought time-sharing property on the ocean in a fabulous recreation area for about $1,200; I resold it a few years later for over $5,000.

Another reason: variety. With a time share, you can visit both your own resort and hundreds of others *around the world,* from Hawaii to Nepal, from the Caribbean to the Alps. For me, the exchange program connected with time sharing is the number-one reason for buying.

At some point, most of us face a real estate dilemma. Do I buy a second home, that dream place where my family and I are going to visit and where we will live when we retire?

Or do I buy two or three weeks of time sharing in one place I enjoy at this time of my life? What about buying two weeks in Las Vegas, two weeks in France, two weeks in Miami Beach? That is what time sharing is all about.

WHAT IS A TIME SHARE?

Time sharing is real estate. It is a vacation home.

A time share, contractually, is a long-term vacation purchase. It gives you the right to use a vacation home, be it a condo apartment, town home or resort unit, with all the goodies attached, for a specified period of time each year for the rest of your life. You can pass it on to your family. Sometimes time sharing is called "interval ownership."

The most common form of time sharing is *fee simple*— a deed to property. You buy the property and you own it. Other ownership plans include *right-to-use* plans, in which you buy the exclusive right to use a unit of a resort for a number of years, after which ownership reverts back to the developer. The right-to-use plan is similar to leasing a car.

While the details of time-share plans differ, the general concept does not. Time sharing allows busy people or those without a lot of money to put into a second home the chance to schuss their favorite ski slopes, relax on their favorite island with a margarita in one hand and a fishing rod in the other, or take board-sailing lessons on their favorite lake— for a *relatively modest investment.*

A TIME SHARE SAVES YOU MONEY

There is a wide range of costs, but the price tag for a week of time sharing can be as low as $3,000, and hardly ever more than $15,000. You pay in installments, much as you would an auto loan, so your initial outlay is small.

A logical question is, "Why not just *rent* the same place every year if you can't afford a full-share vacation home?"

The answer: time sharing saves you money by locking in current vacation prices and locking out inflation. Furthermore, when a time share is paid for, it becomes a usable, sellable asset.

For example, if you bought a time-share unit near Disney World, you might pay $5,000 for a unit, thus locking in the $1,000-a-week price for five years. After that, you could use it *free,* except for the cost of your yearly maintenance fee.

In addition, you are making an investment in fun. You receive *tangible* pleasures from it. Did you ever try to take a vacation with a stock certificate? It does not work.

Some resorts, rather than sell one unit to 52 different people, sell it to 15 or 16 people who buy two or three weeks each. Is this a good deal? That depends on how much time you want to use a place.

Theoretically, multiweek sales cut down on a developer's marketing costs, which can run as high as 50 percent. Theoretically, the developer passes the savings along to you, the buyer, in terms of reduced prices.

It is typical to offer one week in high season, one in low season, one in the "shoulder" or in-between season. For instance, I know people who have bought a three-week grouping at a ski and summer resort in the mountains. One week is in winter (the high season), one in summer (shoulder) and one in May (also known as mud month, during which the town is nearly empty). After two years, the owners have already made back their initial investment by renting out their week in winter rather than using it themselves.

EVEN IF YOU CAN'T BUY A VACATION HOME, YOU CAN BUY A VACATION

Is time sharing a good alternative to buying a full-share vacation home? To answer that, you have to know a *good time-share offer* when you see one.

The first sign of a good time share is lots of activity, and I am *not* talking about sales activity. I am talking about people swimming in the pool, dining in the clubhouse, strolling in and out of the main lobby.

The second sign is satisfied owners. Look for the smiles on their faces. Believe it or not, a good time-sharing resort is one where those who have already bought are happy with their purchase.

Talk to at least five people at random in the resort. I suggest five, because you might happen to pick a member of the staff, who will not identify himself or herself as an employee of the resort.

You also have to know what to ask local bankers, and how to check the offer and the developer. Either write to the National TimeSharing Council, 1220 L Street, N.W., 5th Floor, Washington, DC 20005, or call the group at (202) 371-6700. Is the developer in question a member in good standing of the group? Does the developer have a good track record in the industry? This organization is quite choosy about its members. It does *not* allow people to stay in the group if they do not adhere to the code of ethics.

I have a simple system for evaluating time sharing as a yearly vacation retreat.

First, *question current owners,* as I emphasized earlier. Second, *never purchase* a time share in a resort that you *do not intend to visit on a regular basis,* no matter how terrific the sales pitch.

Third, *do not* buy a time-sharing unit *without seeing it.*

Fourth, *never close* the deal if you are visiting on a *fly-buy* program, until after you see the resort. On a "fly-buy," you give a deposit to a developer in your home city, and then fly out to the development. If you decide to buy a time share, the developer deducts the deposit from your purchase price.

What if you are not happy with your unit? Make sure there is a provision on the deposit slip that states your *right to a refund* of at least the portion of your deposit that exceeds the cost of the trip.

HOW TO AVOID TIME-SHARING RIP-OFF ARTISTS

Let me tell you how time sharing got a bad reputation in the past, so you can spot a fast-buck artist who has snuck into what is now a very regulated, very image-conscious industry.

In the 1970s, con men could sell people time shares in everything from swamp land to the Brooklyn Bridge through fraudulent "predevelopment sales." The developer would offer phony prizes such as yachts and money jackpots in order to rake in the bucks. Then the company would disappear—and so would investors' money.

There are far fewer schemes today. All but four states have tough laws governing time shares. Most states now have a registration requirement for developers of resorts who are selling properties out of the state in which you live. Developers are required by law to give you an offering statement. This statement gives you names of people to call to check the credibility of the developer.

But con artists never give up. A developer in Texas recently had a very strong sales organization in the Northeast. This outfit took in in excess of $8 million of deposits on a particular Gulf Coast development that was not even built yet. He advertised on television, promising free information about time shares. Viewers who responded were visited by salesmen who came armed with contracts to their homes. Some respondents were invited to a party at a nearby hotel, where they were shown enticing slides and movies of the upcoming vacation paradise.

Afterward, the sales agent put on a full-court press. Consumers were pressured to put down a deposit on the spot and given a piece of paper for a future visit.

No one has heard from the guy or the resort since. In the meantime, customers ended up with nothing but a piece of paper marked "Deposit." They had nothing to show for it.

Occasionally, time-share buyers are hurt by poor resort managers. One man told me about trouble with a resort in Hawaii. "For the first two years it was great. Then the management changed," he began. When the fellow returned to his unit for the third year, the furniture was so beat up it looked like Marvin Hagler had trained there for his last fight. And the original refrigerator had been exchanged for a smaller, older one.

This kind of diminishing return can be avoided first by purchasing only from a first-rate company, and second by going over your time-share offering statement with a fine-tooth comb before signing. The offering states how often your furniture is supposed to be replaced.

I should add that the time-share resorts I have personally visited do a better job than hotels as far as keeping the units looking good.

COOLING OFF THE HARD SELL

An important regulation governing time-share sales gives you the right to *change your mind*.

Let us say you are seduced by an irresistible offer of two weeks a year in an oceanfront condo with free golf, tennis and horses. You sign on the dotted line.

A few days later, after calling the National TimeSharing Council and your state attorney general, you discover the truth. The beach on that part of the ocean washed away in the last hurricane. The tennis is at public courts five miles away. The horses are on view at the local racetrack and the golf is a putting green.

Back out. The law is on your side.

Under federal and state statutes, you have *between 7 and 15 days* to withdraw from an agreement after signing a contract to buy a time share. Some developers ask you to waive that provision and promise a discount in exchange. This is illegal. Wave good-bye to the developer instead.

THIS YEAR IN THE ROCKIES, NEXT YEAR IN JERUSALEM

Perhaps the best part of the new time-sharing industry is the flexibility it allows you. Any time-share owner can plug into *time-sharing exchanges* that let you trade some of your time for vacations in other time-share resorts all over the world.

If you are not going to use your unit every year, I encourage you to buy a membership in one of the national exchange services.

There are only two that I recommend: Resort Condominiums International in Indiana, and Interval International in Florida. (See the end of the chapter for addresses and phone numbers.)

Spend the money—it is less than $100—to join one of these exchanges. You can place your unit into a time-share bank and withdraw from that bank a unit of like value. One New York couple recently spent one week in their Aspen condo time share, then traded in their second week to sample the lush greenery of Kauai.

Some of the more sophisticated and newer time-sharing developers are selling *floating* time shares. This means that within a period of time —usually 3 to 4 months—you can utilize any one of the weeks. The big catch in this arrangement is that you must *make your reservation early,* sometimes a year in advance, in order to secure a particular week.

PROFITING FROM "PRIME-TIME" SHARING

I do not advocate buying time shares as a resale or investment unit, with two exceptions.

Perhaps you have bought a "prime-time" sharing unit. This is a *high-season* week, in the most desirable time of year, which varies from region to region. The developer is either 90 percent sold out or wants to close out the balance of the units.

Investigate buying one of the remaining shares, because the place is a winner. You can resell one of your purchases for a profit, usually within five years.

Or perhaps you meet a private individual who for some reason— divorce, death, health or financial problems—wishes to unload a time-share unit for *less than it is worth.* The value of a time share in, say, an oceanfront resort is easily determined. What is the individual seller's asking price? What is the going rate on the open market?

Compare the two. If there is a 40 to 50 percent difference in the private person's price, you can safely bet that you can make money.

URBAN AND CAMPING TIME SHARES

Opportunities now exist to buy *urban time shares* in cities such as New Orleans, San Francisco and New York. This could be an excellent alternative to annual stays in a hotel.

Time-share campgrounds, located in all fifty states, are a fast-growing segment of the vacation home market. An outfit called Camp Coast to Coast arranges for exchanges, for a small fee. See the end of the chapter for its address.

BUYING EQUITY IN A RESORT

A final note: there is a new concept under which you can buy a share of a resort, called an *undivided resort interest.* It is being touted as an alternative to buying a resort condo or time share.

As *The Wall Street Journal* has pointed out, marketers of this concept would like buyers to believe that it is an improved version of time sharing. However, the *Journal* also noted that the undivided resort interest has yet to prove itself. An early version, the first R Ranch in the Atlanta area, took seven years to sell out.

Buy one of these equity plans *only* if you plan to use it. R Ranch appealed to people who love riding, fishing and camping. It makes a lot of sense to purchase a unit for $5,000 (which is what units sold for some years ago) if you take advantage of its saddle horses and campsites on an unlimited basis.

Under the new tax laws, you will *not* receive any tax benefits for shares in an undivided resort.

Recommended Time-Share Exchange Companies

Resort Condominiums International, 9333 North Meridian Street, Indianapolis, IN 46240; telephone: (317) 846-4724

Interval International, 7000 SW 62nd Avenue, South Miami, FL 33142; telephone: (305) 666-1861

Time-Share Information Sources

National TimeSharing Council, 1220 L Street, N.W., 5th Floor, Washington, DC 20005

Camp Coast to Coast, 1000 16th Street, N.W., Washington, DC 20005

Chapter 17

Homeowner's Insurance, or, Are You Sure Your Policy Covers *Everything* That Could Be Stolen or Destroyed by Fire Tonight?

When was the last time you pulled your homeowner's policy out of the drawer and made sure it covers every valuable item that could be lost, stolen or destroyed by fire tonight? When was the last time you updated your list of valuables? Does your policy include flood insurance?

Most of us look for the best buy we can get on homeowner's insurance. Then we forget about it, except to pay the premium each year. In fact, your policy needs to be updated every *12 months.*

With inflation always a factor, the silverware you paid $100 for a year ago could be worth $200 today. And how many large-ticket items—a VCR, a new air conditioner, a fancy computer and printer, a music synthesizer, a new fur coat—have you bought since that first policy list?

Armed with my list of questions to ask an insurance sales agent (at the end of this chapter), you will be able to get a policy that covers your cash, your guests, perhaps even your Steinway grand piano. And you will know when it is better to keep valuables in a safe-deposit box than in your home.

THE SEVEN BASIC POLICIES

You can shop for insurance more intelligently by familiarizing yourself with the insurance industry's lingo.

The industry categorizes its policies in seven basic forms. Each begins with the letters *HO,* standing for "home owners." Grasping the difference between HO-1 and HO-5 can help you sidestep *the classic mistake —underinsuring* your residence.

1. "Basic" policy HO-1 covers fire, lightning, windstorm, hail, explosions, riot, civil commotion, aircraft crashes, vehicle damage, smoke, vandalism and malicious mischief, theft and breakage of glass constituting a part of the building. Although this is the *least* expensive, I advise you to *avoid* this policy. It does not offer enough.

2. HO-2, called the "broad-form" coverage, includes the losses mentioned above, *plus* an additional seven: falling objects; weight of ice, snow or sleet; collapse of buildings; sudden and accidental damage to a steam or hot water heating system, or to appliances for heating water; accidental discharge, leakage or overflow of water or steam from a plumbing or air-conditioning system, or from another appliance using water; freezing of plumbing, heating or air-conditioning system; and sudden, accidental injury from artificially generated currents to electrical appliances such as stoves or refrigerators but not television sets.

3. HO-3, the "special form," gives you *maximum* protection for your residence but *skimps* on coverage of personal belongings.

4. HO-4 is strictly a *tenant policy* for those who rent rather than own. It gives you comprehensive coverage of personal property and liability, but there is no coverage of the structure itself.

5. HO-5, the "comprehensive" form, is the *minimum* that I recommend for homeowners. This policy puts the burden of proof on the insurance agency where damage is concerned. It is an "all-risk" policy, costing 35 to 45 percent more than the HO-2. However, the peace of mind in the coverage is definitely worth the price.

6. HO-6 is for *condominium owners.* It covers everything within the space occupied.

7. HO-8 (there is no HO-7) is a special policy for older homes. This expensive policy is for homes with distinctive workmanship and details that cannot be duplicated. It is useful for a home so valuable that it cannot be replaced under the "replacement-cost" approach. But you pay an *extraordinarily high premium.*

Under this policy, you are paid for the replacement of your house at its actual cash value. For example, if you owned a historic landmark in downtown Boston, with 1,200 square feet, it is worth more than an equivalent space because of its historic value.

INSURANCE AGENTS AND INSURANCE COMPANIES

Now it is time for a visit with your insurance person. Like a good travel agent or mortgage broker, he or she will do the shopping and compare rates for you.

I prefer doing business with those known as *general agents*. They do not represent one company exclusively. Establish a rapport with a good general agent, let the agent handle all of your insurance (car, life etc.), and that person will work harder for you.

You can recognize a good insurance agent when one telephones to say he or she has found a better policy for you to replace your current one. Have the agent review your policies once a year.

How do you recognize unacceptable agents? They are the ones who try to foist sales tricks on you—like offering the slightly cheaper policy that promises "market value" replacement instead of actual replacement costs.

Probably the most important word in your insurance policy is "replacement."

This refers to the type of insurance you receive. Most policies on the standard end will give you *market value* for items lost or damaged. Market value policies pay a pittance.

You are not interested. You want *replacement cost*. That—not what you paid for it—is what it will cost to replace your ten-year-old set of silverware five years from now, should you be robbed by a friendly neighborhood burglar.

One of the best ways to make sure you get good insurance is to *have one insurance agent bid against the other.* Two things happen: first, you might become the object of a price war. Second, and most important, competing insurance agencies will be quick to point out *what their policy covers* and *what the competition's policy does not.* (In fact, it is extremely difficult to read insurance policies. If you do not understand your policy completely, a $50 or $100 session with an insurance attorney might save you thousands of dollars in the future.)

It is better to change policies than to change agents, once you have found a winner.

* * *

As for policies themselves, the coverage is far more meaningful than the brand name of a famous company on the cover. Some of the *heavy advertisers* are not necessarily rated the best, as shown in a *Consumer Reports* survey published in 1985.

The magazine based ratings on responses from 218,000 subscribers. They were asked how satisfied they were with their company's access, courtesy, paperwork, final settlement, speed in claims handling and speed of payment.

The companies with the four *highest scores* on a satisfaction index were Amica, USAA, Erie and U.S. Fidelity & Guarantee. Those with the five *lowest scores* (two were tied) were Liberty Mutual, Allstate, Metropolitan Property, Prudential and Geico.

COVERING ALL THE BASES IN YOUR NEWLY BOUGHT HOME

More than half the people who purchase homes in a new area take over the insurance policy from the previous owner. Do not do this.

Go through the house with your insurance agent and point out those items you want covered. For example, what about water damage for broken pipes on the carpet. Do you want standard fire insurance? How much coverage do you need? How do you maximize that coverage by including every item you should?

I do *not* agree that you should insure your house for 80 percent of its replacement value, but some companies will give you only that much insurance.

Try to get a policy that will give you *100 percent replacement value.* However, you do not insure the ground under which your house stands, so most companies take the market value of the house, and deduct 20 percent for the land, which is fair.

Do you want flood insurance if you live in a coastal area? This is special insurance that has to be bought through the federal government.

Items such as valuable art, jewelry and furs must be "scheduled"— listed separately in your policy. All policies have a cutoff price, a maximum on which they will pay. You may want to store very expensive art and jewels in a bank vault, which would also reduce your premium payments.

I am happy to report that the current trend is to put a limit on the amount of money insurance companies can charge you for liability coverage, the coverage that takes care of such things as guests breaking a leg in your house and suing you for damages. Some states, Florida, for instance, have passed legislation cutting back rates as much as 40 percent.

After walking your agent through the house, be extra smart. *Make your own home video.* Take your video camera (rent one if necessary) and record on tape each item in your house, as well as the cost of its replacement. I will lead you through each video step at the end of this chapter.

MAKING A YEARLY UPDATE

Each year, you should look at the maximum amount that you are covered for in case of damage or burglary. If that maximum is between $25,000 and $50,000, review the items in your house again.

Add up what it will cost to replace all of them at this year's prices; include those you have had for many years, but consider *especially the new ones*—the antiques you bought in Europe, the new television in the guest room, the crystal vase that was this year's anniversary present.

Call your agent and *increase your coverage* to cover everything as indicated by your yearly updated inventory. Do not forget to schedule new items not covered by the maximum amount of dollars in your general policy.

GOOD NEWS AND BAD ABOUT CLAIMS

The easiest thing about buying insurance is making the payments. *The hardest thing is collecting a claim,* even a legitimate one.

The insurance industry hires professional people who are taught to make sure that your claim is legitimate. These people look for ways to discredit a faulty or false claim.

While it is true that the insurance industry has suffered a tremendous amount of fraud against it during the past decade, this is no excuse for harassing legitimate claimants.

If you make a claim, the chances are that one of two things will occur: your premium will be raised the next time around, or the company will cancel your policy when the current one runs out.

That is the bad news. The good news is that by shopping around, and by making a few changes in your home, you could *reduce the premium* significantly.

The insurance premium on your home in one neighborhood of a city can differ greatly from that in another neighborhood. It might be because of a lack of adequate fire protection, your distance from the nearest hydrant or a high crime rate.

Also, premiums vary according to basic risk factors determined by a company's actuarial department. (That is the department that determines the odds on your place being damaged or burglarized.)

If you move from one city to another, you might ask your present insurance agent which areas of your new city have the lowest insurance rates. That information is available to agents across the nation.

Here are four additional measures to *reduce* your insurance rates:

• Check with local insurance companies and ask which security system has been certified by them as one that would reduce your premium. A premium can be reduced in most parts of the country if you have a recommended security system.

(For free information on security protection, call ADT Security Systems toll-free at [800] 624-9000.)

• Consider installing an inside sprinkler system. This might lower rates in some parts of the country where fire protection is not adequate. If you amortize the cost of installing a sprinkler system over the life of a less expensive insurance policy, you might find it makes economic sense.

For example, suppose you install a sprinkler system inside the house for $5,000. Perhaps it will reduce your premiums by that much over a ten-year period. Meanwhile, your house is safer to live in and becomes more valuable at the time of sale.

• Ask for a higher deductible. Most policies have a standard $100 deductible for a claim. But you CAN get a lower premium in exchange for a higher deductible. The insurance company figures that if you are willing to pay more money on the initial deductible item, it can afford to give you a lower premium.

• Pay the whole premium annually instead of paying quarterly or semiannual installments. Insurance companies charge you interest on delayed payments.

EVEN IF YOU LOSE YOUR JOB, YOU DO NOT LOSE YOUR HOME

Morgard is an insurance whose time has come. Finally, you can buy insurance that will pay your mortgage each month should you happen to lose your job.

It is called Morgard Job-Loss Insurance and it is brand-new. Some pioneering lenders pay the premium—an average of about $200 per year—themselves.

Under the plan, your monthly payments for a full year would be paid directly to your mortgage holder if you are out of work. As of September 1986, the one state in which this default protection would *not* be offered was New York, because its insurance laws do not provide for job-loss underwriting. Ask your lender about it.

Another home buyer protection plan I am very much in favor of is the *Home Owners Warranty*. This insurance covers problems that might crop up in new and resale homes *after* the purchase. Obviously, it is a great plus to offer a buyer when you are selling your house.

In a typical case, the warranty lasts one year and covers major heating, cooling, plumbing and wiring systems in a house, plus appliances. There is a $100 deductible. More and more real estate chains and individual brokers are picking up the premium on such a warranty for homes they list.

Firms that sell this policy include ERA (Electronic Realty Associates) and American Home Shield Corporation. Among the chains are Realty World and some branches of Century 21. If you are selling your house, ask the brokers you interview whether they provide this coverage.

What happens when your Chippendale gets chipped en route from your old house to your new one? The mover will pay for the damage through automatic *moving insurance*.

This insurance is provided by the moving company. But find out in advance what the *automatic insurance limit* is. In most cases, you have to buy additional insurance to cover yourself fully.

I have found moving insurance to be extremely cost-effective. Nevertheless, play it safe.

Stand right beside the truck when your movers unload your items, holding the check-off list they give you. *Call attention* to any scratches or damage *at that moment.* The mover's employee will have to initial the space on the sheet on which you write what the item is and what happened to it. Otherwise, you will *not* be able to collect.

MAJOR APPLIANCE SERVICE POLICIES

Do you have terrible luck with electronic appliances? Even if not everyone has experienced problems, all of us are relying more and more on gadgets that can be very expensive and time-consuming to repair. One of the best buys on the market today is an insurance policy that covers the appliances in your home. Among the appliances that can be covered: refrigerator, stove, television set, washer, dryer, video equipment.

Special companies write such policies. Sears offers policies on its own appliances for use when a new appliance warranty runs out. Other companies are Montgomery Ward; Homeowners Marketing Services in Hollywood, Florida; and Safeco Appliance Warranty Company, which has offices throughout the country.

We have all been through the annoyance of a television set going on the fritz, then the double whammy when the authorized repair shop tells you it will cost you a $50 minimum just to leave the set at the shop for the next week for an estimate of the total cost of repairs.

When you have a total appliance service policy, you do not pay for estimates. The company has agents in every city. Just as members of the AAA auto club would call someone on the AAA list of authorized towing companies, you would call one of the repair agencies on your list to repair your broken appliance without an estimate beforehand.

UNUSUAL INSURANCE, AND INSURING THE UNUSUAL

Grace's brother-in-law faced a crisis. He is a musician who turned his garage into a state-of-the-art recording studio—and then could not find an insurance company that would cover the full replacement cost of his computer, synthesizers, piano and other equipment, even though he had a first-rate security system installed.

As a musician myself, I suggested two sources: his union, the American Federation of Musicians, and Lloyds of London. Lloyds will insure *anything*—for a price. You do not have to be British. Just have an agent contact one of their American offices. If your recording studio or other valuables are that unique, Lloyds is worth an inquiry.

Many unions, not just the musicians' union, offer policies to members. In the case of musicians, the union policy can cover instruments that travel with you. Other unions are equally sensitive to the special needs of the trade. It pays to ask.

Another source of insurance, for those who are told that theirs is a high-crime area, is the federal government.

Federal Crime Insurance is available to anyone with satisfactory locks. It covers losses due to robbery and burglary *only,* but it may be cheaper than private insurance in your neighborhood. Although this program was created to help people in high-crime areas, almost any community within a major city qualifies.

I suggest including Federal Crime Insurance in your comparison-shopping. Call (800) 638-8780 for information.

Unfortunately, there is no federal *earthquake* insurance similar to federal crime and flood insurance programs. If you live in an earthquake-prone region, you probably already have been denied earthquake coverage by private companies.

I am sorry to report that insurance companies are deleting earthquake insurance from their policies. I *do not know of a single company* at the moment that will insure you for an earthquake in a quake-prone area.

However, after a community is designated a disaster area, the government does give you an opportunity to pick up a low-cost loan to replace damaged residences.

If you are worried about *tornado* coverage, ask your insurance agent to show you how your policy covers you for this particular disaster. If the policy does not mention tornadoes in its coverage section, chances are you are *not* covered.

CO-OP AND CONDO POLICIES

Co-op and condo policies are different from single-family dwelling insurance because the property is different. Whether you must pay more for condo or co-op insurance depends on actuarial studies, not on the nature of your condo or co-op itself.

For instance, you will pay higher insurance in New York City than in Portland, Oregon, simply because, on a percentage basis, there are not as many claims coming out of Portland.

UMBRELLA INSURANCE

If you can afford the premium, *there is no such thing as being overinsured* on your home. On the contrary, too often you find out you are underinsured only after you are robbed or suffer a fire.

The *umbrella policy,* if you qualify, is the *best insurance bargain* on the market. This policy gives you the broadest liability coverage obtainable. It is ideal for someone who owns several properties, such as a residence, country home, business building and fleet of cars. If you have that much exposure—and could be sued by anyone who has an accident on any one of those properties—you could benefit. Ask your agent to quote you a price.

*   *   *

Once you have bought the best insurance for you, following the guidelines in the test below, you can make your home video tape.

You will be astonished at how much you have accumulated during your lifetime—and how much you have forgotten you own!

Why not simply take plain old color snapshots or Polaroids? I prefer video because I can *talk* about each item as I tape it, and because I can photograph myself with my possessions. There is nothing wrong with color snapshots or Polaroids. But as court cases show, a *videotape is more effective* in proving ownership and identification.

To verify a date, hold up that day's newspaper with you and the item in the same frame. To lock in a date further, turn on the TV news and show it playing next to the item. Store the completed videotape in your *bank safe-deposit box,* not your home.

The video session is tedious, but once you have finished it, you have taped yourself some peace of mind. Preparing for taping also helps you clean out your house. What a handy way to put together a garage sale, and get rid of unwanted furniture, books, semi-antiques and old clothes!

Best of all, the garage sale could pay at least a portion of your new insurance premium.

VIDEO INSURANCE GUIDE
10 Steps to Making a Video Inventory of Your Valuables

Step 1: Tape room by room, floor by floor, wall by wall, ceiling by ceiling, window by window, including basement and garage. (Do not bring items into one room for video-taping. That is too time-consuming.)

Step 2: Start with bedrooms. Those are the places people usually store jewelry and furs.

Step 3: List *everything*—even items like an expensive electric shaver in the bathroom.

Step 4: Check the floor. Is your rug or Oriental carpet an expensive item?

Step 5: If you are making still photos rather than a video, as you walk through rooms, talk into a portable audio tape recorder about each item.

Step 6: Go back and make sure you included wall coverings, hangings, drapes and other window and wall dressings.

Step 7: Review ceilings. Have you included expensive light fixtures?

Step 8: Review closets, and drawers of bureaus and desks.

Step 9: In the basement, open boxes you have not looked at for years, plus books stored.

Step 10: In the garage, do not forget lawn mowers, fertilizer spreaders and tools.

17 Questions to Ask About Your Homeowner's Insurance

1. How long has the company to whom I pay premiums been in business?
2. What is the company's record of satisfying claims?
3. Does the company have a local claims office?
4. Is there another comparable company that will give me the same coverage for less money?
5. Does my policy have a replacement cost provision?
6. Do I have to call my agent every time I buy something new in order to add it to my policy?
7. If so, how much can I add before I begin paying more premiums?
8. Does my policy include additional living expenses if my house is so damaged that I have to move elsewhere temporarily?
9. Does my policy cover the loss of my credit cards and cash, or do I need a separate policy?
10. What is the maximum liability coverage I can get in case somebody gets hurt on my property?
11. Does my policy cover damages that are done by my pets?
12. What kind of legal representation will the insurance company give me if I am sued by somebody who gets hurt at my home?
13. What items will the company *not* insure in my geographic area, such as expensive jewelry, furs, antiques and paintings?
14. What kind of appraisal will the company accept for the coverage of these high-risk items?
15. Does the company offer the $1 million umbrella policy that covers me for such things as false arrest, wrongful eviction, libel, slander, defamation of character and invasion of privacy?
16. What discount can I get on my homeowner's insurance

premium if I include my auto policies in the package?
17. What is my deduction in the premium for installing smoke alarms, burglar alarms and a sprinkler system?

PART III

Selling

Chapter 18

Profiling Your Comfort Zone Before the Sale

Once you think the time has come to sell your house, you should examine your Comfort Zone every bit as much as you would if you were buying. What is the price you should set? Are you willing to compromise? Should you sell with or without a real estate broker? How long are you willing to wait for the right deal? Do you want to spruce up your home or sell "as is"?

No matter how lovely your house is, you *can* improve its marketability before you put it on public display. I will advise you on how to "package" your house for a sale: putting vanilla to boil on the stove, curb appeal, and all the other little things that make a house more salable.

Do you need to make a sale fast? How quickly you sell is in part a function of how you price the house, as well as of the marketplace. If you price a house too low, it may sell *too* fast. If you price it too high, it will sell slowly or not at all.

You will need to assemble a major-league team for this effort, including a top-notch broker (unless you are selling without one), your real estate attorney, your certified public accountant, an appraiser and your friendly banker or mortgage broker.

This chapter and the following ones will discuss how the team can bring you a winning sale. But the first question to ask yourself is, should I sell at all?

WHY YOU SHOULD *NOT* SELL YOUR HOUSE

The biggest mistake people make is selling a house when *they do not need to.* Your reasons for selling should be very clear to you.

"Wait a minute!" you protest. "I'm being transferred out of town. I don't have a choice."

Yes, you do have a choice. Even if you are moving to another market, consider the option of *not* selling.

I know this may sound like heresy, but hear me out.

First, answer these three questions:

1. Is your home located right now in a hot marketplace?
2. Is there a lack of residential properties for sale nearby?
3. Do you have a large equity in your home?

If you answered yes to all three, *you would be much better off not selling.*

Instead, you can put yourself in an enviable financial position. You could keep your current home, lease (rent) it to others, and use the equity in it to buy your new home in your new location. In this fashion, you would start to build a real estate portfolio for later in life, since homes in certain parts of the country are increasing in value at a rate of 10 percent or more a year.

Let us imagine your house is worth about $200,000. You owe only $50,000 on it. Somebody else will *make those payments for you* by paying you rent. You can sit back in your new location with the understanding that your previous home, now your $200,000 "investment" house, will increase in value by about $20,000 every year.

Where else could you find such a safe investment that would allow you to build up that much equity tax-free, until you sell it?

There is no better road to wealth than through real estate. And you would be embarking on that road with almost no risk. Your first investment property is one you yourself are knowledgeable about and have enjoyed.

Think of it this way: if you cannot replace your current house with an investment that is going to be paid for by your tenants, you had better think twice about selling.

* * *

You also should analyze the tax advantages and disadvantages of selling your house.

If you are moving into a house that is *more* expensive, you can benefit from the 1034 rollover provision in the Internal Revenue Code. It lets you defer paying taxes on the house that you just sold, in order to buy the new house. For more details, see chapter 28 on buying and selling a house at the same time.

However, if you are under the age of fifty-five and buy a *less* expensive house, you are subject to taxes on the profit of the sale of your previous home. (If you are over fifty-five, you are allowed a one-time *exemption* from this tax.)

If you think you should put your house on the market because homes are selling well in your area and you will make a lot of money, that is not a good reason to sell, since taxes will eat into your profit.

Perhaps you are about to sell because your house is not large enough for you or your growing family.

Why not investigate what it would cost to add rooms or enlarge your space by remodeling? You do need to make sure in the process that you would not be not overbuilding for your area. (This happens when yours becomes the most expensive house in the neighborhood.) But remodeling or enlarging is cheaper and less disruptive than moving.

Or perhaps you are an empty-nester or older American, and you have decided to sell because your family suggests it. "What do you need that big house for?" grown children often ask.

Your answer almost always should be, "Peace of mind."

Unfortunately, some older homeowners are persuaded to sell. To my way of thinking, this is one of the saddest misjudgments they can make.

"I have this dilemma," one radio friend said. "I have been living in this home for forty-five years. My husband passed away two years ago. My children are telling me to sell the house and move into a condominium. But I am very comfortable here. I am healthy. What should I do?"

My advice to the woman was *not* to sell her home. This kind of place was more than just brick, wood, glass and mortar. It was a refuge, a place where she knew the neighborhood. To move into a condominium at her stage in life did not make any sense.

Many older Americans *have* sold their homes, moved elsewhere, and found themselves becoming *very unhappy.* Yet they cannot move back to their former neighborhood because prices have gone up.

PRICES GOING DOWN? BLOCK THAT SALE!

People living in a depressed economic region with declining real estate prices may think they should sell anyway, because they are moving or because they have found a house that suits them better. What I counsel is, if you do not need the money, keep the house.

Why take a bath when, in nine cases out of ten, the market will eventually improve? You do not have to make the monthly payments, because you can get them from someone else, in the form of rent.

A woman called my radio show about a gorgeous condo in Fort Lauderdale, which she bought thinking she might like to retire there. She had a very small mortgage of $9,000. One winter, she rented the place out for $900 a month—$3,600 for the season. That covered her mortgage payment and more. Still, she thought she should sell, since she had changed her mind about retiring. "Wait," I told her.

At the time, South Florida condo prices were down. However, in a few years, I expected that she would be able to get more than her original $42,000 back. Condominium construction had virtually halted in the area. Yet people were moving to Florida at the rate of 1,000 a day. The excess condos would gradually be absorbed and prices would rise.

In another case, a central Oregon family rented out the house they had bought in 1979 for $52,500 when they transferred to a new job in Albuquerque six years later.

Then the economic slump hit Oregon. The value of the rental house plummeted too. The owner wondered if he should put the Oregon property on the market. I urged him to keep it. The rent still covered the monthly payments. "Somebody else is building equity for you while you sleep," I said. "It is as if your tenants are putting money into a savings account for you!" They could sell the Oregon home when prices there improved.

HOW QUICKLY MUST YOU SELL?

"Sorry, Sonny. I'm not in any of the situations you have described," you reply. "I am not a retiree. And I am not cut out to be a landlord. After my transfer I will be three thousand miles away. I don't want to get calls at seven A.M. from my tenant about trouble with the septic tank. I don't have the mentality for maintaining this investment, no matter how sound it may be."

That is fine. Once you have considered all the reasons *not* to sell your house, and your conclusion is that you truly *must* sell it, the next move is to figure out when.

The time frame puts you in a position to get the most for your house or to sell it quickly and take a lower price. Chapter 19 supplies you with details on setting the proper price. Meanwhile, take a moment to calculate the amount of time you have to ready yourself and your family and to prepare your house to be listed.

In a good market, with a well-chosen broker, a multilisted house should be sold within 30 days. In an average market, 60 to 90 days is good. Get an estimate from your real restate broker of the time frame in which you are dealing. An honest broker will tell you how houses have been selling in your area. That way, you will not get upset if your house is still on the market after a week.

SPRUCING UP YOUR HOUSE FOR A SALE

Most houses are not ready to be "marketed." What looks merely lived in to you looks a trifle worn, sloppy or troublesome to an outsider. I guarantee that if you take care and time to enhance, clean and beautify your house, the additional few dollars and days spent will translate into *thousands* of dollars in a higher selling price.

Packaging is a selling tool; there are are many products you would never pick up in the grocery or drug store unless they had eye appeal.

You need to package your house in a similar manner. Let me "talk you through" the jobs first. Then you can follow up with the Step-by-Step Spruce-Up Guide at the end of this chapter.

CURB APPEAL

Begin where your prospective buyer does—at the curb at the point that your *landscaping* begins.

In the winter, if there is snow on the ground, you do not have to be concerned with landscaping. But it is good to *get rid of dead bushes and branches* drooping from the tree in the front yard.

Make sure the *lawn is edged. Neatness counts.* Freshly cut grass smells marvelous. Once the date of your open house is set, let the grass grow for a week, then *mow the lawn* the morning of the showing. The scent of freshly cut grass does wonders for a buyer's olfactory nerves, and perhaps more.

Do you have a mailbox? Is it rusty? You can *get a new mailbox* for under $25. How about the *street numbers* on your house? Are they displayed in an obvious place? Have they been painted over time after time? Why not buy new numbers? They cost less than a dollar apiece.

Does your last exterior paint job still look fresh? If any part of the exterior looks shoddy—inspect the trim area in particular—spend the money for a *touch-up or complete repainting.* You will be rewarded by selling the house for many more extra dollars than the painting costs.

The next stop for a visitor is your *front door.* Does it say *"Welcome"* *on a mat* out front? Why not? When was the last time you painted your front door? A quart of paint and a few hours of your time can be the difference between a sale and no sale.

What about your *front door knocker?* If it is worn, replace it with a new one. It takes only four screws. If you have an old *doorbell* that sounds like a buzz saw, why not replace it with a new, mellifluous ringing one?

Do not forget the *doorknob,* the first thing visitors touch when they think about buying your house. Why not a newly polished one or a brand-new one?

Does your *door* look as if it had been beaten with a heavy chain? You may want to invest in a new door. It is a great psychological plus for people who buy. The door makes a first, and last, impression.

STEP INSIDE AND SEE MY MIRRORS

A good interior designer trick is the use of *mirrors and mirrored panels.* Floor-to-ceiling mirrors can make a narrow entrance hall look wider. Mirrors at right angles to windows consolidate and double the light.

Mirrors on closet doors are excellent selling points. Young couples are delighted to see mirrors on the wall or ceiling in the bedroom. You can install mirrored tiles yourself. They are inexpensive and are sold in your local hardware store.

For information on decorating with mirrors, write for a free booklet called "Mirror Magic" from the National Association of Mirror Manufacturers, 9005 Congressional Court, Potomac, MD 20859. There is also a book on do-it-yourself mirroring with mirror tiles; write to Hoyne Mirrors, Marketing Department, PO Box 697, McDonough, GA 30253.

VANILLA WAFTING THROUGH THE KITCHEN

Put a pot of boiling water on top of the range, pour a teaspoon of vanilla extract into it, and add some cinnamon and cloves. Or bake bread or muffins in the oven. A house that smells delicious sells itself.

Otherwise, *clean* the oven so it is spotless. Characteristically, women open oven doors. For heaven's sake, do *not* leave dishes in the sink. Scrub those countertops.

It is not necessary to replace that ten-year-old refrigerator if it looks decent; you should replace it if it is rusty or smelly. The same goes for your ten-year-old stove. It should be sparkling clean. There is no reason to buy a dishwasher if you do not have one.

Have your *dining table set* with your best china and glassware, as if someone special is coming to dinner. Put *pleasant, soft music* on the stereo. (You may love Bruce Springsteen, but Schubert or Vangelis makes a better sales agent.)

Regardless of what part of the country you are in, or whether you have been bothered by pests, have a professional exterminator go through the entire house. Get a certificate from the exterminator showing the deed has been done, and include this in your selling tools. By the way, ask the exterminator to use the latest improvement, a non-smelling chemical that does the job without leaving lingering odors.

If you have a dog, put it in the backyard. Or send the dog and the kids to a friend's house, so people will feel comfortable moving around your house.

Many homes appear *too "busy," too crowded with furniture.* Move some of the furniture into storage so the house looks bigger. This is the perfect time to have a garage sale (in your part of the country perhaps it is called a yard sale or tag sale) to clear out those things you no longer need.

You could even time it to coincide with the open house that a broker holds to "show" your house to potential buyers. (Yes, the more people who see that your house is for sale, the better chance you have to sell it. Garage sales create traffic.)

Take the *knicknacks off the tops of bureaus, dressers, tables, desks.* Where to put the stuff? In a bedroom, you can store plenty of things under the bed, as long as the bedspread is a decent length. Nobody gets down on hands and knees to peer under a bed. (Well, now every reader of this book can!)

Make sure all personal-care utensils, bottles and jars in the bathrooms are put away. Get rid of the junk in the closets, in the attic, in the basement, under the bathroom sink and in the kitchen that you have sworn you would clean out. Clutter always makes a home look smaller. This is most critical in closets, because *stuffed closets look small.* In a buyer's mind, that translates into "not enough closet space."

Are all your light bulbs working? Try each switch, including lamps. Flip the switch that runs your garbage disposal, the automatic air-conditioning fan switch, and other electric switches that a visitor is sure to try out.

Your house can never be *too* clean. Begin with the windows. We all notice dirty windows, so if yours need washing, call in a pro to do them as close to your open house as possible. Do the windows open easily? Visitors will try them, especially during the warm-weather months. Rub a bar of soap on each side of a window to facilitate opening and closing.

Imagine walking into a bathroom or hallway and seeing fingerprints or crayon marks. Go through your visible wall space like Mr. or Ms. Clean, rag and spray can of Fantastik in hand.

Systematically *examine your baseboards* in every room as well for chips and spots from skateboards, furniture moving and so on. Is there a spot that will not come off with elbow grease? If necessary, invest a few dollars in a can of paint for touch-up jobs.

Consider a *single-coat paint job* for those areas that are spotty or dark. It may have suited your taste to have a small area like a hallway painted purple, brown or black, but that is *not* everyone's idea of spacious. A cheaper solution would be a brighter light bulb.

A freshly painted off-white or beige wall always does the trick in brightening any room. It creates open space, and gives people an opportunity to judge where they would hang their own pictures.

Think, too, about *painting ceilings white.* This opens up a room without calling attention to the paint job. It is very useful in a kitchen whose ceiling has been darkened by cooking.

Taste is subjective. Items that bring fond memories to *you* (family photos on a bureau, for instance) can make visitors uneasy. Once, Grace had trouble subletting a fabulous apartment because the living room was dominated by a "supergraphic" of bright stripes painted across an entire wall. She loved it, but she should have spent a few dollars to have it painted into oblivion before the place was listed.

Have your teenagers put giant posters of Twisted Sister or Tom Cruise on their walls? They might not bother people who have children the same age. Still, it is best to remove this kind of decoration, to create a sense of space as well as neutrality.

It is *not* expensive but it is worthwhile to *have your carpets cleaned* professionally. They look fresh only for a while, so time your cleaning as close as possible to your open house.

If there is a worn spot on a carpet, and you do not want to replace it, use an old real estate trick: cover the spot with an area rug.

What if the carpet is worn to a complete frazzle or hopelessly dirty? What kind of floors are underneath? Handsome *hardwood floors now sell faster than carpeted floors* because new owners prefer neutral wood grains to the colors of someone else's carpet. A professionally sanded and polished floor will help sell your house quickly.

Check every faucet in your kitchen and bathrooms to make sure they do not drip. Particularly in areas where water bills are high, smart people know what extra costs a dripping faucet can cause. Recently, in my Washington, D.C., home, a faucet was leaking for thirty days before I noticed it. My water bill was up $100 that month! Cost to fix the faucet? Twenty-five cents, for a rubber ring.

While you are in the bathrooms, clean out the grout areas between the shower tiles. If a bathroom has no window, be generous with deodorizer spray or solid sticks.

Somewhere in the house, you are bound to come upon a door that does not close completely. First, try rubbing soap on the door jamb. If that does not work, hire a handyman for a few dollars to shave the door so it closes properly.

In your basement, work room or garage, weed out the clutter. That includes old toys, rusted garden tools and lawn furniture, ancient backyard swings. Once you are in the backyard, check to see that your dog, whom you have sent to visit a friend, did not leave behind anything for potential buyers to step on.

Once you are through with your own inspection, it is time for a professional one. This will reveal any major problems with your operating systems—heat, cooling, wiring, water, sewage, plumbing, roof, subsidence.

Should your house be in excellent condition, by all means let buyers know. If there are things that need to be improved, the home inspection report shows that you have taken trouble to point out what must be done to make the house perfect. The cost of an inspection is modest—$125 to $225.

As you have guessed by now, I lean toward as much cosmetic work and theatrically appealing lighting, expanding and emptying as possible. *I do as little renovation work as possible.* Why spend thousands of dollars on renovations such as the construction of a fireplace or an extra bath, when you could tuck that money away as part of the nest egg you are building to buy your next house?

The remodeling industry has done an excellent job of marketing the idea that if you add to your home it increases in value. The real question is, *how much?* The answer is, usually *not enough.*

Unless you are in the remodeling or building business, the chore and inconvenience of remodeling your home in order to sell it is filled with self-imposed stress.

To a seller, the question of fixing a house up or selling it as is boils down to economics. If you add a room to your $100,000 home at a cost of $20,000, how much more will you get for that house afterward? Chances are, not much more than $20,000. So why go through the aggravation of adding the room in the first place?

Even if the added room brings you a $2,000 to $3,000 profit over your costs, are the time, inconvenience and stress worth it? You also must consider the time lag in getting your house ready to be put on the market. It is another matter if you do the remodeling yourself or if you are in the business of remodeling homes.

Items that bring *very little* back in terms of resale value include:

- above-ground swimming pool
- tennis court
- solarium
- hot tub or sauna

If you insist that you want to add a room, remodel a kitchen, add an extra bath, or enclose your garage area, be sure you are not increasing the value of your house beyond the price of the average home in your neighborhood. Perhaps homes in your community sell for $100,-000 to $120,000. You spend an additional $30,000 to $40,000 remodeling. You are now in a *poor marketing position:* your home is now overpriced for your market. Such homes are the hardest to sell.

On the other hand, if you have an $80,000 house in a $120,000 neighborhood, you would be safe in spending $30,000 to $40,000 on improvements. But why not just sell for $80,000 and let the new buyer have construction people tramping in and out for six months to a year?

Why do I feel so strongly about this? I have had the ulcerated privilege of remodeling over a dozen homes in my lifetime. In three cases, I was living in the house that was being remodeled. After each job was completed, I realized that it was absolutely *not* worth it!

Your aim, as a seller, is to be a great set designer. Take your production—your home—and stage it in professional, Broadway style with lights, flowers, cleanliness and charm. Your buyers will be impressed, even if they do not applaud out loud.

EXTRA PACKAGING FOR A CO-OP OR CONDO

The selling of an apartment, whether condo or co-op, begins at the front door, just as it does with a single-family home, but you cannot be there to greet every visitor.

When I approach an apartment house, I always get a fleeting but strange feeling: "My goodness, we're going into a strange building, and these people don't know who we are!"

Therefore, your job should be to insure that guests feel welcome. What about slipping your doorman an extra tip? Tell him Mr. and Mrs. Buyer are on their way to view your apartment, and suggest that he be exceptionally sweet to them. A big smile and greeting *by name* from a doorman never fails to warm a visitor's heart—and establish the right frame of mind for buying.

For those who believe in extra public relations gestures, you might want to have your next-door neighbors standing in the foyer talking to you. Then you can introduce a prospective buyer to these friendly folks.

You have a much more difficult problem if the common areas of your condo development or building appear unkempt. A purchaser buys not just your apartment, but common areas as well.

Can you convince your resident manager or handyman to do a little sprucing up as a personal favor to you (perhaps for a tip)? If not, you might show prospective buyers a comparable price situation in your area, *plus* an appraisal.

And then, *drop the price* of your apartment.

You can make excuses from today until Christmas about how the place is about to change management companies. It might help momentarily, although I doubt it. A first impression that is not a happy one turns into a "no sale." The exception could be a very sophisticated buyer who must have your specific location—but do not hold your breath for such a buyer to come along.

"AS IS": SELLING WITHOUT A FUSS

There is no law that says you must brighten and enhance your house before you sell it. Perhaps you simply do not have the time. Perhaps it is the wrong time in your life to cope with those details—there has been a death in the family, or you are in divorce proceedings, and you just want to get the sale over with.

That is when maintaining your Comfort Zone means selling your house in as-is condition. You will have to accept a reduced price. But you will invariably find a buyer, as long as you do *not* mislead people. There are plenty of hungry buyers waiting for handyman specials just like yours.

Suppose your kitchen looks like a war zone (or a roach-infested slum, or a museum piece from the previous century). Your selling tactic might be to allow $5,000 off the purchase price so the buyer can create his or her own new kitchen. (For more hints, see chapter 24 on negotiating.)

A woman from New Jersey who called my show was worried about how marketable her house was in a very vigorous buying climate.

She was eager to sell but *did not want to spend a penny* to spruce up the residence. I told her, "Take a sheet of paper and write down the description of your house. This is how big the property is, this is how many bedrooms there are, how many bathrooms, and this is the price."

At the bottom of the piece of paper, I told her, she should write in big letters—in lipstick, if she wanted to—HOUSE BEING SOLD IN AS-IS CONDITION.

The woman was selling without a broker. She could hand the paper to any prospective buyer. Since "as is" is code for "Let's negotiate," I told her to set the asking price higher than the price she would actually accept as the final one.

Expect to take a 5- to 10-percent reduction in price for a house sold as is.

SELL LOCATION, LOCATION, LOCATION

Using the guide at the end of this chapter, type out and have ready copies of a list of the selling points of your area. Is there an accessible country club, jogging trail, community swimming pool or park nearby? What are the school districts? Are there colleges nearby?

How long does it take—in minutes, not miles—to get to various places such as the convenience store, gas station, shopping center, churches, hospitals, commuter bus or train?

Have a list ready with telephone numbers of police, fire department, hospitals. People like to have those things at their fingertips. How about a community or neighborhood map? Real estate companies often stock these.

A good broker will have all this information put together for you. If you are selling the house yourself, *you* need to prepare this material.

Also have a complete description sheet of your house, based on the one at the end of this chapter. It should include the following:

- Dimensions of property.
- Names of water, gas, oil, electric and telephone companies, and service people.
- Floor plan, if possible, with dimensions of rooms in feet, as well as total square footage. (You need not include the dimensions of bathrooms, just state whether they are full or half.)
- Copies of the professional inspection report and of the one-year warranty you have on those items inspected. This is a remarkably effective selling tool, well worth the cost (under $250). See chapter 4 on appraisals for details on professional home inspections with warranties.

Seller's Comfort Zone Test

1. Do I really need to sell my house? Why?
2. Can I list three good reasons for *not* selling it?
3. How soon do I actually need to sell it?
4. Do I want to sell it myself? Do I have the time?
5. Would I rather sell it through a real estate broker?
6. Have I reviewed the checklist for choosing a broker on page 278 of chapter 20?
7. How much have other houses similar to mine in my neighborhood sold for within the past six months?
8. What is the price I would like to place on my house?
9. What is the least I will accept?
10. How much cash do I need from the buyer to make a deal?
11. Am I willing to finance part of the down payment myself?
12. Am I willing to finance the entire purchase myself, if necessary?
13. Have I made arrangements for a replacement residence?
14. If my home sells before I buy or rent a replacement house, have I arranged to pay rent to the buyer of my home so I can remain there for a while?

Seller's Time-Frame Comfort Zone Worksheet

I am due to start my new job on _____ , which is _____ weeks from now.

Time needed for interviewing brokers: 7 days.

Time needed for cleaning up house interior: _____ days.

Time needed for cleaning up front yard and exterior of house: _____ days.

Time needed for work by professional on landscaping and pruning: _____ days. Landscaper appointment is for _____ (date).

Time needed for paint jobs: _____ days. Painter appointment is for: ___ _____ (date).

Target date for yard sale: _____ , which is _____ days from now.

Target date for first open house: _____ , which is in _____ days.

Step-by-Step Spruce-Up Guide
(Check items as they are done.)

Curb Appeal

Fence: Painted? _____ Slats missing? _____

Mailbox: New enough? _____ Painted? _____ Replaced? _____

Front lawn: Edged? _____

Front yard trees: Pruned? _____

Front yard bushes: Pruned? _____ Replanted? _____

House numbers: Easily seen? _____ Replaced? _____

Porch: Clutter removed ? _____ Chairs and flowers (in summer)? _____

Do windows sparkle? _____

Front Door

Needs repainting? _____ Replacement? _____

Knocker polished? _____ Replaced? _____

New welcome mat? _____ Or old one replaced? _____

Doorbell or chimes working? _____

Doorknob polished? _____ Replaced? _____

Entrance Hall and Other Hallways

Mirrors needed? _____ Installed? _____

Living Room

Some furniture removed? _____

Carpet cleaned? _____

Holes covered with area rugs? _____

Floors polished? _____

Fireplace swept? _____ Fresh logs in place? _____

Fire lit (in winter)? _____

Family Room

Some furniture removed? _____

Soft music playing? _____

Toys put away? _____

Step-by-Step Spruce-Up Guide (continued)

Kitchen

Ceiling painted white? _____

Vanilla boiling? _____

Floor scrubbed? _____

Appliances clean inside and out? _____

Inside of cupboards clean? _____

Pantry

Swept and arranged neatly? _____

Empty boxes thrown out? _____

Dining Room

Full table set? _____

Flowers? _____

Master Bedroom

Bureau tops neat? _____

Bed made? _____

Carpets cleaned and/or vacuumed? _____

Drapes neat? _____

Closets uncluttered (items stored under bed)? _____

Master Bath

Toilet flushing properly? _____

Faucets checked for drips? _____

Clean towels folded on racks? _____

Utensils put away? _____

Tiles checked? _____

Grout cleaned? _____

Mirrors polished? _____

Other Bedrooms

Beds made? _____

Bureau tops neat? _____

Step-by-Step Spruce-Up Guide (continued)

Other Baths

Toilets flushing? _____

Clean towels? _____

Utensils put away? _____

Tiles checked? _____

Closets, Doors

Closets cleaned? _____

Doors closing properly? _____

Attic

Loose items boxed? _____

Basement

Walls painted? _____

Floor washed? _____

Loose items boxed and stored neatly? _____

Backyard or Patio

Rusty items discarded or painted? _____

Barbeque grill cleaned? _____

Cleaned up after dog? _____

Carport or Garage

Clutter removed? _____

Seller's Neighborhood Selling Points for Buyers

Seller's Name and Address(es) _____

_____

_____

_____

Public Transportation

Train station (location: driving distance in minutes) _____

Bus stop _____

Schools

Day-care center: _____

Elementary school and district _____

Intermediate school and district _____

High school _____

College or university _____

Parks, Playgrounds, Community Centers, Recreational Facilities

Nearest park _____

Other (pool, tennis, riding trails, health club, country club)

_____

_____

_____

_____

Nearest Convenience Store _____

Nearest Gas Station _____

Seller's Neighborhood Selling Points for Buyers (continued)

Nearest Bank with Auto-Teller _____

Shopping Center or Mall _____

_____

Churches and/or Synagogues

Name and Address _____

Name and Address _____

Public and/or Private Sanitation Service

Name, address, telephone _____

Frequency of pick-ups _____

Fire Department

Nearest station (address) _____

Telephone _____

Police Department

Precinct _____

Nearest police station (address) _____

Driving distance (in minutes) _____

Telephone _____

Captain _____

Hospitals and/or Walk-In Medical Office

Hospital name and address _____

Driving distance (minutes) _____

Medical office name and address _____

Driving distance (minutes) _____

Fact Sheet on the _____ Residence
(Description of your house, attached to floor plan if possible)

Address _____

Size of lot _____

Total square feet of dwelling _____

Number of bedrooms _____ Sizes _____

_____

_____

_____

Full baths _____ Half baths _____

Living room size _____

Family room and/or den size _____

Window treatments (drapes, shutters, blinds, if included) _____

_____

Kitchen size _____ Eat-in space? yes/no

    Appliances included: _____

    _____

Dining area size _____

Attic _____

Basement _____

Front yard and/or porch _____

Backyard and/or patio _____

Carport and/or garage: _____

Special amenities (such as brass switch plates, chandelier, etc.) _____

_____

_____

Practicalities

 Type of heat/air _____

    Gas and/or oil company name and address _____

_____

 Water heater capacity _____

    Water company name and address _____

_____

 Electrical capacity _____

    Electric company name and address _____

_____

 Telephone company name and number _____

_____

Fact Sheet on the _____ **Residence** (continued)

Practicalities (continued)
Reliable service personnel and companies
Appliance repair _____

Alarm systems _____

Auto mechanic _____

Auto towing _____

Cable TV _____

Carpenter _____

Chimneysweep _____

Electrician _____

Exterminator _____

Firewood _____

Floor sanding and polishing _____

Furniture refinishing and upholstering _____

House painting _____

Landscaping _____

Lawn services _____

Locksmith _____

Masonry _____

Plumber _____

Roofer _____

Septic tank service _____

Snow removal _____

Tree work _____

Trash removal _____

Water pumps/wells _____

Window cleaning _____

## Chapter 19

How to Set the Right Price for Your House — Appraising the Appraisers

A big question at cocktail parties is, "How much do you think your house is worth?" That is *not* the question that matters. The real issue is, "How shall I price this house so it sells?"

People tend to *overprice* their homes. They call several realtors and get the asking prices for homes in their neighborhood. The asking price is always higher than the actual selling price, except in a very hot market.

Check with local realtors, certainly. But also get a professional appraisal. In addition, look up courthouse records to see how much homes in your neighborhood have brought in the past six months.

If you have a friend who has sold a house like yours recently in your neighborhood, ask the friend about the price negotiations. Explain that you are selling your house. You will find that people like to talk about real estate and *will* share that information.

On the flip side, nothing is worse than feeling you have sold your house *too cheaply*.

Once you advertise a house for a specific asking price, the worst thing that can happen is that the house does not sell. Perhaps the market is in flux, or your price is simply too high. You always can negotiate the price downward. But if you mistakenly start out with too low a price, it is extremely difficult to raise it.

This chapter reviews the ways to determine a *fair* price—and to find an honest appraiser. I also describe how to skip the boilerplate in an appraisal and get to the meat of it, how to know when a broker is setting too high or too low a price, and how to do the legwork yourself.

You can be sure your potential buyers will want to know how you arrived at your asking price.

Suppose you say, "Joan down the street got $150,000 for her house, so I think mine is worth the same." You are likely to get a skeptical, "wrinkled-forehead" look.

But if you pull out an appraisal from a reputable appraiser who belongs to a nationally recognized organization, it could be the exclamation point that ends the discussion.

TRACKING DOWN A RELIABLE APPRAISER

Some appraisals are worthless, while others are useful. As we explained in chapter 4, the honest, licensed appraiser with credentials whom you need is likely to be one with the initials MAI or ASA after his or her name. MAI indicates a member of the Appraisal Institute (the American Institute of Real Estate Appraisers) and ASA a member of the American Society of Appraisers.

These professional organizations have excellent codes of ethics. Only 10 percent of the appraisers in this country belong to them. Unfortunately, there are no industry-wide standards and few state regulations governing this field.

A good appraiser charges about $200 to $300 for a full-fledged market-value appraisal. Problems crop up because the bank, not the buyer or seller, usually orders the appraisal.

However, you can beat the bank to the punch.

The people who listen to my programs order their own appraisal before selling. There is a certain respect a real estate pro will have for a seller who has an appraisal in his or her possession *before* listing the house. This puts the pro on notice that this is not amateur night.

Because you clearly are an informed seller, a broker will hesitate playing the price game with you. This game comes in two parts.

The first part involves the broker's telling you that your house is worth a heck of a lot more than it is, in order to get the listing, and then bring you offers that are much lower. The second part of the game takes place when your house is listed way below market value and then sold to someone the broker knows, in order to make a quick profit.

Please keep in mind that only a tiny fraction of con artists will attempt to pull this stunt. On the contrary, a good broker, realizing that you are price-sensitive, can be an invaluable member of your team.

APPRAISAL PRICES VERSUS COMPUTERIZED MULTILIST PRICES

Over 90 percent of the professionals in real estate, believe it or not, accept the first appraisal presented, or the appraisal presented by the bank.

Unfortunately, banks tend to use *in-house appraisers.* In most cases these people may be cheaper but they seldom are certified by a national appraisal organization.

If you really are serious about getting the most for your house or apartment, compare the appraisal price with a price that has been called up by a computer tied in with the local Multiple Listing Service.

Up-to-date real estate offices now have computerized sales analyses of comparable houses on the multilist. When a sale is made, that information is retrievable. A report that once took five or six days now can be done in minutes.

There are times when a professional appraisal comes in low, or "short," as the industry refers to it. Your first reaction is disbelief. The worst time for it to happen is after you have made a deal and your buyer has applied for a mortgage. Then the bank appraisal turns up, with a dollar figure that is lower than the amount in the contract.

Stop wringing your hands. Errors can be rectified. In my experience, underpriced appraisals happen in just 2 or 3 percent of cases. Most appraisals come in within 2 or 3 percent of each other if the appraiser is doing his job.

Here are three steps to battle a short appraisal:

1. Ask to inspect the appraisal if you think it is incorrect. Certain lending institutions refuse to give a seller the actual appraiser's report on grounds of confidentiality. Case law holds that a bank *cannot* withhold documents for which you have paid, so call your lawyer if you run up against a brick wall.

2. Go to another appraiser for a second opinion, which will cost anywhere from $50 to $100. (Of course, you might also check a real estate agency computer as well, since sales in recent weeks could change the appraiser's facts and figures.)

3. *Challenge the low appraisal.* If you lose a deal based on an incorrect appraisal, you might be in a strong legal position.

There have been court cases stating that an appraiser can be sued for the difference in the money that the client lost because the appraisal was incorrect. The courts have held that the client is relying on a professional opinion. If the appraiser blew it, he or she will have to make up the difference.

Keep in mind that an appraisal is always an *opinion.* Different appraisers may offer widely disparate views. More troubling than the small percentage of short appraisals is the larger percentage of unduly high estimates. Client advocacy appraising—providing the conveniently high appraisal needed to support a bank loan—has caused enough bank defaults to warrant a congressional investigation.

Defective appraisals, whether low or high, can be terribly damaging. One recent House subcommittee report charged that "taxpayers and lenders are losing billions of dollars" through this kind of ineptitude, according to syndicated columnist Kenneth Harney.

I have heard about inept appraisals firsthand. One radio friend complained to me that the first appraisal on the house he was selling was $58,000, but the sale in question did not go through. A second appraisal came in at only $43,000, killing the second deal. Finally a third appraisal, at $56,000, was accepted and the sale went ahead. Clearly, the second appraiser did *not* know the area in which the house was located.

The story illustrates why you, as a seller, should have in hand right from the start an appraisal that you believe to be fair. If there turns out to be a tremendous difference between yours and the bank's, at least you have a professional opinion upon which to base your case.

HOW TO READ AN APPRAISAL

There is another route to fair, successful pricing.

If you want to hasten your deal, you, the seller, can set up the financing at a bank right at the beginning. Then, well before you enter into negotiations, obtain your appraisal from that bank's appraisal firm, provided it is an outside firm.

You will notice that your appraisal document is quite lengthy. Because of legal exposure, the appraiser includes several pages in the beginning discussing the document as, indeed, an opinion. This boilerplate also states that the appraiser is not responsible if an error is made under certain conditions.

Skip this material until you get to the phrase about market value, as well as the information just preceding it. Here is where you find a list of homes like yours in the area that have been sold recently, and information on when they were sold and for how much.

Urge your banker to find out how up to date the service he uses is, and what its credentials are. If an appraiser botches a job, let his or her professional organization know about it.

This route cuts the time it takes for your buyer, who would need an appraisal for the bank anyway. It is a terrific sales tool, since you have done much of the work for the buyer. (If the appraisal is more than six months old, of course, it must be updated.)

YOU CAN'T JUDGE A HOUSE BY ITS COVER

Not sure how much your house is worth compared to similar ones in your area now on the market?

You *cannot* go by the price of the house next door, although, as mentioned earlier, it is not a bad idea to find out about actual sales prices in your neighborhood in general. On the next block, a house that from the curb appears to be the twin of yours might be offered for $20,000 more than yours—or $20,000 less.

Prices are determined by several factors, including the condition of the home, plus extra added attractions. The "twin" may have a finished basement, an extra bathroom, brand-new carpeting, a better air-conditioning system, a pool. It may be a "twin" on the outside, but it is quite different in terms of improvements, amenities and repairs.

As I mentioned in the previous chapter, some improvements—such as an interior paint job, replacement of doors, fresh landscaping, plus a major cleaning effort—will bring you *more money* from the sale of the house than the actual cost of making those improvements.

Amenities such as in-ground swimming pools in subtropical areas, remodeled bathrooms and remodeled kitchens (provided you do not go overboard on gold fixtures or the like) will bring you back approximately the *same amount* of money as you put into those amenities. The major advantage of a large remodeling job is that in some cases, it will help you sell the house *faster.*

Special additions—a tennis court or a sauna, for example—will *not* add dollars to the sale price. However, since a tennis court would appeal to an avid tennis family, you might want to advertise a house with a court in a tennis magazine.

* * *

You can do appraisal legwork yourself. In the records book for your neighborhood in the local courthouse, documentary stamps indicate the sales prices of property. These books are available to everyone. You can see with your own eyes how much homes like yours have sold for in the past six months.

Do *not* bother with prices from two years or even one year ago. Regional developments can drastically alter a community's real estate market in the course of a few months.

Recently, in Texas, where the residential market and the entire economy were tied to the price of oil, the bottom dropped out of the economy, including real estate. The price of residences in some parts of Texas dropped as much as 22 percent within a four-month period.

INSPECTIONS AND WARRANTIES SPEED UP SALES

Let me mention once more that homeowners who want to upgrade their houses can get the same kind of professional home inspection that we recommended in chapter 4 for buyers, *before* putting a house on the market.

Remember, there is a difference between an *appraisal* and an *inspection*. An appraisal tells you the fair market price of your house. An inspection tells you what is physically wrong with it, if anything.

After a professional inspection, you will know if your roof needs repairs, if your electrical wiring is in good condition, if your plumbing is sound.

Then, when a prospective buyer walks in the front door and says, "What kind of condition is this house in?" you can hand the buyer a certificate from a respected firm, complete with a one-year warranty. Imagine how much more comfortable your visitor will feel—and how quickly you might be able to shake hands on a sale.

A home inspection coupled with a warranty covering such systems as heating, wiring, roofing and plumbing is a powerful magnet for buyers. In a competitive market, the home with the inspection and a warranty starts out giant strides ahead of others. Smart brokers suggest these sales tools; if yours does not, ask about them.

Information on House Inspection Firms

Write the American Society of Home Inspectors, 1010 Wisconsin Avenue, N.W., Washington, DC 20007; or call (202) 842-3096.

Information on Appraisals

Write or phone for the free booklet "Standards of Professional Practice and Conduct," from the Society of Real Estate Appraisers, 645 North Michigan Avenue, Chicago, IL 60611; or call (312) 346-7422 or toll-free (800) 331-7732.

Chapter **20**

Finding the Broker Who Is Right for You

There are plenty of real estate brokers hanging their shingles out across the country who would be delighted to list your house. What makes one better than another? Should you list your house with more than one?

If you do your homework, you will never get into a situation like that a woman on my staff got herself into. She told me, "I put my house on the market yesterday, and somebody bought it today for the full price, without even making an offer."

I replied, "You haven't been listening to me. You priced your house too low."

Who priced it for her? A real estate broker. Who bought it? His mother-in-law.

I will return to this scam in a moment. First, let me offer a few clues to leading brokers, which you can pick up merely by taking an hour's drive through your community.

An active broker has "For Sale" signs up around town. Ask the owners of those houses if they are happy with the broker's service.

Stop in at the courthouse or hall of records. Are there any lawsuits pending against a broker you plan to interview? Does the state licensing board have any complaints on record? If you are relocating, see if your new area has a branch of a national brokerage firm.

Once you have the names of several real estate firms that seem promising, make an appointment and interview the broker or sales agent. You will find a list of questions at the end of this chapter as a guide. Check the references you are given.

Incidentally, there is a practical reason for scouting the neighborhood and visiting other homes that a broker is trying to sell. Those other houses could be competition for your own. Do not be shy about questioning the broker on this point. Perhaps there have been some improvements made on a nearby, fast-selling home that you would do well to copy.

EXCLUSIVE VERSUS OPEN LISTINGS

A good broker will ask you for an *exclusive-right-to-sell* listing. In this arrangement, no matter who sells the property—the "exclusive" broker, another firm or broker, or you personally—the broker who has the listing gets a commission.

A second alternative, the *exclusive-agency* listing, is going out of style. This agreement states that if the real estate broker sells the house, that brokerage gets the commission, but if you sell it yourself, *you* keep the commission. Brokers are fleeing this agreement like the plague.

A final agreement is the *open* listing. You tell every broker in town that your home is on the market. The broker who brings the first acceptable deal to you gets the commission.

I recommend giving a broker an exclusive-right-to-sell listing, because in nine out of ten cases, that person will work harder and sell your home more quickly.

The only problem with exclusive listings is the one suggested in the scam I mentioned earlier, in which a broker's relative bought the house. No matter how often sellers are warned, there are those who get trapped.

An unscrupulous broker has an anxious seller sign an exclusive-right-of-sale form. The broker underprices the house. Then the broker sets up the straw man (such as a relative) to buy the house the same day. The broker ends up getting the house, through the straw man, for a lower price than it is worth.

Only a tiny percentage of the 700,000 brokers in this country are unscrupulous enough to seek these exclusive-right-of-sale scams aggressively. But those are the ones to beware of!

Inviting several brokers to make presentations helps you avoid both underpricing and overpricing. The good brokers—and there are loads of them—use the comparable price information available through the Multiple Listing Service and thus will be within the same general price range.

The first question a broker will ask you is "May I have an exclusive-right-to-sell listing?" The second question will probably be "How long can you wait for a sale?"

Do not let a broker list your home for a long period of time. *Never list a home for more than 90 days.*

Tell the broker that if homes are selling in your market generally within 30 days, you want an agreement for a 30-day listing *only.* If it takes 60 days at this time in your area, give the broker a 60-day listing.

Good brokers *will* accept a shorter listing period, because they know they will bring plenty of positive activity. If you have a good relationship, both you and your broker understand that *you* can *extend* the listing agreement.

Too many people mistakenly give a house to a broker for six months, or an unspecified period of time. They wait . . . and *nothing happens.* They are stuck six months later when they are planning to move to their next house. This is one of the most frequently voiced complaints on my call-in radio show.

Once you have made an exclusive arrangement, it is hard to get out of it. One woman sought my advice after signing one such agreement. It seemed that she almost sold her house *without* a broker to an acquaintance, but the deal fell through. She then signed a three-month exclusive with a broker that promised him a 7-percent commission.

The initial buyer came back into the picture. "I can't discuss any business with you now," she explained. "You have to contact my broker."

The fellow did just that. The broker helped finalize the deal . . . and asked for his full 7-percent commission.

"It was *my* acquaintance, my contact," protested the woman. "Do I have a way out for a lesser commission? He hardly did any work!"

I asked if her contract said on the top of the page, "exclusive right of sale." It did.

Since she had signed it, that broker had every right to that commission, no matter who made the first contact with the buyer. There was *no* way of getting out of it, unless she had excluded her acquaintance from the listing, in writing, with the broker's signature as proof.

Before your house is listed, examine the agreement with the broker. Ask for a *jump-out clause* should you be unhappy with the broker's work. Discuss the wording with your attorney before signing, or at least write on the agreement that it is *subject to your attorney's approval.* (See chapter 22 for more on your attorney's job.) Then, if the broker does nothing in the first two to six weeks, you can get out of the agreement legally and ethically.

Be wary of a broker who tells you your house is worth *more* than you think it is. Ask the broker for examples of *actual* sales of comparable houses in your area from the past three months, so you and the broker can determine a realistic asking price. Wise sellers also get a professional appraisal.

HOW MUCH OF A COMMISSION SHOULD YOU PAY?

A good broker's job is to sell your house for as much money as possible and as quickly as possible. Brokers are not in the business of listing houses and sitting on them. When you find a good broker, hang on to that broker. A winner is worth the commission you pay.

What should that commission be?

The Sonny Bloch Rule Number One here is, *all commissions are negotiable.*

Sure, a common one is 6 or 7 percent of the sale price. But it is not carved in stone. If you are in a seller's market, you can request a smaller commission. If the broker says this is not so, show him or her this paragraph. There is always another broker waiting in the wings, anxious for your business at a lower commission.

How high a commission should you pay a well-recommended broker? It depends on the broker's services. Some brokers put together a tremendous promotion package and deserve as high as 7 percent. Other brokers will sell your house for a flat fee, or a smaller percentage.

Reduced-fee brokers can be every bit as aggressive and successful as full-fee ones. There is nothing crucial that you must give up for a reduced fee. The analogy might be a full-service stock brokerage versus a discount brokerage. The real estate broker working for a reduced commission is one who makes it up in volume business, as opposed to the full-fee broker in a small office without that many clients.

Here and there, a broker may counter your suggestion of a reduced commission with a *reduction in service*—such as not listing your house with the local Multiple Listing Service.

Don't bite. There are other brokers who do use the multilist who will be fishing for your business at a lower commission.

Nor should you compromise on advertising. A broker who says your house will sell simply through the multilist either is overly optimistic or is working in a very, very hot market, where desperate buyers are roaming the streets night and day knocking on doors. Nor is it a good idea to haggle over paying for each separate ad.

Be a thorough comparison-shopper. What is a full-commission broker offering you, compared to a reduced-fee broker? Make a decision based on the services rendered, not the fee charged.

You might be talking about substantial sums, so talk dollars, not percentages. If you want $200,000 or more for your house, a 7-percent commission runs $14,000 or more. When you speak to a broker in terms of dollars, you will find the broker more amenable to discussing a discount. This trend is becoming more prevalent and will continue.

HIKING YOUR ASKING PRICE TO COVER A COMMISSION

Take the commission into account when you calculate the asking price. Raise your price initially by that percentage, so that when you negotiate with a buyer, you can lower it by that percentage. Usually, in a 7-percent commission scenario, the selling broker gets 3½ percent and the listing broker gets 3½ percent.

Here is how three of us—a caller, a real estate broker and I—discussed negotiating the size of a commission, on my radio show. The caller had an estate in Westchester County, New York, for which she wanted $450,000.

I asked the broker what the normal commission is on a $450,000 house. His answer: $27,000, or 6 percent.

The caller had a choice. She could tell brokers whom she interviewed that her asking price was $450,000, and negotiate a commission, or she could raise the figure to $477,000, which would automatically cover the commission.

Her concern was that she was susceptible to the hard sell, and that a broker might talk her into a lower asking price.

"Write a note to yourself on a three-by-five index card that says *'No less than $450,000,'* " I suggested. "Every time you talk to someone about what amount you must have, put the card in front of you." No matter how hard a broker tried to get her to change her mind, she could answer, "That's it guys, I wrote this note as a contract with myself." In her market, at the time she called, she had no trouble getting the money she wanted, regardless of the commission.

Be sure you negotiate the commission with an authorized person. Do you understand the difference between a broker and a sales agent? *The broker is licensed by the state.* This person has passed a test indicating knowledge of real estate law. A broker hires sales agents to work under the broker. Everything a sales agent does has to be approved by a broker.

Thus, all decisions about your property are the responsibility, ultimately, of the broker, even if they are negotiated by an underling. It is the broker's license that is on the line if something goes awry, if, for example, the sales agent misrepresents the time and money to be spent selling your property.

The sales listing agreement will, in fact, be with the broker, not with the sales agent. By law, the sales agent and the broker *work solely for you, the seller.* Therefore, do not be timid about requesting open houses, signs, ads, activity reports and proposed deals.

OPEN HOUSE: Y'ALL COME!

What does a broker do to earn his or her commission? A good one makes up a floor plan of your home, does a market study of the neighborhood, and suggests ways to spruce up the place for sale, as shown in chapter 18.

When the house is ready, the broker discusses dates for open houses. These are vehicles for making the product you have now attractively packaged available to the consumer, at a time that is convenient for the buying public. Saturday and Sunday are the most popular days, because most working people and both spouses have the time to drop by.

Open houses are customary in selling a house, whether you are working with or without a broker. These days, an open house is *essential* in the sale of residential property.

Dismiss any broker who will not take the trouble to announce and arrange one for you. All it takes is a classified ad in your local paper and some strategically placed signs in your area.

Individual appointments may also be arranged, but the open house often comes first. Among other things, an open house brings other brokers who belong to the Multiple Listing Service to see your home. The more exposure your product gets, the more likely you are to get a quick, profitable sale.

Open houses tend to last from a half to a full day. It is a wonderful idea to invite friends to this event, to "paper the house." But do not spend all your time chatting with your pals. Your job is to make yourself available to strangers who have questions about the property that your broker cannot answer. (Some brokers prefer that you *not* be there.)

It is one thing to be a gracious host and quite another to follow prospective purchasers around the house like a puppy. Leave them alone, especially in the kitchen, the backyard, the living room. Give them a chance to talk to each other about the place. Let them get a sense of the house on personal terms. This is the treatment you would want if you were shopping for clothes, for instance; you would want to try on a dress or suit in a dressing room without the salesperson staring or disturbing you.

If visitors start asking questions, they are potential buyers; answer them courteously.

When a broker shows your home to a specific client, do *not* hover. The broker and the client should be left alone. *Do* leave a telephone number where you can be reached during a private showing, just in case the client has a question that the broker cannot answer.

Be sure to *put away* personal items that can be pocketed. Stash valuable jewelry in your safe-deposit box.

HOW LOCKED IS A LOCKBOX?

Among real estate people, a lockbox is a convenient method of allowing their fellow professionals to show a house. I disagree. It is a convenience to them, but it could be trouble for you.

A lockbox holds your house keys. The box is placed on your front door. The only people with access to the lockbox are members of the realty board and the real estate agency with your listing.

But some people have had bad experiences with lockboxes. If you are in a high-crime area, you are better off making definite appointments with the broker to meet a client at the door. If you are out of town while your house is on the market, insist that the broker keep the keys under his or her control at all times, rather than use a lockbox.

CHECKLIST:
What to Ask Brokers Who Want to Sell Your House

1. Are you a full-time broker?
2. How long have you sold full-time in this region?
3. Do you have any special professional designations from the National Association of Realtors?
4. Have you sold any homes in the immediate vicinity in the past two years? (Request to see the sold listing in the multilist.)
5. Did you get the asking price? If not, how close to it? (Remember, this is public information, verifiable in the courthouse.)
6. Do you have other homes you are showing in my neighborhood?
7. Is your commission negotiable?
8. Will you give me the names of people for whom you have sold houses in the past year? (A good broker gladly gives references. Do not stop there—call them!)
9. If you are a salesperson, may I have some references to check your brokerage firm?
10. Which mortgage brokers or bankers do you work with on financing?
11. Do you work with a particular real estate attorney?
12. Will you give me a written advertising campaign?
13. How much will you spend, and where and when will the ads appear?
14. How many times will you hold an open house?
15. Will my home be listed with the Multiple Listing Service?

## Chapter 21

Can You Save Thousands by Selling Your Home Without a Broker?

Sometimes.

But I must warn you about the dangers of selling your house yourself. Unless you are slightly masochistic and have a lot of time, you will be much better off working with a broker.

In fact, you can go halfway by using FSBO services.

Each year, thousands of homes are sold by their owners, mainly because they cannot afford the real estate broker's commission. The trouble is, most people do *not* know how to price their home or how to market it. They do not understand what a closing is. They do not realize what title insurance is.

You can save thousands selling without a broker *only* when you know what you are doing.

UNSCRUPULOUS BUYERS WHO STALK YOUR HOME

Let us say you own a house with a $97,000 mortgage. You bought it recently, made a down payment, and suddenly you get a new job that requires moving to another city.

If a broker sells the house for you quickly at the market price of $100,000, you would use $97,000 of that to pay off your mortgage, leaving you with $3,000 toward the broker's commission of $6,000 (the common 6 percent).

Rather than be faced with coughing up $3,000 in cash you do not have, you decide to advertise the house yourself. You figure if you sell it yourself, you can pocket $3,000 instead of paying out $6,000.

Unfortunately, there are unscrupulous buyers who prey on such sellers. These con artists end up getting houses for far less than they are worth. The seller is the loser.

In Seattle not long ago, a man from Alaska went all over town making offers on houses. He was willing to pay what the seller was asking, or even higher. The man would put down a small deposit of less than $500, explaining to the prospective seller that he was liquidating his Alaska gold mine. He would show people gold mine stock in his briefcase. (It proved to be phony.)

The closing on the gold mine would take place in six months, he told the sellers. At that time, he would be able to close on the houses. The gold miner brought with him a contract, an offer to purchase, which at the top said "Standard—State of Washington." He had sellers sign it. He pointed to small print that said: "Buyer will pay seller cash within six months."

The sellers, seeing the gold drip from the fast-talking miner, believed they were selling their houses for as much as or more than they wanted. They signed and collected $500.

What they failed to realize was that the miner was a con man who had studied his marks. He knew that in some cases the seller was being transferred and had to move within the year. In other cases there was an impending divorce or a death in the family.

He did *not* point out to the sellers an additional tiny line of print on the contract. It stated that in the event the seller was unable to close the sale within six months, either the buyer would take over the seller's existing mortgage in exchange for a note, meaning *no cash,* or, at the *buyer's* option, the buyer could extend the agreement for as long as 24 months.

This extra clause had the effect of taking the house off the market for two and a half years, for a deposit of $500.

A WORKABLE STRATEGY

How can you work yourself out of this kind of predicament, yet still sell *without* a broker? Here is my outline of a safe strategy.

Begin by asking yourself some hard questions. (Just because you bought your house at a good price some years ago does *not* mean you are an expert in selling it.) Ask yourself the following:

• Am I willing to pay for an appraisal in order to price my house correctly?

• Do I know how to write ads for marketing my house?

• Will I hire a professional sign painter to paint a deluxe "For Sale by Owner" sign to put in front of my house?

• Am I willing to make appointments with people and have them meet with me at their convenience so I can show the home?

• Am I willing to hold open houses?

• Am I willing to cooperate with a legitimate broker who might see the sign and bring a client in?

• Am I willing to pay that broker a decent commission?

• Will I hire an attorney to direct me on the initial paperwork?

• Finally, can I spend the time that it takes (lots of it!) to sell my home by myself?

If you cannot reply with a hearty yes to these questions, go back to the beginning of this chapter. Do not pass Go, and do not collect $200. You might be terrific at Monopoly, but you need a real estate pro to sell your house for you in the real world.

However, if you are still enthusiastic, it is time to learn the basics through which you can achieve success in the For Sale by Owner game.

Do you want to spend a few hundred dollars for an appraisal that will tell you how much your house is worth? If not, *beware of the grave error of overpricing your home.* This is the single biggest mistake made by most do-it-yourself sellers.

Drop by your local courthouse to find actual prices paid for nearby homes in recent months. To see what people are saying about houses like yours, check the ads in local real estate magazines and newspapers, often found in convenience store racks. Also check the classified ads in the Sunday newspaper. "Owner" ads are generally clearly identified.

The next maneuver is not entirely cricket, but some owners do it anyway. They invite a few real estate brokers to visit and make presentations. They ask these brokers for comparable sales figures for the neighborhood. Even if you are not successful selling the house by yourself, this is a good way to get to know some professional brokers.

Next, put a classified ad in your local paper. Describe your house properly; for example: "Turn-of-the-century colonial; totally reno-

vated, three bedrooms, two baths; huge yard, swimming pool . . ."
Include the price, and your phone number. For safety reasons, do *not*
give your exact street address.

Your phone may start ringing off the hook. Surprised? Not when you
hear who is on the line.

Nearly *half the calls* undoubtedly will be from real estate agents.
That is how they get listings. Make it clear that you do *not* want to sign
an exclusive-right-to-sell agreement, but that if they want to look at
your place it is fine.

A woman from Cape Canaveral, Florida, was having trouble selling
her home, despite ads she placed in her local paper. I felt she had to
devise a better marketing campaign.

Instead of the headline for her ad "Home for Sale," I suggested:
"Owner must move! Will sacrifice deluxe ranch home. Florida coastal
area. Move in now. $84,500 *full price.*" Having thus limited her appeal
to truly interested buyers who were looking for her type of place in her
area at her price, she could run the ad for $50 in a national newspaper,
USA Today, on its biggest day, Friday. This is an example of a *qualifying* ad. It gets rid of curiosity seekers.

The first week you place a *good* ad, this is what could happen:

Ace Realty calls. "I have a buyer who is in town for only four days,"
the broker tells you. "This person is perfect for your house. I can get
you your price, or pretty close, plus my commission."

If you say "all right" without any paperwork, if you tell the agent
to bring the client to see your house, you will be *required* to pay that
commission, under the open-listing laws. Although you have not signed
a listing agreement, once you allow agents to show your house you are
liable for the commission.

To protect yourself, have your attorney prepare a memo for brokers
to sign *before* they step over your threshold with a client in tow. The
memo should say that you are giving permission to the named broker
to show the house for this day *only.* You understand that the broker
will deliver the price you name in the memo. This piece of paper limits
the "open listing" to the day specified. An example of a one-time
commission agreement can be found at the end of this chapter.

BILLBOARD YOUR SALE

Now that you have gotten your feet wet by placing your first ad, is your
professionally painted sign ready?

Both sides of the sign should list your phone number and additional descriptions, such as "swimming pool, 3 bedrooms, 2 baths, owner financing." The sign should say "By Appointment Only," except on those days you are holding an open house. Post the sign close to the curb in your front yard.

Why all this detail about a sign? People driving by and stopping because of a sign are the best prospects you could possibly want. They have already searched the neighborhood and they are genuine buyers.

Like a good scout, though, be prepared. Your doorbell could ring at almost any time. If you have not made an appointment, you are putting yourself and your family's safety *at risk* by leading an unannounced stranger through your property. Reject people who want to make impromptu visits.

HOW TO BE COURTEOUS AND NOSY AT THE SAME TIME

If you are working, you need to take the time, trouble and money to hire an answering service to take calls.

Prospective buyers expect *you* to be there when they call your number. They are not concerned about the fact that you are away from home, especially if they are from out of town. Do *not* use an electronic answering machine. People are intimidated by them.

Your answering service should have living, breathing, friendly operators on the answering end. You do not want to miss a valuable call. Real estate brokers pay up to $50 for a qualified call to come in to their office. If you miss ten calls, that is $500 worth of calls a pro would be happy to pay for.

It might be useful to have a toll-free 800 number. Several toll-free answering services advertise for clients in the classified section of *USA Today* under "Answering Services." The cost for hiring a toll-free message center to take your calls can run as low as $35 a month.

When you call back, what is your telephone demeanor? Are you answering with a smiling voice, even if the voice on the other end sounds like your ex-husband? Thank whoever calls, take down the name and phone number for follow-up calls, and make an appointment for a specific time to show the house.

Again, *take reasonable precautions.* If callers say they are in town only for the day, get the number of their hotel and verify that they are there. Also check names and out-of-town addresses with directory information.

The simplest way to verify all names and numbers is by phoning to reconfirm all appointments. The proper language is, "I'm calling back to make sure our appointment is at such-and-such a time, and to double-check that you have the right directions to my house."

If the phone number is fake, or if you cannot get a caller to leave a number, you are asking for trouble by inviting the person for a tour. If this advice makes you nervous, reconsider the idea of using a broker. (I am addressing older people particularly, and women who live alone, among others.)

OWNER-PLANNED OPEN HOUSES

Plan an open house, preferably on a weekend, and make sure your ads and sign announce it to the world.

Give people clear, concise directions to your home. You may know about making that right-hand turn at the second stop sign and then a left at the 7-Eleven, but spell it out for strangers. Use street names, including the distance between points that you mention.

Thus, you should say, "Take a left on Elm Street, drive six blocks to Park Place, and make a right at the 7-Eleven. Drive four and a half blocks. It is the third driveway on the left. The house is a two-story white clapboard with red trim. The number 123 is on the right of the front door."

Why risk losing a sale because someone gets lost—and ticked off— en route?

Showing your house to a prospect, room by room, is a minor art form. Pretend you are half game-show host, half college professor. Enthusiastic, knowledgeable . . . and sensitive.

Thus, as you and your guest enter the living room, point out the bay window, the recently installed double-glass insulation and the working fireplace. In the kitchen, call attention to the new dishwasher and the window that catches the morning sun.

You do *not* want to sound like a kindergarten teacher. So remind yourself not to introduce rooms ("This is the living room") when the function is obvious. By all means ask your visitors questions, whether they have any children, for instance, so you can offer subtle marketing information about schools, recreation and so on.

It is prudent to have two of you in the house when showing it to a visitor, for safety reasons. (One person should conduct the tour, the other remain out of the way.) If you are alone, you could arrange to have a friend call every twenty minutes, just to be sure you are all right.

PLAN FOR HEAVY TRAFFIC AND PLENTY OF PAPERWORK

Schedule individual appointments *twenty minutes apart* throughout the day. You gain a tremendous psychological advantage when the doorbell rings with the next "customer" on the threshold. I have seen homes sold at this point; a buyer, upon hearing the bell, turns to the owner and says, "Don't show it; we will buy it."

It is time for more homework because you will soon be negotiating a deal with someone. Consult a banker or mortgage broker about financing. What kinds of mortgages are they offering? How many points are they charging? What down payment is required? How quickly can one be arranged? Many banks have the material prepared in a brochure. You can grease the sale wheels by showing financing information to prospective buyers after a tour. Doing so makes you seem almost as professional as a real estate agent.

A few days have passed following your open house and two days of private showings. One potential buyer calls to make an offer over the phone.

No matter what the offer is, you should give the following answer: "Thank you. Why don't you come to the house for a cup of coffee so we can talk further?" *Telephone negotiating does not work.*

When you are sitting around the kitchen table sipping coffee, what you want the buyer to disclose is not what he or she is offering you, but what the buyer really will pay.

It is thus inappropriate to say, "I'm insulted by your low offer." As a smart seller, handle the first offer by explaining how you arrived at your price, display your appraisal, and pull out the market listings for your area that you have collected from local real estate agencies.

Always have your bottom-line price in the back of your mind. But do *not* announce that price immediately. A little bargaining at a time goes a long way.

Your trump card is the fact that you are selling without a broker, so instead of paying a commission you are passing thousands of dollars in savings along to the lucky buyer.

A clever buyer will ask you immediately to take 7 percent (the standard commission) *off* your asking price. Anticipate this from the start. Show the house at 7 percent *above* what you wish to sell it for.

Then you can *gradually* bring down your asking price, if necessary. In fact, in the course of negotiations, you may lower your price only

1 or 2 percent from the price of a similar house being sold by a broker. But if the purchase price of the similar home is $150,000, and yours is $147,000, the 2-percent difference translates into a weighty-sounding $3,000. Always talk in terms of dollars, not percentages.

CHECKMATE, NOT STALEMATE

Never burn your bridges in a negotiating session. If you are deadlocked, ask your prospect to give you some time to mull over his or her offer. Make an appointment to meet again the next day, or the next after that.

Prospective buyers inevitably have second thoughts after they leave; they fall more deeply in love with your house and call the next day to say they are coming over to accept your last counteroffer.

Even at this moment, do *not* react quickly. When a potential buyer says, "We will pay what you want," your response should be, "I think we can get together and do a deal. Why don't you come over and give us a deposit, which I can take to my lawyer in order to draw up an agreement."

Before putting your house on the market, you have notified your real estate lawyer about your plans. Now work with your lawyer on the final stages. Have your attorney prepare an offer to purchase (see the example at the end of this chapter) and a "binder" or good-faith deposit receipt (see the example in chapter 6 on negotiating).

THE "IN-BETWEEN" FOR-SALE-BY-OWNER SERVICES

In some areas of the country, brokers are jumping in on the "for-sale-by-owner" bandwagon, offering a service that is a *great compromise* between hiring a broker and selling completely by yourself.

Such brokers give you all the necessary paperwork needed to sell your house and teach you how to use it, help you get a professional, custom-made sign, come through and do an inspection, give you a checklist to follow, and write the ads for you.

In addition, the broker charges you a flat fee *in case* he or she sells the house for you.

This is an in-between service, somewhere between using a broker and doing it entirely by yourself, for a smaller fee than a full-service broker might charge. The fee runs anywhere from $300 to $750, or it could be 1½ percent of the sale price. It is absolutely a free market.

WHAT IF YOURS IS A BROKERED SALE IN THE END?

Nine times out of ten in FSBO (for sale by owner) situations, you end up with a referral broker bringing in a client.

In this case, you have a written agreement with a broker negotiated before the person looks at the house. It is important to quote a price to a broker that includes the commission, as I indicated in the previous chapter, if you are looking for a specific net price.

For example, if you want to get $97,000 and you know the broker wants a $3,000 commission, simply quote the price as $100,000 to the broker. The broker will ask whether this includes his commission. Your answer is yes.

The important thing is not that a broker ultimately collects a fee. What is important is that you have sold your house for *your* price.

Sample Offer to Purchase

Property: To the owner or person who has the right to sell the property described below: I (we) agree to purchase the following property situated in the

City of _____, County of_____,

State of _____, known as _____, being (address

and brief description go here) _____

_____

_____ (for

a more detailed description of the property, reference is hereby made to the

deed thereof), together with all lighting, heating and plumbing fixtures, window shades, screen and storm doors and windows, if any, water heater, water

meter and all fixtures and fittings belonging to or used in the operation of the

property and owned by you.

Legal description, including lot and block number: _____

_____

_____

_____

_____

Price and Deposit: At the price of (in words) _____

dollars, $_____ payable as follows:

$_____ cash, deposited with _____,

to be held until this offer is accepted, at which time it shall become part of

the purchase price, or returned if not accepted.

Balance: Balance of $_____ cash, on or before _____

on passing of deed.

Special Terms: (Cross out those that do not apply.)

1. Seller financing (details) _____

2. Subject to obtaining financing at _____ percent over _____ years

3. Subject to sale of purchaser's present home

4. Subject to purchaser's approval of appraisal

5. Subject to purchaser's approval of professional physical inspection

---

Sample Offer to Purchase (continued)

6. Subject to purchaser's attorney's approval

7. Other special terms: _____

_____

Searches, Taxes, Restrictions, Etc.: You are to deliver to me or my attorney, at least five (5) days before closing, a forty-year abstract of title and ten-year search of tax receipts showing the property free and clear of all liens and encumbrances, except as herein set forth, and except building and use restrictions, pole and wire easements of record, and subject to zoning ordinance and to any taxes for local improvements not now completed, or a current title binder from a recognized title company.

Closing and Deed: Transfer to be completed at the office of _____

_____, (address) _____,

on or before _____, or as soon thereafter as the abstracts can be brought to date. At that time you are to convey to me by

_____deed, good title to the property free of all liens and encumbrances, except as above set forth, subject to rights of tenants, if any.

Adjustments: Interest, insurance premiums, rents, and taxes shall be prorated and adjusted as of _____ , 19_____. _____

_____

_____

City, State and County Taxes shall be adjusted and apportioned on a calendar year beginning January 1 and ending December 31. School Taxes outside the city shall be adjusted and apportioned for the fiscal year beginning July 1 and ending the following June 30, and Village Taxes shall be adjusted and apportioned for the fiscal year beginning June 1 and ending the last day of May following or as otherwise provided by law.

Possession, Mortgage Expenses, Assignment, Risk of Loss: Possession of premises shall be delivered on or before _____, 19_____, on

Sample Offer to Purchase (continued)

passing of deed _____.

Upon any purchase money mortgage given, I (we) agree to pay the usual mortgage tax and recording fee and revenue stamps on bond where required.

This offer may be assigned to an individual or corporation for the purpose of holding title thereto. However, I (we) shall remain responsible for the faithful performance of the contract.

The risk of loss or damage to the property by fire or other causes until the delivery of the deed is assumed by you.

Broker, Persons Bound: I (we) represent that _____ is the broker in this transaction and that no other real estate broker or agent has helped to bring about this sale.

This offer, when accepted, shall be a binding contract. It shall bind the parties hereto and their respective executors, administrators, distributees, successors and assigns.

Dated _____, 19_____ (signed) _____

Witness _____ (signed) _____

Acceptance: The undersigned hereby accepts this offer, agrees to sell on the terms and conditions set forth, and agrees to pay _____, the authorized agent, _____ commission.

The deposit made or as much as covers the commission may be applied to payment of the commission.

Dated _____, 19_____ (signed) _____

Witness _____ (signed) _____

Salesmen are not permitted to change the regular rates of commission.

[*Note:* This is a generic form that may need to be modified, depending on your state laws.]

Sample Commission Agreement
(for single transaction only)

In consideration of the presentation of the Purchase Agreement and Deposit Receipt dated _____, relating to the real property commonly known as _____, the undersigned Owner of said property agrees to pay to

_____

_____,

as compensation for services rendered, a fee of _____ percent of the selling price.

If suit is brought to collect the compensation or if Broker successfully defends any action brought against Broker by Owner relating to this agreement, Owner agrees to pay all costs incurred by Broker in connection with such action, including a reasonable attorney's fee.

The undersigned Owner warrants that he/she is the owner of record of the property and has the authority to execute this agreement.

Signed _____ (Seller)

Printed _____ (Seller)

Address _____

Phone _____

Dated: _____

[*Note:* The amount or rate of real estate commissions is not fixed by law. It is set by each Broker individually, and may be negotiable between Seller and Broker.]

[Adapted from Professional Publishing Corp. Form 101-L. Used with permission.]

Chapter **22**

Can a Real Estate Attorney Make the Sale Easier?

In a word, yes. But make sure you hire the right person.

After deciding to sell your home, but *before* signing an agreement with a broker and *before* running any ads, if you are doing the sale yourself, find yourself a good real estate attorney. Every seller needs a lawyer to go over all the papers involved—the listing agreement with a broker, any deposits, binders, offers to purchase, all of which are part of the legal documentation.

Friends whom you trust (or lawyers who handle your other legal matters) usually can recommend real estate attorneys. A specialist in real estate, not an all-purpose attorney, is crucial, because property laws can be intricate.

Besides, when you put your home on the market, you are putting your most valuable asset on the line. The last thing you want to happen is to let anybody tie it up in legal red tape.

The usual things an attorney picks up, (which even the sharpest lay person might miss) are items like forged signatures, or an element in the chain of title that would cause you not to deliver good title. The latter could saddle you with a suit at closing.

So do not wait until someone presents you with a listing agreement or someone wants to make an offer to purchase. Line up the attorney for your team right now.

A seller's attorney should be ready to handle title research, a title insurance policy, the approval of a listing agreement, as well as the drafting and approval of an offer to purchase. A good attorney could also help expedite financing, should that be necessary.

Interview more than one person. Comparison-shop, just as you would for any other service.

My first question always is, "How much will you charge me to close this transaction?"

My second question: "Do you charge an additional fee for title insurance?" (Some attorneys receive a commission from title insurance companies.)

My third question: "Will you give me a letter confirming the price you have quoted with a list of items you will handle up to and including the closing?"

A good attorney will gladly answer these questions and put the answers in writing.

GET A FLAT FEE, NOT HOURLY RATES

Lawyers prefer to charge by the hour. I prefer to pay *flat fees only,* because it saves both time and money.

The normal fee for a closing, from start to finish, for a house with no complicated problems, runs from $500 to $1,000, depending on the price of the house. Some lawyers might want a percentage of the selling price, rather than a fee. This is ludicrous! If it takes the same amount of work to close on a $200,000 house as on a $100,000 house, why should your pocket be picked for extra dollars?

Ask for flat fees beginning with the listing agreement, the offer to purchase and all the way through the closing. Then, have the attorney write you a letter confirming all the prices that were quoted, including the title insurance price (more about this in a moment).

Is the attorney unwilling to put the fees in writing? End the conversation and hunt up another lawyer.

LAWYERS AND TITLE COMPANIES

Once a fee is agreed on, you need to know if your lawyer writes title insurance, which guarantees that you own the property. If so, what company does he or she use, and what are the fees? Will the insurance company give you a discount if you buy title insurance through that attorney? Lawyers do get commissions and/or fees from title insurance companies.

The typical fee for title insurance runs from ½ to 1 percent of the purchase price.

Typically an attorney will receive a commission for writing the title policy. Out of a $1,000 policy fee, some attorneys have received as much as 40 percent. I also know attorneys who will reduce their legal fees to the client, since a commission is being paid to them from the title insurance company.

There is nothing wrong with title insurance companies offering attorney commissions. But why not negotiate a lower legal fee? In many states, the attorney cannot share the commission with you, so you are in a better position to ask for a reduced fee. (For details on what title insurance is, and why you need it, see the next chapter.)

HAVE YOUR ATTORNEY WRITE JUMP-OUT CLAUSES

An attorney provides a service and acts as a *safety valve*. Have your attorney's card with you when you are asked to sign documents, starting with the broker's listing agreement. That way, you either call on the spot or hand the card to the broker and have the broker submit the documents for your attorney's review before you sign.

"Review" sounds mundane, and it should be a simple matter. Your attorney looks at what kind of performance the broker promises, what the commission is, and whether there is a *cancellation clause*, or *jump-out clause*, in case the broker does not perform up to your expectations.

Suppose the broker does not advertise your house, or is slow to bring prospective buyers to see it. Your attorney can write a jump-out clause into the listing agreement.

In simple English, here is how it might read: "This contract is cancellable by either party with written notice to Charles Broker at 175 Enhancement Avenue, Newark, NJ. It is further understood that the broker will have 7 days to present to the seller a list of clients to whom the home has been presented. If those clients buy within the next 30 days, the broker's selling commission will be payable to the former listing broker."

PROTECTION AGAINST FRAUD

A lawyer's most important role in the selling of your house might be keeping you out of hot water somewhere en route to the closing.

Remember the story I told about the Alaska gold miner who conned a number of Seattle people and took their houses off the market for years? Whether you are selling with or without a broker, you can see how a lawyer could have saved some folks from that swindle.

The sellers signed Golden Boy's offer to purchase contract *without noticing the fine print* that allowed him to claim their existing mortgages or option their homes for 24 months.

An attorney would *never* have allowed the seller to sign the agreement, unless the seller understood the fine print.

There are a handful of attorneys in this country whose tremendous knowledge qualifies them as good real estate negotiators. Unless you have this kind of attorney—chances are you do not—let your attorney deal with the legal questions of the documents you are about to sign, not the business questions.

Do let your attorney handle communications with your buyer's attorney. You should not be involved in direct talks with someone else's lawyer. Your own lawyer can give you the instructions you need. In general, attorneys kill more deals than they save. So keep your attorney's focus where it belongs—on the legal aspects of the deal.

HOW ELSE CAN A LAWYER HELP A SELLER?

For starters, lawyers are good at putting pressure on a bank to expedite your loan.

Untangling the complications caused by divorce and the subsequent sale of jointly owned property calls for a lawyer too.

Under normal conditions on a $100,000 house, with the buyer putting $20,000 as a down payment, a bank would give the buyer an $80,000 mortgage. The bank would then turn over the cash to the seller.

With a divorce situation, the divorcing husband and wife each would walk away with $40,000 in cash. But what if the two of them disagree? Perhaps the house was his, or hers, before the marriage. Perhaps he, or she, did major remodeling after the breakup. These issues crop up time and time again.

Who is entitled to what, and for how much? When these are the questions, the sale can be held up until a lawyer steps in to mediate.

LET A LAWYER TACKLE AN ASSESSMENT CHALLENGE

A sudden increase in property taxes drives many people, especially those about to sell their homes, to the tax collector's office, demanding an explanation. You are safer turning the matter over to a lawyer.

An Anchorage woman called my show with a typical story: "I was getting ready to sell my house when I received a notification from my tax collector. It doubled the assessment value of my home!"

I responded by asking her, "Do you understand what tax assessors do and how they arrive at the assessment value?"

In most states the assessor reevaluates your home no less than once every two years. The assessment tax is based on what the market value of your home is—a price someone will pay at any given time, and the price a person will sell for at any given time.

After an assessor decides your home is worth more than it was the last time around, you receive a new assessment, or reassessment. This is the assessor's opinion. In some markets, it is linked to the economy of that area, and your assessment may go down if the economy has gone down.

You have a right to challenge an assessment, but the burden of proof is on you.

At the assessor's office, there are forms you can fill out to file an objection. The laws and procedure vary from state to state. Usually, you need to appear before a review board, armed with documentation, such as appraisals and reports of sales in your area. Should your request for a lower assessment be denied, there are further remedies in court.

However, if the assessment *raises* your tax bill more than 25 percent, I recommend that you do *not* handle the dispute yourself. Let an expert fight for you.

At the courthouse, the clerk can show you other cases currently pending. Make a list of lawyers whose specialty is representing owners in these disputes. Lawyers in this field take cases on a percentage basis, which is good for you because a lawyer will work harder for a percentage. The percentage is a portion of the amount of tax that the lawyer saves you in a given year. If there are many cases in your community, the lawyers clearly feel the assessor has made an error.

If you plan to stay in your home for several years, a higher assessment can be quite a load. The assessment raises your taxes every year. So if your taxes went up $250 this year, you will pay $2,500 or more in the next 10 years. In a hot real estate market, you can also count on having that assessment raised as often as every year or at least every two years.

DO YOU PAY AN ATTORNEY IF A SALE FALLS THROUGH?

How do you avoid attorney fees when a deal falls through? It would be naive to expect your attorney to suggest anything in this area.

However, as a seller, you might build into a binder or contract a clause that makes the *buyer liable* for some of your legal bills.

One man called my show to complain that he had arranged to sell his condo to an apparently enthusiastic local resident. A binder contract and check had been mailed by this caller's lawyer. However, the buyer lost his enthusiasm and the deal collapsed.

The caller was left holding a $300 bill from his lawyer, but no sale.

An attorney is entitled to a fee for his or her time. But why put gas in someone else's car? The next time, I told this gentleman, do not accept an offer unless the buyer, *in the very first agreement,* signs a liquidated-damages clause that reimburses his legal fees. These legal fees would be deducted from the earnest money by your lawyer, who should be holding that money in his trust account.

If you think this kind of situation could crop up in your sale, discuss a liquidated-damages clause covering legal fees with your attorney.

Sample Letter
(How an attorney might outline terms with a seller)

Dear Mr. and/or Ms. Seller:

Thank you for the courtesy extended to me during our discussion in my offices concerning the representation of you as the seller of your home at 123 Pine Street, Virginia Beach, VA.

My fee for handling all the items necessary for the sale of your house will be $1,500. This includes the following:

Title Research
Title Insurance Policy
Approval of Listing Agreement
Drafting and approving Offer to Purchase
Assisting with and expediting financing
Attending the closing

If you have any further questions concerning this, please feel free to contact me.

Yours truly,

Legal Eagle, Esq.

Chapter 23

Is Your House on Somebody Else's Lot? What You Need to Know About Title Insurance

Do you really own your own home? Or do you face the possibility of finding a bulldozer instead of a newspaper on your doorstep one day?

You probably have title insurance. But it would be a shock if, on the eve of a sale, someone knocked on your door and said he had the right to build a road through the living room because he has a claim on your property. This chapter will, I hope, convince you of the importance of a title policy.

Title insurance does *not* insure your home, condo or co-op; home insurance does. A title policy insures the ground on which a house stands, or the ground under the building where an apartment is located.

What does it do? Title insurance protects you against a missing link in the chain of title, which could allow someone to knock on your door and say, "My great-grandfather's signature was forged on a deed fifty years ago. Therefore I have an interest in your property."

Believe me, without title insurance, such things can happen. With title insurance, if it happens, you are paid the amount for which you have insured your title.

Title insurance is the *least costly* insurance you will ever buy. If you do not intend to use title insurance, you should not be in the real estate market.

The nice thing about title insurance is that, as is not the case with health, home, auto or life insurance, you pay only once. The premium is commonly a percentage of the total amount of the insurance.

For example, if your title is being insured for $175,000, you will pay less than someone who insures a $500,000 property. It does not hurt to compare two or three companies for title insurance, just as you would when shopping for home insurance.

Once you have your title policy, put it in an envelope with a copy of your deed and all your closing documents, mark the envelope "House Papers" and keep it in your safe-deposit box. When you are ready to sell, you can pull out the title insurance and advise your prospective purchaser of the name of the insurer. The company that wrote your policy usually will give a better price to your buyer, since the research has already been done.

TITLE BINDERS

As a buyer, I always ask for a title insurance policy binder. The binder answers the following:

1. Are the taxes paid and up to date?

2. Have there been any claims against the property, such as tax liens, lawsuits against the individuals or anything else that would prevent me from obtaining "clear title" to the property?

But a seller should act first.

My radio friend Sam in Winter Haven, Florida, for example, was thrown into a panic just before a closing because of a title problem. His buyer's attorney said that the title binder, which had been ordered just a week before, stated that Sam owed Sears $4,200 on appliance purchases and that Sears had filed a lien against his property.

Sam explained to the buyer that there was a dispute on some defective appliances. The bill was finally paid and Sears advised him over the phone that it had filed a "satisfaction of lien." The red tape took three weeks for Sam to get Sears to give him this "satisfaction." When he filed it in the courthouse, it removed the cloud from his title.

If Sam had ordered a title binder himself, he could have sidestepped this embarrassing glitch in his sale.

As a seller, order a binder (usually it is free or costs under $250) to see if anything has happened to your title since you bought your home. If there are some clouds on your title, it is better to know about them and clear them up now, rather than hold up your closing.

ENDORSEMENTS, EXCEPTIONS AND CLOUDS

All the items on a title policy that are listed under "Exceptions" are known as "clouds" on the title. To avoid a thunderstorm in your life, it is essential to deal with such matters in the policy.

Go for maximum protection when buying title insurance by having your lawyer request from the title company what are known as specific endorsements. In some cases, an endorsement negates a restriction on the coverage mentioned elsewhere in the policy. Ask your attorney to get an endorsement that invalidates what are known as "Schedule B exceptions," which involve liens on a property and similar problems.

Another popular endorsement is known as the "inflation endorsement." It increases your protection as the value of your property goes up and is usually tied to some government cost-of-living index. Ask for it.

From a seller's point of view, it is an excellent idea to show your prospective purchaser that there is title insurance on your condo, co-op or home. You always order an updated title binder, showing the potential buyer that you have a clear title, without any clouds.

Naturally, you should do business with a reputable title insurance firm. Many have been in business for close to 100 years.

The top companies nationally are Lawyers Title Insurance Company of Virginia, American Title of Florida and Chicago Title Company. Major companies such as Sears and Safco have their own title companies. Stay away from title insurance companies that are local or are not tied into a national, Fortune 500 company.

WATCH OUT FOR LAWYERS' "ABSTRACTS" LETTERS

Let your attorney know you are shopping, since he or she probably can come up with a discount. As I mentioned previously, real estate lawyers often write policies for title insurance companies, and can pass some savings on to you in the form of a discount on their fee for closing the sale.

In some states attorneys will write you a letter stating they have examined your abstract. Such a letter would tell you, "Your title is good. Go ahead and close the deal."

Warning! This is an *archaic and dangerous way* to close a real estate transaction.

What the attorney is doing is examining the history (that is what the abstract is), going as far back as he or she can go—sometimes back to the land grant from the king before the Revolution. If all the papers in that history are in order legally, the attorney writes the letter.

But what if the attorney dies, or is put in jail for fraud? The only thing you have to guarantee your title to the property is a worthless piece of paper.

A classic case showing the value of title insurance happened in a small town outside Dallas. A woman bought a piece of property without buying title insurance to go with it. Six months later, someone did, in fact, show up at her door—with a bulldozer.

A road builder wanted to tear her house down in order to put a road through. If she had purchased title insurance, the title company would have paid for her property in full. But since she had none, what she got instead was a lot of national publicity but no money—and she lost her house.

She sat on her front porch with a loaded double-barreled shotgun in her lap. She swore to all who came near her house that she would "blow them away." The woman was arrested and taken to jail. Now there is a road where her house used to be.

INSURANCE AGAINST DIVORCE BATTLES

Time and time again, homeowners receive letters from divorced spouses who claim their ex sold the property without the necessary spouse's signature on the deed. They insist they still have a right to the property. In most cases, the title insurance company settles with the claimant, if the claim is legitimate. The title insurance company also defends you if you are sued over the title for this or other reasons.

A final word in title insurance. In the New York metropolitan area, there is a rather sleazy tradition of title company representatives who demand cash tips after closings. The buyer pays the tip, which can run anywhere from $5 to $60. I have never heard of title tipping anywhere else.

Chapter 24

Negotiating—Key Strategies That Win You a Better Deal

My philosophy on negotiating is that each no is one step closer to a yes.

Selling a piece of property is *not* like selling a pair of socks at K-Mart or cereal at the grocery. Prices, in real estate, are *never* fixed; they are negotiable. Most Americans are not comfortable negotiating. We do not go to the marketplace and bargain on a daily basis.

In real estate, you are expected to negotiate. If, in a normal real estate market, you pay the asking down payment and the asking price, the owner and the broker will think something is wrong.

Once that idea sinks in, many of the negative feelings associated with bargaining start to dissolve. Besides, bargaining, stripped of its bad connotations, is really *talking with one another,* an activity in which we all have plenty of experience.

What makes real estate negotiations doubly difficult for some of us is the fact that the purchase of a home is laced with deep emotions. We tend to view a home as an extension of ourselves, a place to spend the majority of our lives, as opposed to the purchase of a commodity that we will use for a period of time.

As a seller, you need to play on those emotions. (As a buyer, of course, you need to put those emotions aside. For insight into how a buyer views negotiations, see chapter 6.)

If you understand what the market value of your home is, and your price is close to the value of homes in your geographic area, negotiating can add as much as *25 to 30 percent* to the price the buyer is offering to you.

YOU ARE CAPTAIN OF THE TEAM

In general, leave the business negotiations to the brokers and the legal issues to the attorneys. But be prepared to join the bargaining table.

Your broker makes the initial contacts for you, in typical sales. However, once the deal nears completion (or earlier, if your broker and buyer have a personality conflict), make an effort to sit down and talk with your buyer, face to face. At that stage, you can display a winning attitude (do not confuse that with being intimidating) to convince the buyer that your home is the best for him.

Some people use brokers to avoid face-to-face negotiations. However, the broker does not have the authority to negotiate for you, unless you specifically contract for that service. The broker's authority is to bring the offer to you, and to bring your counteroffer back to the buyer. Keep in mind that *you* are the quarterback calling the plays. The broker is basically a messenger.

One rule is extremely important, no matter how the negotiations proceed: *never tell your real estate agent what your absolute bottom dollar is on selling.*

Your broker works on commission. If you let the bottom-line cat out of the bag, the broker's next move may be to call the potential buyer, whispering, "Offer Mrs. Jones $75,000 for her $100,000 house, and I know she will take the deal."

The bottom-line price is for your eyes only. With the techniques you learn in this book, you will in most cases get a higher price.

Never use your attorney to negotiate the dollar aspects of the deal. The only time you ask your attorney to negotiate is when the buyer's attorney has a legal point to be discussed.

For example, you do not need to be involved if there is a question on what kind of title insurance to get, or what kind of a deed to draw for the transferral of the property.

Never talk to the prospective buyer's attorney. Always have that attorney talk to yours. In most jurisdictions it is unethical for a buyer's attorney even to ask to talk to you.

THE ART OF LISTENING

"Can we talk?"

Joan Rivers understands my theory: the prime ingredient in your negotiating technique is communication. The second most important item is learning how to listen.

At the stage that a deal is in the making, your task is to *keep those lines of communication open.* How? First, by asking questions.

"What did you have on your mind?"

"What would be the most perfect situation that I could set forth for the purchase of my home?"

"How do you feel about this part of the deal?"

"What are you looking for?"

"How would you like me to present this to you?"

If you *ask those kinds of questions,* and most important, if you *listen carefully,* your potential buyer will tell you directly or indirectly what he or she wants.

THE NEGOTIATION MENU

The main negotiable elements in a real estate deal are

- purchase price
- down payment
- date of possession
- seller financing
- "personal property"

The last is the term for other items that are not permanently "affixed" (attached) to the house, such as drapes and furniture. It is best to leave off as many such items as possible. Do you have a washer and dryer, refrigerator, stove, fancy fixtures? Put a price for each in your mind, or on an index card to keep in your pocket. When the time comes, use those items as negotiating points.

For example, when you first decide to sell, you might think of your price as $100,000, everything included.

Think again. Offer your house without personal property. Then, when someone negotiates the price down to $95,000, you can say, "For an extra $5,000 you can have my drapes and my special window treatments, light fixtures and some other items."

OFFERS AND COUNTEROFFERS

When you put your house on the market, the dollar figure you place on it is not the *sales* price. It is the *asking* price.

Who gets the asking price? A few lucky souls—perhaps 2 percent of all sellers. And those are people in areas where the demand far exceeds the supply.

You always raise the asking price 15 to 20 percent above the market. Then, during negotiations, you can earn a lot of money, provided you have done research on what prices houses like yours are commanding.

Let us say that you are asking $150,000 for your home, in a reasonably healthy market. Your bottom-line figure is $130,000, a fact you have *not* mentioned to your broker. Mr. and Mrs. Buyer make an offer through the broker, of $100,000.

The broker is obligated by law to relay all offers, no matter how low, to the seller.

Once you are presented with an offer, insist that it be in writing, not verbal. When a buyer puts the offer in writing, you know you have a serious prospective purchaser. I know that in places such as metropolitan New York, verbal offers are the rule, rather than the exception. I do *not* approve.

The offer should be accompanied by a *good-faith,* or *binder, check.* The check can be for anywhere from $500 to $5,000, depending on the price of the house. The norm is 1 percent of the purchase price.

What happens next? Most brokers like to bring the offer to you, the seller, in writing, have you write the counteroffer in longhand on the contract, and have you initial it. Then they bring it back to the potential buyer.

This is not a good technique. It creates confusion.

Instead, insist that your broker write a *new* contract with new terms that you have submitted. Then have the broker submit it to the buyer, who either accepts your deal or comes back with another counteroffer.

In our imaginary case, you counter with an offer of $140,000, plus your $10,000 worth of custom drapes, cornices and carpets.

CREATIVE BIDDING

Now you are at a critical stage. You have received an initial offer. You have replied with a counteroffer. The buyer might accept it, or come back with yet another offer. However many times you go back and forth, your goal is to get as close to your asking price as you can.

You need to be creative to bring the bidding up. In addition, you need to know what your buyer's needs are.

Perhaps the buyer is in a time squeeze and needs to get into the house in 30 days. You are *not* in a hurry, so you use the time as a negotiating point. You counter with an offer of $140,000 . . . and the buyer can move in right away.

Perhaps this same "buyer in a hurry" would be willing to pay your rent on a place you will have to move to temporarily, or perhaps he or she will pay more money up front. After all, if you must wait longer for a new buyer, you could end up losing money because of the time wasted waiting for that next prospect. Time is money in real estate, as in anything else.

You may have researched your community enough to know that three houses similar to yours have sold for $134,000, $138,000 and $151,000 in recent weeks. Advise your broker to *show* the potential buyer the sales records that indicate your house really is being sold for the same price as, or at a lower price than, houses of like value.

In a normal three-bedroom, two-bath house in the United States today, custom draperies can cost anywhere from $3,500 to $6,000. In most cases, people do not want to take draperies with them. You can add $2,000 to $3,000 to the price you get, if the buyer likes your draperies.

Some people's trash is other people's treasure. Have you hated the armoire in the guest room since the day you bought it on impulse at an auction? Maybe your buyer adores it. Moving anything from one place to another costs a lot. What's more, you will get 60 to 80 percent *less* on anything you sell at a garage sale or to an auction house than if you sell the items in place and as part of the home package.

"HOT" PROSPECTS, "COLD" BUYERS

Listen to the buyer. At some point, you will hear a phrase that signals that your buyer is ready to *stand firm.*

The phrase is: "We can't afford any more than that." Now you know that the buyer has put pride aside and is at his limit.

At that point, instead of saying, "Well, if you can't afford my house, you'd better buy one for less money," thus insulting the buyer even further, the best thing to say is, "Let's see if we can work out a deal that will make this house affordable for you."

Then it is time to talk about down payments, seller financing, notes and additional inducements.

Angela, a radio friend, called from Seattle with a problem along these lines. "I have a buyer for my home. The price of the house is $65,000. There is a $50,000 mortgage on the house and the buyer has $10,000 to give me toward the down payment, leaving him $5,000 short. The buyer finally said he could not afford the house," she said. "What do I do next?"

After determining that Angela did not need the full $15,000 right away, I suggested that she offer to accept the $10,000 toward the down payment. Then, after the buyer received financing, she could have him *sign a note for the balance of $5,000,* either payable on a monthly basis or due within 3 to 5 years, with interest rates charged at the current level.

Angela proposed this deal. The buyer was so grateful to her for letting him move into the house for $10,000 down that he agreed to pay her an extra $5,000 over a 10-year period. It turned out he had a trust-fund inheritance coming to him in 7 years.

On another deal, however, you may hear key phrases that indicate your prospect has become a *cold buyer.*

The potential buyer may say, "Now that we have thought this over, this house will not work for us. We don't like it because it does not have enough room. We don't like the neighborhood. We don't like the lay-out," and so on.

Clearly, this buyer no longer has an emotional feeling for your house. Say thank you and good-bye.

THE ETIQUETTE OF NEGOTIATIONS

In the course of negotiating a sale, you may want to drive a point home with no room for misunderstanding. I suggest the following words: "Am I correct in assuming that what you mean is . . . ?"

For example, let us say you are asking $100,000 for your house. Your potential buyer offers only $90,000. You ask him to give you a $20,000 down payment, and the buyer says he will give you twice that—$40,000 —with $90,000 remaining as the total offer.

You want to drive home the idea that you are *not* arguing about the down payment but are discussing the house price. You then say: "Am I correct in assuming that you are willing to give me $20,000 more cash for the down payment, but $10,000 less overall for my house?"

At that point, it would be appropriate to talk about possibly getting less of a down payment—for example, $30,000—and $5,000 more for the total price of the house.

In this particular case, if you are taking back a second mortgage in order for the person to buy the house, you are in an excellent negotiating position. For example, if your mortgage on the house was $50,000, and you got a $40,000 down payment, the second mortgage due to you would be $10,000.

You are zeroing in on what your prospective buyer is bothered with in this case—that second $10,000 mortgage.

Since the buyer is sensitive about a second mortgage and has cash on hand, tell him you will meet him halfway. You could simply say, "If you give me an additional $5,000 cash, the house is yours."

By clarifying a negotiating point, you make sure your prospective purchaser knows that *you* know where he is coming from.

It is both good manners and good business to end your negotiating sessions or telephone conversations with pleasant clichés—phrases such as these:

"Thank you for calling."

"Thank you for your offer" (even if it was ridiculous).

"I'm going to discuss this with my spouse."

"I'm going to give this serious consideration."

"I hope we can talk again very soon."

"Please call me if there are further questions."

"Here are all the telephone numbers where you can reach me. . . ."

I cannot emphasize enough how valuable it is to have *face-to-face talks*. Nevertheless, there are times when you have to do business long-distance.

In talking on the phone, take extra care to avoid misconceptions and misunderstandings. Have in front of you your home-selling file or a loose-leaf notebook, with definite ideas of your parameters. These include time of possession, financing, lowest price and lowest down payment you will accept. Take careful notes.

Afterward, confirm your conversation in writing, even if the person lives just across town.

If you are selling without a broker, pay particular attention to the genuine prospect on the other end of the telephone line. When the caller makes an offer over the phone that is within your comfort zone, and the person is in the same town, meet with that person face to face *as soon as possible,* even if it is inconvenient for you. Reduce the offer to writing through the simple use of a binder.

Common telephone courtesy tells you not to call people at inconvenient times or at all hours of the day or night. Always ask if it is all right to call people at work, or what the best time is for them to receive calls.

If a person is in another city, and it is urgent to get the deal completed, use Western Union telegrams to confirm the offer. Or you can have the buyer's broker or lawyer send you a Telefax or a Federal Express, Purolator or postal service Express Mail overnight envelope. (Do *not* rely on regular mail.)

Be quick and sincere about admitting mistakes. One of my listeners called because he was having insomnia over an error most of us commit sooner or later. It is normal, and it is called greed.

He had advertised his co-op in Manhattan for $170,000. After the first ad ran, he received an offer for $16,000 below that. Two weeks went by. He placed another ad offering the co-op in the "high $100,000s" and told callers his price was $190,000. The first people called back with a new offer—$171,000. The seller turned them down, insisting on a few thousand more. They said, "Forget the whole thing."

After a few more weeks passed, he regretted that move. But how could he accept the $171,000 offer without looking like a fool?

"Invite the first people back to the scene of the crime for a cup of coffee," I urged. "Once they are there, admit that you made a mistake. Tell them that if they still want this apartment, you will honor their offer before you put the ad back in the paper." He did. They bought the apartment. Happy endings are worth a few words of apology.

STRATEGIES FOR NEGOTIATING IN A SOFT MARKET

How long the bargaining continues depends on the market. In a normal market, the bargaining can last anywhere from a week to three weeks.

A soft market presents a challenge. The *buyer has more time* for bargaining. You, of course, want to shorten the time because there are too many other houses for sale.

But you also must be flexible. It does not make sense to kill a deal because of a delay in the closing. If a buyer needs 90 days rather than 30 to close, check to see how fast houses have been selling. Why should it make a difference to wait an extra 60 days, when you have an actual purchaser in an area where houses are languishing, unsold, for 6 to 9 months?

There are two creative negotiating techniques that will sell your house even *in the worst market* imaginable.

Number 1 is the *lease-with-option-to-purchase offer.*

If you must unload a residence in a bad market, and you do not have the time or the inclination to lease it until the market bounces back, propose a lease with option to purchase to prospects. (You will find complete details in chapter 8 on this alternative.) It is one of the best "win-win" situations that all too few people employ.

Place an ad in the paper seeking a young couple with great potential who cannot afford a down payment. You lease your house to them for a rental fee slightly higher than normal, over a 36-month (3-year) period. For instance, if your home is in a $300-a-month rental district, charge them an extra $100. The extra $100 over 3 years equals $3,600. That money goes toward the down payment.

If the down payment is $10,000, that means the young couple owes only $6,400 at the end of the 3 years to make your house their own. Meanwhile, you have gotten the house off the market, and you have put people into it who will take much better care of it than normal tenants. They start out with the pride of ownership.

Number 2 is *equity participation,* or *shared appreciation,* as it is sometimes called. (There are complete details in chapter 7 on buyer financing.)

In this scenario, you place a classified ad stating, "House for Sale. I will make your down payment, if you pick up the monthly payments."

In essence, your buyers take over the mortgage. They sign a note over to you for the down payment. No cash comes out of your pocket.

When the house is sold, in 3 to 5 years, you split the profits with your equity participation "partners." This gives *you* real gains on the sale. Once again, the people caring for your residence have pride of ownership.

Incidentally, if you have taken the trouble to make sure your "partners" have a good credit standing, you can use the note they signed at a bank as security on a loan from another bank, for a home you want to buy, or for cash you need to start a business.

Or you can use the note as an actual down payment on a house *you* are buying elsewhere. In effect, you have the money you need in the form of a negotiable instrument, known as a "promissory note."

In using either of these "soft-market" techniques, you do *not* have to lower the price of your house. Your flexibility gives others a chance to own a residence—a chance they would not otherwise have found. They are not in a position to bargain on your asking price.

Even in the worst markets in the nation, people are looking for homes to buy. In San Antonio not too long ago, I had at least four calls, most of them from young people, asking, "How can I take advantage of this soft market? I have no money, but I have a good job and a good future."

A lease with option to purchase or a shared-equity arrangement is perfect for those youngsters. Everybody benefits.

MAKING THE MOST OF A HOT MARKET

"Wait a minute!" hundreds of Bostonians cry. "We have just the *opposite* kind of market here. There are twenty buyers for every house that goes on sale!"

Congratulations. When you are in a hot market, you are in the driver's seat. The pressure is on the buyer to get *you* to accept an offer as soon as possible, because others are lining up to offer you a better deal.

Let us imagine that thanks to a job transfer you must move out of the hottest real estate market in the country, and you do not want to keep your house.

You put your house on the market and presto! Within hours, the broker brings you four qualified buyers, checkbooks in hand. Three are ready to buy at the asking price.

What you have on your hands is a certifiable "bidding war." If you have a broker, ask the broker to bring you the highest bid within 24 to 48 hours. Believe me, the broker is as excited as you are. The more money paid for the property, the bigger the commission the broker makes.

Analyze the other parts of the deal. Sales price is important, but it is not everything. Make sure of the following elements:

- All the bids must include the amount of the down payment.
- The closing date should be the one most convenient for *you.*
- Most important, the bidders must be "qualified" in advance by the broker. ("Qualifying" is the real estate term for determining that the buyer has the income and financing to purchase your house without any difficulties.)

Finally, in a bidding situation, the broker should put you in a position to *accept a good lower bid* that might not have every term that you want, just in case your first choice among the buyers moves out of the picture.

One way to arrange this "fall-back" position is to give the second or third bidder a right of first refusal within the time frame of the closing period. Thus, if you have a closing set for 30 days, you would want to give the second bidder a chance to buy within those 30 days should your first bidder drop out.

One last note. *Never close the door on negotiations,* even when you feel you have reached an impasse. As long as your prospect will accept a telephone call or an invitation to sit down for lunch, negotiations can continue.

Only communication ends; negotiation does not.

Chapter 25

A Seller's Guide to Smart Financing
. . . and Refinancing

If a teller's window in your neighborhood bank had a sign: "Put your money here and earn 12 percent," and next to it was a window marked: "Money Market Funds, 6 percent," to which window would you take your money? I am going to tell you how to locate that 12-percent window when you sell your house.

In the course of selling a house, not only can you earn additional money. You can also make it easier for your buyer to finance the purchase. Even if you decide to keep your house, you can lower your monthly payments, as well as pick up tax-free cash, by refinancing your mortgage, an opportunity that arises when interest rates drop.

Which would you rather have? A big hunk of taxable cash right away? Or a safe investment that will generate income for you year after year, and let you sleep at night too?

If your answer is "a safe, income-producing investment," you should become the 12-percent banker by financing the sale of your home.

The phrase "seller financing" is misunderstood by all too many homeowners. They think it is a last resort for selling one's house in a soft market.

'Taint so! In fact, the opposite is true. Especially in light of tax reform, with many once-lucrative investment opportunities having fallen by the wayside, *seller financing is one of the most secure financial ventures around.*

Yes, there are risks involved. But they are outweighed by the advantages. The most important advantage is that you invest in something with which you are totally familiar—your own home.

BECOMING A "BANKER"

Let me underline the fact that you do *not* have to be a desperate seller to enter into seller financing. Rather, it is a viable strategy for those who prefer to "carry their own paper," ("Paper" means accepting notes and mortgages signed by your buyer that are fully secured by the house. The house becomes the collateral for the loan you have granted to the seller —a loan that takes no cash out of your pocket.)

By financing the sale of your own home, you, in effect, become a "banker." You have a chance to make the equity in your home bring you a monthly payment with interest.

In addition, you postpone the tax bite on the sale of your house and you can earn more interest than you would from such "safe" investments as certificates of deposit, money market funds or treasury bills.

For example, what if you bought a house some years ago for $50,000? You are selling it now for $100,000. Your current mortgage is $25,000, at 8 percent.

You can sell this house to a qualified buyer for $100,000 at *12-percent interest,* creating an annuity for yourself and sparing your buyer the inconvenience and expenses associated with bank mortgages.

Have I captured your attention yet?

Good. Let us examine in more detail what it takes to be a part-time banker.

The reason you can make money is that interest rates on seller financing are *higher* than the going rate at the bank—usually 1 to 1½ points higher.

In our current example, you would finance $75,000 of the sale. (Remember, you already owe a $25,000 mortgage on that $100,000 house.) If you put that $75,000 in the open financial market, there is no way you could earn a guaranteed 12 percent on it. Better yet, you have it secured with real estate that you know is worth $100,000.

The risk is very low, because instead of trading that money for a stock that could tumble, or a bond that fluctuates, or a fund that performs poorly, you *know* the value of your home.

The worst possible scenario? Your buyer could stop making the payments, and you would have to take back the home. You end up with what you started with anyway. And you have collected some payments on it—the down payment plus the monthly payments made before the default.

BANKING MADE SIMPLE

Since few of us are bankers by trade, the idea of becoming even a part-time banker through seller financing might seem scary and complicated.

Naturally there are risks. Your buyer might default, repeatedly make late payments, or damage your house, forcing you to take legal action. But these risks can be made more tolerable through a few precautions.

One is a *deed in lieu of foreclosure,* which puts the deed to your house in the hands of your attorney. As soon as it is recorded, the person in your house becomes a trespasser once you give that person proper notice. (More about the deed in lieu of foreclosure in a moment.) As a last resort, the local sheriff's department will remove a person declared a trespasser from your house.

If your buyer turns out to be destructive, you would have to repair the home. The overwhelming majority of sellers who repossess their homes usually spend a maximum of $2,500 for a complete cosmetic paint job and replacement of worn carpet.

If you are willing to take these risks, the easiest way to sell your home is with an *agreement for deed.*

An agreement for deed is a classic win-win arrangement that benefits both you and your buyer. To begin with, it eliminates the closing costs that the buyer would normally pay, such as points to the bank, appraisal fee and all those other numbers that can add as much as 6 percent of the sales price to the closing cost.

An agreement for deed (also called a contract for deed or land contract) should be drawn by a knowledgeable attorney. You will find a sample at the end of this chapter. Your attorney's fee for the agreement should range from $300 to $500.

An agreement for deed states that you will deliver the deed upon full payment of all money agreed to be paid by the purchaser. Under this arrangement, the buyers first give you a down payment, commonly 5 percent or more. (Often, sellers will take a lower down payment than they would with a bank-financed mortgage.) Or you might accept the buyers' equity in another property as part of the down payment.

The buyers move into your house. For a set number of years, they make monthly payments to you, which you use to continue paying your mortgage on that house. You pass the property title to your buyers when either they pay you cash, because they have obtained a new mortgage, or you have received all the payments as stated in the agreement for deed.

WHOOPS! I SUDDENLY NEED CASH!

What happens if an emergency arises, or another investment of yours goes bust, and you find yourself needing cash?

There are many financial institutions—private mortgage brokers, investment groups and individuals—that advertise constantly for "paper" on real estate in *The Wall Street Journal* as well as other financial publications.

You can take your agreement for deed, which has a promissory note attached to it, to one of these institutions. You then discount your agreement anywhere from 8 to 20 percent, depending on how much interest your purchaser is paying you. Now, you convert the sale of your home into instant cash, by assigning it to a third party that gives you the cash.

Discounting is a normal practice in the financial community. If a note has a balance of, say, $100,000 due, at 12 percent, you would sell it for less than $100,000 cash (the face value), since the person paying you cash for the note is entitled to a profit.

All paper secured by real estate—which includes notes, agreements for deeds, and mortgages—is convertible into cash at a discount, depending on the yield. The yield is the interest the buyer is paying you, plus the discount you have given the person handing you the cash.

If you are structuring your seller financing with the idea that you will, or might, sell the paper to the *secondary mortgage market* (the people who buy this kind of paper), make sure you visit your friendly savings and loan association at the outset.

For a fee, usually between $150 and $300, a savings and loan officer will structure your loan for you. The savings and loan gives you the documents your attorney needs to fill out in order to make the loan salable under the procedures required by the secondary mortgage market.

A good real estate attorney will have the standard documents in his office. Do keep in mind that if you are not going to hold the paper yourself but may sell it, your loan package must meet the standards of the secondary market.

An alternative kind of seller financing—and another very easy way for you to sell a house—is on a lease with option to purchase. We have discussed this in detail in its own chapter.

The most attractive feature is that buyers can move into the house for almost no down payment, without any closing costs or points to a bank. The lease generally expires in 3 to 5 years. At that time the buyer would have to obtain financing and cash you out.

If in this case the buyer does not purchase the house, you, of course, get it back. Generally, it is worth more by the time this happens than it was 3 to 5 years earlier. And you still keep the money paid to you during the period the buyer lived in the house.

In the unlikely event that the buyer has not kept the house in good condition, the maximum amount most owners end up paying for repairs and painting is about $2,500.

An additional point: sometimes a buyer knows that at a definite point down the road he or she will get an infusion of money from a bonus, from the settlement of an estate or from some other source.

In such cases—and only these cases—you, as a seller, would enter into an agreement for the buyer to pay you what is known as a *balloon payment* at that future time, commonly in 3 to 5 years.

Charles Gregg, a Kansas widower, landed in that situation. Having lost his wife, he no longer wanted to stay in the house he had shared with her. He had bought the house for $50,000. He owed a $25,000 mortgage on it, at 8 percent. A young couple, both of whom were medical students, offered to buy it.

The house had a market value of $100,000. The buyers did not have enough income yet to qualify for a mortgage, because they were still in school. However, they made an arrangement to receive a lump sum of money from their families and other sources upon graduation in 3 years.

They arranged this future income in order to pay Charles the full amount in cash by giving a bank $20,000 (20 percent of the purchase price) and getting a loan for the remaining 80 percent.

At the time they wanted to buy the house, they could not finance it. But they had saved $5,000, in addition to having the guarantee of that stipend coming later.

Charles, once he heard the details of the couple's situation, was happy to accept the $5,000 as a good-faith payment. The couple agreed to pay 12-percent interest on a "wraparound mortgage" for $95,000.

(A wraparound mortgage, as was discussed earlier, is a mortgage carried by the seller. It is an alternative to an agreement for deed for $95,000. Some attorneys, and some states, prefer to use mortgages and notes rather than agreements for deed. The end results are the same.)

To simplify the arrangement further, the couple issued a deed to Charles to be held by a third party—title insurance company, trust officer at a bank, or attorney approved by both parties. This is known as a *deed in lieu of foreclosure.*

The couple now makes monthly payments of $950 to Charles. He puts that money in his bank account and then cuts a check for $214.80 to the bank that still holds his first mortgage of $25,000.

The medical students owe Charles a balloon payment—a big lump sum—at the end of their 3 years.

If, after 3 years, the young couple decides not to buy the house, Charles is not in a bad position. He has received $950 each month. His first mortgage has been covered for 3 years. He has earned 4 percent interest on the first mortgage money because it was costing him 8 while they paid 12 percent. And he has been earning 12 percent interest for 3 years on the balance of the contract, which is $70,000.

If he repossesses the house there would be no litigation, thanks to the deed in lieu of foreclosure. Instead, the deed is merely recorded back to Charles. He would have his house back. More likely than not, the house would be worth more than the original $100,000 from 3 years previously.

Seller financing does not necessarily involve balloon payments. However, if such a deal does end with a balloon, it should be linked with a deed in lieu of foreclosure, held by a trust agent. This eliminates the awful litigation that occurs when you try to repossess a property.

ESCAPING THE NIGHTMARE OF REPOSSESSION

Are you an owner interested in seller financing but still nervous about the possibility that your buyer might default, dragging you into the swamp of foreclosure?

Hundreds of people get into trouble because they do not have the right documentation. With seller financing, the very first step is to secure the deal properly.

Have your real estate attorney prepare and record your documents so that at the very least, you are second in line, right behind the bank that holds the first mortgage, if it is necessary to repossess the property.

The best route around nightmarish litigation and huge costs is to do what Charles and the medical students did: have a deed in lieu of foreclosure held by a trust officer or third party acceptable to all.

Charles Gregg's story illustrates also how older people can sell their homes in return for a good, steady income and at the same time *avoid the capital gains bite.*

Since capital gains taxes are higher now, thanks to the 1986 tax law, seller financing is more than ever a boon to those who choose it.

The other tax advantage in seller financing is the fact that if you sell your home with an agreement for deed or wraparound mortgage, you pay taxes on the money only as it is received, as opposed to paying a tax on one big lump of cash involved in a sale.

On the other hand, you can avoid these taxes through the use of the over-fifty-five one-time $125,000 exemption (see the chapter on the new tax law) or the rollover delayed tax provision (see the chapter on buying and selling at the same time) or the 1031 Tax-Free Exchange (see chapter 27 on trading your house).

SECOND MORTGAGES: A VARIATION ON SELLER FINANCING

Another variety of seller financing is the *second mortgage.* Here is one example:

Jane Allison, of Birmingham, Michigan, newly divorced, was living in a large home that she could no longer afford. After shopping around, she located a smaller residence that was more suitable for her, but she needed about $20,000 for the down payment.

Enter Tom and Susan. This couple wanted to purchase the Allison home, which carried a price tag of $150,000. The mortgage that Jane owed on it was for $100,000.

Tom and Susan could handle the monthly payments on the $100,000 mortgage, plus even more, because they owned a successful florist shop in downtown Birmingham.

In order for Jane to get the $20,000 for the down payment on her new residence, I advised her to structure the following deal: Take the $20,000 in cash from Tom and Susan as a down payment on the big house. (That left a balance of $130,000, of which $100,000 was Jane's existing first mortgage.) Have Tom and Susan sign a second mortgage for $30,000, plus a note for $30,000 with monthly payments paid to Jane, plus interest.

Record that second mortgage in the courthouse; this would give Jane her $20,000 cash, plus a secured $30,000 investment payable to her.

Meanwhile, Tom and Susan take over her $100,000 first mortgage.

If the couple defaults on either the first or second loan, Jane Allison has still gotten $20,000 on her $150,000 house. It is probably worth more than that now, and Jane has the right to take back the house without the legal costs, provided her attorney holds a deed in lieu of foreclosure for her.

Why? Because by law, the bank holding the first mortgage would have to file all the legal papers necessary. At the time of foreclosure, Jane could go in with a loan already in place to buy the house back for the $100,000 that the bank would require.

In fact, the bank would negotiate for her either to take over the $100,000 loan or to pay the bank the cash that she could get from another bank to buy back the house and then resell it.

So, if a foreclosure occurs, in 5 years, and the house increases in value 5 percent a year, Jane walks away with several profits: first, the $20,000 down payment, and second, a $150,000 house that appreciates over 5 years at 5 percent per year.

Thanks to appreciation, the house is now worth $37,500 more than she sold it for in the first place. This gives her a neat $57,500 profit, in the unlikely event that she is forced to take the house back.

Seller financing, *if done properly,* makes for an excellent, well-secured investment, especially in areas where residential real estate is appreciating at a rate of at least 3 to 10 percent a year.

WHAT IF I DON'T WANT TO PLAY BANKER?

For reasons of temperament, personal financial obligations or a time bind—key elements in your Financial Comfort Zone—you may not share my enthusiasm for seller financing.

However, you can still make your home much more attractive to a buyer—and sell it faster—by lining up *information on mortgages* before you meet your first prospective purchaser.

Do you have a spare hour for a few phone calls or visits to local banks? That is all the time you need to reap a quicker sale.

Explain to your banker that you are getting ready to sell your house. Show the banker the recent appraisal that you obtained from an appraiser approved by the bank.

Let us assume that you expect your sales price to be $125,000, and that you currently have a $25,000 mortgage. Ask your banker for a letter stating that the bank will lend up to 80 or 90 percent of the stated value of the house, provided you bring in a qualified buyer.

With just a little effort, you have overcome the most frequent objection and the time constraint that buyers are likely to face—acquiring the right financing.

When the right buyer shows up, you can whip out the bank letter and say, "I have already arranged for financing. All you have to do is go to this bank, and if you have a decent income and credit record, you will have your loan in a flash."

One Connecticut radio listener wanted to line up a mortgage in advance, so he could advertise that his home was on sale with good financing. A mortgage broker who visited my radio show told him that a good mortgage broker could *match various mortgage products* to the appraised value of the house. This would give the buyer a selection of financial choices instead of just one.

Then prospective buyers could be told what kind of financing was open to them. Although interest rates most likely would vary, according to when a mortgage commitment was made, the seller in some cases could lock into a 30- to 60-day rate. That becomes a powerful sales tool.

IS YOUR MORTGAGE PAID IN FULL?

One of the most welcome documents a homeowner gets is the satisfaction of mortgage. You receive it after all your debts are paid on a home. However, a major stumbling block to a sale could occur if someone has forgotten to *record* this document. Be sure that yours, with the notarized signature of the bank officer, is recorded in the appropriate courthouse.

It is customary for the lender to record this paper, but as the years pass, items like this can slip through the cracks.

A ROAD MAP TO REFINANCING

Many homeowners are saddled with mortgages at interest rates much higher than those available today, or they are looking for ways to withdraw some equity out of their homes, even if they do not plan to sell immediately. When interest rates drop or tax reforms throw real estate plans into disarray, the word "refinancing" is on everyone's lips.

Actually, refinancing is not always the most efficient road to lower monthly payments or taxes. Let me tell you about *renegotiated mortgages*—an express lane—that can keep you out of the refinancing traffic jam.

Rather than lose mortgage refinancing to rival lenders during a period of relatively low interest rates, banks have opened their doors a bit to owners who wish to renegotiate, rather than refinance, their old, expensive loans.

Call the lender who gave you your high-interest mortgage. Ask that it be amended to reflect current, lower rates. This renegotiated mortgage requires no big closing costs the way refinancing does.

The bank charges you a single fee, usually ½ to 1 percent of the amount of the new loan. Moreover, renegotiation takes just a few days, rather than weeks (or months, in a true "mortgage mania" market).

Rehearse your pitch in front of a mirror at home, if necessary, before you visit your lender. *Be firm.* You can get a good rate on renegotiating if you let the financial institution know that you are serious about going to an outside source for refinancing unless this lender cooperates.

Chances are that you will get the cooperation you need. No banker likes to lose a client.

Another version of the renegotiated mortgage is a *blended mortgage.* It is useful for pulling equity out of a house, yet not enough consumers know about it.

Let us say you have an existing loan for 7 percent and the current rate is 12 percent. The bank wants to get out of the 7 percent mortgage. You want additional money. Your banker can blend the two rates and give you a renegotiated loan at 9 or 10 percent.

THE REFINANCING WALTZ

Refinancing suddenly came back into vogue when interest rates fell to 10 percent and below in 1986. Perhaps you, like others, thought to yourself, why pay $800 per month on a high-interest mortgage when lenders all over town are advertising refinancing that will bring that monthly nut down to $600?

Unfortunately, everyone got the same idea at the same time and the result was refinancing gridlock. Homeowners fumed as banks fell behind in processing the paperwork. By the time many loans were cleared, the 60- or 90-day commitment period for which the bank had locked in the new low rate had expired.

Thousands of homeowners *did* get refinancing eventually, but it was not a smooth waltz around the financial dance floor; it was more like break dancing.

Is refinancing still worth it? Yes, if . . .

Under tax reform, it still pays to refinance your house if the mortgage interest rate you have been paying is *2 percent or more higher* than the rate now offered on refinancing.

The kicker is that you can deduct the interest on your newly refinanced mortgage only for the amount of the original purchase price of the home, plus the cost of any improvements, such as adding a room, a pool and so on.

There are two exceptions. You *can* deduct interest on an amount refinanced above the original purchase price plus improvements if that money is used for medical bills, or for educational tuition for any member of your family including yourself.

Imagine that you paid $100,000 for your home, and you put in $50,000 in improvements—an additional room, a pool, a remodeled kitchen and so on. You are thinking about refinancing your mortgage for $300,000, your home's current worth.

Only the interest on $150,000 (purchase price plus improvements) of that refinanced mortgage is tax deductible; the interest on the entire $300,000 is not.

Of course, if you are paying a high interest rate on your original mortgage and you cannot renegotiate that mortgage, it is worth shopping for refinancing. But beware of the points, origination fees and other fees the lender will charge. Comparison-shopping among several lenders is essential here.

The arithmetic works like this: multiply by 12 the difference each month between one mortgage and another. That gives you the yearly savings. Multiply this by the number of years you will stay in your house. That gives you the overall savings on one mortgage versus another, and shows you how many years it will take to reach the savings position.

You will find that if you plan to stay in your current home a long enough time, extra points charged by the lender will eventually be absorbed.

You might be offered a choice of a fixed-rate or adjustable-rate mortgage (ARM) when you refinance. (See chapter 7 for details on each.) ARMs often come with an *assumable* clause, which allows a purchaser to take over that mortgage. Fixed-rate mortgages tend not to be assumable.

For those of you planning to sell your home shortly, a newly refinanced, assumable ARM can be perfect.

After all, you are pretty sure you are leaving the house. Let us say your sales price is $100,000; you have only a small mortgage left—

$10,000 to $30,000—and you want to get cash out of that house *before* you sell. By all means, get a new assumable, adjustable-rate mortgage for $90,000.

The fact that it is assumable will make it easier to sell your house quickly, because the buyer will not have to wait on line at the bank quite as long as someone applying for a brand-new loan. The cost will be low —"assumption" fees run from $250 to $1,000. Furthermore, you will not have to worry about the adjustable rate inching up. That will be your buyer's headache.

The main difficulty with assumable ARMs is that the buyer will have to meet all credit and income requirements.

Since I am outspoken against ARMs for buyers, my radio friends are surprised by my occasional nod in favor of one.

For instance, I spoke to one Eastern listener who had a property worth over $350,000. As interest rates dipped, she shopped for a refinancing worth $250,000. She wanted to retire the $40,000 mortgage left on this house and have enough left over to move to San Diego. She planned to hold on to her house in the East for three years.

Her shopping trip turned up two offers:

One was a 30-year adjustable mortgage starting at 7 percent that could go up no more than 2 percent a year to a maximum of 14½ percent, with 3½ points up front. It was assumable. Another institution offered her a 30-year fixed mortgage at 14¼ percent with no points. It was not assumable.

In this case, the first choice, the adjustable mortgage, was more attractive because the savings in the first year alone, at 7 percent with 3½ points (which equaled 10½ percent), would be better than on the higher fixed rate.

Since she planned to sell within three years anyway, the fact that it was assumable was another plus. I recommended she take the adjustable loan, so she could move to San Diego in a few years with money already in her pocket.

To see if refinancing is right in your situation, fill out the following chart I call "Doing the Numbers."

HOME EQUITY LOANS—THE HIGHER-PRICED SPREAD

If a refinanced mortgage with a better than 2-percent interest rate spread is the equivalent of margarine, then a *home equity loan* is a higher-priced spread.

Doing the Numbers: A Refinancing Worksheet

Present Mortgage Balance $ _____
  (principal only)

Present Mortgage Rate _____% Present Mortgage Payment $_____
Anticipated Mortgage Rate _____% New Mortgage Payment $_____
                                              (from Monthly Payment Table)

Subtract the New Mortgage Payment from Present Mortgage
  Payment. This is your Monthly Savings (or Additional
  Payment). $_____

Closing Costs (in dollars)

Points $_____   (Each point = 1% of your
                                                                          Present Mortgage Balance
                                                                          or amount to be bor-
                                                                          rowed.)

Application Fee $_____
Reappraisal(s) $_____
Inspections $_____
Lender's Attorney's Review Fee $_____
Your Attorney's Review Fee $_____
Prepayment Penalty, if any $_____
Miscellaneous $_____   (title search, title insu-
                                                                          rance, credit reports, etc.)

Total of Closing Costs $_____

Doing the Numbers. To determine how long it should take you to recoup
your closing costs, divide the Closing Costs by your Monthly Savings:

Closing Costs $_____ ÷ Monthly Savings $_____ = _____ months
The result is the number of months needed to recoup your outlay of refinance closing costs.

Do not confuse a home equity loan with refinancing, no matter what the bank advertisements say. The *only* time to seek a home equity loan is if you need cash, whether to spruce up your house, pay a medical bill, take a trip, send a child to college or make a business investment.

A home equity loan is an amount of money that a financial institution lends you on the amount of money your home is worth, over and above all current debts.

For example, let us say a home is worth $100,000. You have a first mortgage of $50,000. You have a second of $20,000. That means you have $30,000 worth of equity in that home against which you can borrow.

Home equity loans come in 2 varieties.

In one you get a fixed amount of money. In the case described above, you could borrow $20,000 or up to 90 percent of the value of your home after subtracting the mortgages, which is the limit banks allow. You can obtain this loan all at once. The lender takes out a second mortgage on your home. You sign it. You then make a fixed amount of monthly payments toward that second mortgage.

The other type of home equity loan is called a revolving or open credit line. Here, the interest rates fluctuate as often as market rates do.

The dangerous part of this second variety of home equity loan is that *at any time* the bank can, in fact, "call" the loan, and require you to pay the *entire* principal balance. The bank does not have to give you a reason.

Remember, if you cannot pay, your house is the collateral.

A *home improvement loan,* on the other hand, is a loan you take out for specific work that is being done on your home—a new roof, the addition of a room, a pool, a new heating system, new air-conditioning and so on.

This is a one-time, fixed-rate interest loan, secured by a second mortgage. The home improvement loan with a fixed interest rate and payment schedule is much better, in the long run, than a home equity loan. Interest rates on home equity loans can skyrocket, and, as mentioned before, the loan itself can be called for payment in full at any time.

In both of the cases stated above, if your home is paid for in full, the loans will become first rather than second mortgages.

Sample Agreement for Deed

Dated _____ , 19_____ .

Articles of Agreement between _____
                                          (name of seller(s))
                              and _____
                                          (name of buyer(s))

   Buyer shall first make the payments and perform the covenants hereinafter stated to Seller. Seller covenants and agrees to convey and assure to Buyer and heirs, executors, administrators or assigns, in fee simple, clear of all encumbrances whatever, by a good and sufficient deed, the lot _____, piece or parcel of land, situated in the County of _____, State of _____, known and described as follows: _____
_____
_____ ,

   Buyer hereby covenants and agrees to pay said Seller the sum of _____
_____ dollars, under the following terms: _____
_____
_____ ,

with interest at the rate of _____ percent yearly, payable annually on the whole sum remaining from time to time unpaid; and to pay all taxes, assessment or impositions that may be legally levied or imposed upon said land subsequent to the year 19_____ , and to keep the buildings upon said premises insured by a company satisfactory to Seller, and payable for the parties, respectively as their interests may appear, in a sum not less than _____ dollars during the term of this agreement. In case of failure of Buyer to make any of the payments or any part thereof, or to perform any of the covenants made and entered into, this contract shall, at the option of Seller, be forfeited and terminated, and Buyer

---

Sample Agreement for Deed (continued)

shall forfeit all payments made on this contract; and such payments shall be retained by Seller in full satisfaction and liquidation of all damages sustained, and Seller shall have the right to reenter and take possession of the premises without being liable to any action.

It is mutually agreed, by and between the parties, that the time of each payment shall be an essential part of this contract, and that all covenants and agreements contained in this agreement shall extend to and be obligatory upon the heirs, executors, administrators and assigns of the respective parties.

In witness whereof, the parties have signed on the day and year written above.

_____ (name of Seller)

_____ (signature of Seller)

_____ (name of Buyer)

_____ (signature of Buyer)

State of _____

County of _____

I hereby certify that on this day, before me, an officer duly authorized in the State and County to take acknowledgments, personally appeared _____
_____,
to me known to be the person(s) described in and who executed the foregoing instrument and acknowledged before me that _____
executed the same.

Witness my hand and official seal in the County and State named above
_____ (date)

_____ (signature and seal).

Note: Always review legal documents with an attorney.

Chapter 26

Preparing for a Hassle-Free Closing

The closing, or settlement, is basically a review of documents and an exchange—you turn over the keys to the house to your buyer in exchange for a certified check covering the sales price.

Top professionals pride themselves on keeping closings *short*—10 to 15 minutes. I did, when I handled up to twenty closings a day some years back as chairman of the board of a title company. If a closing goes beyond 30 minutes, there is either too much social chatter or something is wrong.

Your job as a seller is to ride herd on your team from the beginning, so that those "wrongs" never develop.

The closing is the mouth of a river of paperwork. All the tributaries —information from the lender, the various attorneys, the brokers, the tax assessor, the pest control company, the house inspection company, everyone else involved—flow into this river. Why do we need a six-inch-thick file of papers? Because there are a series of laws and customs designed to guarantee that you are, in fact, selling what you think you own. The closing is a formality, confirming that all these laws have been observed.

People in the real estate business once kept closings a deep, dark, mystic procedure that gave sellers, as well as buyers, sweaty palms. Finally, in 1974, the federal government passed the Real Estate Settlement Procedures Act (RESPA), which gives you the right to receive all the information on closing costs.

Do not allow anyone to stall you by saying, "We will get you everything," and then to hand you material as you walk in the door at the closing itself. (A copy of the uniform Settlement Statement appears in chapter 9.)

READY: KEEPING YOUR TEAM ON ITS TOES

Nobody likes to be a pest, but once you have made a deal to sell, you are within your rights to call the title company, your attorney or both *regularly.*

Step 1 is to push for a *firm closing date.* This step should be taken right after you shake hands on a sale.

Step 2, done at the same time, is to *review your file yourself* at your attorney's office. If anything is missing, have your attorney keep you posted weekly on progress. Otherwise, you could be faced with the same dilemma as my friend Jack.

The day before his closing, Jack learned that the buyer's attorney had not delivered a certain document. The closing was about to be postponed. Jack had to leave for a new job in three days.

What should he have done to avoid the problem? Follow through— this is as necessary to closing on time as it is to a golfer's long tee shot. In Jack's case, a few telephone calls could have pushed the document along. Instead, Jack either had to fly back to San Francisco three weeks later to attend the closing or give his West Coast lawyer power of attorney to close the sale.

A sure-fire means of speeding up a closing is to include in the actual sales contract and agreement to purchase all of the adjusted items, such as taxes, insurance premiums, utility deposits and everything else listed as seller expenses in the closing documents.

SET: THE FINAL WEEK

Four or five days before the closing, take a last-minute look at the personal property list that should be attached to your sales contract.

This is the list of items you have agreed—or declined—to include in the sale, such as your custom drapes, light fixtures, dishwasher, refrigerator and other "extras."

What if your daughter has taken a favorite lamp back to her college dorm, not realizing you promised it to the buyers in your negotiations?

The buyers will look for it on their final inspection. It sounds petty, but this sort of thing can turn a closing into a shouting match.

It is a good idea to have a *written memo* ready for the buyers to sign on the day before closing, stating that the buyers have actually made their inspection and found all personal property in place.

GO: CALCULATING YOUR CLOSING COSTS

About two or three days before the closing, be sure to get a copy of the seller's portion of Estimated Closing Costs, as required by federal law, from whoever is running the closing—the title insurance official or your lawyer. The closing charges are smaller for you (the buyer pays most settlement costs), but you do not want to let bills sneak up on you.

Contact your bank if you have a present mortgage. Will there be any additional charges as the result of your prepaying your loan early? The Estimated Closing Costs sheet should include this, but it does not hurt to double-check.

Depending on the practice in your part of the country, you may be responsible for paying the full cost of title insurance. Also, in some states you are responsible for a local and state revenue tax. In other states, you are required to pay for a termite inspection. On some mortgages, such as those from the Veterans Administration, the seller must pay some of the buyer's up-front loan costs.

If you have paid attention to my suggestions on attorney fees and real estate broker commissions, you will know well in advance how much you owe these important members of your team.

Finally, in the hectic time right before a closing, it is easy to forget little things—like cancelling your newspaper delivery, forwarding your mail and, above all, arranging disconnect dates (or transfer dates) with your utility companies. One envelope you do not want to receive two months later at your new address is a $350 electric bill from your former home!

Use the Good-bye Guide provided in this chapter to cover those bases. To keep track of your papers and costs, follow the Seller's Closing Worksheet at the end of this chapter.

Now you can feel confident that you are up to date on the status of all the documents and on the costs you will be expected to pay.

Congratulations! You are ready for a hassle-free, 10-minute closing.

Seller's Closing Worksheet
(Use this to estimate net proceeds from your sale.)

A. **Sales Price** $_____

B. **Estimated Selling Costs**

    Title fees $_____

    Local revenue tax $_____

    State revenue tax $_____

    Mortgage prepayment penalty (if any) $_____

    Loan points $_____

    Tax proration $_____

    Appraisal fee $_____

    Document preparation fee $_____

    Recording and transfer fees $_____

    Survey preparation $_____

    Real estate commission $_____

    Legal fees $_____

    Special assessments $_____

    Termite inspection $_____

    House inspection $_____

    Required repairs $_____

C. **Total Estimated Selling Costs**   = $_____

D. **Credits and Rebates to Seller**

    Prepaid property taxes $_____

    Prepaid utilities (including oil) $_____

    Prepaid homeowner's insurance $_____

E. **Total Credits to Seller**   = $_____

F. Add A and E for your **Gross Proceeds**   = $_____

G. Subtract C for **Gross** before Mortgage Payoff   − $_____

H. Subtract existing Mortgage Balance   − $_____

I. This is your **Estimated Net Proceeds**   = $_____

Good-bye Guide

(Have you made arrangements for the following?)

Electricity disconnect date _____

Gas company disconnect date _____

Water company notice _____

Oil company notice _____

Forwarding address to post office _____

Local telephone forwarding and/or disconnect _____

Notify long-distance telephone company _____

Empty safe-deposit box (if moving to a new community) _____

Stop newspaper delivery _____

Cable TV cutoff _____

Garbage company notice _____

End landscaping, snow removal, lawn-mowing services _____

End pool service _____

Give final thank-you tips to handymen and service people in apartment
   building _____

Give buyer appliance manuals and warranties _____

Chapter 27

Can't Sell Your House? Here's How to Trade It

One Sunday morning I got a call on my national radio show from Mary, a Texas woman who was trying to talk through her tears.

She had done everything she could to sell her home. But the market in her town was weak. She could not get enough cash to move with her out-of-work husband to Harrisburg, Pennsylvania, where she had a job offer from a major company.

Her best bet, I told her, might be a *tax-free exchange.*

Under Internal Revenue Code 1031, anyone can *trade one property for another of like value* without paying taxes. This resourceful real estate arrangement has received little publicity. Tax-free swaps are not done very often by lay people. But under proper supervision, you can benefit from them.

Exchanges should be investigated by anyone in the market for a home, especially if you have one in a soft market, or want to purchase one in such an area.

But there are other valuable swaps available as well. Owners of rental property in a suburban area of a major city can exchange that property for a resort home on a lake or in the mountains.

There are *thousands* of properties out there, waiting to be exchanged. You can check into them via local or state exchange clubs, which are run by real estate agents across the country. The trading process available under Internal Revenue Code 1031 is not terribly complex.

By plugging in to this exchange network, you can accomplish these multiple gains:

- You can swap your house for one in a community to which you wish to move.
- You defer *all* capital gains or income taxes.
- You find out about properties that are not necessarily in the multi-list or available through normal real estate channels.
- You might be able to do more creative financing, since people in the exchange mode are always open to deals that are overlooked or not considered in the more conventional real estate market.

YOU CAN DUPLICATE THIS SWAP SUCCESS STORY

In order to find a home in Harrisburg, I advised Mary to place an ad every day for one week in a Harrisburg paper, offering to exchange her $85,000 home for a home of like value in the Harrisburg region. She should also state the equity she had in her current home, which was $10,000.

By the following Sunday, she had received eight calls from Pennsylvania retirees who wanted to retire to the Sunbelt! "Now what do I do?" she asked.

"Your first step is to make sure your attorney and accountant know how to put together the correct documentation for a 1031 exchange," I said.

Mary would then make a trip immediately to Harrisburg, to examine personally the eight properties, their neighborhoods, their financing, and do everything else a buyer does in evaluating a property. Naturally, she would never agree to accept a home without seeing it or going through a standard title search and professional home inspection.

She would also hire a Harrisburg lawyer to handle her legal work on the Pennsylvania side of the exchange. (It is wise to hire attorneys in both towns when doing a 1031. But if you do not want the expense of two attorneys, use one in the community to which you are moving, rather than your hometown attorney.)

As soon as Mary reached a decision on which Harrisburg residence worked for her, her attorney and the attorney for the person on the other end of the exchange would complete the paperwork. An exchange closing is very much like a standard real estate closing, except that the documents are different.

HOW DO YOU RECONCILE AN UNEQUAL SWAP?

Rarely do you find an exchange in which both homes are *exactly* equal in value. This is not a major deterrent, however.

Let us assume that Mary chooses the Johnsons' home in Harrisburg. It is worth $95,000, and the Johnsons have a $20,000 equity in it. Her house, remember, is worth $85,000, with only a $10,000 equity. Thus, Mary would owe the Johnsons a total of $10,000, the difference between her equity of $10,000 and theirs of $20,000.

Either she makes a deal to give them the cash difference, or she and the Johnsons enter into a second mortgage and note arrangement such as the one we discussed in chapter 25 on seller financing.

Another option for Mary might be new financing from a Harrisburg lender. That would take longer than a straightforward exchange. However, she could structure the deal so the exchange goes through right away, while she has as little as six months or as long as a year or two to get the financing and pay off the Johnsons.

It is also common, with an unequal exchange, to add a commodity other than money or a note as a "sweetener" to even the deal. Mary might want to give the Johnsons a nice collection of jewelry, which she does not wear anymore, as part of the house exchange. Then nobody owes anybody anything.

Typically, homeowners do use jewelry, loan-free boats or cars as sweeteners. Still, this is the barter system. You can sweeten the pot with almost anything your exchange partner will accept, including vacant land, registered livestock, art objects or additional property.

Yet another option: commercial property. Mary might trade her house for a store in Harrisburg. This would generate income while she looked for a house—and at the same time might provide her husband with a temporary job as storekeeper.

Are you getting the impression that tax-free exchanges involve only small-time deals? Not so. Recently, a broker representing Arizona millionaire Gordon Hall offered to trade his $10 million Paradise Valley mansion for a Caribbean island!

You do have to be careful that you work within the rules. One hitch, to reap the tax advantages, is that you cannot exchange your house for gold or silver alone. The swap has to include property.

NETWORKING ON TAX-FREE EXCHANGES

Contact your local realty board for information on exchange groups in local areas, as well as statewide. The people who handle these arrangements are called exchangors. Some list themselves at their real estate offices or in the yellow pages as members of the National Exchangors Association.

The head of the National Exchangors Association is A. D. Kessler, Drawer L, Rancho Santa Fe, CA 92067; phone, (619) 755-0505.

Exchange groups operate much in the same fashion as the stock market, with a computer bulletin board. Various properties are listed on a group's board. If you get involved with an exchange group, which I recommend, your property might wind up being taken by somebody you never even see.

For instance, perhaps you are looking for a house in upstate New York. You also happen to own a house in Dallas that someone in Harrisburg might want. Meanwhile, someone in upstate New York wants a house in Harrisburg. An exchange group can match you with the others in order to arrange a three-way swap.

The tax-free exchange is neither exotic nor underhanded. It is simply the process of buying a house with another house, instead of with money. It is time that more Americans knew that there are imaginative, unconventional, *eminently workable* ways to buy and sell residential real estate.

Chapter 28

When You Are Buying and Selling a House at the Same Time

One day a woman in Frankfort, Kentucky, called my show in a tizzy. Her husband had just been notified that he was being promoted to a new assignment in his company's Atlanta headquarters.

Her assignment: to sell their home in Frankfort and buy a new one in Atlanta, a city she barely knew . . . all within 90 days. How was she supposed to go about it?

Her situation was one with which many of us are familiar, since few of us buy or sell a home in a vacuum. Commonly, we sell our current house—or *think* we need to sell it—because we are buying another. There are special problems associated with doing both at the same time.

For people like these folks in Kentucky, driving around a strange city or being taken around by a broker day after day can become exhausting. After a while, you become bleary-eyed from viewing too many homes in too short a time, and that is an uncomfortable, blurred viewpoint from which to make a decision as important as buying a home.

Take a deep breath, stop peeking at your watch, and *relax.* You have more time than you think.

"Unless you are moving from a very hot real estate market to a very slow market, your best bet, right off the bat, is to put your current house on the market and rent a place in Atlanta," I told the Kentucky woman.

Most of the real estate industry disagrees with this philosophy because it does not sell enough homes. Still, it is silly (and fiscally harmful) to sell in a panic for too low a price, and then buy another house for too high a price in a new market that you do not understand.

THE "RENT/RENT" APPROACH

The rent/rent approach is one I recommended to another couple from California. You can use the same questions I put to them to decide if it is the proper one for you.

The call came from Atwater, California, near Modesto. In a few months, the two of them, both in their thirties, were transferring to Washington, D.C. Should they sell? Buy? Rent?

"What kind of a town is Atwater?" I asked.

"It is supported by an air force base and farming."

"How long have you owned your current house?"

"Three years."

"What's the mortgage?"

"Close to $70,000."

"What is the house worth?"

"Probably $85,000."

"So you have a $15,000 equity," I continued. "What are the monthly payments?"

"Between $750 and $800."

"Could you rent it for that much?"

"No. A maximum of $600 would be more like it."

Aha! My listeners were thinking that it would not be a good idea to keep the house, because they would have a loss of $150 per month, or negative cash flow.

Wrong. I had not asked enough questions yet. "Do you consider Atwater 'home'?" I asked.

"No, but we don't know how long we'll be in Washington. Perhaps three to seven years. There is a possibility of returning to Atwater some day."

"Do you have enough for a down payment on a house in Washington?"

"Yes."

"There are many people listening right now who wish they had kept their first two or three homes they owned," I began. "Today, those places are probably worth a lot more. So if you can get a good licensed, bonded property manager in Atwater, I would keep the California home."

The manager would charge between 3 and 6 percent of the rent a month to handle the affairs of the Atwater house, I explained.

How could they be better off financially holding on to the property? A national survey indicated that residential real estate in that area of California was appreciating at 9 to 11 percent per year. In 10 years their house would be worth twice the $85,000 it was currently worth.

"Even with the $150-plus loss each month, the renter winds up paying for your investment," I said. Rents would increase—they always do—and the loss would be deductible in any case even under tax reform, because it was within the new tax guidelines.

Meanwhile, the couple could lease with an option to purchase (see chapter 8) as a risk-free experiment in Washington, until they decided exactly where they wanted to live, and how big a place they could afford.

It takes a while to feel "at home" in a new community. No one puts a gun to your head to *buy* the week you transfer to a new job (or get promoted, or get the yen for more space), so why not take a few months to scout the residential marketplace, using the suggestions in chapter 1 about discovering your Comfort Zone?

WHICH DO I DO FIRST—BUY OR SELL?

This is the overriding question everyone asks. The answer? Do both *simultaneously,* if your situation merits it.

Yes, you can stay sane in the process, as long as you keep in focus the two prime considerations: *money* (the amount needed for both moving and paying for the new house) and *time.*

Do not buy a new house first and worry yourself sick about selling your old house, unless you have tremendous amounts of cash.

Your first visit, as both a buyer and a seller, might be to Housing Consumer Libraries or Home Buying Centers. (See chapter 1 for more details.)

"THE METER IS RUNNING" STRATEGIES

What if the clock is ticking—loudly and rapidly? You do not have the time to do all the homework that I have assigned on selling your house. This is a situation where hiring a good real estate broker is a must. Get a sales whiz who knows how to create action and a positive climate for a fast sale, while still getting *you* top dollar.

What if someone wants to buy your current house before you are ready to move?

You have two basic choices: (1) sell the house and pay the new owner rent during the time you are looking for your new house; or (2) lease a temporary place—there are many apartments with short-term, 2- to 6-month leases in major cities.

THE "ONE BROKER, TWO HOUSES" STRATEGY

Here is another strategy, but you must consider how far you are moving.

If you are selling and looking to buy in the *same town,* find the savviest real estate broker you can. Make a deal with that broker to help you find a new home and sell your current one *at a reduced commission rate on both sides.*

Both of you win. He gets a sure commission, and you save thousands on the selling end.

Let us assume the broker is in a marketplace where the going rate for commissions is 7 percent. Offer him a 10-percent package deal—5 percent on the sale of the old house, 5 percent on the purchase of the new house. If you are selling a $100,000 home and buying another for the same price, you *save* $4,000 in commissions.

"BUY THE NEW WHILE STUCK WITH THE OLD" STRATEGIES

Perhaps the most anxiety-producing situation occurs when you put your house on the market, and then find the perfect house that you want to purchase right away. Where do you get the money for the down payment on the new house, since you were counting on the proceeds of the sale on the current home?

This is where your mortgage broker or banker comes in. The broker or banker has your down payment in the form of an *equity loan* or *bridge loan* that will cover the down payment. Both these loans use your equity in your present house as security.

All you have to do is show your banker documentation on the market value of your home. You will be able to sign a note on the mortgage on your present home. A provision in it says the note will be paid from the proceeds of the sale of your old house.

Your interest rate on a short-term loan such as this will be higher. Expect to pay from 2 to 4 percent *more* on a bridge loan than on a 30-year fixed-rate mortgage.

The Kentucky people mentioned earlier in this chapter, for example, were sitting in a $150,000 home in Frankfort. It was listed with the local branch of a well-known national real estate company. Their present mortgage was $50,000. Therefore, they had a $100,000 equity in it. Before you could whistle Dixie, they found a house in Roswell, Georgia, they were crazy about. It was priced at $250,000.

The woman called me, saying she would like to make a $50,000, or 20-percent, down payment, and get a 30-year fixed-rate mortgage on the remaining 80 percent. An Atlanta bank decided that the couple could definitely afford the payments on a $200,000 mortgage and thus lent them the $50,000 based on the equity in the old Kentucky home.

Why go for an expensive short-term loan? In this case, because it put my radio friend in a position of not being overly anxious to sell the Kentucky house for too low a price. Quite the reverse: she was now in a stronger position to get her original asking price in Frankfort because the question of how to get cash to cover costs on the Georgia dream house had been settled.

What happens if the buyer you have lined up for your present home backs out at the last minute? Suddenly you are expected at a closing table with, say, $50,000 as a down payment on a $250,000 house.

Where's the money? You don't have it. The people from whom you are buying your new house can sue you for nonperformance—not going through with the closing.

Sidestep this trap with a subject-to clause. In your contract to purchase the new house, write a clause making the contract *subject to the sale of your present home and/or to your obtaining a bridge loan,* as explained above.

There is another way around this stumbling block. If the sellers do not need cash right away, arrange to show them the equity position that you have in the house you are selling. Then give them a note *without* borrowing a bridge loan from a bank. That note is actually a second mortgage on your present house, giving them a $50,000 interest in it, in lieu of your borrowing fresh money.

Once the sale of your present house finally goes through, you can present these sellers with their $50,000, plus some dollars in interest, and they give you back the note, marked "paid." This is done quite often.

Cover yourself, rather than cover up. Put these situations on the table. Do not keep secrets from your broker, buyer or seller. Everyone will sleep better—and have more confidence in you.

THE "SOMEONE IS SLEEPING IN MY BEDROOM" STRATEGY

What if your new house is not vacant when you are ready to move in? This happens when the people from whom you have bought the house are also closing on a new house of their own.

See to it that your sellers also have a subject-to provision in the contract with you, saying they will pay rent to you while they are waiting to move out. Put a time limit on this provision. The norm is 90 to 120 days.

In addition, this rent should cover both the monthly payment on the house and the money necessary for you to move your belongings twice or to rent a temporary place to live.

Be wary of people who tell you they will move and give you possession of your new house "as soon as our builder finishes our new house." Always add 90 days to 6 months (that's right, 3 to 6 months!) to the completion date quoted by your seller's builder.

Am I really telling you that it is safer to buy a house that is already vacant or to buy from someone else who is being transferred?

Absolutely.

THE "SELL NOW, KEEP POSSESSION" STRATEGY

This is the *most conservative approach* to buying and selling at the same time. Sell your house first, but have a clause in your contract that does not give possession of the house to your buyer for as long as it takes YOU to find your next house.

You usually receive less money—5 to 10 percent—for the house with such a clause, especially if your buyer wants immediate occupancy. But if you are the conservative type, and you are willing to take a minor loss by selling a bit *below* market value, then sell first.

Another version of this is the "sell now, rent now" plan. Use it when you know in your heart that you are going to sell your current home rather than keep it and rent it while it grows in value.

Put that house on the market right away. Begin your search for the new one right away. If you are moving to a new town, ease your mind at the outset by renting a temporary place, or arrange a lease with option to purchase. (Again, see chapter 8 on such leases for details.)

With both "sell now" techniques, you allow yourself precious time to try out an area and/or the house. You can always buy later on, after the initial traumas of moving and job transfer have passed.

GUARANTEED . . . TO BRING YOU A LOWER PRICE

Some brokers promote the idea of a *guaranteed sale.* It can sound enticing if you are in a rush, or if you do not want to spend another minute living in your old residence.

The broker lists your house at a price *lower* than the market price. The trade-off is that if your house is not sold within a specific period, usually 6 months, the broker will *buy it back* from you at the guaranteed price.

My recommendation is, *stay away* from guaranteed sale or buy-back arrangements, because you will get approximately *15 to 20 percent less* for your home than you would if you sold it on a straight commission basis.

WHAT IF YOU ARE TRADING UP?

The next time you shop for a home, perhaps because you have been transferred to a higher-paying job in another state, or because you have a growing family, you might think about "trading up" to a bigger, *more expensive* house. You will be more experienced shopping for money. But you will also have to budget for greater expenses.

You tend to put more money down as you trade up. One reason is that you have equity in the home that you are selling, equity that you can pull out of that home to put into your trade-up home.

You do not want to get rid of that money. You want to *roll it over* into the next house to get the tax benefit of clause 1034 of the Internal Revenue Code.

ROLLOVER—A RARE BREAK FROM THE IRS

Rollover Residence Replacement Rule 1034 is a seller-friendly section of the Internal Revenue Code.

If you move, selling one residence to buy another, and your new residence is equal in value to or more expensive than the old one, you can *defer taxes on profits* made from the sale of the old home. The sale price is what determines your gain. So if you are living in a house valued at $100,000 and you buy one for $150,000, you are okay.

The worth of the home you sell is determined on an *adjusted-cost basis.* Here is how it works:

The adjusted cost of the old home is the total purchase cost (including closing costs such as title fee, escrow fee, transfer fees, but not loan fees), plus the cost of improvements made, minus depreciation deductions or casualty loss. To qualify for the 1034 rollover, you must have lived in the house for at least 24 months.

So let us say you bought the first house for $50,000. You spent $25,000 on capital improvements, and you kept a record of the improvements. After 24 months, you sold the house for $100,000. You have made a profit of $25,000. As long as you buy a house for $100,000 or more within two years the tax on your $25,000 profit is deferred under the 1034 IRS rollover.

The IRS realizes that you are using that profit to buy a replacement residence, and thus it would be unfair to make you pay taxes on that money. If you *trade down,* so that the second house costs less than the one you previously owned, you pay *full income tax* on the difference.

HOW YOUR EMPLOYER CAN HELP

There is one final source of help in buying and selling—your company. If a job transfer is involved, most large companies will help executives make the move smoothly.

Check with your employee benefits department. Ask about the following:

• If the transfer does not allow you enough time to sell your home, or if the market is soft, will the company pick up your mortgage payments? Or will the company buy your home, so you have the resources to buy another in your new location?

• Will the company lease a home for you in your new location, at least for a transition period?

• Will the company pay for the cost of your move?

• If you must go to your new job before your family moves (or before the school term ends), will the company pay your hotel or temporary apartment costs?

Many larger companies have guidelines that outline how much they will contribute to moving costs. Even those without formal rules often are willing to ease the trauma of a transfer.

Chapter **29**

How the New Tax Laws Affect Buying and Selling a Home

The Tax Simplification and Reform Act of 1986, along with its revisions in 1987 and 1988, instituted the most radical and comprehensive tax changes in the past half century. The spirit of these acts, which amount to the ninth tax law revisions since 1964, was to redistribute the tax burden from the individuals who could not carry that burden to corporations that could. The irony is that corporations will pass the cost back to those individuals as consumers.

Certain portions of recent tax reforms affect homeowners, buyers and sellers *directly,* but the acts do not destroy the advantages homeowners already have. Mortgage interest deductions are still allowed. You still can sell your home and buy a more expensive one without paying any taxes. You still have the right to a one-time lifetime exemption from the capital gains tax up to $125,000 of profit on the sale of your home if you are over the age of fifty-five, provided you have owned and lived in the residence three of the past five years. (If the owner was in a qualified nursing home for that period of time, he or she may be able to declare the home as a principal residence and make use of the lifetime exemption.)

But the new laws make it essential to update your strategy on real estate. What is your basic goal? To see that you have as many legal deductions as possible.

STRATEGIES FOR ONE- AND TWO-HOME OWNERS

One of the most important changes in the law since 1986 involves deducting mortgage interest. Although mortgage interest on your first and second homes may be fully deductible, there is a new twist.

You may deduct all of your mortgage interest payment where the amount of your loan is up to the amount of the acquisition cost of your first and second properties. *Acquisition cost* refers to the amount of debt you incurred when you first bought the property. The loan must be in place within 90 days from the time you buy the house; otherwise you lose the acquisition debt classification forever on that property. Those who buy a home for cash must incur a debt within 90 days from the date of closing in order to claim an acquisition debt deduction.

For instance, if you bought a house in December 1987 for $200,000, you would be allowed to have a mortgage of up to $200,000, and that entire mortgage would be fully deductible. But if you borrowed only $180,000 when you bought that house, that is your "acquisition cost" mortgage amount. Only the interest on that much may be deducted from your taxes.

This acquisition mortgage amount declines as you make mortgage principal payments month after month. If, at some time in the future, you refinance this mortgage, you can refinance only up to the acquisition amount. Thus, if you had a $200,000 mortgage and after 2 years you had paid off $2,000 worth of mortgage principal, your balance would be $198,000. You could only refinance that mortgage for $198,-000 and still have it deductible as home mortgage acquisition cost interest.

In addition, you cannot extend the term of the mortgage. So if you have a 30-year mortgage and after 2 years you decide to refinance, you can deduct only the acquisition interest for the first 28 years of the new mortgage. (An exception exists for balloon mortgages.)

Happily, there is a loan for which the interest is deductible: a home equity loan of any type. You can take out a home equity loan, a second mortgage or refinancing of your first mortgage for up to $100,000 more than your acquisition cost on either or both your first and second homes and deduct the interest payments. The $100,000 home equity loan is the fully deductible amount you can have on your first and second homes combined.

All debt in place as of October 13, 1987, is considered acquisition debt. Did you have a first mortgage of $200,000 on October 13, 1987? Even though it might have exceeded your initial acquisition cost of your home, you can still claim the entire amount as acquisition debt, and you can still borrow up to $100,000 in home equity debt above that total.

In addition, acquisition cost can be increased if you make improvements on your home. Let's go back to the home mentioned above, with a $200,000 first mortgage, which is the acquisition cost. After 2 years, you spend $10,000 making improvements on the house. You can include that $10,000 in your deductions by taking out a home equity loan or a home improvement loan or by refinancing the mortgage to pay for those improvements.

How are *improvements* defined? You can obtain a complete list from the IRS or your accountant. The basic rule is that improvements are permanent changes that are not removable—a new roof, a porch, an extra room, a patio or new windows. Be sure to save receipts.

There is one loophole. If, for the purpose of business or investments, you borrow money on your house above the allowable acquisition debt, including improvements, plus home equity debt of $100,000, you may be permitted deductions. If the money is used to start your own business, you can deduct *every penny* of the interest on the loan.

If you put the money directly into a new investment real estate property, that interest will be deductible against that property on Schedule E of your tax return. The amount of losses from the same property will be subject to the passive loss rules. (More about those rules below.)

A recommended strategy: if you have not made use of your deductible home equity debt allowance, which is up to $100,000 of home equity debt on your first and second homes, you should think seriously about borrowing this amount. By all means, get the additional money out of your home up to the limit when you are ready to invest in real estate.

For example, your current mortgage is $50,000. Your house is worth $300,000. You may be be able to borrow up to $150,000 on that home via a new first mortgage, a $100,000 second mortgage or a $100,000 home equity loan.

You can use this refinancing money for any purpose. You might want to pay off credit card interest, which you get at a much higher rate than a home equity loan. You also can buy such things as cars, boats, vacation packages, a new living room furniture ensemble, jewelry, a stereo/home entertainment system, a fur coat or other consumer goods.

The interest on the $150,000 is fully deductible. The interest on the installment loan for a car or other consumer item is no longer deductible. By paying off consumer loans with a new home equity loan, you can shift nondeductible debt into the fully deductible category and thus lower your taxes.

STRATEGIES FOR TWO- AND THREE-HOME OWNERS

Thinking about renting your second home or buying a rental property as your third home? The deductibility of mortgage interest on rental property has changed drastically.

Mortgage interest on rental property is deductible only if the loan was in place on the property at the time of purchase. If you refinance later for an amount greater than the initial mortgage, the new loan must be used to put improvements into that home or to buy and/or improve another rental property. Otherwise that interest is not deductible.

If you buy a rental property for cash and later try to take out a mortgage on it, the 90-day rule that applies to first and second residences does not apply here. Instead, you incur nondeductible interest on this rental property.

You must carefully trace where the money from a refinanced rental property goes. Let's say you have a $50,000 mortgage on the rental and you refinance it for $100,000. Only $50,000 of the refinancing would be deductible against income from this rental property.

If you deposited the additional $50,000 in a bank account, the interest on this $50,000 would be deductible up to your interest income. Obviously, the goal is to put the money to work in such a way that the interest is an allowable deduction.

The mortgage interest and property taxes on a weekend or vacation home that you use occasionally but do not rent continues to be fully deductible. You do not have to live in that second home, but you must use the place 14 days a year, or 10 percent of the time it is rented, whichever is greater.

If you rent out that vacation home for fewer than 15 days a year, you do not have to report the rental income on your tax return, but you cannot deduct the operating expenses.

If you rent out that vacation home, you must actively manage the place to retain the benefits of the interest deduction. There no longer are tax benefits available to those who do not manage their own properties. Rental pools apparently do qualify as active management.

If you have a third home, it is classified as a passive rental property, provided you personally use it fewer than 14 days out of the year. If you use it more than that, you can deduct the mortgage interest only up to the amount of your rental income.

There are exceptions to these deduction rules on third homes that depend on adjusted gross incomes and other losses. Those who earn more than $100,000 should consult their CPAs.

The rules on passive investments—those managed by other people, such as real estate limited partnerships—have been tightened as a result of laws passed since 1986. You cannot use losses from these investments to offset income from other sources, such as wages, stocks and bond dividends. However, losses from actively managed rental real estate are in a special category of passive investments, which allows up to $25,000 in losses to be used against other income types. Thus, if you have rental property that shows a loss after all payments and expenses have been met, you can deduct up to $25,000 against any other kind of income.

If you have a loss of more than $25,000, you can use the additional loss only to offset other passive income. The deductibility of losses on actively managed rental real estate are phased out beginning with an adjusted gross income of $100,000 or more. When you reach the $150,-000 level, you lose the right to deduct any of the loss. You can accumulate these losses and deduct them from the profit when you sell the property.

All profits on property are now taxed as ordinary income, not at the once-lower capital gains rate.

STRATEGIES FOR BUYING OLDER BUILDINGS

Thinking of buying an older building? If you purchase one built prior to 1936, the new law gives you a renovation break. If you spend $50,000 renovating the property, you are eligible to reduce your tax bite by $5,000, or 10 percent of the rehab cost. This tax credit applies only to nonresidential property.

Thus, should your tax bill at the end of the year be $10,000 and you spent $50,000 renovating a pre-1936 or older building, your tax bill is cut in half. That is because you deduct $5,000, or 10 percent of the $50,000 renovation work.

If you are thinking of renovating the pre-1936 building that you already own, you will receive a tax break on the renovations *under certain conditions.* Please consult your accountant before proceeding.

If you do renovation in a designated historic district, or you renovate a building designated as a historic landmark, you get a 20 percent reduction instead of 10.

STRATEGIES FOR DEPRECIATION

There are also new depreciation rules that cover the money that you deduct each year on the basis of the life cycle of a property. Residential real estate formerly had a useful tax life cycle of 19 years; now it is 27½. Nonresidential property has a tax life cycle of 31½ years.

Thus, in many cases you can depreciate your property at 3.6 percent per year. On a $100,000 property, that amounts to a $3,600 tax break a year. The depreciation schedule on properties that you owned before the 1986 tax law went into effect will not be changed.

If you have further questions on depreciation, check with your accountant. There are special rules depending on whether you use your home as a place of business and depending on which home you claim as your primary residence.

STRATEGIES FOR SELLERS

The new laws allow you to spread your profit on the sale of property by accepting a small down payment and receiving monthly payments during the term of the contract. This applies to all sales except those considered "dealer" property. (You are a dealer if you are a builder, a developer or in a similar business involving housing. Real estate agents are not considered dealers unless they "flip" properties often.)

You will be taxed only on the portion of the principal payment or down payment you receive in relation to your gross profit percentage.

Here is how you figure your gross profit percentage: Determine the amount of installment sale income that will be taxed by taking your net profit from the sale of the property and dividing it by your total sale price. This percentage is then multiplied by the amount of principal payments you receive on the installment plan during the year.

For example, you sell a home that originally cost you $100,000 for $150,000, making a profit of $50,000. Divide the $50,000 profit by $150,000. That leaves you with a profit percentage of 33 percent. Thus, if you get $21,000 in principal payments during the year, 33 percent of the amount, or $7,000, is taxable.

Any interest payments that you receive during the year should be included as taxable income on your tax return and will be taxed at your current income tax rate.

The lesson here is be very careful when selling a property you no longer use personally, such as a vacation home you have stopped visiting.

CHEERS! SOME REAL ESTATE TAX BREAKS REMAIN

The recent laws were passed to reduce tax shelters (including real estate shelters) and tax-advantaged purchases, but there are still some available tax breaks within the realm of real estate.

If you have not read chapter 27 about tax-free exchanges, we urge you to do so now, because the *1031 exchange* is still available to you.

Also still available—and worth reading about again in chapter 28—is the *1034 rollover*. The latter provision saves you taxes when you sell one house and buy another. To report the transaction, use IRS Form 2119.

For those whose adjusted gross income is less than $150,000 a year, the recent tax reforms have spotlighted single-family residential homes as the safest, most profitable investment of the next decade. We predict that people will pull money out of the stock market and other investments to build their future and enhance their wealth by investing in single-family residential properties, including detached homes, condominiums, co-ops, vacation homes and even mobile homes.

The reasons? For one thing, single-family residences are easy to finance. Mortgage money is available from lenders all over the country. For another, they are among the easiest investments to buy; homes are advertised in every Sunday newspaper in every town. It is not difficult to determine the value of houses in a particular area, and there is such a broad base of ownership that no one group of megamoney managers can control the market for single-family homes.

And single-family properties are more comfortable to manage than a multifamily dwelling. In financial terms, single-family residences are the most liquid of all real estate investments, with the exception of REITs—real estate investment trusts, which are sold as shares in the same way as stocks. If you need cash, it is hard to pull it out of a 20-unit dwelling, but if you own 20 single-family residences, you can always sell one. Finally, it is easier to be an active manager of single-family homes under the provisions of recent tax laws.

In sum, real estate owned by millions of American homeowners and soon-to-be owners remains a great investment.

PART IV

Sonny Bloch's Checklist

360 Questions

TO TAKE ALONG EN ROUTE TO MAKING THE MOST INTELLIGENT PURCHASE OR SALE OF A HOUSE, CONDO OR CO-OP

Buyer's Comfort Zone—Questions to Ask Yourself

1. Have I used my magic pencil to draw the dream house that I really want and need?

2. Have I evaluated my yearly income (plus that of my spouse or roommate) to see what my price range is?

3. Have I included all my outside income as well as my salary?

4. Have I added up all my current expenses, as shown on the Financial Comfort Zone Worksheet (page 20)?

5. Have I calculated on the worksheet what my available income is, then added to it my current rent and taxes, so that I know how much I actually can spend each month on a mortgage?

6. How far from my workplace, in time and miles, is the home I am considering?

7. How far are the schools my children would attend?

8. How far are the commuter train and the airport?

9. How far are other things that mean a lot to me, such as a shopping mall, church, recreation?

10. Have I checked the present zoning?

11. Can I use the house for the purpose I am buying it?

12. Have I decided on the style of home I want, with a second and third choice?

13. Do I want a pool? Hot tub? Other amenities?

14. How many bedrooms do I need?

15. How many bathrooms do I really need?

16. Is the living room the size that suits me?

17. Have I measured the rooms that are most important to me?

18. What is an absolute must for me in a kitchen?

19. Does the home have the study/laundry/workshop that I really need?

20. Am I satisfied with the exterior spaces—porch, front and back yards, garage?

21. Are the closets adequate?

22. If I am looking at a condo/co-op apartment or town home, are the common areas such as the lobby satisfactory?

23. Are the condo/co-op staff and service people satisfactory?

24. Is the parking adequate?

25. Will I pay an exorbitant price for certain built-ins, such as a stereo system, that are being left with the house?

26. Am I buying the house just because of gimmicks, such as a heart-shaped swimming pool?

Questions to Ask a Real Estate Broker

27. Are you a licensed broker or a sales associate?

28. How long have you been licensed?

29. Are you a member of the National Association of Realtors?

30. Do you work full-time as a real estate professional?

31. Do you have special designations, credentials or expertise?

32. How long have you been involved in this town/neighborhood/county?

33. Can you give me three references of recent clients?

34. What houses have you sold in the past 60 days?

35. Can you give me banking and credit references?

36. Are you showing me any properties that are your own listings?

37. Can we negotiate your commission if I choose one of your listings?

38. Will you put that in writing?

Questions to Ask a Real Estate Attorney

39. May I have a written schedule of the fees you will charge me for this deal?

40. What does each charge cover?

41. Are there contingency fees?

42. Will you do this deal on a flat-fee basis? If so, how much?

43. Is your practice limited to real estate?

44. Do you have an attorney-client relationship with either the lender or the seller in my situation?

45. (If he or she is a stranger) Can you give me a few references among your clients?

46. Can you get a discount on title insurance and pass it along to me?

47. Will you include jump-out clauses in this contract, giving me breathing room if I have trouble with the financing?

48. Have you double-checked zoning laws on this house?

49. (If you are doing an equity-sharing deal) Have you prepared shared-equity documents recently?

Inspecting a Home—Questions to Ask Yourself

50. Have I inspected the house I am thinking of buying in the company of a professional inspector?

51. What is the condition of the exterior structure—roof, siding, foundation?

52. What is the condition of the appliances being sold with the house?

53. Are warranties still in effect on appliances such as washer, dryer, garbage compactor, refrigerator, water heater?

54. What will it cost to repair elements of the house that are in unsatisfactory condition?

55. Is the wiring capacity adequate—at least 100 amps, plus spares and circuits for future electric appliances?

56. Is the septic tank at least 900 gallons in capacity, with adequate drain fields, or leaching fields?

57. Has a percolation test been done to show the septic system is working in the ground?

58. Is the plumbing supply line from the street at least three-fourths of an inch in diameter to avoid backup?

59. Have I looked closely at the bathroom fixtures and accessories? Am I going to have to replace them?

60. Does the kitchen have a good, solid countertop? Will it have to be replaced? Are there ample lighting and good ventilation?

61. Does the insulation conform to the minimum R factor (insulation value standard)?

62. Is the heating system guaranteed to maintain the house at 70 degrees even when the temperature is zero outside? In other words, is the heating system large enough for the house?

63. Do the heating and air-conditioning work quickly and quietly? (Turn them on.)

64. Are large window areas shaded and insulated to keep down air-conditioning bills in summer?

65. If the house does not have central air-conditioning, are heating ducts already installed through the furnace blower system to allow installation of a central air-conditioning system?

66. Is the door hardware made of solid brass, solid bronze, solid aluminum with deadbolt lock mechanisms on the exterior doors?

67. Is the roofing material of high quality and of adequate weight, with sealed-down roof shingles?

Questions to Help Get the Best Price

68. Has the home been appraised by a member of a respected appraisal associaton?

69. What is the appraised value?

70. What are other recent sales prices in the area?

Questions on Timing a Purchase

71. How long have houses in the area stayed on the market—for less than a month? For 1 to 3 months? For 3 to 5 months? For 6 months or more?

72. What was the price of a home in your style and size a year ago?

73. By how much has the population grown in the area in the last 5 years?

74. Have any major industries left the area lately, or are any ready to leave?

75. Are any major industries moving in?

76. How does the local chamber of commerce rate the business climate?

77. Does a check of courthouse records show an unusually high number of real estate transactions? An unusually high number of foreclosures?

78. In shopping and commercial areas, is the number of vacancies proportionally low? Moderate? High?

Questions on Negotiating

79. Is your binder refundable if the deal does not go through?

80. Have you put buyer-protection clauses in the binder and/or purchase agreement that make the deal subject to the approval of your attorney?

81. Have you made the deal contingent upon qualifying for a mortgage?

Questions on Getting a Mortgage

82. Will the bank that is carrying the present mortgage let you assume that mortgage or give you a new one for fewer points?

83. Have you called at least ten other banks and/or mortgage brokers in order to shop for a better deal? (Use the Comparison-Shopping Scorecard on pages 102–3).

84. What are the total points charged by each lender?

85. Have you counted total fees (application, origination, credit report, survey, appraisal)?

86. Have you factored in the years you expect to stay in the house before selling?

87. Do you qualify for VA or FHA loans to get a lower down payment and interest savings?

Questions on the Closing

88. Have you used the RESPA settlement form (pages 121–22) to calculate how much the closing will cost you?

89. In advance of the closing, have you contacted the seller, the bank, real estate brokers and your attorney to make sure everyone has the same closing date?

90. Have you received your good-faith estimate of closing costs, due 3 business days after the written loan application, according to federal law?

91. Have you notified the seller's security agency (or, in the case of a co-op or condo, the name of the security person at the building) that you are the new owner as of the closing date, so you can gain entrance to the property and change the code on a house security system?

92. Have you notified the utility companies (electric, water, gas, telephone) of the change of ownership?

93. Have you instructed the post office to forward mail, and have you filled out a change-of-address form?

94. Did you receive the federally mandated (RESPA) copy of the final settlement costs at least 1 day before the closing?

95. On closing day, has your attorney or title company checked court records for last-minute liens?

96. If there is oil remaining in the tank for heat, has the seller received credit for it?

97. Has the electric or gas meter been read for final charges?

98. Has the water meter been read?

99. Have you made your closing-day inspection of the new home?

100. Do you have your certified check for closing costs?

101. Is there additional money in your checking account for last-minute expenses?

102. Do you have a copy of the loan commitment letter in the folder you bring to the closing table?

103. Do you have a copy of your contract to purchase?

104. Have you received a copy of your new home insurance policy or a statement of ownership change from the seller's insurance agency?

105. Has the seller or a real estate person been reminded to bring the keys to your new residence?

Questions on Buying a Fixer-Upper

Have you received at least three estimates on the cost of renovating or repairing the following:

106. The house's roof?

107. The heating/cooling system?

108. The wiring and electrical system?

109. The plumbing?

110. The waste removal system?

111. Any sag?

112. The drainage system?

113. The water heater?

114. The landscaping and other repairs?

115. Have you estimated the cost of remodeling and other cosmetic changes in baths, kitchen, additional fixtures, painting, window replacement, floor covering?

116. Have you added these renovation, repair and remodeling costs to the purchase price of the house?

117. Have you multiplied this total cost by ⅓ for sweat equity or profit to calculate the market value of the house after renovation?

118. How does this market value compare with other houses in perfect condition in the same neighborhood?

119. If your market value will be greater than that of comparable houses, are you willing to pay a premium for your fixer-upper?

Questions on Buying a Custom-Built Home

120. Have you determined how much extra money the special features you want will cost?

121. How long has the builder been established in business?

122. Has the builder always operated under the present company name?

123. Do previous customers say the builder does come back to finished homes to fix things that go wrong?

124. What does the local bank say about the builder?

125. What kind of credit rating does the builder have with a local credit bureau?

126. Is the builder willing to show you houses already built?

127. Will the builder supply you with the names of at least six buyers of this builder's homes?

128. Do local building-material suppliers and subcontractors give the builder a good rating?

129. Does the builder belong to the local chapter of the National Association of Homebuilders?

130. What does the Association say about this builder?

131. Is the builder a member of the Home Owners Warranty program?

132. What do the Better Business Bureau, chamber of commerce and especially the local consumer-protection agency say about the builder?

133. Does the builder have a listed telephone number?

Questions on Buying a Condo (first or second home)

134. Have you comparison-shopped for the best condo buy in the neighborhood you have chosen?

135. Have you added the down payment and total closing costs to determine the initial outlay?

136. What are the monthly mortgage payments?

137. What are the yearly property taxes?

138. What is the monthly maintenance fee?

139. Are there any special assessments?

140. Are there extra fees for parking, club membership and so on?

141. Have you compared costs of condos versus co-ops in the neighborhood?

Questions on Buying a Co-op

142. Do you like the neighborhood?

143. Have you talked to the people in the building to ask them how they feel about living there?

144. Do you like the people you have met in the building?

145. Are you willing to be cross-examined by strangers on the board in order to live there?

146. Have you examined the outside of the building, the common areas, the hallways and the elevators for visual signs of good housekeeping?

147. Is financing available, and can you, in fact, finance this co-op, or must it be an all-cash deal?

148. Are banks lending money on this particular building? Where are those banks located?

149. Can you get a second loan in case you cannot come up with the cash to pay for a large assessment?

150. Do you like the level of personal service the building offers?

151. Will you be content with the restrictions on guests, subleases, children, pets and so on?

152. Are you getting as much for your money in this co-op as you would buying into a similarly located condo?

153. Have you learned who your common-wall neighbors are and whether they share a similar lifestyle in terms of noise, comings and goings, parties?

154. Does the apartment have good appreciation potential, should you decide to sell within a few years?

Questions for a Co-op Board

155. How old is the building?

156. What was the most recent major capital improvement?

157. What other improvements are being discussed?

158. How is the board of directors selected?

159. How often do directors rotate or change?

160. May we see some annual or semiannual reports?

161. How often does the board meet?

162. What income is required of incoming shareholders?

163. What are other considerations?

164. How much of the apartment's purchase price can be financed?

165. Are there restrictions on refinancing?

166. Has the board rejected anyone recently? Why?

167. How many (or what percentage of) apartments are investor-owned?

168. Are washers/dryers permitted in apartments?

169. Can a Jacuzzi or whirlpool be added?

170. What are the subleasing restrictions?

171. Who manages the building's day-to-day operations?

Questions on Buying a Second Home

172. How much did you spend last year for recreation lodging?

173. Have you multiplied this amount by 4 percent inflation over 10 years to define your 10-year vacation home kitty?

174. Have you calculated how much you can afford to pay for a mortgage on a second home?

175. Are you buying a vacation property for enjoyment, not for investment?

176. Have you "test-driven" your vacation locale by renting there before buying?

177. Have you asked if the developer of a resort you like is offering an inexpensive "try-out" vacation to prospective buyers?

178. Would you like to retire to this place eventually?

179. Have you inspected your vacation home choice as carefully as you would inspect a primary residence?

180. Are you shopping in the off season to find better deals?

181. Have you asked at least five owners in the same resort area if they are happy with their choice?

182. Have you given yourself a "cooling-off" period after hearing a sales pitch, before you sign any papers?

183. Did you get all the details about renting out your second home when you are not using it?

184. Have you checked the developer's credentials with the local resort association, Better Business Bureau and Association of Resort and Residential Developers?

185. Would it make better sense to buy a time share rather than a vacation home?

Questions for Resort Management Companies

186. Can you provide references from at least three current clients before I sign a contract for you to manage my vacation home?

187. How do you find customers for your rental units?

188. Can I see the rental records for the past 3 years for the unit I expect to purchase?

189. May I have the names and phone numbers of clients who have used your service for the past 3 years?

190. What is your annual management fee?

191. What dollar amount or percentage of each rental fee do you take in each season?

192. Does this cover daily, semiweekly or weekly linen changes and maid service? If so, which?

193. If the answer to the above question is no, what is the charge for these services?

194. How much of a reduction in the fee do I get if I refer a rental customer to you?

195. Is rental income distributed to owners via a pool or unit by unit?

196. How do you decide which unit to rent first?

197. Will I get a preferred place in the rental pool if I add such items as new furniture or new kitchen appliances to my property?

198. If you rent units on the basis of a rating system, who does the rating?

199. If there is such a rating system, how high a position would my unit hold right now?

200. Can I have a list of your charges for minor maintenance, such as fixing leaky faucets and changing light bulbs?

Questions on Insurance

201. Have you videotaped your residence, room by room, floor by floor, wall by wall, window by window, including basement and garage?

202. How long has your insurance company been in business?

203. What is the company's record of satisfying claims?

204. Does the company have a local claims office?

205. Is there another, comparable company that will give you the same coverage for less money?

206. Does your policy have a replacement cost provision?

207. Do you have to call your agent every time you buy something new in order to add it to your policy?

208. If so, how much can you add before you begin paying more premiums?

209. Does your policy include additional living expenses if your house is so damaged that you have to move elsewhere temporarily?

210. Does your policy include the loss of credit cards and cash, or do you need a separate policy?

211. What is the maximum liability coverage in case somebody gets hurt on your property?

212. Does your policy cover damages that are done by your pets?

213. What kind of legal representation will the insurance company offer if you are sued by somebody who gets hurt at your home?

214. What are the items that the company will *not* insure in your geographic area, such as jewelry, furs, antiques and paintings?

215. What kind of appraisal will the company accept for the coverage of these high-risk items?

216. Does this company offer the $1 million umbrella policy that covers you for such things as false arrest, wrongful eviction, libel, slander, defamation of character and invasion of privacy?

217. What discount can you get on your homeowner's insurance premium if you include auto policies in the package?

218. What is your deduction in the premium for installing smoke alarms, burglar alarms and sprinkler systems?

Job Transfer—Questions for Your Company

219. If the transfer does not allow you enough time to sell your home, or if the market is soft, will the company pick up your mortgage payments? Or perhaps buy your home, so you have the resources to buy another in your new location?

220. Will the company lease a home for you in your new location, at least for a transition period?

221. Will the company pay for the cost of your move?

222. If you must start your new job before your family moves (or before the school term ends), will the company pay your hotel or temporary apartment costs?

Selling a House—Questions to Ask Yourself

223. Do I really need to sell my house? Why?

224. Can I list three good reasons for *not* selling it?

225. How soon do I actually need to sell it?

226. Do I want to sell it myself? Do I have the time?

227. Would I rather sell it through a real estate broker?

228. Have I reviewed the "thermometer" for judging a real estate market? (See pages 67–68.)

229. How much have other houses similar to mine in my neighborhood sold for within the past 6 months?

230. What is the price I would like to place on my house?

231. What is the least I will accept?

232. How much cash do I need from the buyer to make a deal?

233. Am I willing to finance part of the down payment myself?

234. Am I willing to finance the entire purchase myself, if necessary? (If the answer is yes, see Questions on Seller Financing below.)

235. Have I considered the tax advantages of a 1034 rollover, under which I pay no taxes on the sale, provided I buy another house within 24 months?

236. Have I made arrangements for a replacement residence?

237. If my home sells before I buy or rent a replacement house, have I arranged to pay rent to the buyer of my home so I can remain there for a while?

238. Have I allowed myself at least a week for interviewing brokers?

239. Have I allowed myself time for cleaning up the house, inside and out?

240. Have I allowed time for work by professionals on landscaping and pruning?

241. Have I allowed time for paint jobs?

242. Have I planned a yard sale?

Questions on Sprucing Up Your House for Sale

243. Is the fence painted and fixed?

244. Are the mailbox and house numbers new enough? Painted? Replaced?

245. Is the front lawn edged, are trees pruned, are bushes tended?

246. Has porch clutter been removed and have chairs and flowers been put out?

247. Do the windows sparkle?

248. Does the front door need repainting or replacement?

249. Is the door knocker polished, is a new welcome mat out, and is the doorbell working?

250. Are mirrors needed in the entrance hall or elsewhere?

251. Has some living room furniture been removed?

252. Is the carpet clean, and are holes covered with area rugs?

253. Are the floors polished, and is closet clutter removed?

254. Is the fireplace swept, with fresh logs in place?

255. Is the family room neat, with some furniture removed?

256. Is soft music playing, and are toys put away?

257. In the kitchen, is the ceiling painted white?

258. Is vanilla boiling on the stove for a sweet smell?

259. Are appliances and cupboards clean, inside and out?

260. Is the pantry swept and neat?

261. Has a full table been set in the dining room, with flowers?

262. In the bedrooms, are bureau tops neat and are the beds made?

263. Are the bedroom carpets cleaned and/or vacuumed, and are the drapes neat?

264. Are the bedroom closets uncluttered, with items stored under the bed?

265. In the bathrooms, are the toilets flushing properly, and have the faucets been checked for drips?

266. Are there clean towels folded on racks, and have utensils been put away?

267. Have the tiles been checked and has grout been cleaned?

268. Do all doors close properly?

269. In the attic, are loose items boxed?

270. In the basement, are the walls painted, is the floor washed, and have loose items been boxed and stored neatly?

271. Has the backyard or patio been tidied and cleaned?

272. Have you cleaned up after the dog?

273. In the carport or garage, has clutter been removed?

Selling Points—Questions for Your Checklist

274. What is the location and driving time, in minutes, to a commuter train and/or bus?

275. What and where are the neighborhood schools and nearest day-care center?

276. Where are the nearest park and nearest recreation facility (pool, tennis courts, riding trails, health club, country club)?

277. Where is the nearest convenience store?

278. Where is the nearest gas station?

279. Where is the nearest bank with automatic teller?

280. Where is the nearest shopping center or mall?

281. What and where are nearby churches and synagogues?

282. What are the name, address and phone number of the public and/or private sanitation service?

283. Where are the nearest fire house and police station? What are their phone numbers?

284. Where is the nearest hospital or walk-in medical office?

Questions for Your Selling Fact Sheet

285. Have you described the style and age of your house?

286. Have you attached a floor plan, if possible?

287. What is the size of the lot, and how many total square feet of dwelling space are there?

288. How many bedrooms are there, and what are their sizes?

289. How many full and half baths?

290. How big are the living room, family room and/or den?

291. If included, what type of window treatments (drapes, shutters, blinds) are there?

292. How big are the kitchen and eat-in space?

293. Which appliances are included?

294. How big is the dining area?

295. Are there special facts on attic, basement, front and/or back porch, yard, patio, carport and/or garage?

296. Are there special amenities (brass switch plates, chandeliers)?

297. What type of heating or air-conditioning system is there?

Have you supplied the following:

298. Gas and/or oil company name and address?

299. Water heater capacity and water company name and address?

300. Electrical capacity and electric company name and address?

301. Telephone company name and business office phone number?

302. Who are reliable service personnel and companies for such jobs as new lock installation, lawn care, snow removal? (See a more complete list on pages 262–63.)

Questions for Brokers Who Want to Sell Your House

303. Are you a full-time broker?

304. How long have you sold full-time in this region?

305. Do you have any special professional designations from the National Association of Realtors?

306. Have you sold any homes in the immediate vicinity in the past 2 years? (Request to see the sold listing in the multilist.)

307. Did you get the asking price? If not, how close to it?

308. Do you still have homes that you are showing in my neighborhood?

309. Is your commission negotiable?

310. Will you give me the names of people for whom you have sold houses in the past year?

311. If you are a salesperson, may I have some references to check your brokerage firm?

312. Which mortgage brokers or bankers do you work with on financing?

313. Do you work with a particular real estate attorney?

314. Will you give me a written advertising campaign?

315. How much will you spend, and where and when will the ads appear?

316. How many times will you hold an open house?

317. Will my home be listed with the Multiple Listing Service?

Questions If You Are Selling Without a Broker

318. Has your attorney prepared an offer to purchase?

319. Has the attorney prepared a commission agreement for a single transaction only?

320. Have you arranged for an answering service to receive calls?

321. Have you prepared ads and signs for your sale?

322. Have you arranged for a friend to call if you show your house alone?

Questions for the Seller's Attorney

323. Are you a full-time real estate attorney?

324. Can you give me, in writing, your flat fee to handle all items necessary for the sale of my house?

325. Does this fee include title research, title insurance policy, approval of listing agreement, drafting and approving offer to purchase, assisting with and expediting financing, and attending the closing?

Questions on Negotiating a Sale

326. Have you set your asking price a small amount higher—10 to 20 percent—than you will accept?

327. Have you waited for the buyer to state his or her position first?

328. Are you giving in by making small concessions, rather than giving up everything you are willing to give all at once?

329. Are you prepared to change your mind before the contract is signed, in case something is amiss?

330. Have you found out what the buyer's needs are?

331. Have you first listened carefully to the buyer, and only then concentrated on your next move?

332. Have you left an opening for the other side?

Questions on Seller Financing

333. Will it help sell your house faster if you offer to finance the sale yourself?

334. Have you considered offering the house on a lease with option to purchase instead of an outright sale?

335. Have you considered an equity participation arrangement if your buyer cannot come up with a down payment?

336. If you are not financing the sale, have you consulted local lenders for information on mortgages that they can offer to qualified buyers?

337. Do you understand the advantages and drawbacks of becoming a "banker"?

338. Have you and your seller signed an agreement for deed drawn up by your attorney?

339. Have you arranged a deed in lieu of foreclosure to avoid the problems of repossession?

340. Have you thought about a tax-free exchange of your house rather than a sale?

Questions on Refinancing

341. Are current interest rates lower now than the rate on your mortgage?

342. Have you tried renegotiating your mortgage through the bank that currently holds that loan in order to obtain lower interest rates?

343. Have you comparison-shopped with other lenders who might refinance your mortgage, to judge whether renegotiating is the best deal?

344. Have you filled out Doing the Numbers Worksheet (page 326) to see how much you can save on refinancing or renegotiating?

Questions on Closing for a Seller

345. Do you know what you must pay for such items and services as title fee, unpaid taxes, mortgage prepayment penalty, loan points, appraisal fee, document preparation fee, recording and transfer fees, survey, real estate commission, legal fees, special assessments, termite inspection, house inspection, repairs? (See page 333.)

346. What will the sale net you after you deduct selling costs, credits to you, and your mortgage balance?

Leaving the House After a Sale

347. Have you arranged for the electricity to be disconnected?

348. The gas?

349. Have you notified the water company?

350. The oil company?

351. Have you given a forwarding address to the post office?

352. Have you given the telephone company a forwarding number and a disconnect order?

353. Have you notified your long-distance phone company?

354. Did you empty your safe-deposit box if you are moving to a new community?

355. Did you stop newspaper delivery?

356. Have you requested a cable TV cutoff?

357. Did you notify the garbage company, if a private service?

358. Have you ended all landscaping, snow removal, lawn care and pool services?

359. Did you give final thank-you tips to handymen and service people in the apartment building or town home development?

360. Have you turned over the appliance manuals and warranties to your buyer?

Glossary

Real Estate Terms from A to Z

Amortization. A schedule of monthly payments which include interest and principal.

APR. Actual percentage rate of interest paid.

Assessment. An amount of money paid to the government or an association with legal rights to force payment.

Assumable. Capable of being taken over by another person, as a mortgage.

Balloon payment. A payment due for the entire balance of a mortgage before monthly payments pay it off.

Binder. Money paid by a buyer to show "good faith" to take a property off the market, accompanied by an agreement very carefully written so the buyer can inspect the property and get his money back if he is not satisfied. (See also *Earnest money.*)

Blended mortgage. A combination of a low-interest first mortgage with a high-interest second mortgage to create a new mortgage with an interest rate in between.

Certificate of occupancy. A document issued by the local government authority giving someone permission to move into a home.

Date of origination. The date a loan begins to be processed.

Default. Failure to pay, or nonperformance of one of the parties to an agreement.

Earnest money. An amount a party pays on a real estate deal, before entering into a formal contract, that says the party is sincere about the transaction; in return the party gets a receipt. Also called *binder, good-faith money, deposit.*

Easement. A portion of one person's property that is legally open for use by another party. Examples include electric poles or underground wires, gas lines, roads, cable TV wires, sewers.

Encumbrance. Literally, a burden. Your mortgage is an encumbrance against your house.

Equity loan. Money borrowed against the difference between a home's worth and what is owed on it. For example, a $150,000 home on which you still owe $75,000 allows you an equity loan of up to $75,000.

Escrow. Money or documents held in trust, usually by a third party such as a bank or title company, until a deal is closed.

FHA loan. A loan insured (guaranteed) by the Federal Housing Administration.

First mortgage. The first loan obtained on a home, which stays as the first mortgage until it is paid off. It also is first in line at foreclosure.

First refusal. A person's right to purchase a home first if another bona fide offer comes in and the person *meets* it.

Interest. The rent you pay on the money you borrow.

Key money. A sum sometimes required from a tenant for residential real estate by a landlord, in return for obtaining a lease on an apartment. (This is illegal in some states.) Also, the amount a subtenant is required to pay to the prime tenant in order to get a sublease. In commercial real estate, key money is neither illegal nor uncommon. It means money for improvements.

Leverage. Controlling a lot of real estate with a little bit of money; in real estate $10,000 controls $100,000.

Liquidated damages. The amount forfeited (usually limited to the deposit) for nonperformance.

Listing broker. The broker who signs a contract with a homeowner to sell his home.

Lock in. A *written* commitment from an institution that lends money for buying a home or that grants a second mortgage or equity loan, saying that the rate quoted at the beginning will be the *same* at the closing.

Mortgage banker. A person working in the mortgage business.

Mortgage broker. A person licensed to find mortgage money from any source.

Note. The document a person signs that makes him personally responsible for the money the person borrows.

Origination fee. The fee paid up front to have paperwork done on a loan.

Plat. A drawing of property.

Prepayment. Payment on principal before it is due.

Points. Money paid to obtain a loan. 1 point equals 1 percent of the loan.

Replacement cost. The actual cost of replacing an item damaged, lost or stolen.

Refinancing. Obtaining a new mortgage and simultaneously paying off the old one, usually for a better rate of interest.

Restrictive covenants. Recorded rules and regulations on how property can be used.

Second mortgage. Additional money borrowed on a home without changing the first mortgage.

Take back. To accept, as in, "I'll take back a second mortgage when I sell you this."

Title company. An institution that issues insurance guaranteeing that a person owns the property he has just bought.

Transfer taxes. Payment for transferring property from one person to another, usually paid to city, county and state governments and to local condo and co-op boards or associations.

Underlying mortgage. A mortgage that exists on a property.

VA loan. A loan insured and guaranteed by the Veterans Administration.

Wraparound mortgage. A mortgage or contract combining all existing mortgages into one, with one payment going to the holder.

Yield. The amount earned on money invested.

Zoning codes. Strict guidelines enforced by local governments on how a property can or cannot be used.

9.00%

MONTHLY

PAYMENT REQUIRED TO AMORTIZE A LOAN

TERM AMOUNT	1 YEAR	2 YEARS	3 YEARS	4 YEARS	5 YEARS	6 YEARS	7 YEARS	8 YEARS	9 YEARS	10 YEARS	11 YEARS	12 YEARS
50	4.38	2.29	1.59	1.25	1.04	.91	.81	.74	.68	.64	.60	.57
100	8.75	4.57	3.18	2.49	2.08	1.81	1.61	1.47	1.36	1.27	1.20	1.14
200	17.50	9.14	6.36	4.98	4.16	3.61	3.22	2.94	2.71	2.54	2.40	2.28
300	26.24	13.71	9.54	7.47	6.23	5.41	4.83	4.40	4.07	3.81	3.59	3.42
400	34.99	18.28	12.72	9.96	8.31	7.22	6.44	5.87	5.42	5.07	4.79	4.56
500	43.73	22.85	15.90	12.45	10.38	9.02	8.05	7.33	6.78	6.34	5.99	5.70
600	52.48	27.42	19.08	14.94	12.46	10.82	9.66	8.80	8.13	7.61	7.18	6.83
700	61.22	31.98	22.26	17.42	14.54	12.62	11.27	10.26	9.49	8.87	8.38	7.97
800	69.97	36.55	25.44	19.91	16.61	14.43	12.88	11.73	10.84	10.14	9.57	9.11
900	78.71	41.12	28.62	22.40	18.69	16.23	14.49	13.19	12.19	11.41	10.77	10.25
1000	87.46	45.69	31.80	24.89	20.76	18.03	16.09	14.66	13.55	12.67	11.97	11.39
2000	174.91	91.37	63.60	49.78	41.52	36.06	32.18	29.31	27.09	25.34	23.93	22.77
3000	262.36	137.06	95.40	74.66	62.28	54.08	48.27	43.96	40.63	38.01	35.89	34.15
4000	349.81	182.74	127.20	99.55	83.04	72.11	64.36	58.61	54.18	50.68	47.85	45.53
5000	437.26	228.43	159.00	124.43	103.80	90.13	80.45	73.26	67.72	63.34	59.81	56.91
6000	524.71	274.11	190.80	149.32	124.56	108.16	96.54	87.91	81.26	76.01	71.77	68.29
7000	612.17	319.80	222.60	174.20	145.31	126.18	112.63	102.56	94.81	88.68	83.73	79.67
8000	699.62	365.48	254.40	199.09	166.07	144.21	128.72	117.21	108.35	101.35	95.69	91.05
9000	787.07	411.17	286.20	223.97	186.83	162.23	144.81	131.86	121.89	114.01	107.65	102.43
10000	874.52	456.85	318.00	248.86	207.59	180.26	160.90	146.51	135.43	126.68	119.61	113.81
11000	961.97	502.54	349.80	273.74	228.35	198.29	176.98	161.16	148.98	139.35	131.57	125.19
12000	1049.42	548.22	381.60	298.63	249.11	216.31	193.07	175.81	162.52	152.02	143.53	136.57
13000	1136.87	593.91	413.40	323.51	269.86	234.34	209.16	190.46	176.06	164.68	155.50	147.95
14000	1224.33	639.59	445.20	348.40	290.62	252.36	225.25	205.11	189.61	177.35	167.46	159.33
15000	1311.78	685.28	477.00	373.28	311.38	270.39	241.34	219.76	203.15	190.02	179.42	170.71
16000	1399.23	730.96	508.80	398.17	332.14	288.41	257.43	234.41	216.69	202.69	191.38	182.09
17000	1486.68	776.65	540.60	423.05	352.90	306.44	273.52	249.06	230.23	215.35	203.34	193.47
18000	1574.13	822.33	572.40	447.94	373.66	324.46	289.61	263.71	243.78	228.02	215.30	204.85
19000	1661.58	868.02	604.20	472.82	394.41	342.49	305.70	278.36	257.32	240.69	227.26	216.23
20000	1749.03	913.70	636.00	497.71	415.17	360.52	321.79	293.01	270.86	253.36	239.22	227.61
21000	1836.49	959.38	667.80	522.59	435.93	378.54	337.88	307.66	284.41	266.02	251.18	238.99
22000	1923.94	1005.07	699.60	547.48	456.69	396.57	353.96	322.31	297.95	278.69	263.14	250.37
23000	2011.39	1050.75	731.40	572.36	477.45	414.59	370.05	336.96	311.49	291.36	275.10	261.75
24000	2098.84	1096.44	763.20	597.25	498.21	432.62	386.14	351.61	325.03	304.03	287.06	273.13
25000	2186.29	1142.12	795.00	622.13	518.96	450.64	402.23	366.26	338.58	316.69	299.03	284.51
26000	2273.74	1187.81	826.80	647.02	539.72	468.67	418.32	380.91	352.12	329.36	310.99	295.89
27000	2361.19	1233.49	858.60	671.90	560.48	486.69	434.41	395.56	365.66	342.03	322.95	307.27
28000	2448.65	1279.18	890.40	696.79	581.24	504.72	450.50	410.21	379.21	354.70	334.91	318.65
29000	2536.10	1324.86	922.20	721.67	602.00	522.75	466.59	424.86	392.75	367.36	346.87	330.03
30000	2623.55	1370.55	954.00	746.56	622.76	540.77	482.68	439.51	406.29	380.03	358.83	341.41
31000	2711.00	1416.23	985.80	771.44	643.51	558.80	498.77	454.16	419.84	392.70	370.79	352.79
32000	2798.45	1461.92	1017.60	796.33	664.27	576.82	514.86	468.81	433.38	405.37	382.75	364.17
33000	2885.90	1507.60	1049.40	821.21	685.03	594.85	530.94	483.46	446.92	418.04	394.71	375.56
34000	2973.36	1553.29	1081.20	846.10	705.79	612.87	547.03	498.11	460.46	430.70	406.67	386.94
35000	3060.81	1598.97	1113.00	870.98	726.55	630.90	563.12	512.76	474.01	443.37	418.63	398.32
36000	3148.26	1644.66	1144.80	895.87	747.31	648.92	579.21	527.41	487.55	456.04	430.59	409.70
37000	3235.71	1690.34	1176.60	920.75	768.06	666.95	595.30	542.06	501.09	468.71	442.55	421.08
38000	3323.16	1736.03	1208.39	945.64	788.82	684.98	611.39	556.71	514.64	481.37	454.52	432.46
39000	3410.61	1781.71	1240.19	970.52	809.58	703.00	627.48	571.36	528.18	494.04	466.48	443.84
40000	3498.06	1827.39	1271.99	995.41	830.34	721.03	643.57	586.01	541.72	506.71	478.44	455.22
41000	3585.52	1873.08	1303.79	1020.29	851.10	739.05	659.66	600.66	555.26	519.38	490.40	466.60
42000	3672.97	1918.76	1335.59	1045.18	871.86	757.08	675.75	615.31	568.81	532.04	502.36	477.98
43000	3760.42	1964.45	1367.39	1070.06	892.61	775.10	691.84	629.96	582.35	544.71	514.32	489.36
44000	3847.87	2010.13	1399.19	1094.95	913.37	793.13	707.92	644.61	595.89	557.38	526.28	500.74
45000	3935.32	2055.82	1430.99	1119.83	934.13	811.15	724.01	659.26	609.44	570.05	538.24	512.12
46000	4022.77	2101.50	1462.79	1144.72	954.89	829.18	740.10	673.91	622.98	582.71	550.20	523.50
47000	4110.22	2147.19	1494.59	1169.60	975.65	847.21	756.19	688.56	636.52	595.38	562.16	534.88
48000	4197.68	2192.87	1526.39	1194.49	996.41	865.23	772.28	703.21	650.06	608.05	574.12	546.26
49000	4285.13	2238.56	1558.19	1219.37	1017.16	883.26	788.37	717.86	663.61	620.72	586.08	557.64
50000	4372.58	2284.24	1589.99	1244.26	1037.92	901.28	804.46	732.52	677.15	633.38	598.05	569.02
55000	4809.84	2512.67	1748.99	1368.68	1141.71	991.41	884.90	805.77	744.86	696.72	657.85	625.92
60000	5247.09	2741.09	1907.99	1493.11	1245.51	1081.54	965.35	879.02	812.58	760.06	717.65	682.82
65000	5684.35	2969.51	2066.99	1617.53	1349.30	1171.66	1045.80	952.27	880.29	823.40	777.46	739.72
70000	6121.61	3197.94	2225.99	1741.96	1453.09	1261.79	1126.24	1025.52	948.01	886.74	837.26	796.63
75000	6558.87	3426.36	2384.98	1866.38	1556.88	1351.92	1206.69	1098.77	1015.72	950.07	897.07	853.53
80000	6996.12	3654.78	2543.98	1990.81	1660.67	1442.05	1287.13	1172.02	1083.44	1013.41	956.87	910.43
85000	7433.38	3883.21	2702.98	2115.23	1764.47	1532.18	1367.58	1245.27	1151.15	1076.75	1016.67	967.33
90000	7870.64	4111.63	2861.98	2239.66	1868.26	1622.30	1448.02	1318.52	1218.87	1140.09	1076.48	1024.23
95000	8307.90	4340.06	3020.98	2364.08	1972.05	1712.43	1528.47	1391.77	1286.58	1203.42	1136.28	1081.13
100000	8745.15	4568.48	3179.98	2488.51	2075.84	1802.56	1608.91	1465.03	1354.30	1266.76	1196.09	1138.04

MONTHLY   9.00%

PAYMENT REQUIRED TO AMORTIZE A LOAN

TERM AMOUNT	13 YEARS	14 YEARS	15 YEARS	16 YEARS	17 YEARS	18 YEARS	19 YEARS	20 YEARS	25 YEARS	30 YEARS	35 YEARS	40 YEARS
50	.55	.53	.51	.50	.48	.47	.46	.45	.42	.41	.40	.39
100	1.09	1.05	1.02	.99	.96	.94	.92	.90	.84	.81	.79	.78
200	2.18	2.10	2.03	1.97	1.92	1.88	1.84	1.80	1.68	1.61	1.57	1.55
300	3.27	3.15	3.05	2.96	2.88	2.81	2.76	2.70	2.52	2.42	2.36	2.32
400	4.36	4.20	4.06	3.94	3.84	3.75	3.67	3.60	3.36	3.22	3.14	3.09
500	5.45	5.25	5.08	4.93	4.80	4.69	4.59	4.50	4.20	4.03	3.92	3.86
600	6.54	6.30	6.09	5.91	5.76	5.62	5.51	5.40	5.04	4.83	4.71	4.63
700	7.63	7.35	7.10	6.90	6.72	6.56	6.42	6.30	5.88	5.64	5.49	5.40
800	8.72	8.40	8.12	7.88	7.68	7.50	7.34	7.20	6.72	6.44	6.28	6.18
900	9.81	9.45	9.13	8.87	8.63	8.43	8.26	8.10	7.56	7.25	7.06	6.95
1000	10.90	10.49	10.15	9.85	9.59	9.37	9.17	9.00	8.40	8.05	7.84	7.72
2000	21.80	20.98	20.29	19.70	19.18	18.73	18.34	18.00	16.79	16.10	15.68	15.43
3000	32.70	31.47	30.43	29.54	28.77	28.10	27.51	27.00	25.18	24.14	23.52	23.15
4000	43.59	41.96	40.58	39.39	38.36	37.46	36.68	35.99	33.57	32.19	31.36	30.86
5000	54.49	52.45	50.72	49.23	47.95	46.83	45.85	44.99	41.96	40.24	39.20	38.57
6000	65.39	62.94	60.86	59.08	57.53	56.19	55.02	53.99	50.36	48.28	47.04	46.29
7000	76.28	73.43	71.00	68.92	67.12	65.56	64.19	62.99	58.75	56.33	54.88	54.00
8000	87.18	83.92	81.15	78.77	76.71	74.92	73.36	71.98	67.14	64.37	62.72	61.71
9000	98.08	94.41	91.29	88.61	86.30	84.29	82.53	80.98	75.53	72.42	70.56	69.43
10000	108.97	104.90	101.43	98.46	95.89	93.65	91.69	89.98	83.92	80.47	78.40	77.14
11000	119.87	115.39	111.57	108.30	105.47	103.01	100.86	98.97	92.32	88.51	86.24	84.85
12000	130.77	125.88	121.72	118.15	115.06	112.38	110.03	107.97	100.71	96.56	94.08	92.57
13000	141.66	136.37	131.86	127.99	124.65	121.74	119.20	116.97	109.10	104.61	101.92	100.28
14000	152.56	146.86	142.00	137.84	134.24	131.11	128.37	125.97	117.49	112.65	109.76	108.00
15000	163.46	157.35	152.14	147.68	143.83	140.47	137.54	134.96	125.88	120.70	117.60	115.71
16000	174.35	167.84	162.29	157.53	153.41	149.84	146.71	143.96	134.28	128.74	125.44	123.42
17000	185.25	178.32	172.43	167.37	163.00	159.20	155.88	152.96	142.67	136.79	133.28	131.14
18000	196.15	188.81	182.57	177.22	172.59	168.57	165.05	161.96	151.06	144.84	141.12	138.85
19000	207.04	199.30	192.72	187.06	182.18	177.93	174.22	170.95	159.45	152.88	148.96	146.56
20000	217.94	209.79	202.86	196.91	191.77	187.29	183.38	179.95	167.84	160.93	156.80	154.28
21000	228.84	220.28	213.00	206.75	201.35	196.66	192.55	188.95	176.24	168.98	164.64	161.99
22000	239.73	230.77	223.14	216.60	210.94	206.02	201.72	197.94	184.63	177.02	172.48	169.70
23000	250.63	241.26	233.29	226.44	220.53	215.39	210.89	206.94	193.02	185.07	180.32	177.42
24000	261.53	251.75	243.43	236.29	230.12	224.75	220.06	215.94	201.41	193.11	188.16	185.13
25000	272.43	262.24	253.57	246.13	239.71	234.12	229.23	224.94	209.80	201.16	196.00	192.85
26000	283.32	272.73	263.71	255.98	249.29	243.48	238.40	233.93	218.20	209.21	203.84	200.56
27000	294.22	283.22	273.86	265.82	258.88	252.85	247.57	242.93	226.59	217.25	211.68	208.27
28000	305.12	293.71	284.00	275.67	268.47	262.21	256.74	251.93	234.98	225.30	219.52	215.99
29000	316.01	304.20	294.14	285.51	278.06	271.57	265.91	260.93	243.37	233.35	227.36	223.70
30000	326.91	314.69	304.28	295.36	287.65	280.94	275.07	269.92	251.76	241.39	235.20	231.41
31000	337.81	325.18	314.43	305.20	297.23	290.30	284.24	278.92	260.16	249.44	243.04	239.13
32000	348.70	335.67	324.57	315.05	306.82	299.67	293.41	287.92	268.55	257.48	250.88	246.84
33000	359.60	346.15	334.71	324.90	316.41	309.03	302.58	296.91	276.94	265.53	258.72	254.55
34000	370.50	356.64	344.86	334.74	326.00	318.40	311.75	305.91	285.33	273.58	266.56	262.27
35000	381.39	367.13	355.00	344.59	335.59	327.76	320.92	314.91	293.72	281.62	274.40	269.98
36000	392.29	377.62	365.14	354.43	345.17	337.13	330.09	323.91	302.12	289.67	282.24	277.70
37000	403.19	388.11	375.28	364.28	354.76	346.49	339.26	332.90	310.51	297.72	290.08	285.41
38000	414.08	398.60	385.43	374.12	364.35	355.85	348.43	341.90	318.90	305.76	297.92	293.12
39000	424.98	409.09	395.57	383.97	373.94	365.22	357.59	350.90	327.29	313.81	305.76	300.84
40000	435.88	419.58	405.71	393.81	383.53	374.58	366.76	359.90	335.68	321.85	313.60	308.55
41000	446.77	430.07	415.85	403.66	393.11	383.95	375.93	368.89	344.08	329.90	321.44	316.26
42000	457.67	440.56	426.00	413.50	402.70	393.31	385.10	377.89	352.47	337.95	329.28	323.98
43000	468.57	451.05	436.14	423.35	412.29	402.68	394.27	386.89	360.86	345.99	337.12	331.69
44000	479.46	461.54	446.28	433.19	421.88	412.04	403.44	395.88	369.25	354.04	344.96	339.40
45000	490.36	472.03	456.42	443.04	431.47	421.41	412.61	404.88	377.64	362.09	352.80	347.12
46000	501.26	482.52	466.57	452.88	441.05	430.77	421.78	413.88	386.04	370.13	360.64	354.83
47000	512.15	493.01	476.71	462.73	450.64	440.13	430.95	422.88	394.43	378.18	368.48	362.54
48000	523.05	503.50	486.85	472.57	460.23	449.50	440.12	431.87	402.82	386.22	376.32	370.26
49000	533.95	513.98	497.00	482.42	469.82	458.86	449.28	440.87	411.21	394.27	384.16	377.97
50000	544.85	524.47	507.14	492.26	479.41	468.23	458.45	449.87	419.60	402.32	392.00	385.69
55000	599.33	576.92	557.85	541.49	527.35	515.05	504.30	494.85	461.56	442.55	431.20	424.25
60000	653.81	629.37	608.56	590.71	575.29	561.87	550.14	539.84	503.52	482.78	470.40	462.82
65000	708.30	681.81	659.28	639.94	623.23	608.69	595.99	584.83	545.48	523.01	509.60	501.39
70000	762.78	734.26	709.99	689.17	671.17	655.52	641.83	629.81	587.44	563.24	548.80	539.96
75000	817.27	786.71	760.70	738.39	719.11	702.34	687.68	674.80	629.40	603.47	588.00	578.53
80000	871.75	839.16	811.42	787.62	767.05	749.16	733.52	719.79	671.36	643.70	627.20	617.09
85000	926.23	891.60	862.13	836.84	814.99	795.98	779.37	764.77	713.32	683.93	666.40	655.66
90000	980.72	944.05	912.84	886.07	862.93	842.81	825.21	809.76	755.28	724.17	705.60	694.23
95000	1035.20	996.50	963.56	935.30	910.87	889.63	871.06	854.74	797.24	764.40	744.80	732.80
100000	1089.69	1048.94	1014.27	984.52	958.81	936.45	916.90	899.73	839.20	804.63	784.00	771.37

MONTHLY

PAYMENT REQUIRED TO AMORTIZE A LOAN

9.25%

TERM AMOUNT	1 YEAR	2 YEARS	3 YEARS	4 YEARS	5 YEARS	6 YEARS	7 YEARS	8 YEARS	9 YEARS	10 YEARS	11 YEARS	12 YEARS
50	4.38	2.29	1.60	1.26	1.05	.91	.82	.74	.69	.65	.61	.58
100	8.76	4.58	3.20	2.51	2.09	1.82	1.63	1.48	1.37	1.29	1.21	1.16
200	17.52	9.16	6.39	5.01	4.18	3.63	3.25	2.96	2.74	2.57	2.42	2.31
300	26.28	13.74	9.58	7.51	6.27	5.45	4.87	4.44	4.11	3.85	3.63	3.46
400	35.03	18.32	12.77	10.01	8.36	7.26	6.49	5.92	5.48	5.13	4.84	4.61
500	43.79	22.90	15.96	12.51	10.44	9.08	8.11	7.40	6.84	6.41	6.05	5.77
600	52.55	27.48	19.15	15.01	12.53	10.89	9.73	8.87	8.21	7.69	7.26	6.92
700	61.30	32.06	22.35	17.51	14.62	12.71	11.36	10.35	9.58	8.97	8.47	8.07
800	70.06	36.64	25.54	20.01	16.71	14.52	12.98	11.83	10.95	10.25	9.68	9.22
900	78.82	41.22	28.73	22.51	18.80	16.34	14.60	13.31	12.31	11.53	10.89	10.37
1000	87.57	45.80	31.92	25.01	20.88	18.15	16.22	14.79	13.68	12.81	12.10	11.53
2000	175.14	91.60	63.84	50.01	41.76	36.30	32.44	29.57	27.36	25.61	24.20	23.05
3000	262.71	137.40	95.75	75.02	62.64	54.45	48.65	44.35	41.03	38.41	36.30	34.57
4000	350.27	183.20	127.67	100.02	83.52	72.60	64.87	59.13	54.71	51.22	48.40	46.09
5000	437.84	229.00	159.59	125.02	104.40	90.75	81.09	73.91	68.38	64.02	60.50	57.61
6000	525.41	274.80	191.50	150.03	125.28	108.90	97.30	88.69	82.06	76.82	72.60	69.13
7000	612.98	320.60	223.42	175.03	146.16	127.05	113.52	103.47	95.74	89.63	84.70	80.66
8000	700.54	366.40	255.33	200.04	167.04	145.20	129.73	118.25	109.41	102.43	96.80	92.18
9000	788.11	412.20	287.25	225.04	187.92	163.35	145.95	133.03	123.09	115.23	108.90	103.70
10000	875.68	458.00	319.17	250.04	208.80	181.50	162.17	147.81	136.76	128.04	121.00	115.22
11000	963.25	503.80	351.08	275.05	229.68	199.65	178.38	162.59	150.44	140.84	133.10	126.74
12000	1050.81	549.60	383.00	300.05	250.56	217.80	194.60	177.37	164.11	153.64	145.20	138.26
13000	1138.38	595.40	414.92	325.06	271.44	235.95	210.82	192.15	177.79	166.45	157.30	149.79
14000	1225.95	641.20	446.83	350.06	292.32	254.10	227.03	206.93	191.47	179.25	169.40	161.31
15000	1313.52	687.00	478.75	375.06	313.20	272.25	243.25	221.71	205.14	192.05	181.49	172.83
16000	1401.08	732.80	510.66	400.07	334.08	290.40	259.46	236.49	218.82	204.86	193.59	184.35
17000	1488.65	778.60	542.58	425.07	354.96	308.55	275.68	251.27	232.49	217.66	205.69	195.87
18000	1576.22	824.40	574.50	450.08	375.84	326.70	291.90	266.05	246.17	230.46	217.79	207.39
19000	1663.79	870.20	606.41	475.08	396.72	344.85	308.11	280.83	259.84	243.27	229.89	218.91
20000	1751.35	916.00	638.33	500.08	417.60	363.00	324.33	295.61	273.52	256.07	241.99	230.44
21000	1838.92	961.80	670.25	525.09	438.48	381.15	340.55	310.39	287.20	268.87	254.09	241.96
22000	1926.49	1007.59	702.16	550.09	459.36	399.30	356.76	325.17	300.87	281.68	266.19	253.48
23000	2014.06	1053.39	734.08	575.10	480.24	417.45	372.98	339.95	314.55	294.48	278.29	265.00
24000	2101.62	1099.19	765.99	600.10	501.12	435.60	389.19	354.73	328.22	307.28	290.39	276.52
25000	2189.19	1144.99	797.91	625.10	522.00	453.75	405.41	369.51	341.90	320.09	302.49	288.04
26000	2276.76	1190.79	829.83	650.11	542.88	471.90	421.63	384.29	355.58	332.89	314.59	299.57
27000	2364.33	1236.59	861.74	675.11	563.76	490.05	437.84	399.07	369.25	345.69	326.69	311.09
28000	2451.89	1282.39	893.66	700.11	584.64	508.20	454.06	413.85	382.93	358.50	338.79	322.61
29000	2539.46	1328.19	925.58	725.12	605.52	526.35	470.28	428.63	396.60	371.30	350.88	334.13
30000	2627.03	1373.99	957.49	750.12	626.40	544.50	486.49	443.41	410.28	384.10	362.98	345.65
31000	2714.60	1419.79	989.41	775.13	647.28	562.65	502.71	458.19	423.95	396.91	375.08	357.17
32000	2802.16	1465.59	1021.32	800.13	668.16	580.80	518.92	472.97	437.63	409.71	387.18	368.70
33000	2889.73	1511.39	1053.24	825.13	689.04	598.95	535.14	487.75	451.31	422.51	399.28	380.22
34000	2977.30	1557.19	1085.16	850.14	709.92	617.10	551.36	502.53	464.98	435.32	411.38	391.74
35000	3064.87	1602.99	1117.07	875.14	730.80	635.25	567.57	517.31	478.66	448.12	423.48	403.26
36000	3152.43	1648.79	1146.99	900.15	751.68	653.40	583.79	532.09	492.33	460.92	435.58	414.78
37000	3240.00	1694.59	1180.90	925.15	772.56	671.55	600.01	546.87	506.01	473.73	447.68	426.30
38000	3327.57	1740.39	1212.82	950.15	793.44	689.70	616.22	561.65	519.68	486.53	459.78	437.82
39000	3415.14	1786.19	1244.74	975.16	814.32	707.85	632.44	576.43	533.36	499.33	471.88	449.35
40000	3502.70	1831.99	1276.65	1000.16	835.20	726.00	648.65	591.21	547.04	512.14	483.98	460.87
41000	3590.27	1877.79	1308.57	1025.17	856.08	744.15	664.87	605.99	560.71	524.94	496.08	472.39
42000	3677.84	1923.59	1340.49	1050.17	876.96	762.30	681.09	620.77	574.39	537.74	508.18	483.91
43000	3765.41	1969.38	1372.40	1075.17	897.84	780.45	697.30	635.55	588.06	550.55	520.27	495.43
44000	3852.97	2015.18	1404.32	1100.18	918.72	798.60	713.52	650.33	601.74	563.35	532.37	506.95
45000	3940.54	2060.98	1436.23	1125.18	939.60	816.75	729.74	665.11	615.41	576.15	544.47	518.48
46000	4028.11	2106.78	1468.15	1150.19	960.48	834.90	745.95	679.90	629.09	588.96	556.57	530.00
47000	4115.68	2152.58	1500.07	1175.19	981.36	853.05	762.17	694.68	642.77	601.76	568.67	541.52
48000	4203.24	2198.38	1531.98	1200.19	1002.24	871.20	778.38	709.46	656.44	614.56	580.77	553.04
49000	4290.81	2244.18	1563.90	1225.20	1023.12	889.35	794.60	724.24	670.12	627.37	592.87	564.56
50000	4378.38	2289.98	1595.82	1250.20	1044.00	907.50	810.82	739.02	683.79	640.17	604.97	576.08
55000	4816.21	2518.98	1755.40	1375.22	1148.40	998.25	891.90	812.92	752.17	704.18	665.47	633.69
60000	5254.05	2747.98	1914.98	1500.24	1252.80	1089.00	972.98	886.82	820.55	768.20	725.96	691.30
65000	5691.89	2976.97	2074.56	1625.26	1357.20	1179.75	1054.06	960.72	888.93	832.22	786.46	748.91
70000	6129.73	3205.97	2234.14	1750.28	1461.60	1270.50	1135.14	1034.62	957.31	896.23	846.96	806.51
75000	6567.56	3434.97	2393.72	1875.30	1566.00	1361.24	1216.22	1108.52	1025.69	960.25	907.45	864.12
80000	7005.40	3663.97	2553.30	2000.32	1670.40	1451.99	1297.30	1182.42	1094.07	1024.27	967.95	921.73
85000	7443.24	3892.97	2712.88	2125.34	1774.80	1542.74	1378.39	1256.32	1162.45	1088.28	1028.45	979.34
90000	7881.08	4121.96	2872.46	2250.36	1879.20	1633.49	1459.47	1330.22	1230.82	1152.30	1088.94	1036.95
95000	8318.91	4350.96	3032.05	2375.38	1983.60	1724.24	1540.55	1404.13	1299.20	1216.32	1149.44	1094.55
100000	8756.75	4579.96	3191.63	2500.40	2087.99	1814.99	1621.63	1478.03	1367.58	1280.33	1209.93	1152.16

MONTHLY 9.25%

PAYMENT REQUIRED TO AMORTIZE A LOAN

TERM AMOUNT	13 YEARS	14 YEARS	15 YEARS	16 YEARS	17 YEARS	18 YEARS	19 YEARS	20 YEARS	25 YEARS	30 YEARS	35 YEARS	40 YEARS
50	.56	.54	.52	.50	.49	.48	.47	.46	.43	.42	.41	.40
100	1.11	1.07	1.03	1.00	.98	.96	.94	.92	.86	.83	.81	.80
200	2.21	2.13	2.06	2.00	1.95	1.91	1.87	1.84	1.72	1.65	1.61	1.59
300	3.32	3.20	3.09	3.00	2.93	2.86	2.80	2.75	2.57	2.47	2.41	2.38
400	4.42	4.26	4.12	4.00	3.90	3.81	3.74	3.67	3.43	3.30	3.22	3.17
500	5.53	5.32	5.15	5.00	4.88	4.77	4.67	4.58	4.29	4.12	4.02	3.96
600	6.63	6.39	6.18	6.00	5.85	5.72	5.60	5.50	5.14	4.94	4.82	4.75
700	7.73	7.45	7.21	7.00	6.82	6.67	6.53	6.42	6.00	5.76	5.62	5.54
800	8.84	8.51	8.24	8.00	7.80	7.62	7.47	7.33	6.86	6.59	6.43	6.33
900	9.94	9.58	9.27	9.00	8.77	8.57	8.40	8.25	7.71	7.41	7.23	7.12
1000	11.05	10.64	10.30	10.00	9.75	9.53	9.33	9.16	8.57	8.23	8.03	7.91
2000	22.09	21.28	20.59	20.00	19.49	19.05	18.66	18.32	17.13	16.46	16.06	15.82
3000	33.13	31.91	30.88	30.00	29.23	28.57	27.99	27.48	25.70	24.69	24.09	23.72
4000	44.17	42.55	41.17	39.99	38.97	38.09	37.32	36.64	34.26	32.91	32.11	31.63
5000	55.21	53.19	51.46	49.99	48.72	47.61	46.65	45.80	42.82	41.14	40.14	39.54
6000	66.25	63.82	61.76	59.99	58.46	57.13	55.97	54.96	51.39	49.37	48.17	47.44
7000	77.29	74.46	72.05	69.98	68.20	66.65	65.30	64.12	59.95	57.59	56.20	55.35
8000	88.33	85.09	82.34	79.98	77.94	76.17	74.63	73.27	68.52	65.82	64.22	63.26
9000	99.37	95.73	92.63	89.98	87.69	85.70	83.96	82.43	77.08	74.05	72.25	71.16
10000	110.41	106.37	102.92	99.97	97.43	95.22	93.29	91.59	85.64	82.27	80.28	79.07
11000	121.45	117.00	113.22	109.97	107.17	104.74	102.61	100.75	94.21	90.50	88.31	86.98
12000	132.49	127.64	123.51	119.97	116.91	114.26	111.94	109.91	102.77	98.73	96.33	94.88
13000	143.54	138.27	133.80	129.97	126.66	123.78	121.27	119.07	111.33	106.95	104.36	102.79
14000	154.58	148.91	144.09	139.96	136.40	133.30	130.60	128.23	119.90	115.18	112.39	110.70
15000	165.62	159.55	154.38	149.96	146.14	142.82	139.93	137.39	128.46	123.41	120.42	118.60
16000	176.66	170.18	164.68	159.96	155.88	152.34	149.25	146.54	137.03	131.63	128.44	126.51
17000	187.70	180.82	174.97	169.95	165.62	161.87	158.58	155.70	145.59	139.86	136.47	134.42
18000	198.74	191.45	185.26	179.95	175.37	171.39	167.91	164.86	154.15	148.09	144.50	142.32
19000	209.78	202.09	195.55	189.95	185.11	180.91	177.24	174.02	162.72	156.31	152.53	150.23
20000	220.82	212.73	205.84	199.94	194.85	190.43	186.57	183.18	171.28	164.54	160.55	158.14
21000	231.86	223.36	216.14	209.94	204.59	199.95	195.89	192.34	179.85	172.77	168.58	166.04
22000	242.90	234.00	226.43	219.94	214.34	209.47	205.22	201.50	188.41	180.99	176.61	173.95
23000	253.94	244.63	236.72	229.94	224.08	218.99	214.55	210.65	196.97	189.22	184.64	181.86
24000	264.98	255.27	247.01	239.93	233.82	228.51	223.88	219.81	205.54	197.45	192.66	189.76
25000	276.02	265.91	257.30	249.93	243.56	238.03	233.21	228.97	214.10	205.67	200.69	197.67
26000	287.07	276.54	267.59	259.93	253.31	247.56	242.54	238.13	222.66	213.90	208.72	205.58
27000	298.11	287.18	277.89	269.92	263.05	257.08	251.86	247.29	231.23	222.13	216.75	213.48
28000	309.15	297.81	288.18	279.92	272.79	266.60	261.19	256.45	239.79	230.35	224.77	221.39
29000	320.19	308.45	298.47	289.92	282.53	276.12	270.52	265.61	248.36	238.58	232.80	229.30
30000	331.23	319.09	308.76	299.91	292.28	285.64	279.85	274.77	256.92	246.81	240.83	237.20
31000	342.27	329.72	319.05	309.91	302.02	295.16	289.18	283.92	265.48	255.03	248.86	245.11
32000	353.31	340.36	329.35	319.91	311.76	304.68	298.50	293.08	274.05	263.26	256.88	253.02
33000	364.35	350.99	339.64	329.91	321.50	314.20	307.83	302.24	282.61	271.49	264.91	260.92
34000	375.39	361.63	349.93	339.90	331.24	323.73	317.16	311.40	291.17	279.71	272.94	268.83
35000	386.43	372.27	360.22	349.90	340.99	333.25	326.49	320.56	299.74	287.94	280.97	276.74
36000	397.47	382.90	370.51	359.90	350.73	342.77	335.82	329.72	308.30	296.17	288.99	284.64
37000	408.51	393.54	380.81	369.89	360.47	352.29	345.14	338.88	316.87	304.39	297.02	292.55
38000	419.55	404.17	391.10	379.89	370.21	361.81	354.47	348.03	325.43	312.62	305.05	300.46
39000	430.60	414.81	401.39	389.89	379.96	371.33	363.80	357.19	333.99	320.85	313.08	308.36
40000	441.64	425.45	411.68	399.88	389.70	380.85	373.13	366.35	342.56	329.08	321.10	316.27
41000	452.68	436.08	421.97	409.88	399.44	390.37	382.46	375.51	351.12	337.30	329.13	324.18
42000	463.72	446.72	432.27	419.88	409.18	399.90	391.78	384.67	359.69	345.53	337.16	332.08
43000	474.76	457.35	442.56	429.87	418.93	409.42	401.11	393.83	368.25	353.76	345.19	339.99
44000	485.80	467.99	452.85	439.87	428.67	418.94	410.44	402.99	376.81	361.98	353.21	347.90
45000	496.84	478.63	463.14	449.87	438.41	428.46	419.77	412.15	385.38	370.21	361.24	355.80
46000	507.88	489.26	473.43	459.87	448.15	437.98	429.10	421.30	393.94	378.44	369.27	363.71
47000	518.92	499.90	483.73	469.86	457.90	447.50	438.42	430.46	402.50	386.66	377.29	371.62
48000	529.96	510.53	494.02	479.86	467.64	457.02	447.75	439.62	411.07	394.89	385.32	379.52
49000	541.00	521.17	504.31	489.86	477.38	466.54	457.08	448.78	419.63	403.12	393.35	387.43
50000	552.04	531.81	514.60	499.85	487.12	476.06	466.41	457.94	428.20	411.34	401.38	395.34
55000	607.25	584.99	566.06	549.84	535.83	523.67	513.05	503.73	471.02	452.48	441.51	434.87
60000	662.45	638.17	617.52	599.82	584.55	571.28	559.69	549.53	513.83	493.61	481.65	474.40
65000	717.66	691.35	668.98	649.81	633.26	618.88	606.33	595.32	556.65	534.74	521.79	513.93
70000	772.86	744.53	720.44	699.79	681.97	666.49	652.97	641.11	599.47	575.88	561.93	553.47
75000	828.06	797.71	771.90	749.78	730.68	714.09	699.61	686.91	642.29	617.01	602.06	593.00
80000	883.27	850.89	823.36	799.76	779.39	761.70	746.25	732.70	685.11	658.15	642.20	632.53
85000	938.47	904.07	874.82	849.75	828.10	809.31	792.89	778.49	727.93	699.28	682.34	672.07
90000	993.68	957.25	926.28	899.73	876.82	856.91	839.53	824.29	770.75	740.41	722.47	711.60
95000	1048.88	1010.43	977.74	949.72	925.53	904.52	886.17	870.08	813.57	781.55	762.61	751.13
100000	1104.08	1063.61	1029.20	999.70	974.24	952.12	932.81	915.87	856.39	822.68	802.75	790.67

9.50%

MONTHLY

PAYMENT REQUIRED TO AMORTIZE A LOAN

TERM AMOUNT	1 YEAR	2 YEARS	3 YEARS	4 YEARS	5 YEARS	6 YEARS	7 YEARS	8 YEARS	9 YEARS	10 YEARS	11 YEARS	12 YEARS
50	4.39	2.30	1.61	1.26	1.06	.92	.82	.75	.70	.65	.62	.59
100	8.77	4.60	3.21	2.52	2.11	1.83	1.64	1.50	1.39	1.30	1.23	1.17
200	17.54	9.19	6.41	5.03	4.21	3.66	3.27	2.99	2.77	2.59	2.45	2.34
300	26.31	13.78	9.61	7.54	6.31	5.49	4.91	4.48	4.15	3.89	3.68	3.50
400	35.08	18.37	12.82	10.05	8.41	7.31	6.54	5.97	5.53	5.18	4.90	4.67
500	43.85	22.96	16.02	12.57	10.51	9.14	8.18	7.46	6.91	6.47	6.12	5.84
600	52.62	27.55	19.22	15.08	12.61	10.97	9.81	8.95	8.29	7.77	7.35	7.00
700	61.38	32.15	22.43	17.59	14.71	12.80	11.45	10.44	9.67	9.06	8.57	8.17
800	70.15	36.74	25.63	20.10	16.81	14.62	13.08	11.93	11.05	10.36	9.80	9.34
900	78.92	41.33	28.83	22.62	18.91	16.45	14.71	13.42	12.43	11.65	11.02	10.50
1000	87.69	45.92	32.04	25.13	21.01	18.28	16.35	14.92	13.81	12.94	12.24	11.67
2000	175.37	91.83	64.07	50.25	42.01	36.55	32.69	29.83	27.62	25.88	24.48	23.33
3000	263.04	137.75	96.10	75.37	63.01	54.83	49.04	44.74	41.43	38.82	36.72	35.00
4000	350.74	183.66	128.14	100.50	84.01	73.10	65.38	59.65	55.24	51.76	48.96	46.66
5000	438.42	229.58	160.17	125.62	105.01	91.38	81.72	74.56	69.05	64.70	61.20	58.32
6000	526.11	275.49	192.20	150.74	126.02	109.65	98.07	89.47	82.86	77.64	73.44	69.99
7000	613.79	321.41	224.24	175.87	147.02	127.93	114.41	104.38	96.67	90.58	85.68	81.65
8000	701.47	367.32	256.27	200.99	168.02	146.20	130.76	119.29	110.48	103.52	97.91	93.31
9000	789.16	413.24	288.30	226.11	189.02	164.48	147.10	134.20	124.29	116.46	110.15	104.98
10000	876.84	459.15	320.33	251.24	210.02	182.75	163.44	149.11	138.10	129.40	122.39	116.64
11000	964.52	505.06	352.37	276.36	231.03	201.03	179.79	164.02	151.91	142.34	134.63	128.31
12000	1052.21	550.98	384.40	301.48	252.03	219.30	196.13	178.94	165.72	155.28	146.87	139.97
13000	1139.89	596.89	416.43	326.61	273.03	237.58	212.48	193.85	179.53	168.22	159.11	151.63
14000	1227.57	642.81	448.47	351.73	294.03	255.85	228.82	208.76	193.34	181.16	171.35	163.30
15000	1315.26	688.72	480.50	376.85	315.03	274.13	245.16	223.67	207.15	194.10	183.58	174.96
16000	1402.94	734.64	512.53	401.98	336.03	292.40	261.51	238.58	220.95	207.04	195.82	186.62
17000	1490.62	780.55	544.57	427.10	357.04	310.67	277.85	253.49	234.76	219.98	208.06	198.29
18000	1578.31	826.47	576.60	452.22	378.04	328.95	294.20	268.40	248.57	232.92	220.30	209.95
19000	1665.99	872.38	608.63	477.34	399.04	347.22	310.54	283.31	262.38	245.86	232.54	221.62
20000	1753.68	918.29	640.66	502.47	420.04	365.50	326.88	298.22	276.19	258.80	244.78	233.28
21000	1841.36	964.21	672.70	527.59	441.04	383.77	343.23	313.13	290.00	271.74	257.02	244.94
22000	1929.04	1010.12	704.73	552.71	462.05	402.05	359.57	328.04	303.81	284.68	269.26	256.61
23000	2016.73	1056.04	736.76	577.84	483.05	420.32	375.92	342.96	317.62	297.62	281.49	268.27
24000	2104.41	1101.95	768.80	602.96	504.05	438.60	392.26	357.87	331.43	310.56	293.73	279.93
25000	2192.09	1147.87	800.83	628.08	525.05	456.87	408.60	372.78	345.24	323.50	305.97	291.60
26000	2279.78	1193.78	832.86	653.21	546.05	475.15	424.95	387.69	359.05	336.44	318.21	303.26
27000	2367.46	1239.70	864.89	678.33	567.06	493.42	441.29	402.60	372.86	349.38	330.45	314.93
28000	2455.14	1285.61	896.93	703.45	588.06	511.70	457.64	417.51	386.67	362.32	342.69	326.59
29000	2542.83	1331.53	928.96	728.58	609.06	529.97	473.98	432.42	400.48	375.26	354.93	338.25
30000	2630.51	1377.44	960.99	753.70	630.06	548.25	490.32	447.33	414.29	388.20	367.16	349.92
31000	2718.19	1423.35	993.03	778.82	651.06	566.52	506.67	462.24	428.10	401.14	379.40	361.58
32000	2805.88	1469.27	1025.06	803.95	672.06	584.80	523.01	477.15	441.90	414.08	391.64	373.24
33000	2893.56	1515.18	1057.09	829.07	693.07	603.07	539.36	492.06	455.71	427.02	403.88	384.91
34000	2981.24	1561.10	1089.13	854.19	714.07	621.34	555.70	506.98	469.52	439.96	416.12	396.57
35000	3068.93	1607.01	1121.16	879.31	735.07	639.62	572.04	521.89	483.33	452.90	428.36	408.24
36000	3156.61	1652.93	1153.19	904.44	756.07	657.89	588.39	536.80	497.14	465.84	440.60	419.90
37000	3244.29	1698.84	1185.22	929.56	777.07	676.17	604.73	551.71	510.95	478.78	452.83	431.56
38000	3331.98	1744.76	1217.26	954.68	798.08	694.44	621.08	566.62	524.76	491.72	465.07	443.23
39000	3419.66	1790.67	1249.29	979.81	819.08	712.72	637.42	581.53	538.57	504.66	477.31	454.89
40000	3507.35	1836.58	1281.32	1004.93	840.08	730.99	653.76	596.44	552.38	517.60	489.55	466.55
41000	3595.03	1882.50	1313.36	1030.05	861.08	749.27	670.11	611.35	566.19	530.53	501.79	478.22
42000	3682.71	1928.41	1345.39	1055.18	882.08	767.54	686.45	626.26	580.00	543.47	514.03	489.88
43000	3770.40	1974.33	1377.42	1080.30	903.09	785.82	702.80	641.17	593.81	556.41	526.27	501.55
44000	3858.08	2020.24	1409.45	1105.42	924.09	804.09	719.14	656.08	607.62	569.35	538.51	513.21
45000	3945.76	2066.16	1441.49	1130.55	945.09	822.37	735.48	670.99	621.43	582.29	550.74	524.87
46000	4033.45	2112.07	1473.52	1155.67	966.09	840.64	751.83	685.91	635.24	595.23	562.98	536.54
47000	4121.13	2157.99	1505.55	1180.79	987.09	858.92	768.17	700.82	649.04	608.17	575.22	548.20
48000	4208.81	2203.90	1537.59	1205.92	1008.09	877.19	784.52	715.73	662.85	621.11	587.46	559.86
49000	4296.50	2249.82	1569.62	1231.04	1029.10	895.46	800.86	730.64	676.66	634.05	599.70	571.53
50000	4384.18	2295.73	1601.65	1256.16	1050.10	913.74	817.20	745.55	690.47	646.99	611.94	583.19
55000	4822.60	2525.30	1761.82	1381.78	1155.11	1005.11	898.92	820.10	759.52	711.69	673.13	641.51
60000	5261.02	2754.87	1921.98	1507.39	1260.12	1096.49	980.64	894.66	828.57	776.39	734.32	699.83
65000	5699.43	2984.45	2082.15	1633.01	1365.13	1187.86	1062.36	969.21	897.61	841.09	795.52	758.15
70000	6137.85	3214.02	2242.31	1758.62	1470.14	1279.23	1144.08	1043.77	966.66	905.79	856.71	816.47
75000	6576.27	3443.59	2402.48	1884.24	1575.14	1370.61	1225.80	1118.32	1035.71	970.49	917.90	874.78
80000	7014.69	3673.16	2562.64	2009.86	1680.15	1461.98	1307.52	1192.88	1104.75	1035.19	979.10	933.10
85000	7453.10	3902.74	2722.81	2135.47	1785.16	1553.35	1389.24	1267.43	1173.80	1099.88	1040.29	991.42
90000	7891.52	4132.31	2882.97	2261.09	1890.17	1644.73	1470.96	1341.98	1242.85	1164.58	1101.48	1049.74
95000	8329.94	4361.88	3043.14	2386.70	1995.18	1736.10	1552.68	1416.54	1311.89	1229.28	1162.68	1108.06
100000	8768.36	4591.45	3203.30	2512.32	2100.19	1827.47	1634.40	1491.09	1380.94	1293.98	1223.87	1166.38

MONTHLY

9.50%

PAYMENT REQUIRED TO AMORTIZE A LOAN

TERM AMOUNT	13 YEARS	14 YEARS	15 YEARS	16 YEARS	17 YEARS	18 YEARS	19 YEARS	20 YEARS	25 YEARS	30 YEARS	35 YEARS	40 YEARS
50	.56	.54	.53	.51	.50	.49	.48	.47	.44	.43	.42	.41
100	1.12	1.08	1.05	1.02	.99	.97	.95	.94	.88	.85	.83	.82
200	2.24	2.16	2.09	2.03	1.98	1.94	1.90	1.87	1.75	1.69	1.65	1.63
300	3.36	3.24	3.14	3.05	2.97	2.91	2.85	2.80	2.63	2.53	2.47	2.44
400	4.48	4.32	4.18	4.06	3.96	3.88	3.80	3.73	3.50	3.37	3.29	3.25
500	5.60	5.40	5.23	5.08	4.95	4.84	4.75	4.67	4.37	4.21	4.11	4.06
600	6.72	6.48	6.27	6.09	5.94	5.81	5.70	5.60	5.25	5.05	4.93	4.87
700	7.84	7.55	7.31	7.11	6.93	6.78	6.65	6.53	6.12	5.89	5.76	5.68
800	8.95	8.63	8.36	8.12	7.92	7.75	7.60	7.46	6.99	6.73	6.58	6.49
900	10.07	9.71	9.40	9.14	8.91	8.72	8.54	8.39	7.87	7.57	7.40	7.30
1000	11.19	10.79	10.45	10.15	9.90	9.68	9.49	9.33	8.74	8.41	8.22	8.11
2000	22.38	21.57	20.89	20.30	19.80	19.36	18.98	18.65	17.48	16.82	16.44	16.21
3000	33.56	32.36	31.33	30.45	29.70	29.04	28.47	27.97	26.22	25.23	24.65	24.31
4000	44.75	43.14	41.77	40.60	39.60	38.72	37.96	37.29	34.95	33.64	32.87	32.41
5000	55.93	53.92	52.22	50.75	49.49	48.40	47.45	46.61	43.69	42.05	41.09	40.51
6000	67.12	64.71	62.66	60.90	59.39	58.08	56.94	55.93	52.43	50.46	49.30	48.61
7000	78.31	75.49	73.10	71.05	69.29	67.76	66.42	65.25	61.16	58.86	57.52	56.71
8000	89.49	86.27	83.54	81.20	79.19	77.44	75.91	74.58	69.90	67.27	65.73	64.81
9000	100.68	97.06	93.99	91.35	89.09	87.12	85.40	83.90	78.64	75.68	73.95	72.91
10000	111.86	107.84	104.43	101.50	98.98	96.80	94.89	93.22	87.37	84.09	82.17	81.01
11000	123.05	118.63	114.87	111.65	108.88	106.48	104.38	102.54	96.11	92.50	90.38	89.11
12000	134.23	129.41	125.31	121.80	118.78	116.15	113.87	111.86	104.85	100.91	98.60	97.21
13000	145.42	140.19	135.75	131.95	128.68	125.83	123.35	121.18	113.59	109.32	106.81	105.31
14000	156.61	150.98	146.20	142.10	138.57	135.51	132.84	130.50	122.32	117.72	115.03	113.41
15000	167.79	161.76	156.64	152.25	148.47	145.19	142.33	139.82	131.06	126.13	123.25	121.51
16000	178.98	172.54	167.08	162.40	158.37	154.87	151.82	149.15	139.80	134.54	131.46	129.61
17000	190.16	183.33	177.52	172.55	168.27	164.55	161.31	158.47	148.53	142.95	139.68	137.72
18000	201.35	194.11	187.97	182.70	178.17	174.23	170.80	167.79	157.27	151.36	147.90	145.82
19000	212.53	204.89	198.41	192.85	188.06	183.91	180.28	177.11	166.01	159.77	156.11	153.92
20000	223.72	215.68	208.85	203.00	197.96	193.59	189.77	186.43	174.74	168.18	164.33	162.02
21000	234.91	226.46	219.29	213.15	207.86	203.27	199.26	195.75	183.48	176.58	172.54	170.12
22000	246.09	237.25	229.73	223.30	217.76	212.95	208.75	205.07	192.22	184.99	180.76	178.22
23000	257.28	248.03	240.18	233.45	227.65	222.62	218.24	214.40	200.96	193.40	188.98	186.32
24000	268.46	258.81	250.62	243.60	237.55	232.30	227.73	223.72	209.69	201.81	197.19	194.42
25000	279.65	269.60	261.06	253.75	247.45	241.98	237.21	233.04	218.43	210.22	205.41	202.52
26000	290.83	280.38	271.50	263.90	257.35	251.66	246.70	242.36	227.17	218.63	213.62	210.62
27000	302.02	291.16	281.95	274.05	267.25	261.34	256.19	251.68	235.90	227.04	221.84	218.72
28000	313.21	301.95	292.39	284.20	277.14	271.02	265.68	261.00	244.64	235.44	230.06	226.82
29000	324.39	312.73	302.83	294.35	287.04	280.70	275.17	270.32	253.38	243.85	238.27	234.92
30000	335.58	323.52	313.27	304.50	296.94	290.38	284.66	279.64	262.11	252.26	246.49	243.02
31000	346.76	334.30	323.71	314.65	306.84	300.06	294.15	288.97	270.85	260.67	254.70	251.12
32000	357.95	345.08	334.16	324.80	316.73	309.74	303.63	298.29	279.59	269.08	262.92	259.22
33000	369.13	355.87	344.60	334.95	326.63	319.42	313.12	307.61	288.32	277.49	271.14	267.33
34000	380.32	366.65	355.04	345.10	336.53	329.09	322.61	316.93	297.06	285.90	279.35	275.43
35000	391.51	377.43	365.48	355.25	346.43	338.77	332.10	326.25	305.80	294.30	287.57	283.53
36000	402.69	388.22	375.93	365.40	356.33	348.45	341.59	335.57	314.54	302.71	295.79	291.63
37000	413.88	399.00	386.37	375.55	366.22	358.13	351.08	344.89	323.27	311.12	304.00	299.73
38000	425.06	409.78	396.81	385.70	376.12	367.81	360.56	354.21	332.01	319.53	312.22	307.83
39000	436.25	420.57	407.25	395.85	386.02	377.49	370.05	363.54	340.75	327.94	320.43	315.93
40000	447.43	431.35	417.69	406.00	395.92	387.17	379.54	372.86	349.48	336.35	328.65	324.03
41000	458.62	442.14	428.14	416.15	405.82	396.85	389.03	382.18	358.22	344.76	336.87	332.13
42000	469.81	452.92	438.58	426.30	415.71	406.53	398.52	391.50	366.96	353.16	345.08	340.23
43000	480.99	463.70	449.02	436.45	425.61	416.21	408.01	400.82	375.69	361.57	353.30	348.33
44000	492.18	474.49	459.46	446.60	435.51	425.89	417.49	410.14	384.43	369.98	361.51	356.43
45000	503.36	485.27	469.91	456.75	445.41	435.57	426.98	419.46	393.17	378.39	369.73	364.53
46000	514.55	496.05	480.35	466.90	455.30	445.24	436.47	428.79	401.91	386.80	377.95	372.63
47000	525.73	506.84	490.79	477.05	465.20	454.92	445.96	438.11	410.64	395.21	386.16	380.73
48000	536.92	517.62	501.23	487.20	475.10	464.60	455.45	447.43	419.38	403.62	394.38	388.83
49000	548.11	528.41	511.68	497.35	485.00	474.28	464.94	456.75	428.12	412.02	402.59	396.94
50000	559.29	539.19	522.12	507.50	494.90	483.96	474.42	466.07	436.85	420.43	410.81	405.04
55000	615.22	593.11	574.33	558.25	544.38	532.36	521.87	512.68	480.54	462.47	451.89	445.54
60000	671.15	647.03	626.54	609.00	593.87	580.75	569.31	559.28	524.22	504.52	492.97	486.04
65000	727.08	700.94	678.75	659.75	643.36	629.15	616.75	605.89	567.91	546.56	534.05	526.55
70000	783.01	754.86	730.96	710.50	692.85	677.54	664.19	652.50	611.59	588.60	575.13	567.05
75000	838.93	808.78	783.17	761.25	742.34	725.94	711.63	699.10	655.28	630.65	616.21	607.55
80000	894.86	862.70	835.38	812.00	791.83	774.33	759.08	745.71	698.96	672.69	657.29	648.05
85000	950.79	916.62	887.60	862.75	841.32	822.73	806.52	792.32	742.65	714.73	698.37	688.56
90000	1006.72	970.54	939.81	913.50	890.81	871.13	853.96	838.92	786.33	756.77	739.46	729.06
95000	1062.65	1024.45	992.02	964.25	940.30	919.52	901.40	885.53	830.02	798.82	780.54	769.56
100000	1118.58	1078.37	1044.23	1014.99	989.79	967.92	948.84	932.14	873.70	840.86	821.62	810.07

9.75%

MONTHLY
PAYMENT REQUIRED TO AMORTIZE A LOAN

TERM AMOUNT	1 YEAR	2 YEARS	3 YEARS	4 YEARS	5 YEARS	6 YEARS	7 YEARS	8 YEARS	9 YEARS	10 YEARS	11 YEARS	12 YEARS
50	4.39	2.31	1.61	1.27	1.06	.93	.83	.76	.70	.66	.62	.60
100	8.78	4.61	3.22	2.53	2.12	1.85	1.65	1.51	1.40	1.31	1.24	1.19
200	17.56	9.21	6.43	5.05	4.23	3.69	3.30	3.01	2.79	2.62	2.48	2.37
300	26.34	13.81	9.65	7.58	6.34	5.53	4.95	4.52	4.19	3.93	3.72	3.55
400	35.12	18.42	12.86	10.10	8.45	7.37	6.59	6.02	5.58	5.24	4.96	4.73
500	43.90	23.02	16.08	12.63	10.57	9.21	8.24	7.53	6.98	6.54	6.19	5.91
600	52.68	27.62	19.29	15.15	12.68	11.05	9.89	9.03	8.37	7.85	7.43	7.09
700	61.46	32.23	22.51	17.67	14.79	12.89	11.54	10.53	9.77	9.16	8.67	8.27
800	70.24	36.83	25.72	20.20	16.90	14.73	13.18	12.04	11.16	10.47	9.91	9.45
900	79.02	41.43	28.94	22.72	19.02	16.57	14.83	13.54	12.55	11.77	11.15	10.63
1000	87.80	46.03	32.15	25.25	21.13	18.41	16.48	15.05	13.95	13.08	12.38	11.81
2000	175.60	92.06	64.30	50.49	42.25	36.81	32.95	30.09	27.89	26.16	24.76	23.62
3000	263.40	138.09	96.45	75.73	63.38	55.21	49.42	45.13	41.84	39.24	37.14	35.43
4000	351.20	184.12	128.60	100.98	84.50	73.61	65.89	60.17	55.78	52.31	49.52	47.23
5000	439.00	230.15	160.75	126.22	105.63	92.01	82.37	75.22	69.72	65.39	61.90	59.04
6000	526.80	276.18	192.90	151.46	126.75	110.41	98.84	90.26	83.67	78.47	74.28	70.85
7000	614.60	322.21	225.05	176.70	147.87	128.81	115.31	105.30	97.61	91.54	86.66	82.65
8000	702.40	368.24	257.20	201.95	169.00	147.21	131.78	120.34	111.55	104.62	99.04	94.46
9000	790.20	414.27	289.35	227.19	190.12	165.61	148.26	135.38	125.50	117.70	111.41	106.27
10000	878.00	460.30	321.50	252.43	211.25	184.01	164.73	150.43	139.44	130.78	123.79	118.07
11000	965.80	506.33	353.65	277.67	232.37	202.41	181.20	165.47	153.39	143.85	136.17	129.88
12000	1053.60	552.36	385.80	302.92	253.50	220.81	197.67	180.51	167.33	156.93	148.55	141.69
13000	1141.40	598.39	417.95	328.16	274.62	239.21	214.14	195.55	181.27	170.01	160.93	153.49
14000	1229.20	644.42	450.10	353.40	295.74	257.61	230.62	210.60	195.22	183.08	173.31	165.30
15000	1317.00	690.45	482.25	378.65	316.87	276.01	247.09	225.64	209.16	196.16	185.69	177.11
16000	1404.80	736.48	514.40	403.89	337.99	294.41	263.56	240.68	223.10	209.24	198.07	188.91
17000	1492.60	782.51	546.55	429.13	359.12	312.81	280.03	255.72	237.05	222.31	210.45	200.72
18000	1580.40	828.54	578.70	454.37	380.24	331.21	296.51	270.76	250.99	235.39	222.82	212.53
19000	1668.20	874.57	610.85	479.62	401.37	349.61	312.98	285.81	264.93	248.47	235.20	224.33
20000	1756.00	920.60	643.00	504.86	422.49	368.01	329.45	300.85	278.88	261.55	247.58	236.14
21000	1843.80	966.63	675.15	530.10	443.61	386.41	345.92	315.89	292.82	274.62	259.96	247.95
22000	1931.60	1012.66	707.30	555.34	464.74	404.81	362.40	330.93	306.77	287.70	272.34	259.75
23000	2019.40	1058.69	739.45	580.59	485.86	423.21	378.87	345.98	320.71	300.78	284.72	271.56
24000	2107.20	1104.72	771.60	605.83	506.99	441.61	395.34	361.02	334.65	313.85	297.10	283.37
25000	2195.00	1150.75	803.75	631.07	528.11	460.01	411.81	376.06	348.60	326.93	309.48	295.18
26000	2282.80	1196.78	835.90	656.31	549.24	478.41	428.28	391.10	362.54	340.01	321.85	306.98
27000	2370.60	1242.80	868.05	681.56	570.36	496.81	444.76	406.14	376.48	353.08	334.23	318.79
28000	2458.40	1288.83	900.20	706.80	591.48	515.21	461.23	421.19	390.43	366.16	346.61	330.60
29000	2546.20	1334.86	932.35	732.04	612.61	533.61	477.70	436.23	404.37	379.24	358.99	342.40
30000	2633.99	1380.89	964.50	757.29	633.73	552.01	494.17	451.27	418.31	392.32	371.37	354.21
31000	2721.79	1426.92	996.65	782.53	654.86	570.41	510.65	466.31	432.26	405.39	383.75	366.02
32000	2809.59	1472.95	1028.80	807.77	675.98	588.81	527.12	481.36	446.20	418.47	396.13	377.82
33000	2897.39	1518.98	1060.95	833.01	697.11	607.21	543.59	496.40	460.15	431.55	408.51	389.63
34000	2985.19	1565.01	1093.10	858.26	718.23	625.61	560.06	511.44	474.09	444.62	420.89	401.44
35000	3072.99	1611.04	1125.25	883.50	739.35	644.01	576.54	526.48	488.03	457.70	433.26	413.24
36000	3160.79	1657.07	1157.40	908.74	760.48	662.41	593.01	541.52	501.98	470.78	445.64	425.05
37000	3248.59	1703.10	1189.55	933.98	781.60	680.81	609.48	556.57	515.92	483.85	458.02	436.86
38000	3336.39	1749.13	1221.70	959.23	802.73	699.21	625.95	571.61	529.86	496.93	470.40	448.66
39000	3424.19	1795.16	1253.85	984.47	823.85	717.61	642.42	586.65	543.81	510.01	482.78	460.47
40000	3511.99	1841.19	1286.00	1009.71	844.97	736.01	658.90	601.69	557.75	523.09	495.16	472.28
41000	3599.79	1887.22	1318.15	1034.96	866.10	754.41	675.37	616.74	571.70	536.16	507.54	484.08
42000	3687.59	1933.25	1350.30	1060.20	887.22	772.81	691.84	631.78	585.64	549.24	519.92	495.89
43000	3775.39	1979.28	1382.45	1085.44	908.35	791.21	708.31	646.82	599.58	562.32	532.30	507.70
44000	3863.19	2025.31	1414.60	1110.68	929.47	809.61	724.79	661.86	613.53	575.39	544.67	519.50
45000	3950.99	2071.34	1446.75	1135.93	950.60	828.01	741.26	676.90	627.47	588.47	557.05	531.31
46000	4038.79	2117.37	1478.90	1161.17	971.72	846.41	757.73	691.95	641.41	601.55	569.43	543.12
47000	4126.59	2163.40	1511.05	1186.41	992.84	864.81	774.20	706.99	655.36	614.63	581.81	554.92
48000	4214.39	2209.43	1543.20	1211.65	1013.97	883.21	790.68	722.03	669.30	627.70	594.19	566.73
49000	4302.19	2255.46	1575.35	1236.90	1035.09	901.61	807.15	737.07	683.24	640.78	606.57	578.54
50000	4389.99	2301.49	1607.50	1262.14	1056.22	920.01	823.62	752.12	697.19	653.86	618.95	590.35
55000	4828.99	2531.63	1768.25	1388.35	1161.84	1012.01	905.98	827.33	766.91	719.24	680.84	649.38
60000	5267.98	2761.78	1929.00	1514.57	1267.46	1104.01	988.34	902.54	836.62	784.63	742.74	708.41
65000	5706.98	2991.93	2089.75	1640.78	1373.08	1196.01	1070.70	977.75	906.34	850.01	804.63	767.45
70000	6145.98	3222.08	2250.50	1766.99	1478.70	1288.01	1153.07	1052.96	976.06	915.40	866.52	826.48
75000	6584.98	3452.23	2411.25	1893.21	1584.32	1380.01	1235.43	1128.17	1045.78	980.78	928.42	885.52
80000	7023.98	3682.37	2572.00	2019.42	1689.94	1472.01	1317.79	1203.38	1115.50	1046.17	990.31	944.55
85000	7462.98	3912.52	2732.75	2145.63	1795.57	1564.01	1400.15	1278.59	1185.22	1111.55	1052.21	1003.58
90000	7901.97	4142.67	2893.50	2271.85	1901.19	1656.01	1482.51	1353.80	1254.93	1176.94	1114.10	1062.62
95000	8340.97	4372.82	3054.25	2398.06	2006.81	1748.01	1564.87	1429.01	1324.65	1242.32	1175.99	1121.65
100000	8779.97	4602.97	3215.00	2524.27	2112.43	1840.01	1647.23	1504.23	1394.37	1307.71	1237.89	1180.69

MONTHLY 9.75%

PAYMENT REQUIRED TO AMORTIZE A LOAN

AMOUNT	TERM 13 YEARS	14 YEARS	15 YEARS	16 YEARS	17 YEARS	18 YEARS	19 YEARS	20 YEARS	25 YEARS	30 YEARS	35 YEARS	40 YEARS
50	.57	.55	.53	.52	.51	.50	.49	.48	.45	.43	.43	.42
100	1.14	1.10	1.06	1.04	1.01	.99	.97	.95	.90	.86	.85	.83
200	2.27	2.19	2.12	2.07	2.02	1.97	1.93	1.90	1.79	1.72	1.69	1.66
300	3.40	3.28	3.18	3.10	3.02	2.96	2.90	2.85	2.68	2.58	2.53	2.49
400	4.54	4.38	4.24	4.13	4.03	3.94	3.86	3.80	3.57	3.44	3.37	3.32
500	5.67	5.47	5.30	5.16	5.03	4.92	4.83	4.75	4.46	4.30	4.21	4.15
600	6.80	6.56	6.36	6.19	6.04	5.91	5.79	5.70	5.35	5.16	5.05	4.98
700	7.94	7.66	7.42	7.22	7.04	6.89	6.76	6.64	6.24	6.02	5.89	5.81
800	9.07	8.75	8.48	8.25	8.05	7.88	7.72	7.59	7.13	6.88	6.73	6.64
900	10.20	9.84	9.54	9.28	9.05	8.86	8.69	8.54	8.03	7.74	7.57	7.47
1000	11.34	10.94	10.60	10.31	10.06	9.84	9.65	9.49	8.92	8.60	8.41	8.30
2000	22.67	21.87	21.19	20.61	20.11	19.68	19.30	18.98	17.83	17.19	16.82	16.60
3000	34.00	32.80	31.79	30.92	30.17	29.52	28.95	28.46	26.74	25.78	25.22	24.89
4000	45.33	43.73	42.38	41.22	40.22	39.36	38.60	37.95	35.65	34.37	33.63	33.19
5000	56.66	54.67	52.97	51.52	50.28	49.20	48.25	47.43	44.56	42.96	42.03	41.48
6000	67.99	65.60	63.57	61.83	60.33	59.03	57.90	56.92	53.47	51.55	50.44	49.78
7000	79.33	76.53	74.16	72.13	70.39	68.87	67.55	66.40	62.38	60.15	58.85	58.07
8000	90.66	87.46	84.75	82.44	80.44	78.71	77.20	75.89	71.30	68.74	67.25	66.37
9000	101.99	98.40	95.35	92.74	90.49	88.55	86.85	85.37	80.21	77.33	75.66	74.67
10000	113.32	109.33	105.94	103.04	100.55	98.39	96.50	94.86	89.12	85.92	84.06	82.96
11000	124.65	120.26	116.53	113.35	110.60	108.23	106.15	104.34	98.03	94.51	92.47	91.26
12000	135.98	131.19	127.13	123.65	120.66	118.06	115.80	113.83	106.94	103.10	100.88	99.55
13000	147.32	142.13	137.72	133.96	130.71	127.90	125.45	123.31	115.85	111.70	109.28	107.85
14000	158.65	153.06	148.32	144.26	140.77	137.74	135.10	132.80	124.76	120.29	117.69	116.14
15000	169.98	163.99	158.91	154.56	150.82	147.58	144.75	142.28	133.68	128.88	126.09	124.44
16000	181.31	174.92	169.50	164.87	160.88	157.42	154.40	151.77	142.59	137.47	134.50	132.73
17000	192.64	185.86	180.10	175.17	170.93	167.25	164.05	161.25	151.50	146.06	142.91	141.03
18000	203.97	196.79	190.69	185.48	180.98	177.09	173.70	170.74	160.41	154.65	151.31	149.33
19000	215.31	207.72	201.28	195.78	191.04	186.93	183.35	180.22	169.32	163.24	159.72	157.62
20000	226.64	218.65	211.88	206.08	201.09	196.77	193.00	189.71	178.23	171.84	168.12	165.92
21000	237.97	229.58	222.47	216.39	211.15	206.61	202.65	199.19	187.14	180.43	176.53	174.21
22000	249.30	240.52	233.06	226.69	221.20	216.45	212.30	208.68	196.06	189.02	184.93	182.51
23000	260.63	251.45	243.66	237.00	231.26	226.28	221.95	218.16	204.97	197.61	193.34	190.80
24000	271.96	262.38	254.25	247.30	241.31	236.12	231.60	227.65	213.88	206.20	201.75	199.10
25000	283.30	273.31	264.85	257.60	251.36	245.96	241.25	237.13	222.79	214.79	210.15	207.39
26000	294.63	284.25	275.44	267.91	261.42	255.80	250.90	246.62	231.70	223.39	218.56	215.69
27000	305.96	295.18	286.03	278.21	271.47	265.64	260.55	256.10	240.61	231.98	226.96	223.99
28000	317.29	306.11	296.63	288.51	281.53	275.47	270.20	265.59	249.52	240.57	235.37	232.28
29000	328.62	317.04	307.22	298.82	291.58	285.31	279.85	275.07	258.43	249.16	243.78	240.58
30000	339.95	327.98	317.81	309.12	301.64	295.15	289.50	284.56	267.35	257.75	252.18	248.87
31000	351.29	338.91	328.41	319.43	311.69	304.99	299.15	294.05	276.26	266.34	260.59	257.17
32000	362.62	349.84	339.00	329.73	321.75	314.83	308.80	303.53	285.17	274.93	268.99	265.46
33000	373.95	360.77	349.59	340.03	331.80	324.67	318.45	313.02	294.08	283.53	277.40	273.76
34000	385.28	371.70	360.19	350.34	341.85	334.50	328.10	322.50	302.99	292.12	285.81	282.05
35000	396.61	382.64	370.78	360.64	351.91	344.34	337.75	331.99	311.90	300.71	294.21	290.35
36000	407.94	393.57	381.38	370.95	361.96	354.18	347.40	341.47	320.81	309.30	302.62	298.65
37000	419.28	404.50	391.97	381.25	372.02	364.02	357.05	350.96	329.73	317.89	311.02	306.94
38000	430.61	415.43	402.56	391.55	382.07	373.86	366.70	360.44	338.64	326.48	319.43	315.24
39000	441.94	426.37	413.16	401.86	392.13	383.69	376.35	369.93	347.55	335.08	327.83	323.53
40000	453.27	437.30	423.75	412.16	402.18	393.53	386.00	379.41	356.46	343.67	336.24	331.83
41000	464.60	448.23	434.34	422.47	412.24	403.37	395.65	388.90	365.37	352.26	344.65	340.12
42000	475.93	459.16	444.94	432.77	422.29	413.21	405.30	398.38	374.28	360.85	353.05	348.42
43000	487.26	470.10	455.53	443.07	432.34	423.05	414.95	407.87	383.19	369.44	361.46	356.72
44000	498.60	481.03	466.12	453.38	442.40	432.89	424.60	417.35	392.11	378.03	369.86	365.01
45000	509.93	491.96	476.72	463.68	452.45	442.72	434.25	426.84	401.02	386.62	378.27	373.31
46000	521.26	502.89	487.31	473.99	462.51	452.56	443.90	436.32	409.93	395.22	386.68	381.60
47000	532.59	513.83	497.91	484.29	472.56	462.40	453.55	445.81	418.84	403.81	395.08	389.90
48000	543.92	524.76	508.50	494.59	482.62	472.24	463.20	455.29	427.75	412.40	403.49	398.19
49000	555.25	535.69	519.09	504.90	492.67	482.08	472.85	464.78	436.66	420.99	411.89	406.49
50000	566.59	546.62	529.69	515.20	502.72	491.92	482.50	474.26	445.57	429.58	420.30	414.78
55000	623.24	601.28	582.65	566.72	553.00	541.11	530.75	521.69	490.13	472.54	462.33	456.26
60000	679.90	655.95	635.62	618.24	603.27	590.30	579.00	569.12	534.69	515.50	504.36	497.74
65000	736.56	710.61	688.59	669.76	653.54	639.49	627.25	616.54	579.24	558.46	546.39	539.22
70000	793.22	765.27	741.56	721.28	703.81	688.68	675.50	663.97	623.80	601.41	588.42	580.70
75000	849.88	819.93	794.53	772.80	754.08	737.87	723.75	711.39	668.36	644.37	630.45	622.17
80000	906.54	874.59	847.50	824.32	804.36	787.06	772.00	758.82	712.91	687.33	672.48	663.65
85000	963.19	929.25	900.46	875.84	854.63	836.25	820.25	806.24	757.47	730.29	714.51	705.13
90000	1019.85	983.92	953.43	927.36	904.90	885.44	868.50	853.67	802.03	773.24	756.54	746.61
95000	1076.51	1038.58	1006.40	978.88	955.17	934.63	916.75	901.10	846.59	816.20	798.56	788.09
100000	1133.17	1093.24	1059.37	1030.40	1005.44	983.83	965.00	948.52	891.14	859.16	840.59	829.56

10.00%
MONTHLY
PAYMENT REQUIRED TO AMORTIZE A LOAN

TERM AMOUNT	1 YEAR	2 YEARS	3 YEARS	4 YEARS	5 YEARS	6 YEARS	7 YEARS	8 YEARS	9 YEARS	10 YEARS	11 YEARS	12 YEARS
50	4.40	2.31	1.62	1.27	1.07	.93	.84	.76	.71	.67	.63	.60
100	8.80	4.62	3.23	2.54	2.13	1.86	1.67	1.52	1.41	1.33	1.26	1.20
200	17.59	9.23	6.46	5.08	4.25	3.71	3.33	3.04	2.82	2.65	2.51	2.40
300	26.38	13.85	9.69	7.61	6.38	5.56	4.99	4.56	4.23	3.97	3.76	3.59
400	35.17	18.46	12.91	10.15	8.50	7.42	6.65	6.07	5.64	5.29	5.01	4.79
500	43.96	23.08	16.14	12.69	10.63	9.27	8.31	7.59	7.04	6.61	6.26	5.98
600	52.75	27.69	19.37	15.22	12.75	11.12	9.97	9.11	8.45	7.93	7.52	7.18
700	61.55	32.31	22.59	17.76	14.88	12.97	11.63	10.63	9.86	9.26	8.77	8.37
800	70.34	36.92	25.82	20.30	17.00	14.83	13.29	12.14	11.27	10.58	10.02	9.57
900	79.13	41.54	29.05	22.83	19.13	16.68	14.95	13.66	12.68	11.90	11.27	10.76
1000	87.92	46.15	32.27	25.37	21.25	18.53	16.61	15.18	14.08	13.22	12.52	11.96
2000	175.84	92.29	64.54	50.73	42.50	37.06	33.21	30.35	28.16	26.44	25.04	23.91
3000	263.75	138.44	96.81	76.09	63.75	55.58	49.81	45.53	42.24	39.65	37.56	35.86
4000	351.67	184.58	129.07	101.46	84.99	74.11	66.41	60.70	56.32	52.87	50.08	47.81
5000	439.58	230.73	161.34	126.82	106.24	92.63	83.01	75.88	70.40	66.08	62.60	59.76
6000	527.50	276.87	193.61	152.18	127.49	111.16	99.61	91.05	84.48	79.30	75.12	71.71
7000	615.42	323.02	225.88	177.54	148.73	129.69	116.21	106.22	98.56	92.51	87.64	83.66
8000	703.33	369.16	258.14	202.91	169.98	148.21	132.81	121.40	112.63	105.73	100.16	95.61
9000	791.25	415.31	290.41	228.27	191.23	166.74	149.42	136.57	126.71	118.94	112.68	107.56
10000	879.16	461.45	322.68	253.63	212.48	185.26	166.02	151.75	140.79	132.16	125.20	119.51
11000	967.08	507.60	354.94	278.99	233.72	203.79	182.62	166.92	154.87	145.37	137.72	131.46
12000	1055.00	553.74	387.21	304.36	254.97	222.32	199.22	182.09	168.95	158.59	150.24	143.41
13000	1142.91	599.89	419.48	329.72	276.22	240.84	215.82	197.27	183.03	171.80	162.76	155.37
14000	1230.83	646.03	451.75	355.08	297.46	259.37	232.42	212.44	197.11	185.02	175.28	167.32
15000	1318.74	692.18	484.01	380.44	318.71	277.89	249.02	227.62	211.19	198.23	187.80	179.27
16000	1406.66	738.32	516.28	405.81	339.96	296.42	265.62	242.79	225.26	211.45	200.32	191.22
17000	1494.58	784.47	548.55	431.17	361.20	314.94	282.23	257.97	239.34	224.66	212.84	203.17
18000	1582.49	830.61	580.81	456.53	382.45	333.47	298.83	273.14	253.42	237.88	225.36	215.12
19000	1670.41	876.76	613.08	481.89	403.70	352.00	315.43	288.31	267.50	251.09	237.88	227.07
20000	1758.32	922.90	645.35	507.26	424.95	370.52	332.03	303.49	281.58	264.31	250.40	239.02
21000	1846.24	969.05	677.62	532.62	446.19	389.05	348.63	318.66	295.66	277.52	262.92	250.97
22000	1934.15	1015.19	709.88	557.98	467.44	407.57	365.23	333.84	309.74	290.74	275.44	262.92
23000	2022.07	1061.34	742.15	583.34	488.69	426.10	381.83	349.01	323.81	303.95	287.96	274.87
24000	2109.99	1107.48	774.42	608.71	509.93	444.63	398.43	364.18	337.89	317.17	300.48	286.82
25000	2197.90	1153.63	806.68	634.07	531.18	463.15	415.03	379.36	351.97	330.38	313.00	298.77
26000	2285.82	1199.77	838.95	659.43	552.43	481.68	431.64	394.53	366.05	343.60	325.52	310.73
27000	2373.73	1245.92	871.22	684.79	573.68	500.20	448.24	409.71	380.13	356.81	338.04	322.68
28000	2461.65	1292.06	903.49	710.16	594.92	518.73	464.84	424.88	394.21	370.03	350.56	334.63
29000	2549.57	1338.21	935.75	735.52	616.17	537.25	481.44	440.06	408.29	383.24	363.08	346.58
30000	2637.48	1384.35	968.02	760.88	637.42	555.78	498.04	455.23	422.37	396.46	375.60	358.53
31000	2725.40	1430.50	1000.29	786.25	658.66	574.31	514.64	470.40	436.44	409.67	388.12	370.48
32000	2813.31	1476.64	1032.56	811.61	679.91	592.83	531.24	485.58	450.52	422.89	400.64	382.43
33000	2901.23	1522.79	1064.82	836.97	701.16	611.36	547.84	500.75	464.60	436.10	413.16	394.38
34000	2989.15	1568.93	1097.09	862.33	722.40	629.88	564.45	515.93	478.68	449.32	425.68	406.33
35000	3077.06	1615.08	1129.36	887.70	743.65	648.41	581.05	531.10	492.76	462.53	438.20	418.28
36000	3164.98	1661.22	1161.62	913.06	764.90	666.94	597.65	546.27	506.84	475.75	450.72	430.23
37000	3252.89	1707.37	1193.89	938.42	786.15	685.46	614.25	561.45	520.92	488.96	463.24	442.18
38000	3340.81	1753.51	1226.16	963.78	807.39	703.99	630.85	576.62	535.00	502.18	475.76	454.13
39000	3428.72	1799.66	1258.43	989.15	828.64	722.51	647.45	591.80	549.07	515.39	488.28	466.09
40000	3516.64	1845.80	1290.69	1014.51	849.89	741.04	664.05	606.97	563.15	528.61	500.80	478.04
41000	3604.56	1891.95	1322.96	1039.87	871.13	759.56	680.65	622.15	577.23	541.82	513.32	489.99
42000	3692.47	1938.09	1355.23	1065.23	892.38	778.09	697.25	637.32	591.31	555.04	525.84	501.94
43000	3780.39	1984.24	1387.49	1090.60	913.63	796.62	713.86	652.49	605.39	568.25	538.36	513.89
44000	3868.30	2030.38	1419.76	1115.96	934.87	815.14	730.46	667.67	619.47	581.47	550.88	525.84
45000	3956.22	2076.53	1452.03	1141.32	956.12	833.67	747.06	682.84	633.55	594.68	563.40	537.79
46000	4044.14	2122.67	1484.30	1166.68	977.37	852.19	763.66	698.02	647.62	607.90	575.92	549.74
47000	4132.05	2168.82	1516.56	1192.05	998.62	870.72	780.26	713.19	661.70	621.11	588.44	561.69
48000	4219.97	2214.96	1548.83	1217.41	1019.86	889.25	796.86	728.36	675.78	634.33	600.96	573.64
49000	4307.88	2261.11	1581.10	1242.77	1041.11	907.77	813.46	743.54	689.86	647.54	613.48	585.59
50000	4395.80	2307.25	1613.36	1268.13	1062.36	926.30	830.06	758.71	703.94	660.76	626.00	597.54
55000	4835.38	2537.98	1774.70	1394.95	1168.59	1018.93	913.07	834.58	774.33	726.83	688.60	657.30
60000	5274.96	2768.70	1936.04	1521.76	1274.83	1111.56	996.08	910.45	844.73	792.91	751.20	717.05
65000	5714.54	2999.43	2097.37	1648.57	1381.06	1204.18	1079.08	986.33	915.12	858.98	813.80	776.81
70000	6154.12	3230.15	2258.71	1775.39	1487.30	1296.81	1162.09	1062.20	985.51	925.06	876.40	836.56
75000	6593.70	3460.87	2420.04	1902.20	1593.53	1389.44	1245.09	1138.07	1055.91	991.14	939.00	896.31
80000	7033.28	3691.60	2581.38	2029.01	1699.77	1482.07	1328.10	1213.94	1126.30	1057.21	1001.60	956.07
85000	7472.86	3922.32	2742.72	2155.82	1806.00	1574.70	1411.11	1289.81	1196.69	1123.29	1064.19	1015.82
90000	7912.43	4153.05	2904.05	2282.64	1912.24	1667.33	1494.11	1365.68	1267.09	1189.36	1126.79	1075.58
95000	8352.01	4383.77	3065.39	2409.45	2018.47	1759.96	1577.12	1441.55	1337.48	1255.44	1189.39	1135.33
100000	8791.59	4614.50	3226.72	2536.26	2124.71	1852.59	1660.12	1517.42	1407.87	1321.51	1251.99	1195.08

MONTHLY

PAYMENT REQUIRED TO AMORTIZE A LOAN

10.00%

TERM / AMOUNT	13 YEARS	14 YEARS	15 YEARS	16 YEARS	17 YEARS	18 YEARS	19 YEARS	20 YEARS	25 YEARS	30 YEARS	35 YEARS	40 YEARS
50	.58	.56	.54	.53	.52	.50	.50	.49	.46	.44	.43	.43
100	1.15	1.11	1.08	1.05	1.03	1.00	.99	.97	.91	.88	.86	.85
200	2.30	2.22	2.15	2.10	2.05	2.00	1.97	1.94	1.82	1.76	1.72	1.70
300	3.45	3.33	3.23	3.14	3.07	3.00	2.95	2.90	2.73	2.64	2.58	2.55
400	4.60	4.44	4.30	4.19	4.09	4.00	3.93	3.87	3.64	3.52	3.44	3.40
500	5.74	5.55	5.38	5.23	5.11	5.00	4.91	4.83	4.55	4.39	4.30	4.25
600	6.89	6.65	6.45	6.28	6.13	6.00	5.89	5.80	5.46	5.27	5.16	5.10
700	8.04	7.76	7.53	7.33	7.15	7.00	6.87	6.76	6.37	6.15	6.02	5.95
800	9.19	8.87	8.60	8.37	8.17	8.00	7.86	7.73	7.27	7.03	6.88	6.80
900	10.34	9.98	9.68	9.42	9.20	9.00	8.84	8.69	8.18	7.90	7.74	7.65
1000	11.48	11.09	10.75	10.46	10.22	10.00	9.82	9.66	9.09	8.78	8.60	8.50
2000	22.96	22.17	21.50	20.92	20.43	20.00	19.63	19.31	18.18	17.56	17.20	16.99
3000	34.44	33.25	32.24	31.38	30.64	30.00	29.44	28.96	27.27	26.33	25.80	25.48
4000	45.92	44.33	42.99	41.84	40.85	40.00	39.26	38.61	36.35	35.11	34.39	33.97
5000	57.40	55.42	53.74	52.30	51.07	50.00	49.07	48.26	45.44	43.88	42.99	42.46
6000	68.88	66.50	64.48	62.76	61.28	60.00	58.88	57.91	54.53	52.66	51.59	50.95
7000	80.35	77.58	75.23	73.22	71.49	69.99	68.69	67.56	63.61	61.44	60.18	59.45
8000	91.83	88.66	85.97	83.68	81.70	79.99	78.51	77.21	72.70	70.21	68.78	67.94
9000	103.31	99.74	96.72	94.14	91.91	89.99	88.32	86.86	81.79	78.99	77.38	76.43
10000	114.79	110.83	107.47	104.60	102.13	99.99	98.13	96.51	90.88	87.76	85.97	84.92
11000	126.27	121.91	118.21	115.05	112.34	109.99	107.94	106.16	99.96	96.54	94.57	93.41
12000	137.75	132.99	128.96	125.51	122.55	119.99	117.76	115.81	109.05	105.31	103.17	101.90
13000	149.23	144.07	139.70	135.97	132.76	129.98	127.57	125.46	118.14	114.09	111.76	110.39
14000	160.70	155.15	150.45	146.43	142.97	139.98	137.38	135.11	127.22	122.87	120.36	118.89
15000	172.18	166.24	161.20	156.89	153.19	149.98	147.19	144.76	136.31	131.64	128.96	127.38
16000	183.66	177.32	171.94	167.35	163.40	159.98	157.01	154.41	145.40	140.42	137.55	135.87
17000	195.14	188.40	182.69	177.81	173.61	169.98	166.82	164.06	154.48	149.19	146.15	144.36
18000	206.62	199.48	193.43	188.27	183.82	179.98	176.63	173.71	163.57	157.97	154.75	152.85
19000	218.10	210.56	204.18	198.73	194.03	189.98	186.44	183.36	172.66	166.74	163.34	161.34
20000	229.57	221.65	214.93	209.19	204.25	199.97	196.26	193.01	181.75	175.52	171.94	169.83
21000	241.05	232.73	225.67	219.64	214.46	209.97	206.07	202.66	190.83	184.30	180.54	178.33
22000	252.53	243.81	236.42	230.10	224.67	219.97	215.88	212.31	199.92	193.07	189.13	186.82
23000	264.01	254.89	247.16	240.56	234.88	229.97	225.69	221.96	209.01	201.85	197.73	195.31
24000	275.49	265.97	257.91	251.02	245.10	239.97	235.51	231.61	218.09	210.62	206.33	203.80
25000	286.97	277.06	268.66	261.48	255.31	249.97	245.32	241.26	227.18	219.40	214.92	212.29
26000	298.45	288.14	279.40	271.94	265.52	259.96	255.13	250.91	236.27	228.17	223.52	220.78
27000	309.92	299.22	290.15	282.40	275.73	269.96	264.94	260.56	245.35	236.95	232.12	229.27
28000	321.40	310.30	300.89	292.86	285.94	279.96	274.76	270.21	254.44	245.73	240.71	237.77
29000	332.88	321.38	311.64	303.32	296.16	289.96	284.57	279.86	263.53	254.50	249.31	246.26
30000	344.36	332.47	322.39	313.78	306.37	299.96	294.38	289.51	272.62	263.28	257.91	254.75
31000	355.84	343.55	333.13	324.23	316.58	309.96	304.20	299.16	281.70	272.05	266.50	263.24
32000	367.32	354.63	343.88	334.69	326.79	319.95	314.01	308.81	290.79	280.83	275.10	271.73
33000	378.79	365.71	354.62	345.15	337.00	329.95	323.82	318.46	299.88	289.60	283.70	280.22
34000	390.27	376.79	365.37	355.61	347.21	339.95	333.63	328.11	308.96	298.38	292.29	288.71
35000	401.75	387.88	376.12	366.07	357.43	349.95	343.45	337.76	318.05	307.16	300.89	297.21
36000	413.23	398.96	386.86	376.53	367.64	359.95	353.26	347.41	327.14	315.93	309.49	305.70
37000	424.71	410.04	397.61	386.99	377.85	369.95	363.07	357.06	336.22	324.71	318.08	314.19
38000	436.19	421.12	408.35	397.45	388.06	379.95	372.88	366.71	345.31	333.48	326.68	322.68
39000	447.67	432.20	419.10	407.91	398.28	389.94	382.70	376.36	354.40	342.26	335.28	331.17
40000	459.14	443.29	429.85	418.37	408.49	399.94	392.51	386.01	363.49	351.03	343.87	339.66
41000	470.62	454.37	440.59	428.82	418.70	409.94	402.32	395.66	372.57	359.81	352.47	348.15
42000	482.10	465.45	451.34	439.28	428.91	419.94	412.13	405.31	381.66	368.59	361.07	356.65
43000	493.58	476.53	462.09	449.74	439.13	429.94	421.95	414.96	390.75	377.36	369.66	365.14
44000	505.06	487.61	472.83	460.20	449.34	439.94	431.76	424.61	399.83	386.14	378.26	373.63
45000	516.54	498.70	483.58	470.66	459.55	449.93	441.57	434.26	408.92	394.91	386.86	382.12
46000	528.02	509.78	494.32	481.12	469.76	459.93	451.38	443.91	418.01	403.69	395.45	390.61
47000	539.49	520.86	505.07	491.58	479.97	469.93	461.20	453.57	427.09	412.46	404.05	399.10
48000	550.97	531.94	515.82	502.04	490.19	479.93	471.01	463.22	436.18	421.24	412.65	407.60
49000	562.45	543.02	526.56	512.50	500.40	489.93	480.82	472.87	445.27	430.02	421.24	416.09
50000	573.93	554.11	537.31	522.96	510.61	499.93	490.63	482.52	454.36	438.79	429.84	424.58
55000	631.32	609.52	591.04	575.25	561.67	549.92	539.70	530.77	499.79	482.67	472.82	467.04
60000	688.71	664.93	644.77	627.55	612.73	599.91	588.76	579.02	545.23	526.55	515.81	509.49
65000	746.11	720.34	698.50	679.84	663.79	649.90	637.82	627.27	590.66	570.43	558.79	551.95
70000	803.50	775.75	752.23	732.14	714.85	699.90	686.89	675.52	636.10	614.31	601.78	594.41
75000	860.89	831.16	805.96	784.43	765.91	749.89	735.95	723.77	681.53	658.18	644.76	636.86
80000	918.28	886.57	859.69	836.73	816.97	799.88	785.01	772.02	726.97	702.06	687.74	679.32
85000	975.68	941.98	913.42	889.02	868.03	849.87	834.08	820.27	772.40	745.94	730.73	721.78
90000	1033.07	997.39	967.15	941.32	919.09	899.86	883.14	868.52	817.84	789.82	773.71	764.24
95000	1090.46	1052.80	1020.88	993.61	970.15	949.86	932.20	916.78	863.27	833.70	816.69	806.69
100000	1147.85	1108.21	1074.61	1045.91	1021.22	999.85	981.26	965.03	908.71	877.58	859.68	849.15

10.25%

MONTHLY
PAYMENT REQUIRED TO AMORTIZE A LOAN

TERM AMOUNT	1 YEAR	2 YEARS	3 YEARS	4 YEARS	5 YEARS	6 YEARS	7 YEARS	8 YEARS	9 YEARS	10 YEARS	11 YEARS	12 YEARS
50	4.41	2.32	1.62	1.28	1.07	.94	.84	.77	.72	.67	.64	.61
100	8.81	4.63	3.24	2.55	2.14	1.87	1.68	1.54	1.43	1.34	1.27	1.21
200	17.61	9.26	6.48	5.10	4.28	3.74	3.35	3.07	2.85	2.68	2.54	2.42
300	26.41	13.88	9.72	7.65	6.42	5.60	5.02	4.60	4.27	4.01	3.80	3.63
400	35.22	18.51	12.96	10.20	8.55	7.47	6.70	6.13	5.69	5.35	5.07	4.84
500	44.02	23.14	16.20	12.75	10.69	9.33	8.37	7.66	7.11	6.68	6.34	6.05
600	52.82	27.76	19.44	15.29	12.83	11.20	10.04	9.19	8.53	8.02	7.60	7.26
700	61.63	32.39	22.67	17.84	14.96	13.06	11.72	10.72	9.96	9.35	8.87	8.47
800	70.43	37.01	25.91	20.39	17.10	14.93	13.39	12.25	11.38	10.69	10.13	9.68
900	79.23	41.64	29.15	22.94	19.24	16.79	15.06	13.78	12.80	12.02	11.40	10.89
1000	88.04	46.27	32.39	25.49	21.38	18.66	16.74	15.31	14.22	13.36	12.67	12.10
2000	176.07	92.53	64.77	50.97	42.75	37.31	33.47	30.62	28.43	26.71	25.33	24.20
3000	264.10	138.79	97.16	76.45	64.12	55.96	50.20	45.93	42.65	40.07	37.99	36.29
4000	352.13	185.05	129.54	101.94	85.49	74.61	66.93	61.23	56.86	53.42	50.65	48.39
5000	440.17	231.31	161.93	127.42	106.86	93.27	83.66	76.54	71.08	66.77	63.31	60.48
6000	528.20	277.57	194.31	152.90	128.23	111.92	100.39	91.85	85.29	80.13	75.98	72.58
7000	616.23	323.83	226.70	178.38	149.60	130.57	117.12	107.15	99.51	93.48	88.64	84.67
8000	704.26	370.09	259.08	203.87	170.97	149.22	133.85	122.46	113.72	106.84	101.30	96.77
9000	792.29	416.35	291.47	229.35	192.34	167.87	150.58	137.77	127.93	120.19	113.96	108.87
10000	880.33	462.61	323.85	254.83	213.71	186.53	167.31	153.07	142.15	133.54	126.62	120.96
11000	968.36	508.87	356.24	280.32	235.08	205.18	184.04	168.38	156.36	146.90	139.28	133.06
12000	1056.39	555.13	388.62	305.80	256.45	223.83	200.77	183.69	170.58	160.25	151.95	145.15
13000	1144.42	601.39	421.01	331.28	277.82	242.48	217.50	198.99	184.79	173.61	164.61	157.25
14000	1232.46	647.65	453.39	356.76	299.19	261.14	234.23	214.30	199.01	186.96	177.27	169.34
15000	1320.49	693.91	485.78	382.25	320.56	279.79	250.96	229.61	213.22	200.31	189.93	181.44
16000	1408.52	740.17	518.16	407.73	341.93	298.44	267.70	244.91	227.44	213.67	202.59	193.54
17000	1496.55	786.43	550.54	433.21	363.30	317.09	284.43	260.22	241.65	227.02	215.25	205.63
18000	1584.58	832.69	582.93	458.70	384.67	335.74	301.16	275.53	255.86	240.38	227.92	217.73
19000	1672.62	878.95	615.31	484.18	406.04	354.40	317.89	290.83	270.08	253.73	240.58	229.82
20000	1760.65	925.21	647.70	509.66	427.41	373.05	334.62	306.14	284.29	267.08	253.24	241.92
21000	1848.68	971.47	680.08	535.14	448.78	391.70	351.35	321.45	298.51	280.44	265.90	254.01
22000	1936.71	1017.73	712.47	560.63	470.15	410.35	368.08	336.75	312.72	293.79	278.56	266.11
23000	2024.75	1063.99	744.85	586.11	491.52	429.00	384.81	352.06	326.94	307.14	291.23	278.20
24000	2112.78	1110.25	777.24	611.59	512.89	447.66	401.54	367.37	341.15	320.50	303.89	290.30
25000	2200.81	1156.52	809.62	637.08	534.26	466.31	418.27	382.67	355.37	333.85	316.55	302.40
26000	2288.84	1202.78	842.01	662.56	555.63	484.96	435.00	397.98	369.58	347.21	329.21	314.49
27000	2376.87	1249.04	874.39	688.04	577.00	503.61	451.73	413.29	383.79	360.56	341.87	326.59
28000	2464.91	1295.30	906.78	713.52	598.37	522.27	468.46	428.59	398.01	373.91	354.53	338.68
29000	2552.94	1341.56	939.16	739.01	619.74	540.92	485.19	443.90	412.22	387.27	367.20	350.78
30000	2640.97	1387.82	971.55	764.49	641.11	559.57	501.92	459.21	426.44	400.62	379.86	362.87
31000	2729.00	1434.08	1003.93	789.97	662.48	578.22	518.65	474.51	440.65	413.98	392.52	374.97
32000	2817.04	1480.34	1036.32	815.46	683.85	596.87	535.39	489.82	454.87	427.33	405.18	387.07
33000	2905.07	1526.60	1068.70	840.94	705.22	615.53	552.12	505.13	469.08	440.68	417.84	399.16
34000	2993.10	1572.86	1101.08	866.42	726.59	634.18	568.85	520.44	483.30	454.04	430.50	411.26
35000	3081.13	1619.12	1133.47	891.90	747.96	652.83	585.58	535.74	497.51	467.39	443.17	423.35
36000	3169.16	1665.38	1165.85	917.39	769.33	671.48	602.31	551.05	511.72	480.75	455.83	435.45
37000	3257.20	1711.64	1198.24	942.87	790.70	690.13	619.04	566.36	525.94	494.10	468.49	447.54
38000	3345.23	1757.90	1230.62	968.35	812.08	708.79	635.77	581.66	540.15	507.45	481.15	459.64
39000	3433.26	1804.16	1263.01	993.83	833.45	727.44	652.50	596.97	554.37	520.81	493.81	471.74
40000	3521.29	1850.42	1295.39	1019.32	854.82	746.09	669.23	612.28	568.58	534.16	506.48	483.83
41000	3609.33	1896.68	1327.78	1044.80	876.19	764.74	685.96	627.58	582.80	547.51	519.14	495.93
42000	3697.36	1942.94	1360.16	1070.28	897.56	783.40	702.69	642.89	597.01	560.87	531.80	508.02
43000	3785.39	1989.20	1392.55	1095.77	918.93	802.05	719.42	658.20	611.23	574.22	544.46	520.12
44000	3873.42	2035.46	1424.93	1121.25	940.30	820.70	736.15	673.50	625.44	587.58	557.12	532.21
45000	3961.45	2081.72	1457.32	1146.73	961.67	839.35	752.88	688.81	639.65	600.93	569.78	544.31
46000	4049.49	2127.98	1489.70	1172.21	983.04	858.00	769.61	704.12	653.87	614.28	582.45	556.40
47000	4137.52	2174.24	1522.09	1197.70	1004.41	876.66	786.35	719.42	668.08	627.64	595.11	568.50
48000	4225.55	2220.50	1554.47	1223.18	1025.78	895.31	803.08	734.73	682.30	640.99	607.77	580.60
49000	4313.58	2266.76	1586.85	1248.66	1047.15	913.96	819.81	750.04	696.51	654.35	620.43	592.69
50000	4401.62	2313.02	1619.24	1274.15	1068.52	932.61	836.54	765.34	710.73	667.70	633.09	604.79
55000	4841.78	2544.33	1781.16	1401.56	1175.37	1025.87	920.19	841.88	781.80	734.47	696.40	665.27
60000	5281.94	2775.63	1943.09	1528.97	1282.22	1119.13	1003.84	918.41	852.87	801.24	759.71	725.74
65000	5722.10	3006.93	2105.01	1656.39	1389.07	1212.40	1087.50	994.95	923.94	868.01	823.02	786.22
70000	6162.26	3238.23	2266.93	1783.80	1495.92	1305.66	1171.15	1071.48	995.01	934.78	886.33	846.70
75000	6602.42	3469.53	2428.86	1911.22	1602.77	1398.92	1254.80	1148.01	1066.09	1001.55	949.64	907.18
80000	7042.58	3700.84	2590.78	2038.63	1709.63	1492.18	1338.46	1224.55	1137.16	1068.32	1012.95	967.66
85000	7482.74	3932.14	2752.70	2166.04	1816.48	1585.44	1422.11	1301.08	1208.23	1135.09	1076.25	1028.14
90000	7922.90	4163.44	2914.63	2293.46	1923.33	1678.70	1505.76	1377.61	1279.30	1201.86	1139.56	1088.61
95000	8363.06	4394.74	3076.55	2420.87	2030.18	1771.96	1589.42	1454.15	1350.37	1268.63	1202.87	1149.09
100000	8803.23	4626.04	3238.47	2548.29	2137.03	1865.22	1673.07	1530.68	1421.45	1335.40	1266.18	1209.57

MONTHLY

PAYMENT REQUIRED TO AMORTIZE A LOAN

10.25%

TERM AMOUNT	13 YEARS	14 YEARS	15 YEARS	16 YEARS	17 YEARS	18 YEARS	19 YEARS	20 YEARS	25 YEARS	30 YEARS	35 YEARS	40 YEARS
50	.59	.57	.55	.54	.52	.51	.50	.50	.47	.45	.44	.44
100	1.17	1.13	1.09	1.07	1.04	1.02	1.00	.99	.93	.90	.88	.87
200	2.33	2.25	2.18	2.13	2.08	2.04	2.00	1.97	1.86	1.80	1.76	1.74
300	3.49	3.37	3.27	3.19	3.12	3.05	3.00	2.95	2.78	2.69	2.64	2.61
400	4.66	4.50	4.36	4.25	4.15	4.07	4.00	3.93	3.71	3.59	3.52	3.48
500	5.82	5.62	5.45	5.31	5.19	5.08	4.99	4.91	4.64	4.49	4.40	4.35
600	6.98	6.74	6.54	6.37	6.23	6.10	5.99	5.89	5.56	5.38	5.28	5.22
700	8.14	7.87	7.63	7.44	7.26	7.12	6.99	6.88	6.49	6.28	6.16	6.09
800	9.31	8.99	8.72	8.50	8.30	8.13	7.99	7.86	7.42	7.17	7.04	6.96
900	10.47	10.11	9.81	9.56	9.34	9.15	8.98	8.84	8.34	8.07	7.91	7.82
1000	11.63	11.24	10.90	10.62	10.38	10.16	9.98	9.82	9.27	8.97	8.79	8.69
2000	23.26	22.47	21.80	21.24	20.75	20.32	19.96	19.64	18.53	17.93	17.58	17.38
3000	34.88	33.70	32.70	31.85	31.12	30.48	29.93	29.45	27.80	26.89	26.37	26.07
4000	46.51	44.94	43.60	42.47	41.49	40.64	39.91	39.27	37.06	35.85	35.16	34.76
5000	58.14	56.17	54.50	53.08	51.86	50.80	49.89	49.09	46.32	44.81	43.95	43.45
6000	69.76	67.40	65.40	63.70	62.23	60.96	59.86	58.90	55.59	53.77	52.74	52.13
7000	81.39	78.63	76.30	74.31	72.60	71.12	69.84	68.72	64.85	62.73	61.52	60.82
8000	93.02	89.87	87.20	84.93	82.97	81.28	79.82	78.54	74.12	71.69	70.31	69.51
9000	104.64	101.10	98.10	95.54	93.34	91.44	89.79	88.35	83.38	80.65	79.10	78.20
10000	116.27	112.33	109.00	106.16	103.71	101.60	99.77	98.17	92.64	89.62	87.89	86.89
11000	127.89	123.56	119.90	116.77	114.09	111.76	109.75	107.99	101.91	98.58	96.68	95.58
12000	139.52	134.80	130.80	127.39	124.46	121.92	119.72	117.80	111.17	107.54	105.47	104.26
13000	151.15	146.03	141.70	138.00	134.83	132.08	129.70	127.62	120.43	116.50	114.26	112.95
14000	162.77	157.26	152.60	148.62	145.20	142.24	139.67	137.44	129.70	125.46	123.04	121.64
15000	174.40	168.50	163.50	159.23	155.57	152.40	149.65	147.25	138.96	134.42	131.83	130.33
16000	186.03	179.73	174.40	169.85	165.94	162.56	159.63	157.07	148.23	143.38	140.62	139.02
17000	197.65	190.96	185.30	180.46	176.31	172.72	169.60	166.88	157.49	152.34	149.41	147.70
18000	209.28	202.19	196.20	191.08	186.68	182.88	179.58	176.70	166.75	161.30	158.20	156.39
19000	220.90	213.43	207.10	201.69	197.05	193.04	189.56	186.52	176.02	170.26	166.99	165.08
20000	232.53	224.66	218.00	212.31	207.42	203.20	199.53	196.33	185.28	179.23	175.78	173.77
21000	244.16	235.89	228.89	222.92	217.79	213.36	209.51	206.15	194.55	188.19	184.56	182.46
22000	255.78	247.12	239.79	233.54	228.17	223.52	219.49	215.97	203.81	197.15	193.35	191.15
23000	267.41	258.36	250.69	244.15	238.54	233.68	229.46	225.78	213.07	206.11	202.14	199.83
24000	279.04	269.59	261.59	254.77	248.91	243.84	239.44	235.60	222.34	215.07	210.93	208.52
25000	290.66	280.82	272.49	265.38	259.28	254.00	249.42	245.42	231.60	224.03	219.72	217.21
26000	302.29	292.06	283.39	276.00	269.65	264.16	259.39	255.23	240.86	232.99	228.51	225.90
27000	313.91	303.29	294.29	286.62	280.02	274.32	269.37	265.05	250.13	241.95	237.30	234.59
28000	325.54	314.52	305.19	297.23	290.39	284.48	279.34	274.87	259.39	250.91	246.08	243.27
29000	337.17	325.75	316.09	307.85	300.76	294.64	289.32	284.68	268.66	259.87	254.87	251.96
30000	348.79	336.99	326.99	318.46	311.13	304.80	299.30	294.50	277.92	268.84	263.66	260.65
31000	360.42	348.22	337.89	329.08	321.50	314.96	309.27	304.31	287.18	277.80	272.45	269.34
32000	372.05	359.45	348.79	339.69	331.87	325.12	319.25	314.13	296.45	286.76	281.24	278.03
33000	383.67	370.68	359.69	350.31	342.25	335.28	329.23	323.95	305.71	295.72	290.03	286.72
34000	395.30	381.92	370.59	360.92	352.62	345.44	339.20	333.76	314.98	304.68	298.82	295.40
35000	406.92	393.15	381.49	371.54	362.99	355.60	349.18	343.58	324.24	313.64	307.60	304.09
36000	418.55	404.38	392.39	382.15	373.36	365.76	359.16	353.40	333.50	322.60	316.39	312.78
37000	430.18	415.61	403.29	392.77	383.73	375.92	369.13	363.21	342.77	331.56	325.18	321.47
38000	441.80	426.85	414.19	403.38	394.10	386.08	379.11	373.03	352.03	340.52	333.97	330.16
39000	453.43	438.08	425.09	414.00	404.47	396.24	389.09	382.85	361.29	349.48	342.76	338.84
40000	465.06	449.31	435.99	424.61	414.84	406.40	399.06	392.66	370.56	358.45	351.55	347.53
41000	476.68	460.55	446.88	435.23	425.21	416.56	409.04	402.48	379.82	367.41	360.34	356.22
42000	488.31	471.78	457.78	445.84	435.58	426.72	419.01	412.30	389.09	376.37	369.12	364.91
43000	499.94	483.01	468.68	456.46	445.95	436.88	428.99	422.11	398.35	385.33	377.91	373.60
44000	511.56	494.24	479.58	467.07	456.33	447.04	438.97	431.93	407.61	394.29	386.70	382.29
45000	523.19	505.48	490.48	477.69	466.70	457.20	448.94	441.74	416.88	403.25	395.49	390.97
46000	534.81	516.71	501.38	488.30	477.07	467.36	458.92	451.56	426.14	412.21	404.28	399.66
47000	546.44	527.94	512.28	498.92	487.44	477.52	468.90	461.38	435.41	421.17	413.07	408.35
48000	558.07	539.17	523.18	509.53	497.81	487.68	478.87	471.19	444.67	430.13	421.86	417.04
49000	569.69	550.41	534.08	520.15	508.18	497.84	488.85	481.01	453.93	439.09	430.64	425.73
50000	581.32	561.64	544.98	530.76	518.55	508.00	498.83	490.83	463.20	448.06	439.43	434.41
55000	639.45	617.80	599.48	583.84	570.41	558.79	548.71	539.91	509.52	492.86	483.38	477.86
60000	697.58	673.97	653.98	636.92	622.26	609.59	598.59	588.99	555.83	537.67	527.32	521.30
65000	755.71	730.13	708.47	689.99	674.11	660.39	648.47	638.07	602.15	582.47	571.26	564.74
70000	813.84	786.29	762.97	743.07	725.97	711.19	698.35	687.16	648.47	627.28	615.20	608.18
75000	871.98	842.46	817.47	796.14	777.82	761.99	748.24	736.24	694.79	672.08	659.15	651.62
80000	930.11	898.62	871.97	849.22	829.68	812.79	798.12	785.32	741.11	716.89	703.09	695.06
85000	988.24	954.78	926.46	902.30	881.53	863.59	848.00	834.40	787.43	761.69	747.03	738.50
90000	1046.37	1010.95	980.96	955.37	933.39	914.39	897.88	883.48	833.75	806.50	790.98	781.94
95000	1104.50	1067.11	1035.46	1008.45	985.24	965.19	947.77	932.57	880.07	851.30	834.92	825.38
100000	1162.63	1123.27	1089.96	1061.52	1037.10	1015.99	997.65	981.65	926.39	896.11	878.86	868.82

10.50%

MONTHLY
PAYMENT REQUIRED TO AMORTIZE A LOAN

TERM AMOUNT	1 YEAR	2 YEARS	3 YEARS	4 YEARS	5 YEARS	6 YEARS	7 YEARS	8 YEARS	9 YEARS	10 YEARS	11 YEARS	12 YEARS
50	4.41	2.32	1.63	1.29	1.08	.94	.85	.78	.72	.68	.65	.62
100	8.82	4.64	3.26	2.57	2.15	1.88	1.69	1.55	1.44	1.35	1.29	1.23
200	17.63	9.28	6.51	5.13	4.30	3.76	3.38	3.09	2.88	2.70	2.57	2.45
300	26.45	13.92	9.76	7.69	6.45	5.64	5.06	4.64	4.31	4.05	3.85	3.68
400	35.26	18.56	13.01	10.25	8.60	7.52	6.75	6.18	5.75	5.40	5.13	4.90
500	44.08	23.19	16.26	12.81	10.75	9.39	8.44	7.73	7.18	6.75	6.41	6.13
600	52.89	27.83	19.51	15.37	12.90	11.27	10.12	9.27	8.62	8.10	7.69	7.35
700	61.71	32.47	22.76	17.93	15.05	13.15	11.81	10.81	10.05	9.45	8.97	8.57
800	70.52	37.11	26.01	20.49	17.20	15.03	13.49	12.36	11.49	10.80	10.25	9.80
900	79.34	41.74	29.26	23.05	19.35	16.91	15.18	13.90	12.92	12.15	11.53	11.02
1000	88.15	46.38	32.51	25.61	21.50	18.78	16.87	15.45	14.36	13.50	12.81	12.25
2000	176.30	92.76	65.01	51.21	42.99	37.56	33.73	30.89	28.71	26.99	25.61	24.49
3000	264.45	139.13	97.51	76.82	64.49	56.34	50.59	46.33	43.06	40.49	38.42	36.73
4000	352.60	185.51	130.01	102.42	85.98	75.12	67.45	61.77	57.41	53.98	51.22	48.97
5000	440.75	231.89	162.52	128.02	107.47	93.90	84.31	77.21	71.76	67.47	64.03	61.21
6000	528.90	278.26	195.02	153.63	128.97	112.68	101.17	92.65	86.11	80.97	76.83	73.45
7000	617.05	324.64	227.52	179.23	150.46	131.46	118.03	108.09	100.46	94.46	89.64	85.69
8000	705.19	371.01	260.02	204.83	171.96	150.24	134.89	123.53	114.81	107.95	102.44	97.94
9000	793.34	417.39	292.53	230.44	193.45	169.02	151.75	138.97	129.16	121.45	115.25	110.18
10000	881.49	463.77	325.03	256.04	214.94	187.79	168.61	154.41	143.51	134.94	128.05	122.42
11000	969.64	510.14	357.53	281.64	236.44	206.57	185.47	169.85	157.86	148.43	140.85	134.66
12000	1057.79	556.52	390.03	307.25	257.93	225.35	202.33	185.29	172.22	161.93	153.66	146.90
13000	1145.94	602.89	422.54	332.85	279.43	244.13	219.19	200.73	186.57	175.42	166.46	159.14
14000	1234.09	649.27	455.04	358.45	300.92	262.91	236.05	216.17	200.92	188.91	179.27	171.38
15000	1322.23	695.65	487.54	384.06	322.41	281.69	252.92	231.61	215.27	202.41	192.07	183.63
16000	1410.38	742.02	520.04	409.66	343.91	300.47	269.78	247.05	229.62	215.90	204.88	195.87
17000	1498.53	788.40	552.55	435.26	365.40	319.25	286.64	262.49	243.97	229.39	217.68	208.11
18000	1586.68	834.77	585.05	460.87	386.90	338.03	303.50	277.93	258.32	242.89	230.49	220.35
19000	1674.83	881.15	617.55	486.47	408.39	356.81	320.34	293.37	272.67	256.38	243.29	232.59
20000	1762.98	927.53	650.05	512.07	429.88	375.58	337.22	308.81	287.02	269.87	256.09	244.83
21000	1851.13	973.90	682.56	537.68	451.38	394.36	354.08	324.25	301.37	283.37	268.90	257.07
22000	1939.27	1020.28	715.06	563.28	472.87	413.14	370.94	339.69	315.72	296.86	281.70	269.32
23000	2027.42	1066.65	747.56	588.88	494.36	431.92	387.80	355.13	330.07	310.36	294.51	281.56
24000	2115.57	1113.03	780.06	614.49	515.86	450.70	404.66	370.57	344.43	323.85	307.31	293.80
25000	2203.72	1159.41	812.57	640.09	537.35	469.48	421.52	386.01	358.78	337.34	320.12	306.04
26000	2291.87	1205.78	845.07	665.69	558.85	488.26	438.38	401.45	373.13	350.84	332.92	318.28
27000	2380.02	1252.16	877.57	691.30	580.34	507.04	455.24	416.89	387.48	364.33	345.73	330.52
28000	2468.17	1298.53	910.07	716.90	601.83	525.82	472.10	432.33	401.83	377.82	358.53	342.76
29000	2556.31	1344.91	942.58	742.50	623.33	544.60	488.96	447.77	416.18	391.32	371.33	355.01
30000	2644.46	1391.29	975.08	768.11	644.82	563.37	505.83	463.21	430.53	404.81	384.14	367.25
31000	2732.41	1437.66	1007.58	793.71	666.32	582.15	522.69	478.65	444.88	418.30	396.94	379.49
32000	2820.76	1484.04	1040.08	819.31	687.81	600.93	539.55	494.09	459.23	431.80	409.75	391.73
33000	2908.91	1530.41	1072.59	844.92	709.30	619.71	556.41	509.53	473.58	445.29	422.55	403.97
34000	2997.06	1576.79	1105.09	870.52	730.80	638.49	573.27	524.97	487.93	458.78	435.36	416.21
35000	3085.21	1623.17	1137.59	896.12	752.29	657.27	590.13	540.41	502.29	472.28	448.16	428.45
36000	3173.35	1669.54	1170.09	921.73	773.79	676.05	606.99	555.85	516.64	485.77	460.97	440.70
37000	3261.50	1715.92	1202.60	947.33	795.28	694.83	623.85	571.29	530.99	499.26	473.77	452.94
38000	3349.65	1762.29	1235.10	972.93	816.77	713.61	640.71	586.73	545.34	512.76	486.57	465.18
39000	3437.80	1808.67	1267.60	998.54	838.27	732.38	657.57	602.17	559.69	526.25	499.38	477.42
40000	3525.95	1855.05	1300.10	1024.14	859.76	751.16	674.43	617.61	574.04	539.74	512.18	489.66
41000	3614.10	1901.42	1332.61	1049.74	881.25	769.94	691.29	633.05	588.39	553.24	524.99	501.90
42000	3702.25	1947.80	1365.11	1075.35	902.75	788.72	708.15	648.49	602.74	566.73	537.79	514.14
43000	3790.39	1994.17	1397.61	1100.95	924.24	807.50	725.01	663.93	617.09	580.23	550.60	526.39
44000	3878.54	2040.55	1430.11	1126.55	945.74	826.28	741.87	679.37	631.44	593.72	563.40	538.63
45000	3966.69	2086.93	1462.61	1152.16	967.23	845.06	758.74	694.81	645.79	607.21	576.21	550.87
46000	4054.84	2133.30	1495.12	1177.76	988.72	863.84	775.60	710.25	660.14	620.71	589.01	563.11
47000	4142.99	2179.68	1527.62	1203.36	1010.22	882.62	792.46	725.69	674.50	634.20	601.81	575.35
48000	4231.14	2226.06	1560.12	1228.97	1031.71	901.40	809.32	741.13	688.85	647.69	614.62	587.59
49000	4319.29	2272.43	1592.62	1254.57	1053.21	920.17	826.18	756.57	703.20	661.19	627.42	599.83
50000	4407.44	2318.81	1625.13	1280.17	1074.70	938.95	843.04	772.01	717.55	674.68	640.23	612.08
55000	4848.18	2550.69	1787.64	1408.19	1182.17	1032.85	927.34	849.21	789.30	742.15	704.25	673.28
60000	5288.92	2782.57	1950.15	1536.21	1289.64	1126.74	1011.65	926.41	861.06	809.61	768.27	734.49
65000	5729.66	3014.45	2112.66	1664.22	1397.11	1220.64	1095.95	1003.61	932.81	877.08	832.29	795.70
70000	6170.41	3246.33	2275.18	1792.24	1504.58	1314.53	1180.25	1080.81	1004.57	944.55	896.32	856.90
75000	6611.15	3478.21	2437.69	1920.26	1612.05	1408.43	1264.56	1158.01	1076.32	1012.02	960.34	918.11
80000	7051.89	3710.09	2600.20	2048.28	1719.52	1502.32	1348.86	1235.21	1148.07	1079.49	1024.36	979.32
85000	7492.64	3941.97	2762.71	2176.29	1826.99	1596.22	1433.16	1312.41	1219.83	1146.95	1088.38	1040.52
90000	7933.38	4173.85	2925.22	2304.31	1934.46	1690.11	1517.47	1389.61	1291.58	1214.42	1152.41	1101.73
95000	8374.12	4405.73	3087.74	2432.33	2041.93	1784.01	1601.77	1466.81	1363.34	1281.89	1216.43	1162.94
100000	8814.87	4637.61	3250.25	2560.34	2149.40	1877.90	1686.07	1544.01	1435.09	1349.36	1280.45	1224.15

PAYMENT REQUIRED TO AMORTIZE A LOAN

TERM AMOUNT	13 YEARS	14 YEARS	15 YEARS	16 YEARS	17 YEARS	18 YEARS	19 YEARS	20 YEARS	25 YEARS	30 YEARS	35 YEARS	40 YEARS
50	.59	.57	.56	.54	.53	.52	.51	.50	.48	.46	.45	.45
100	1.18	1.14	1.11	1.08	1.06	1.04	1.02	1.00	.95	.92	.90	.89
200	2.36	2.28	2.22	2.16	2.11	2.07	2.03	2.00	1.89	1.83	1.80	1.78
300	3.54	3.42	3.32	3.24	3.16	3.10	3.05	3.00	2.84	2.75	2.70	2.67
400	4.72	4.56	4.43	4.31	4.22	4.13	4.06	4.00	3.78	3.66	3.60	3.56
500	5.89	5.70	5.53	5.39	5.27	5.17	5.08	5.00	4.73	4.58	4.50	4.45
600	7.07	6.84	6.64	6.47	6.32	6.20	6.09	6.00	5.67	5.49	5.39	5.34
700	8.25	7.97	7.74	7.55	7.38	7.23	7.10	6.99	6.61	6.41	6.29	6.22
800	9.43	9.11	8.85	8.62	8.43	8.26	8.12	7.99	7.56	7.32	7.19	7.11
900	10.60	10.25	9.95	9.70	9.48	9.30	9.13	8.99	8.50	8.24	8.09	8.00
1000	11.78	11.39	11.06	10.78	10.54	10.33	10.15	9.99	9.45	9.15	8.99	8.89
2000	23.56	22.77	22.11	21.55	21.07	20.65	20.29	19.97	18.89	18.30	17.97	17.78
3000	35.33	34.16	33.17	32.32	31.60	30.97	30.43	29.96	28.33	27.45	26.95	26.66
4000	47.11	45.54	44.22	43.09	42.13	41.29	40.57	39.94	37.77	36.59	35.93	35.55
5000	58.88	56.93	55.27	53.87	52.66	51.62	50.71	49.92	47.21	45.74	44.91	44.43
6000	70.66	68.31	66.33	64.64	63.19	61.94	60.85	59.91	56.66	54.89	53.89	53.32
7000	82.43	79.70	77.38	75.41	73.72	72.26	70.99	69.89	66.10	64.04	62.87	62.20
8000	94.21	91.08	88.44	86.18	84.25	82.58	81.14	79.88	75.54	73.18	71.86	71.09
9000	105.98	102.46	99.49	96.96	94.78	92.91	91.28	89.86	84.98	82.33	80.84	79.98
10000	117.76	113.85	110.54	107.73	105.31	103.23	101.42	99.84	94.42	91.48	89.82	88.86
11000	129.53	125.23	121.60	118.50	115.84	113.55	111.56	109.83	103.86	100.63	98.80	97.75
12000	141.31	136.62	132.65	129.27	126.37	123.87	121.70	119.81	113.31	109.77	107.78	106.63
13000	153.08	148.00	143.71	140.05	136.91	134.19	131.84	129.79	122.75	118.92	116.76	115.52
14000	164.86	159.39	154.76	150.82	147.44	144.52	141.98	139.78	132.19	128.07	125.74	124.40
15000	176.63	170.77	165.81	161.59	157.97	154.84	152.13	149.76	141.63	137.22	134.73	133.29
16000	188.41	182.15	176.87	172.36	168.50	165.16	162.27	159.75	151.07	146.36	143.71	142.18
17000	200.18	193.54	187.92	183.14	179.03	175.48	172.41	169.73	160.52	155.51	152.69	151.06
18000	211.96	204.92	198.98	193.91	189.56	185.81	182.55	179.71	169.96	164.66	161.67	159.95
19000	223.73	216.31	210.03	204.68	200.09	196.13	192.69	189.70	179.40	173.81	170.65	168.83
20000	235.51	227.69	221.08	215.45	210.62	206.45	202.83	199.68	188.84	182.95	179.63	177.72
21000	247.28	239.08	232.14	226.23	221.15	216.77	212.97	209.66	198.28	192.10	188.61	186.60
22000	259.06	250.46	243.19	237.00	231.68	227.10	223.12	219.65	207.72	201.25	197.59	195.49
23000	270.83	261.84	254.25	247.77	242.21	237.42	233.26	229.63	217.17	210.40	206.58	204.38
24000	282.61	273.23	265.30	258.54	252.74	247.74	243.40	239.62	226.61	219.54	215.56	213.26
25000	294.38	284.61	276.35	269.32	263.28	258.06	253.54	249.60	236.05	228.69	224.54	222.15
26000	306.16	296.00	287.41	280.09	273.81	268.38	263.68	259.58	245.49	237.84	233.52	231.03
27000	317.93	307.38	298.46	290.86	284.34	278.71	273.82	269.57	254.93	246.98	242.50	239.92
28000	329.71	318.77	309.52	301.63	294.87	289.03	283.96	279.55	264.38	256.13	251.48	248.80
29000	341.48	330.15	320.57	312.41	305.40	299.35	294.11	289.54	273.82	265.28	260.46	257.69
30000	353.26	341.54	331.62	323.18	315.93	309.67	304.25	299.52	283.26	274.43	269.45	266.58
31000	365.03	352.92	342.68	333.95	326.46	320.00	314.39	309.50	292.70	283.57	278.43	275.46
32000	376.81	364.30	353.73	344.72	336.99	330.32	324.53	319.49	302.14	292.72	287.41	284.35
33000	388.58	375.69	364.79	355.50	347.52	340.64	334.67	329.47	311.58	301.87	296.39	293.23
34000	400.36	387.07	375.84	366.27	358.05	350.96	344.81	339.45	321.03	311.02	305.37	302.12
35000	412.13	398.46	386.89	377.04	368.58	361.28	354.95	349.44	330.47	320.16	314.35	311.00
36000	423.91	409.84	397.95	387.81	379.11	371.61	365.10	359.42	339.91	329.31	323.33	319.89
37000	435.68	421.23	409.00	398.58	389.65	381.93	375.24	369.41	349.35	338.46	332.31	328.78
38000	447.46	432.61	420.06	409.36	400.18	392.25	385.38	379.39	358.79	347.61	341.30	337.66
39000	459.23	443.99	431.11	420.13	410.71	402.57	395.52	389.37	368.24	356.75	350.28	346.55
40000	471.01	455.38	442.16	430.90	421.24	412.90	405.66	399.36	377.68	365.90	359.26	355.43
41000	482.78	466.76	453.22	441.67	431.77	423.22	415.80	409.34	387.12	375.05	368.24	364.32
42000	494.56	478.15	464.27	452.45	442.30	433.54	425.94	419.32	396.56	384.20	377.22	373.20
43000	506.33	489.53	475.33	463.22	452.83	443.86	436.08	429.31	406.00	393.34	386.20	382.09
44000	518.11	500.92	486.38	473.99	463.36	454.19	446.23	439.29	415.44	402.49	395.18	390.98
45000	529.88	512.30	497.43	484.76	473.89	464.51	456.37	449.28	424.89	411.64	404.17	399.86
46000	541.66	523.68	508.49	495.54	484.42	474.83	466.51	459.26	434.33	420.79	413.15	408.75
47000	553.43	535.07	519.54	506.31	494.95	485.15	476.65	469.24	443.77	429.93	422.13	417.63
48000	565.21	546.45	530.60	517.08	505.48	495.47	486.79	479.23	453.21	439.08	431.11	426.52
49000	576.98	557.84	541.65	527.85	516.01	505.80	496.93	489.21	462.65	448.23	440.09	435.40
50000	588.76	569.22	552.70	538.63	526.55	516.12	507.07	499.19	472.10	457.37	449.07	444.29
55000	647.63	626.14	607.97	592.49	579.20	567.73	557.78	549.11	519.30	503.11	493.98	488.72
60000	706.51	683.07	663.24	646.35	631.85	619.34	608.49	599.03	566.51	548.85	538.89	533.15
65000	765.38	739.99	718.51	700.21	684.51	670.95	659.20	648.95	613.72	594.59	583.79	577.58
70000	824.26	796.91	773.78	754.07	737.16	722.56	709.90	698.87	660.93	640.32	628.70	622.00
75000	883.13	853.83	829.05	807.94	789.82	774.18	760.61	748.79	708.14	686.06	673.61	666.43
80000	942.01	910.75	884.32	861.80	842.47	825.79	811.32	798.71	755.35	731.80	718.51	710.86
85000	1000.88	967.67	939.59	915.66	895.12	877.40	862.02	848.63	802.56	777.53	763.42	755.29
90000	1059.76	1024.60	994.86	969.52	947.78	929.01	912.73	898.55	849.77	823.27	808.33	799.72
95000	1118.63	1081.52	1050.13	1023.39	1000.43	980.62	963.44	948.47	896.98	869.01	853.23	844.15
100000	1177.51	1138.44	1105.40	1077.25	1053.09	1032.23	1014.14	998.38	944.19	914.74	898.14	888.58

10.75%

MONTHLY
PAYMENT REQUIRED TO AMORTIZE A LOAN

TERM AMOUNT	1 YEAR	2 YEARS	3 YEARS	4 YEARS	5 YEARS	6 YEARS	7 YEARS	8 YEARS	9 YEARS	10 YEARS	11 YEARS	12 YEARS
50	4.42	2.33	1.64	1.29	1.09	.95	.85	.78	.73	.69	.65	.62
100	8.83	4.65	3.27	2.58	2.17	1.90	1.70	1.56	1.45	1.37	1.30	1.24
200	17.66	9.30	6.53	5.15	4.33	3.79	3.40	3.12	2.90	2.73	2.59	2.48
300	26.48	13.95	9.79	7.72	6.49	5.68	5.10	4.68	4.35	4.10	3.89	3.72
400	35.31	18.60	13.05	10.29	8.65	7.57	6.80	6.23	5.80	5.46	5.18	4.96
500	44.14	23.25	16.32	12.87	10.81	9.46	8.50	7.79	7.25	6.82	6.48	6.20
600	52.96	27.90	19.58	15.44	12.98	11.35	10.20	9.35	8.70	8.19	7.77	7.44
700	61.79	32.55	22.84	18.01	15.14	13.24	11.90	10.91	10.15	9.55	9.07	8.68
800	70.62	37.20	26.10	20.58	17.30	15.13	13.60	12.46	11.60	10.91	10.36	9.92
900	79.44	41.85	29.36	23.16	19.46	17.02	15.30	14.02	13.04	12.28	11.66	11.15
1000	88.27	46.50	32.63	25.73	21.62	18.91	17.00	15.58	14.49	13.64	12.95	12.39
2000	176.54	92.99	65.25	51.45	43.24	37.82	33.99	31.15	28.98	27.27	25.90	24.78
3000	264.80	139.48	97.87	77.18	64.86	56.72	50.98	46.73	43.47	40.91	38.85	37.17
4000	353.07	185.97	130.49	102.90	86.48	75.63	67.97	62.30	57.96	54.54	51.80	49.56
5000	441.33	232.46	163.11	128.63	108.09	94.54	84.96	77.87	72.45	68.17	64.74	61.95
6000	529.60	278.96	195.73	154.35	129.71	113.44	101.95	93.45	86.93	81.81	77.69	74.33
7000	617.86	325.45	228.35	180.07	151.33	132.35	118.94	109.02	101.42	95.44	90.64	86.72
8000	706.13	371.94	260.97	205.80	172.95	151.26	135.94	124.60	115.91	109.08	103.59	99.11
9000	794.39	418.43	293.59	231.52	194.57	170.16	152.93	140.17	130.40	122.71	116.54	111.50
10000	882.66	464.92	326.21	257.25	216.18	189.07	169.92	155.74	144.89	136.34	129.48	123.89
11000	970.92	511.42	358.83	282.97	237.80	207.97	186.91	171.32	159.37	149.98	142.43	136.27
12000	1059.19	557.91	391.45	308.70	259.42	226.88	203.90	186.89	173.86	163.61	155.38	148.66
13000	1147.45	604.40	424.07	334.42	281.04	245.79	220.89	202.47	188.35	177.25	168.33	161.05
14000	1235.72	650.89	456.69	360.14	302.66	264.69	237.88	218.04	202.84	190.88	181.28	173.44
15000	1323.98	697.38	489.31	385.87	324.27	283.60	254.87	233.61	217.33	204.51	194.22	185.83
16000	1412.25	743.87	521.93	411.59	345.89	302.51	271.87	249.19	231.81	218.15	207.17	198.21
17000	1500.51	790.37	554.55	437.32	367.51	321.41	288.86	264.76	246.30	231.78	220.12	210.60
18000	1588.78	836.86	587.17	463.04	389.13	340.32	305.85	280.34	260.79	245.41	233.07	222.99
19000	1677.04	883.35	619.79	488.77	410.75	359.22	322.84	295.91	275.28	259.05	246.02	235.38
20000	1765.31	929.84	652.41	514.49	432.36	378.13	339.83	311.48	289.77	272.68	258.96	247.77
21000	1853.57	976.33	685.03	540.21	453.98	397.04	356.82	327.06	304.25	286.32	271.91	260.15
22000	1941.84	1022.83	717.65	565.94	475.60	415.94	373.81	342.63	318.74	299.95	284.86	272.54
23000	2030.10	1069.32	750.28	591.66	497.22	434.85	390.80	358.20	333.23	313.58	297.81	284.93
24000	2118.37	1115.81	782.90	617.39	518.84	453.76	407.80	373.78	347.72	327.22	310.76	297.32
25000	2206.63	1162.30	815.52	643.11	540.45	472.66	424.79	389.35	362.21	340.85	323.70	309.71
26000	2294.90	1208.79	848.14	668.84	562.07	491.57	441.78	404.93	376.69	354.49	336.65	322.09
27000	2383.16	1255.29	880.76	694.56	583.69	510.47	458.77	420.50	391.18	368.12	349.60	334.48
28000	2471.43	1301.78	913.38	720.28	605.31	529.38	475.76	436.07	405.67	381.75	362.55	346.87
29000	2559.69	1348.27	946.00	746.01	626.93	548.29	492.75	451.65	420.16	395.39	375.50	359.26
30000	2647.96	1394.76	978.62	771.73	648.54	567.19	509.74	467.22	434.65	409.02	388.44	371.65
31000	2736.22	1441.25	1011.24	797.46	670.16	586.10	526.73	482.80	449.13	422.65	401.39	384.03
32000	2824.49	1487.74	1043.86	823.18	691.78	605.01	543.73	498.37	463.62	436.29	414.34	396.42
33000	2912.75	1534.24	1076.48	848.91	713.40	623.91	560.72	513.94	478.11	449.92	427.29	408.81
34000	3001.02	1580.73	1109.10	874.63	735.02	642.82	577.71	529.52	492.60	463.56	440.24	421.20
35000	3089.28	1627.22	1141.72	900.35	756.63	661.72	594.70	545.09	507.09	477.19	453.18	433.59
36000	3177.55	1673.71	1174.34	926.08	778.25	680.63	611.69	560.67	521.57	490.82	466.13	445.97
37000	3265.81	1720.20	1206.96	951.80	799.87	699.54	628.68	576.24	536.06	504.46	479.08	458.36
38000	3354.08	1766.70	1239.58	977.53	821.49	718.44	645.67	591.81	550.55	518.09	492.03	470.75
39000	3442.34	1813.19	1272.20	1003.25	843.11	737.35	662.66	607.39	565.04	531.73	504.98	483.14
40000	3530.61	1859.68	1304.82	1028.98	864.72	756.26	679.66	622.96	579.53	545.36	517.92	495.53
41000	3618.87	1906.17	1337.44	1054.70	886.34	775.16	696.65	638.54	594.01	558.99	530.87	507.91
42000	3707.14	1952.66	1370.06	1080.42	907.96	794.07	713.64	654.11	608.50	572.63	543.82	520.30
43000	3795.40	1999.15	1402.68	1106.15	929.58	812.97	730.63	669.68	622.99	586.26	556.77	532.69
44000	3883.67	2045.65	1435.30	1131.87	951.19	831.88	747.62	685.26	637.48	599.90	569.72	545.08
45000	3971.93	2092.14	1467.93	1157.60	972.81	850.79	764.61	700.83	651.97	613.53	582.66	557.47
46000	4060.20	2138.63	1500.55	1183.32	994.43	869.69	781.60	716.40	666.45	627.16	595.61	569.85
47000	4148.46	2185.12	1533.17	1209.05	1016.05	888.60	798.59	731.98	680.94	640.80	608.56	582.24
48000	4236.73	2231.61	1565.79	1234.77	1037.67	907.51	815.59	747.55	695.43	654.43	621.51	594.63
49000	4324.99	2278.11	1598.41	1260.49	1059.28	926.41	832.58	763.13	709.92	668.06	634.46	607.02
50000	4413.26	2324.60	1631.03	1286.22	1080.90	945.32	849.57	778.70	724.41	681.70	647.40	619.41
55000	4854.58	2557.06	1794.13	1414.84	1188.99	1039.85	934.52	856.57	796.85	749.87	712.14	681.35
60000	5295.91	2789.52	1957.23	1543.46	1297.08	1134.38	1019.48	934.44	869.29	818.04	776.88	743.29
65000	5737.24	3021.98	2120.33	1672.08	1405.17	1228.91	1104.44	1012.31	941.73	886.21	841.62	805.23
70000	6178.56	3254.43	2283.44	1800.70	1513.26	1323.44	1189.39	1090.18	1014.17	954.38	906.36	867.17
75000	6619.89	3486.89	2446.54	1929.33	1621.35	1417.98	1274.35	1168.05	1086.61	1022.55	971.10	929.11
80000	7061.21	3719.35	2609.64	2057.95	1729.44	1512.51	1359.31	1245.92	1159.05	1090.71	1035.84	991.05
85000	7502.54	3951.81	2772.74	2186.57	1837.53	1607.04	1444.26	1323.79	1231.49	1158.88	1100.58	1052.99
90000	7943.86	4184.27	2935.85	2315.19	1945.62	1701.57	1529.22	1401.66	1303.93	1227.05	1165.32	1114.93
95000	8385.19	4416.73	3098.95	2443.81	2053.71	1796.10	1614.18	1479.53	1376.37	1295.22	1230.06	1176.87
100000	8826.51	4649.19	3262.05	2572.43	2161.80	1890.63	1699.13	1557.40	1448.81	1363.39	1294.80	1238.81

MONTHLY   10.75%

PAYMENT REQUIRED TO AMORTIZE A LOAN

TERM AMOUNT	13 YEARS	14 YEARS	15 YEARS	16 YEARS	17 YEARS	18 YEARS	19 YEARS	20 YEARS	25 YEARS	30 YEARS	35 YEARS	40 YEARS
50	.60	.58	.57	.55	.54	.53	.52	.51	.49	.47	.46	.46
100	1.20	1.16	1.13	1.10	1.07	1.05	1.04	1.02	.97	.94	.92	.91
200	2.39	2.31	2.25	2.19	2.14	2.10	2.07	2.04	1.93	1.87	1.84	1.82
300	3.58	3.47	3.37	3.28	3.21	3.15	3.10	3.05	2.89	2.81	2.76	2.73
400	4.77	4.62	4.49	4.38	4.28	4.20	4.13	4.07	3.85	3.74	3.68	3.64
500	5.97	5.77	5.61	5.47	5.35	5.25	5.16	5.08	4.82	4.67	4.59	4.55
600	7.16	6.93	6.73	6.56	6.42	6.30	6.19	6.10	5.78	5.61	5.51	5.46
700	8.35	8.08	7.85	7.66	7.49	7.35	7.22	7.11	6.74	6.54	6.43	6.36
800	9.54	9.23	8.97	8.75	8.56	8.39	8.25	8.13	7.70	7.47	7.35	7.27
900	10.74	10.39	10.09	9.84	9.63	9.44	9.28	9.14	8.66	8.41	8.26	8.18
1000	11.93	11.54	11.21	10.94	10.70	10.49	10.31	10.16	9.63	9.34	9.18	9.09
2000	23.85	23.08	22.42	21.87	21.39	20.98	20.62	20.31	19.25	18.67	18.36	18.17
3000	35.78	34.62	33.63	32.80	32.08	31.46	30.93	30.46	28.87	28.01	27.53	27.26
4000	47.70	46.15	44.84	43.73	42.77	41.95	41.23	40.61	38.49	37.34	36.71	36.34
5000	59.63	57.69	56.05	54.66	53.46	52.43	51.54	50.77	48.11	46.68	45.88	45.42
6000	71.55	69.23	67.26	65.59	64.16	62.92	61.85	60.92	57.73	56.01	55.06	54.51
7000	83.48	80.76	78.47	76.52	74.85	73.41	72.16	71.07	67.35	65.35	64.23	63.59
8000	95.40	92.30	89.68	87.45	85.54	83.89	82.46	81.22	76.97	74.68	73.41	72.68
9000	107.33	103.84	100.89	98.38	96.23	94.38	92.77	91.38	86.59	84.02	82.58	81.76
10000	119.25	115.37	112.10	109.31	106.92	104.86	103.08	101.53	96.21	93.35	91.76	90.84
11000	131.18	126.91	123.31	120.24	117.61	115.35	113.39	111.68	105.84	102.69	100.93	99.93
12000	143.10	138.45	134.52	131.17	128.31	125.84	123.69	121.83	115.46	112.02	110.11	109.01
13000	155.03	149.99	145.73	142.10	139.00	136.32	134.00	131.98	125.08	121.36	119.28	118.10
14000	166.95	161.52	156.94	153.03	149.69	146.81	144.31	142.14	134.70	130.69	128.46	127.18
15000	178.88	173.06	168.15	163.97	160.38	157.29	154.62	152.29	144.32	140.03	137.63	136.26
16000	190.80	184.60	179.36	174.90	171.07	167.78	164.92	162.44	153.94	149.36	146.81	145.35
17000	202.72	196.13	190.57	185.83	181.77	178.26	175.23	172.59	163.56	158.70	155.98	154.43
18000	214.65	207.67	201.78	196.76	192.46	188.75	185.54	182.75	173.18	168.03	165.16	163.52
19000	226.57	219.21	212.99	207.69	203.15	199.24	195.85	192.90	182.80	177.37	174.33	172.60
20000	238.50	230.74	224.19	218.62	213.84	209.72	206.15	203.05	192.42	186.70	183.51	181.68
21000	250.42	242.28	235.40	229.55	224.53	220.21	216.46	213.20	202.04	196.04	192.68	190.77
22000	262.35	253.82	246.61	240.48	235.22	230.69	226.77	223.36	211.67	205.37	201.86	199.85
23000	274.27	265.36	257.82	251.41	245.92	241.18	237.08	233.51	221.29	214.71	211.03	208.94
24000	286.20	276.89	269.03	262.34	256.61	251.67	247.38	243.66	230.91	224.04	220.21	218.02
25000	298.12	288.43	280.24	273.27	267.30	262.15	257.69	253.81	240.53	233.38	229.38	227.10
26000	310.05	299.97	291.45	284.20	277.99	272.64	268.00	263.96	250.15	242.71	238.56	236.19
27000	321.97	311.50	302.66	295.13	288.68	283.12	278.31	274.12	259.77	252.04	247.73	245.27
28000	333.90	323.04	313.87	306.06	299.37	293.61	288.61	284.27	269.39	261.38	256.91	254.36
29000	345.82	334.58	325.08	317.00	310.07	304.09	298.92	294.42	279.01	270.71	266.08	263.44
30000	357.75	346.11	336.29	327.93	320.76	314.58	309.23	304.57	288.63	280.05	275.26	272.52
31000	369.67	357.65	347.50	338.86	331.45	325.07	319.54	314.73	298.25	289.38	284.43	281.61
32000	381.59	369.19	358.71	349.79	342.14	335.55	329.84	324.88	307.87	298.72	293.61	290.69
33000	393.52	380.72	369.92	360.72	352.83	346.04	340.15	335.03	317.50	308.05	302.78	299.78
34000	405.44	392.26	381.13	371.65	363.53	356.52	350.46	345.18	327.12	317.39	311.96	308.86
35000	417.37	403.80	392.34	382.58	374.22	367.01	360.77	355.34	336.74	326.72	321.13	317.94
36000	429.29	415.34	403.55	393.51	384.91	377.50	371.07	365.49	346.36	336.06	330.31	327.03
37000	441.22	426.87	414.76	404.44	395.60	387.98	381.38	375.64	355.98	345.39	339.48	336.11
38000	453.14	438.41	425.97	415.37	406.29	398.47	391.69	385.79	365.60	354.73	348.66	345.20
39000	465.07	449.95	437.17	426.30	416.98	408.95	402.00	395.94	375.22	364.06	357.83	354.28
40000	476.99	461.48	448.38	437.23	427.68	419.44	412.30	406.10	384.84	373.40	367.01	363.36
41000	488.92	473.02	459.59	448.16	438.37	429.92	422.61	416.25	394.46	382.73	376.18	372.45
42000	500.84	484.56	470.80	459.09	449.06	440.41	432.92	426.40	404.08	392.07	385.36	381.53
43000	512.77	496.09	482.01	470.03	459.75	450.90	443.23	436.55	413.70	401.40	394.53	390.62
44000	524.69	507.63	493.22	480.96	470.44	461.38	453.53	446.71	423.33	410.74	403.71	399.70
45000	536.62	519.17	504.43	491.89	481.14	471.87	463.84	456.86	432.95	420.07	412.88	408.78
46000	548.54	530.71	515.64	502.82	491.83	482.35	474.15	467.01	442.57	429.41	422.06	417.87
47000	560.47	542.24	526.85	513.75	502.52	492.84	484.46	477.16	452.19	438.74	431.23	426.95
48000	572.39	553.78	538.06	524.68	513.21	503.33	494.76	487.31	461.81	448.08	440.41	436.04
49000	584.31	565.32	549.27	535.61	523.90	513.81	505.07	497.47	471.43	457.41	449.58	445.12
50000	596.24	576.85	560.48	546.54	534.59	524.30	515.38	507.62	481.05	466.75	458.76	454.20
55000	655.86	634.54	616.53	601.19	588.05	576.73	566.92	558.38	529.16	513.42	504.63	499.62
60000	715.49	692.22	672.57	655.85	641.51	629.16	618.45	609.14	577.26	560.09	550.51	545.04
65000	775.11	749.91	728.62	710.50	694.97	681.59	669.99	659.90	625.37	606.77	596.38	590.46
70000	834.73	807.59	784.67	765.15	748.43	734.01	721.53	710.67	673.47	653.44	642.26	635.88
75000	894.36	865.28	840.72	819.81	801.89	786.44	773.07	761.43	721.57	700.12	688.13	681.30
80000	953.98	922.96	896.76	874.46	855.35	838.87	824.60	812.19	769.68	746.79	734.01	726.72
85000	1013.60	980.65	952.81	929.11	908.81	891.30	876.14	862.95	817.78	793.46	779.88	772.14
90000	1073.23	1038.33	1008.86	983.77	962.27	943.73	927.68	913.71	865.89	840.14	825.76	817.56
95000	1132.85	1096.02	1064.91	1038.42	1015.72	996.16	979.21	964.47	913.99	886.81	871.63	862.98
100000	1192.47	1153.70	1120.95	1093.07	1069.18	1048.59	1030.75	1015.23	962.10	933.49	917.51	908.40

MONTHLY
PAYMENT REQUIRED TO AMORTIZE A LOAN

TERM AMOUNT	1 YEAR	2 YEARS	3 YEARS	4 YEARS	5 YEARS	6 YEARS	7 YEARS	8 YEARS	9 YEARS	10 YEARS	11 YEARS	12 YEARS
50	4.42	2.34	1.64	1.30	1.09	.96	.86	.79	.74	.69	.66	.63
100	8.84	4.67	3.28	2.59	2.18	1.91	1.72	1.58	1.47	1.38	1.31	1.26
200	17.68	9.33	6.55	5.17	4.35	3.81	3.43	3.15	2.93	2.76	2.62	2.51
300	26.52	13.99	9.83	7.76	6.53	5.72	5.14	4.72	4.39	4.14	3.93	3.77
400	35.36	18.65	13.10	10.34	8.70	7.62	6.85	6.29	5.86	5.52	5.24	5.02
500	44.20	23.31	16.37	12.93	10.88	9.52	8.57	7.86	7.32	6.89	6.55	6.27
600	53.03	27.97	19.65	15.51	13.05	11.43	10.28	9.43	8.78	8.27	7.86	7.53
700	61.87	32.63	22.92	18.10	15.22	13.33	11.99	11.00	10.24	9.65	9.17	8.78
800	70.71	37.29	26.20	20.68	17.40	15.23	13.70	12.57	11.71	11.03	10.48	10.03
900	79.55	41.95	29.47	23.27	19.57	17.14	15.42	14.14	13.17	12.40	11.79	11.29
1000	88.39	46.61	32.74	25.85	21.75	19.04	17.13	15.71	14.63	13.78	13.10	12.54
2000	176.77	93.22	65.48	51.70	43.49	38.07	34.25	31.42	29.26	27.56	26.19	25.08
3000	265.15	139.83	98.22	77.54	65.23	57.11	51.37	47.13	43.88	41.33	39.28	37.61
4000	353.53	186.44	130.96	103.39	86.97	76.14	68.49	62.84	58.51	55.11	52.37	50.15
5000	441.91	233.04	163.70	129.23	108.72	95.18	85.62	78.55	73.13	68.88	65.47	62.68
6000	530.29	279.65	196.44	155.08	130.46	114.21	102.74	94.26	87.76	82.66	78.56	75.22
7000	618.68	326.26	229.18	180.92	152.20	133.24	119.86	109.96	102.39	96.43	91.65	87.75
8000	707.06	372.87	261.91	206.77	173.94	152.28	136.98	125.67	117.01	110.21	104.74	100.29
9000	795.44	419.48	294.65	232.61	195.69	171.31	154.11	141.38	131.64	123.98	117.84	112.82
10000	883.82	466.08	327.39	258.46	217.43	190.35	171.23	157.09	146.26	137.76	130.93	125.36
11000	972.20	512.69	360.13	284.31	239.17	209.38	188.35	172.80	160.89	151.53	144.02	137.90
12000	1060.58	559.30	392.87	310.15	260.91	228.41	205.47	188.51	175.52	165.31	157.11	150.43
13000	1148.97	605.91	425.61	336.00	282.66	247.45	222.60	204.21	190.14	179.08	170.21	162.97
14000	1237.35	652.51	458.35	361.84	304.40	266.48	239.72	219.92	204.77	192.86	183.30	175.50
15000	1325.73	699.12	491.09	387.69	326.14	285.52	256.84	235.63	219.39	206.63	196.39	188.04
16000	1414.11	745.73	523.82	413.53	347.88	304.55	273.96	251.34	234.02	220.41	209.48	200.57
17000	1502.49	792.34	556.56	439.38	369.63	323.58	291.09	267.05	248.64	234.18	222.57	213.11
18000	1590.87	838.95	589.30	465.22	391.37	342.62	308.21	282.76	263.27	247.96	235.67	225.64
19000	1679.26	885.55	622.04	491.07	413.11	361.65	325.33	298.47	277.90	261.73	248.76	238.18
20000	1767.64	932.16	654.78	516.92	434.85	380.69	342.45	314.17	292.52	275.51	261.85	250.72
21000	1856.02	978.77	687.52	542.76	456.60	399.72	359.58	329.88	307.15	289.28	274.94	263.25
22000	1944.40	1025.38	720.26	568.61	478.34	418.75	376.70	345.59	321.77	303.06	288.04	275.79
23000	2032.78	1071.99	753.00	594.45	500.08	437.79	393.82	361.30	336.40	316.83	301.13	288.32
24000	2121.16	1118.59	785.73	620.30	521.82	456.82	410.94	377.01	351.03	330.61	314.22	300.86
25000	2209.55	1165.20	818.47	646.14	543.57	475.86	428.07	392.72	365.65	344.38	327.31	313.39
26000	2297.93	1211.81	851.21	671.99	565.31	494.89	445.19	408.42	380.28	358.16	340.41	325.93
27000	2386.31	1258.42	883.95	697.83	587.05	513.93	462.31	424.13	394.90	371.93	353.50	338.46
28000	2474.69	1305.02	916.69	723.68	608.79	532.96	479.43	439.84	409.53	385.71	366.59	351.00
29000	2563.07	1351.63	949.43	749.53	630.54	551.99	496.56	455.55	424.15	399.48	379.68	363.54
30000	2651.45	1398.24	982.17	775.37	652.28	571.03	513.68	471.26	438.78	413.26	392.78	376.07
31000	2739.84	1444.85	1014.91	801.22	674.02	590.06	530.80	486.97	453.41	427.03	405.87	388.61
32000	2828.22	1491.46	1047.64	827.06	695.76	609.10	547.92	502.67	468.03	440.81	418.96	401.14
33000	2916.60	1538.06	1080.38	852.91	717.50	628.13	565.05	518.38	482.66	454.58	432.05	413.68
34000	3004.98	1584.67	1113.12	878.75	739.25	647.16	582.17	534.09	497.28	468.36	445.14	426.21
35000	3093.36	1631.28	1145.86	904.60	760.99	666.20	599.29	549.80	511.91	482.13	458.24	438.75
36000	3181.74	1677.89	1178.60	930.44	782.73	685.23	616.41	565.51	526.54	495.91	471.33	451.28
37000	3270.13	1724.50	1211.34	956.29	804.47	704.27	633.54	581.22	541.16	509.68	484.42	463.82
38000	3358.51	1771.10	1244.08	982.13	826.22	723.30	650.66	596.93	555.79	523.46	497.51	476.36
39000	3446.89	1817.71	1276.82	1007.98	847.96	742.33	667.78	612.63	570.41	537.23	510.61	488.89
40000	3535.27	1864.32	1309.55	1033.83	869.70	761.37	684.90	628.34	585.04	551.01	523.70	501.43
41000	3623.65	1910.93	1342.29	1059.67	891.44	780.40	702.02	644.05	599.67	564.78	536.79	513.96
42000	3712.03	1957.53	1375.03	1085.52	913.19	799.44	719.15	659.76	614.29	578.56	549.88	526.50
43000	3800.42	2004.14	1407.77	1111.36	934.93	818.47	736.27	675.47	628.92	592.33	562.98	539.03
44000	3888.80	2050.75	1440.51	1137.21	956.67	837.50	753.39	691.18	643.54	606.11	576.07	551.57
45000	3977.18	2097.36	1473.25	1163.05	978.41	856.54	770.51	706.88	658.17	619.88	589.16	564.10
46000	4065.56	2143.97	1505.99	1188.90	1000.16	875.57	787.64	722.59	672.79	633.66	602.25	576.64
47000	4153.94	2190.57	1538.72	1214.74	1021.90	894.61	804.76	738.30	687.42	647.43	615.35	589.18
48000	4242.32	2237.18	1571.46	1240.59	1043.64	913.64	821.88	754.01	702.05	661.21	628.44	601.71
49000	4330.71	2283.79	1604.20	1266.44	1065.38	932.67	839.00	769.72	716.67	674.98	641.53	614.25
50000	4419.09	2330.40	1636.94	1292.28	1087.13	951.71	856.13	785.43	731.30	688.76	654.62	626.78
55000	4861.00	2563.44	1800.63	1421.51	1195.84	1046.88	941.74	863.97	804.43	757.63	720.08	689.46
60000	5302.90	2796.48	1964.33	1550.74	1304.55	1142.05	1027.35	942.51	877.56	826.51	785.55	752.14
65000	5744.81	3029.51	2128.02	1679.96	1413.26	1237.22	1112.96	1021.05	950.69	895.38	851.01	814.82
70000	6186.72	3262.55	2291.72	1809.19	1521.97	1332.39	1198.58	1099.59	1023.82	964.26	916.47	877.49
75000	6628.63	3495.59	2455.41	1938.42	1630.69	1427.56	1284.19	1178.14	1096.94	1033.13	981.93	940.17
80000	7070.54	3728.63	2619.10	2067.65	1739.40	1522.73	1369.80	1256.68	1170.07	1102.01	1047.39	1002.85
85000	7512.45	3961.67	2782.80	2196.87	1848.11	1617.90	1455.41	1335.22	1243.20	1170.88	1112.85	1065.53
90000	7954.35	4194.71	2946.49	2326.10	1956.82	1713.07	1541.02	1413.76	1316.33	1239.76	1178.32	1128.20
95000	8396.26	4427.75	3110.18	2455.33	2065.54	1808.24	1626.64	1492.31	1389.46	1308.63	1243.78	1190.88
100000	8838.17	4660.79	3273.88	2584.56	2174.25	1903.41	1712.25	1570.85	1462.59	1377.51	1309.24	1253.56

MONTHLY

PAYMENT REQUIRED TO AMORTIZE A LOAN

11.00%

AMOUNT	13 YEARS	14 YEARS	15 YEARS	16 YEARS	17 YEARS	18 YEARS	19 YEARS	20 YEARS	25 YEARS	30 YEARS	35 YEARS	40 YEARS
50	.61	.59	.57	.56	.55	.54	.53	.52	.50	.48	.47	.47
100	1.21	1.17	1.14	1.11	1.09	1.07	1.05	1.04	.99	.96	.94	.93
200	2.42	2.34	2.28	2.22	2.18	2.14	2.10	2.07	1.97	1.91	1.88	1.86
300	3.63	3.51	3.41	3.33	3.26	3.20	3.15	3.10	2.95	2.86	2.82	2.79
400	4.84	4.68	4.55	4.44	4.35	4.27	4.19	4.13	3.93	3.81	3.75	3.72
500	6.04	5.85	5.69	5.55	5.43	5.33	5.24	5.17	4.91	4.77	4.69	4.65
600	7.25	7.02	6.82	6.66	6.52	6.40	6.29	6.20	5.89	5.72	5.63	5.57
700	8.46	8.19	7.96	7.77	7.60	7.46	7.34	7.23	6.87	6.67	6.56	6.50
800	9.67	9.36	9.10	8.88	8.69	8.53	8.38	8.26	7.85	7.62	7.50	7.43
900	10.87	10.53	10.23	9.99	9.77	9.59	9.43	9.29	8.83	8.58	8.44	8.36
1000	12.08	11.70	11.37	11.10	10.86	10.66	10.48	10.33	9.81	9.53	9.37	9.29
2000	24.16	23.39	22.74	22.19	21.71	21.31	20.95	20.65	19.61	19.05	18.74	18.57
3000	36.23	35.08	34.10	33.28	32.57	31.96	31.43	30.97	29.41	28.57	28.11	27.85
4000	48.31	46.77	45.47	44.37	43.42	42.61	41.90	41.29	39.21	38.10	37.48	37.14
5000	60.38	58.46	56.83	55.46	54.27	53.26	52.38	51.61	49.01	47.62	46.85	46.42
6000	72.46	70.15	68.20	66.55	65.13	63.91	62.85	61.94	58.81	57.14	56.22	55.70
7000	84.53	81.84	79.57	77.64	75.98	74.56	73.33	72.26	68.61	66.67	65.59	64.99
8000	96.61	93.53	90.93	88.73	86.84	85.21	83.80	82.58	78.41	76.19	74.96	74.27
9000	108.68	105.22	102.30	99.82	97.69	95.86	94.28	92.90	88.22	85.71	84.33	83.55
10000	120.76	116.91	113.66	110.91	108.54	106.51	104.75	103.22	98.02	95.24	93.70	92.83
11000	132.83	128.60	125.03	122.00	119.40	117.16	115.23	113.55	107.82	104.76	103.07	102.12
12000	144.91	140.29	136.40	133.09	130.25	127.81	125.70	123.87	117.62	114.28	112.44	111.40
13000	156.98	151.98	147.76	144.18	141.10	138.46	136.18	134.19	127.42	123.81	121.81	120.68
14000	169.06	163.67	159.13	155.27	151.96	149.11	146.65	144.51	137.22	133.33	131.18	129.97
15000	181.13	175.36	170.49	166.36	162.81	159.76	157.12	154.83	147.02	142.85	140.55	139.25
16000	193.21	187.05	181.86	177.45	173.67	170.41	167.60	165.16	156.82	152.38	149.92	148.53
17000	205.28	198.74	193.23	188.54	184.52	181.06	178.07	175.48	166.62	161.90	159.29	157.82
18000	217.36	210.43	204.59	199.63	195.37	191.71	188.55	185.80	176.43	171.42	168.66	167.10
19000	229.44	222.13	215.96	210.72	206.23	202.36	199.02	196.12	186.23	180.95	178.03	176.38
20000	241.51	233.82	227.32	221.81	217.08	213.01	209.50	206.44	196.03	190.47	187.40	185.66
21000	253.59	245.51	238.69	232.90	227.93	223.67	219.97	216.76	205.83	199.99	196.77	194.95
22000	265.66	257.20	250.06	243.99	238.79	234.32	230.45	227.09	215.63	209.52	206.14	204.23
23000	277.74	268.89	261.42	255.08	249.64	244.97	240.92	237.41	225.43	219.04	215.51	213.51
24000	289.81	280.58	272.79	266.17	260.50	255.62	251.40	247.73	235.23	228.56	224.87	222.80
25000	301.89	292.27	284.15	277.26	271.35	266.27	261.87	258.05	245.03	238.09	234.24	232.08
26000	313.96	303.96	295.52	288.35	282.20	276.92	272.35	268.37	254.83	247.61	243.61	241.36
27000	326.04	315.65	306.89	299.44	293.06	287.57	282.82	278.70	264.64	257.13	252.98	250.64
28000	338.11	327.34	318.25	310.53	303.91	298.22	293.29	289.02	274.44	266.66	262.35	259.93
29000	350.19	339.03	329.62	321.62	314.77	308.87	303.77	299.34	284.24	276.18	271.72	269.21
30000	362.26	350.72	340.98	332.71	325.62	319.52	314.24	309.66	294.04	285.70	281.09	278.49
31000	374.34	362.41	352.35	343.80	336.47	330.17	324.72	319.98	303.84	295.23	290.46	287.78
32000	386.41	374.10	363.72	354.89	347.33	340.82	335.19	330.31	313.64	304.75	299.83	297.06
33000	398.49	385.79	375.08	365.98	358.18	351.47	345.67	340.63	323.44	314.27	309.20	306.34
34000	410.56	397.48	386.45	377.07	369.03	362.12	356.14	350.95	333.24	323.79	318.57	315.63
35000	422.64	409.17	397.81	388.16	379.89	372.77	366.62	361.27	343.04	333.32	327.94	324.91
36000	434.71	420.86	409.18	399.25	390.74	383.42	377.09	371.59	352.85	342.84	337.31	334.19
37000	446.79	432.56	420.55	410.34	401.60	394.07	387.57	381.91	362.65	352.36	346.68	343.47
38000	458.87	444.25	431.91	421.43	412.45	404.72	398.04	392.24	372.45	361.89	356.05	352.76
39000	470.94	455.94	443.28	432.52	423.30	415.37	408.52	402.56	382.25	371.41	365.42	362.04
40000	483.02	467.63	454.64	443.61	434.16	426.02	418.99	412.88	392.05	380.93	374.79	371.32
41000	495.09	479.32	466.01	454.70	445.01	436.68	429.47	423.20	401.85	390.46	384.16	380.61
42000	507.17	491.01	477.38	465.79	455.86	447.33	439.94	433.52	411.65	399.98	393.53	389.89
43000	519.24	502.70	488.74	476.88	466.72	457.98	450.41	443.85	421.45	409.50	402.90	399.17
44000	531.32	514.39	500.11	487.97	477.57	468.63	460.89	454.17	431.25	419.03	412.27	408.45
45000	543.39	526.08	511.47	499.06	488.43	479.28	471.36	464.49	441.06	428.55	421.64	417.74
46000	555.47	537.77	522.84	510.15	499.28	489.93	481.84	474.81	450.86	438.07	431.01	427.02
47000	567.54	549.46	534.21	521.24	510.13	500.58	492.31	485.13	460.66	447.60	440.38	436.30
48000	579.62	561.15	545.57	532.33	520.99	511.23	502.79	495.46	470.46	457.12	449.74	445.59
49000	591.69	572.84	556.94	543.42	531.84	521.88	513.26	505.78	480.26	466.64	459.11	454.87
50000	603.77	584.53	568.30	554.51	542.70	532.53	523.74	516.10	490.06	476.17	468.48	464.15
55000	664.15	642.98	625.13	609.96	596.96	585.78	576.11	567.71	539.07	523.78	515.33	510.57
60000	724.52	701.44	681.96	665.41	651.23	639.03	628.48	619.32	588.07	571.40	562.18	556.98
65000	784.90	759.89	738.79	720.86	705.50	692.29	680.86	670.93	637.08	619.02	609.03	603.40
70000	845.27	818.34	795.62	776.31	759.77	745.54	733.23	722.54	686.08	666.63	655.88	649.81
75000	905.65	876.80	852.45	831.76	814.04	798.79	785.60	774.15	735.09	714.25	702.72	696.23
80000	966.03	935.25	909.28	887.21	868.31	852.04	837.98	825.76	784.10	761.86	749.57	742.64
85000	1026.40	993.70	966.11	942.66	922.58	905.30	890.35	877.37	833.10	809.48	796.42	789.06
90000	1086.78	1052.15	1022.94	998.11	976.85	958.55	942.72	928.97	882.11	857.10	843.27	835.47
95000	1147.16	1110.61	1079.77	1053.56	1031.12	1011.80	995.10	980.58	931.11	904.71	890.11	881.88
100000	1207.53	1169.06	1136.60	1109.01	1085.39	1065.05	1047.47	1032.19	980.12	952.33	936.96	928.30

11.25%

MONTHLY

PAYMENT REQUIRED TO AMORTIZE A LOAN

TERM AMOUNT	1 YEAR	2 YEARS	3 YEARS	4 YEARS	5 YEARS	6 YEARS	7 YEARS	8 YEARS	9 YEARS	10 YEARS	11 YEARS	12 YEARS
50	4.43	2.34	1.65	1.30	1.10	.96	.87	.80	.74	.70	.67	.64
100	8.85	4.68	3.29	2.60	2.19	1.92	1.73	1.59	1.48	1.40	1.33	1.27
200	17.70	9.35	6.58	5.20	4.38	3.84	3.46	3.17	2.96	2.79	2.65	2.54
300	26.55	14.02	9.86	7.80	6.57	5.75	5.18	4.76	4.43	4.18	3.98	3.81
400	35.40	18.69	13.15	10.39	8.75	7.67	6.91	6.34	5.91	5.57	5.30	5.08
500	44.25	23.37	16.43	12.99	10.94	9.59	8.63	7.93	7.39	6.96	6.62	6.35
600	53.10	28.04	19.72	15.59	13.13	11.50	10.36	9.51	8.86	8.36	7.95	7.62
700	61.95	32.71	23.01	18.18	15.31	13.42	12.08	11.10	10.34	9.75	9.27	8.88
800	70.80	37.38	26.29	20.78	17.50	15.33	13.81	12.68	11.82	11.14	10.60	10.15
900	79.65	42.06	29.58	23.38	19.69	17.25	15.53	14.26	13.29	12.53	11.92	11.42
1000	88.50	46.73	32.86	25.97	21.87	19.17	17.26	15.85	14.77	13.92	13.24	12.69
2000	177.00	93.45	65.72	51.94	43.74	38.33	34.51	31.69	29.53	27.84	26.48	25.37
3000	265.50	140.18	98.58	77.91	65.61	57.49	51.77	47.54	44.30	41.76	39.72	38.06
4000	354.00	186.90	131.43	103.87	87.47	76.65	69.02	63.38	59.06	55.67	52.96	50.74
5000	442.50	233.62	164.29	129.84	109.34	95.82	86.28	79.22	73.83	69.59	66.19	63.42
6000	530.99	280.35	197.15	155.81	131.21	114.98	103.53	95.07	88.59	83.51	79.43	76.11
7000	619.49	327.07	230.01	181.77	153.08	134.14	120.78	110.91	103.36	97.42	92.67	88.79
8000	707.99	373.80	262.86	207.74	174.94	153.30	138.04	126.75	118.12	111.34	105.91	101.48
9000	796.49	420.52	295.72	233.71	196.81	172.47	155.29	142.60	132.88	125.26	119.14	114.16
10000	884.99	467.24	328.58	259.68	218.68	191.63	172.55	158.44	147.65	139.17	132.38	126.84
11000	973.49	513.97	361.43	285.64	240.55	210.79	189.80	174.28	162.41	153.09	145.62	139.53
12000	1061.98	560.69	394.29	311.61	262.41	229.95	207.06	190.13	177.18	167.01	158.86	152.21
13000	1150.48	607.42	427.15	337.58	284.28	249.12	224.31	205.97	191.94	180.92	172.09	164.90
14000	1238.98	654.14	460.01	363.54	306.15	268.28	241.56	221.82	206.71	194.84	185.33	177.58
15000	1327.48	700.86	492.86	389.51	328.01	287.44	258.82	237.66	221.47	208.76	198.57	190.26
16000	1415.98	747.59	525.72	415.48	349.88	306.60	276.07	253.50	236.24	222.68	211.81	202.95
17000	1504.48	794.31	558.58	441.45	371.75	325.77	293.33	269.35	251.00	236.59	225.04	215.63
18000	1592.97	841.00	591.44	467.41	393.62	344.93	310.58	285.19	265.76	250.51	238.28	228.32
19000	1681.47	887.76	624.29	493.38	415.48	364.09	327.83	301.03	280.53	264.43	251.52	241.00
20000	1769.97	934.48	657.15	519.35	437.35	383.25	345.09	316.88	295.29	278.34	264.76	253.68
21000	1858.47	981.21	690.01	545.31	459.22	402.41	362.34	332.72	310.06	292.26	277.99	266.37
22000	1946.97	1027.93	722.86	571.28	481.09	421.58	379.60	348.56	324.82	306.18	291.23	279.05
23000	2035.47	1074.66	755.72	597.25	502.95	440.74	396.85	364.41	339.59	320.09	304.47	291.74
24000	2123.96	1121.38	788.58	623.22	524.82	459.90	414.11	380.25	354.35	334.01	317.71	304.42
25000	2212.46	1168.10	821.44	649.18	546.69	479.06	431.36	396.09	369.12	347.93	330.94	317.10
26000	2300.96	1214.83	854.29	675.15	568.56	498.23	448.61	411.94	383.88	361.84	344.18	329.79
27000	2389.46	1261.55	887.15	701.12	590.42	517.39	465.87	427.78	398.64	375.76	357.42	342.47
28000	2477.96	1308.28	920.01	727.08	612.29	536.55	483.12	443.63	413.41	389.68	370.66	355.16
29000	2566.46	1355.00	952.86	753.05	634.16	555.71	500.38	459.47	428.17	403.59	383.89	367.84
30000	2654.95	1401.72	985.72	779.02	656.02	574.88	517.63	475.31	442.94	417.51	397.13	380.52
31000	2743.45	1448.45	1018.58	804.99	677.89	594.04	534.88	491.16	457.70	431.43	410.37	393.21
32000	2831.95	1495.17	1051.44	830.95	699.76	613.20	552.14	507.00	472.47	445.35	423.61	405.89
33000	2920.45	1541.90	1084.29	856.92	721.63	632.36	569.39	522.84	487.23	459.26	436.84	418.57
34000	3008.95	1588.62	1117.15	882.89	743.49	651.53	586.65	538.69	502.00	473.18	450.08	431.26
35000	3097.45	1635.34	1150.01	908.85	765.36	670.69	603.90	554.53	516.76	487.10	463.32	443.94
36000	3185.94	1682.07	1182.87	934.82	787.23	689.85	621.16	570.37	531.52	501.01	476.56	456.63
37000	3274.44	1728.79	1215.72	960.79	809.10	709.01	638.41	586.22	546.29	514.93	489.79	469.31
38000	3362.94	1775.52	1248.58	986.75	830.96	728.18	655.66	602.06	561.05	528.85	503.03	481.99
39000	3451.44	1822.24	1281.44	1012.72	852.83	747.34	672.92	617.90	575.82	542.76	516.27	494.68
40000	3539.94	1868.96	1314.29	1038.69	874.70	766.50	690.17	633.75	590.58	556.68	529.51	507.36
41000	3628.44	1915.69	1347.15	1064.66	896.56	785.66	707.43	649.59	605.35	570.60	542.74	520.05
42000	3716.93	1962.41	1380.01	1090.62	918.43	804.82	724.68	665.44	620.11	584.51	555.98	532.73
43000	3805.43	2009.14	1412.87	1116.59	940.30	823.99	741.93	681.28	634.87	598.43	569.22	545.41
44000	3893.93	2055.86	1445.72	1142.56	962.17	843.15	759.19	697.12	649.64	612.35	582.46	558.10
45000	3982.43	2102.58	1478.58	1168.52	984.03	862.31	776.44	712.97	664.40	626.27	595.69	570.78
46000	4070.93	2149.31	1511.44	1194.49	1005.90	881.47	793.70	728.81	679.17	640.18	608.93	583.47
47000	4159.43	2196.03	1544.30	1220.46	1027.77	900.64	810.95	744.65	693.93	654.10	622.17	596.15
48000	4247.92	2242.76	1577.15	1246.43	1049.64	919.80	828.21	760.50	708.70	668.02	635.41	608.83
49000	4336.42	2289.48	1610.01	1272.39	1071.50	938.96	845.46	776.34	723.46	681.93	648.64	621.52
50000	4424.92	2336.20	1642.87	1298.36	1093.37	958.12	862.71	792.18	738.23	695.85	661.88	634.20
55000	4867.41	2569.82	1807.15	1428.20	1202.71	1053.94	948.98	871.40	812.05	765.43	728.07	697.62
60000	5309.90	2803.44	1971.44	1558.03	1312.04	1149.75	1035.26	950.62	885.87	835.02	794.26	761.04
65000	5752.40	3037.06	2135.73	1687.87	1421.38	1245.56	1121.53	1029.84	959.69	904.60	860.44	824.46
70000	6194.89	3270.68	2300.01	1817.70	1530.72	1341.37	1207.80	1109.06	1033.51	974.19	926.63	887.88
75000	6637.38	3504.30	2464.30	1947.54	1640.05	1437.18	1294.07	1188.27	1107.34	1043.77	992.82	951.30
80000	7079.87	3737.92	2628.58	2077.37	1749.39	1532.99	1380.34	1267.49	1181.16	1113.36	1059.01	1014.72
85000	7522.36	3971.54	2792.87	2207.21	1858.73	1628.81	1466.61	1346.71	1254.98	1182.94	1125.19	1078.14
90000	7964.85	4205.16	2957.16	2337.04	1968.06	1724.62	1552.88	1425.93	1328.80	1252.53	1191.38	1141.56
95000	8407.35	4438.78	3121.44	2466.88	2077.40	1820.43	1639.15	1505.15	1402.62	1322.11	1257.57	1204.98
100000	8849.84	4672.40	3285.73	2596.71	2186.74	1916.24	1725.42	1584.36	1476.45	1391.69	1323.76	1268.40

MONTHLY 11.25%

PAYMENT REQUIRED TO AMORTIZE A LOAN

TERM AMOUNT	13 YEARS	14 YEARS	15 YEARS	16 YEARS	17 YEARS	18 YEARS	19 YEARS	20 YEARS	25 YEARS	30 YEARS	35 YEARS	40 YEARS
50	.62	.60	.58	.57	.56	.55	.54	.53	.50	.49	.48	.48
100	1.23	1.19	1.16	1.13	1.11	1.09	1.07	1.05	1.00	.98	.96	.95
200	2.45	2.37	2.31	2.26	2.21	2.17	2.13	2.10	2.00	1.95	1.92	1.90
300	3.67	3.56	3.46	3.38	3.31	3.25	3.20	3.15	3.00	2.92	2.87	2.85
400	4.90	4.74	4.61	4.51	4.41	4.33	4.26	4.20	4.00	3.89	3.83	3.80
500	6.12	5.93	5.77	5.63	5.51	5.41	5.33	5.25	5.00	4.86	4.79	4.75
600	7.34	7.11	6.92	6.76	6.62	6.49	6.39	6.30	5.99	5.83	5.74	5.69
700	8.56	8.30	8.07	7.88	7.72	7.58	7.46	7.35	6.99	6.80	6.70	6.64
800	9.79	9.48	9.22	9.01	8.82	8.66	8.52	8.40	7.99	7.78	7.66	7.59
900	11.01	10.67	10.38	10.13	9.92	9.74	9.58	9.45	8.99	8.75	8.61	8.54
1000	12.23	11.85	11.53	11.26	11.02	10.82	10.65	10.50	9.99	9.72	9.57	9.49
2000	24.46	23.70	23.05	22.51	22.04	21.64	21.29	20.99	19.97	19.43	19.13	18.97
3000	36.69	35.54	34.58	33.76	33.06	32.45	31.93	31.48	29.95	29.14	28.70	28.45
4000	48.91	47.39	46.10	45.01	44.07	43.27	42.58	41.98	39.93	38.86	38.26	37.94
5000	61.14	59.23	57.62	56.26	55.09	54.09	53.22	52.47	49.92	48.57	47.83	47.42
6000	73.37	71.08	69.15	67.51	66.11	64.90	63.86	62.96	59.90	58.28	57.39	56.90
7000	85.59	82.92	80.67	78.76	77.12	75.72	74.51	73.45	69.88	67.99	66.96	66.38
8000	97.82	94.77	92.19	90.01	88.14	86.53	85.15	83.95	79.86	77.71	76.52	75.87
9000	110.05	106.61	103.72	101.26	99.16	97.35	95.79	94.44	89.85	87.42	86.09	85.35
10000	122.27	118.46	115.24	112.51	110.17	108.17	106.43	104.93	99.83	97.13	95.65	94.83
11000	134.50	130.30	126.76	123.76	121.19	118.98	117.08	115.42	109.81	106.84	105.22	104.31
12000	146.73	142.15	138.29	135.01	132.21	129.80	127.72	125.92	119.79	116.56	114.78	113.80
13000	158.95	153.99	149.81	146.26	143.22	140.62	138.36	136.41	129.78	126.27	124.35	123.28
14000	171.18	165.84	161.33	157.51	154.24	151.43	149.01	146.90	139.76	135.98	133.91	132.76
15000	183.41	177.68	172.86	168.76	165.26	162.25	159.65	157.39	149.74	145.69	143.48	142.24
16000	195.63	189.53	184.38	180.01	176.27	173.06	170.29	167.89	159.72	155.41	153.04	151.73
17000	207.86	201.37	195.90	191.26	187.29	183.88	180.93	178.38	169.71	165.12	162.61	161.21
18000	220.09	213.22	207.43	202.51	198.31	194.70	191.58	188.87	179.69	174.83	172.17	170.69
19000	232.31	225.06	218.95	213.76	209.33	205.51	202.22	199.36	189.67	184.54	181.74	180.17
20000	244.54	236.91	230.47	225.01	220.34	216.33	212.86	209.86	199.65	194.26	191.30	189.66
21000	256.77	248.75	242.00	236.26	231.36	227.15	223.51	220.35	209.64	203.97	200.87	199.14
22000	268.99	260.60	253.52	247.51	242.38	237.96	234.15	230.84	219.62	213.68	210.43	208.62
23000	281.22	272.44	265.04	258.76	253.39	248.78	244.79	241.33	229.60	223.40	220.00	218.10
24000	293.45	284.29	276.57	270.01	264.41	259.59	255.43	251.83	239.58	233.11	229.56	227.59
25000	305.67	296.13	288.09	281.26	275.43	270.41	266.08	262.32	249.56	242.82	239.13	237.07
26000	317.90	307.98	299.61	292.51	286.44	281.23	276.72	272.81	259.55	252.53	248.69	246.55
27000	330.13	319.82	311.14	303.76	297.46	292.04	287.36	283.30	269.53	262.25	258.26	256.03
28000	342.35	331.67	322.66	315.01	308.48	302.86	298.01	293.80	279.51	271.96	267.82	265.52
29000	354.58	343.51	334.18	326.26	319.49	313.67	308.65	304.29	289.49	281.67	277.39	275.00
30000	366.81	355.36	345.71	337.51	330.51	324.49	319.29	314.78	299.48	291.38	286.95	284.48
31000	379.03	367.20	357.23	348.77	341.53	335.31	329.93	325.27	309.46	301.10	296.52	293.96
32000	391.26	379.05	368.76	360.02	352.54	346.12	340.58	335.77	319.44	310.81	306.08	303.45
33000	403.49	390.89	380.28	371.27	363.56	356.94	351.22	346.26	329.42	320.52	315.65	312.93
34000	415.72	402.74	391.80	382.52	374.58	367.76	361.86	356.75	339.41	330.23	325.21	322.41
35000	427.94	414.58	403.33	393.77	385.60	378.57	372.51	367.24	349.39	339.95	334.78	331.90
36000	440.17	426.43	414.85	405.02	396.61	389.39	383.15	377.74	359.37	349.66	344.34	341.38
37000	452.40	438.27	426.37	416.27	407.63	400.20	393.79	388.23	369.35	359.37	353.91	350.86
38000	464.62	450.12	437.90	427.52	418.65	411.02	404.43	398.72	379.34	369.08	363.47	360.34
39000	476.85	461.96	449.42	438.77	429.66	421.84	415.08	409.21	389.32	378.80	373.04	369.83
40000	489.08	473.81	460.94	450.02	440.68	432.65	425.72	419.71	399.30	388.51	382.60	379.31
41000	501.30	485.65	472.47	461.27	451.70	443.47	436.36	430.20	409.28	398.22	392.17	388.79
42000	513.53	497.50	483.99	472.52	462.71	454.29	447.01	440.69	419.27	407.93	401.73	398.27
43000	525.76	509.34	495.51	483.77	473.73	465.10	457.65	451.19	429.25	417.65	411.30	407.76
44000	537.98	521.19	507.04	495.02	484.75	475.92	468.29	461.68	439.23	427.36	420.86	417.24
45000	550.21	533.03	518.56	506.27	495.76	486.73	478.93	472.17	449.21	437.07	430.43	426.72
46000	562.44	544.88	530.08	517.52	506.78	497.55	489.58	482.66	459.20	446.79	439.99	436.20
47000	574.66	556.72	541.61	528.77	517.80	508.37	500.22	493.16	469.18	456.50	449.56	445.69
48000	586.89	568.57	553.13	540.02	528.81	519.18	510.86	503.65	479.16	466.21	459.12	455.17
49000	599.12	580.41	564.65	551.27	539.83	530.00	521.51	514.14	489.14	475.92	468.69	464.65
50000	611.34	592.26	576.18	562.52	550.85	540.82	532.15	524.63	499.12	485.64	478.25	474.13
55000	672.48	651.48	633.79	618.77	605.93	594.90	585.36	577.10	549.04	534.20	526.08	521.55
60000	733.61	710.71	691.41	675.02	661.02	648.98	638.58	629.56	598.95	582.76	573.90	568.96
65000	794.75	769.94	749.03	731.28	716.10	703.06	691.79	682.02	648.86	631.32	621.73	616.37
70000	855.88	829.16	806.65	787.53	771.19	757.14	745.01	734.48	698.77	679.89	669.55	663.79
75000	917.01	888.39	864.26	843.78	826.27	811.22	798.22	786.95	748.68	728.45	717.38	711.20
80000	978.15	947.61	921.88	900.03	881.35	865.30	851.44	839.41	798.60	777.01	765.20	758.61
85000	1039.28	1006.84	979.50	956.28	936.44	919.38	904.65	891.87	848.51	825.58	813.02	806.02
90000	1100.41	1066.06	1037.12	1012.53	991.52	973.46	957.86	944.34	898.42	874.14	860.85	853.44
95000	1161.55	1125.29	1094.73	1068.79	1046.61	1027.54	1011.08	996.80	948.33	922.70	908.67	900.85
100000	1222.68	1184.51	1152.35	1125.04	1101.69	1081.63	1064.29	1049.26	998.24	971.27	956.50	948.26

11.50% MONTHLY
PAYMENT REQUIRED TO AMORTIZE A LOAN

TERM AMOUNT	1 YEAR	2 YEARS	3 YEARS	4 YEARS	5 YEARS	6 YEARS	7 YEARS	8 YEARS	9 YEARS	10 YEARS	11 YEARS	12 YEARS
50	4.44	2.35	1.65	1.31	1.10	.97	.87	.80	.75	.71	.67	.65
100	8.87	4.69	3.30	2.61	2.20	1.93	1.74	1.60	1.50	1.41	1.34	1.29
200	17.73	9.37	6.60	5.22	4.40	3.86	3.48	3.20	2.99	2.82	2.68	2.57
300	26.59	14.06	9.90	7.83	6.60	5.79	5.22	4.80	4.48	4.22	4.02	3.85
400	35.45	18.74	13.20	10.44	8.80	7.72	6.96	6.40	5.97	5.63	5.36	5.14
500	44.31	23.43	16.49	13.05	11.00	9.65	8.70	7.99	7.46	7.03	6.70	6.42
600	53.17	28.11	19.79	15.66	13.20	11.58	10.44	9.59	8.95	8.44	8.04	7.70
700	62.04	32.79	23.09	18.27	15.40	13.51	12.18	11.19	10.44	9.85	9.37	8.99
800	70.90	37.48	26.39	20.88	17.60	15.44	13.91	12.79	11.93	11.25	10.71	10.27
900	79.76	42.16	29.68	23.49	19.80	17.37	15.65	14.39	13.42	12.66	12.05	11.55
1000	88.62	46.85	32.98	26.09	22.00	19.30	17.39	15.98	14.91	14.06	13.39	12.84
2000	177.24	93.69	65.96	52.18	43.99	38.59	34.78	31.96	29.81	28.12	26.77	25.67
3000	265.85	140.53	98.93	78.27	65.98	57.88	52.16	47.94	44.72	42.18	40.16	38.50
4000	354.47	187.37	131.91	104.36	87.98	77.17	69.55	63.92	59.62	56.24	53.54	51.34
5000	443.08	234.21	164.89	130.45	109.97	96.46	86.94	79.90	74.52	70.30	66.92	64.17
6000	531.70	281.05	197.86	156.54	131.96	115.75	104.32	95.88	89.43	84.36	80.31	77.00
7000	620.31	327.89	230.84	182.63	153.95	135.04	121.71	111.86	104.33	98.42	93.69	89.84
8000	708.93	374.73	263.81	208.72	175.95	154.33	139.10	127.84	119.23	112.48	107.07	102.67
9000	797.54	421.57	296.79	234.81	197.94	173.63	156.48	143.82	134.14	126.54	120.46	115.50
10000	886.16	468.41	329.77	260.90	219.93	192.92	173.87	159.80	149.04	140.60	133.84	128.34
11000	974.77	515.25	362.74	286.98	241.92	212.21	191.26	175.78	163.95	154.66	147.22	141.17
12000	1063.39	562.09	395.72	313.07	263.92	231.50	208.64	191.76	178.85	168.72	160.61	154.00
13000	1152.00	608.93	428.69	339.16	285.91	250.79	226.03	207.74	193.75	182.78	173.99	166.84
14000	1240.62	655.77	461.67	365.25	307.90	270.08	243.42	223.72	208.66	196.84	187.37	179.67
15000	1329.23	702.61	494.65	391.34	329.89	289.37	260.80	239.70	223.56	210.90	200.76	192.50
16000	1417.85	749.45	527.62	417.43	351.89	308.66	278.19	255.67	238.46	224.96	214.14	205.34
17000	1506.46	796.29	560.60	443.52	373.88	327.95	295.57	271.65	253.37	239.02	227.52	218.17
18000	1595.08	843.13	593.57	469.61	395.87	347.25	312.96	287.63	268.27	253.08	240.91	231.00
19000	1683.69	889.97	626.55	495.70	417.86	366.54	330.35	303.61	283.17	267.14	254.29	243.84
20000	1772.31	936.81	659.53	521.79	439.86	385.83	347.73	319.59	298.08	281.20	267.68	256.67
21000	1860.92	983.65	692.50	547.87	461.85	405.12	365.12	335.57	312.98	295.26	281.06	269.50
22000	1949.54	1030.49	725.48	573.96	483.84	424.41	382.51	351.55	327.89	309.31	294.44	282.33
23000	2038.15	1077.33	758.45	600.05	505.83	443.70	399.89	367.53	342.79	323.37	307.83	295.17
24000	2126.77	1124.17	791.43	626.14	527.83	462.99	417.28	383.51	357.69	337.43	321.21	308.00
25000	2215.38	1171.01	824.41	652.23	549.82	482.28	434.67	399.49	372.60	351.49	334.59	320.83
26000	2304.00	1217.85	857.38	678.32	571.81	501.58	452.05	415.47	387.50	365.55	347.98	333.67
27000	2392.61	1264.69	890.36	704.41	593.81	520.87	469.44	431.45	402.40	379.61	361.36	346.50
28000	2481.23	1311.53	923.33	730.50	615.80	540.16	486.83	447.43	417.31	393.67	374.74	359.33
29000	2569.84	1358.37	956.31	756.59	637.79	559.45	504.21	463.41	432.21	407.73	388.13	372.17
30000	2658.46	1405.21	989.29	782.68	659.78	578.74	521.60	479.39	447.11	421.79	401.51	385.00
31000	2747.07	1452.05	1022.26	808.76	681.78	598.03	538.99	495.37	462.02	435.85	414.89	397.83
32000	2835.69	1498.90	1055.24	834.85	703.77	617.32	556.37	511.34	476.92	449.91	428.28	410.67
33000	2924.30	1545.74	1088.21	860.94	725.76	636.61	573.76	527.32	491.83	463.97	441.66	423.50
34000	3012.92	1592.58	1121.19	887.03	747.75	655.90	591.14	543.30	506.73	478.03	455.04	436.33
35000	3101.53	1639.42	1154.17	913.12	769.75	675.20	608.53	559.28	521.63	492.09	468.43	449.17
36000	3190.15	1686.26	1187.14	939.21	791.74	694.49	625.92	575.26	536.54	506.15	481.81	462.00
37000	3278.76	1733.10	1220.12	965.30	813.73	713.78	643.30	591.24	551.44	520.21	495.19	474.83
38000	3367.38	1779.94	1253.09	991.39	835.72	733.07	660.69	607.22	566.34	534.27	508.58	487.67
39000	3455.99	1826.78	1286.07	1017.48	857.72	752.36	678.08	623.20	581.25	548.33	521.96	500.50
40000	3544.61	1873.62	1319.05	1043.57	879.71	771.65	695.46	639.18	596.15	562.39	535.35	513.33
41000	3633.22	1920.46	1352.02	1069.65	901.70	790.94	712.85	655.16	611.06	576.45	548.73	526.16
42000	3721.84	1967.30	1385.00	1095.74	923.69	810.23	730.24	671.14	625.96	590.51	562.11	539.00
43000	3810.45	2014.14	1417.97	1121.83	945.69	829.52	747.62	687.12	640.86	604.57	575.50	551.83
44000	3899.07	2060.98	1450.95	1147.92	967.68	848.82	765.01	703.10	655.77	618.62	588.88	564.66
45000	3987.68	2107.82	1483.93	1174.01	989.67	868.11	782.40	719.08	670.67	632.68	602.26	577.50
46000	4076.30	2154.66	1516.90	1200.10	1011.66	887.40	799.78	735.06	685.57	646.74	615.65	590.33
47000	4164.91	2201.50	1549.88	1226.19	1033.66	906.69	817.17	751.04	700.48	660.80	629.03	603.16
48000	4253.53	2248.34	1582.85	1252.28	1055.65	925.98	834.56	767.01	715.38	674.86	642.41	616.00
49000	4342.14	2295.18	1615.83	1278.37	1077.64	945.27	851.94	782.99	730.28	688.92	655.80	628.83
50000	4430.76	2342.02	1648.81	1304.46	1099.64	964.56	869.33	798.97	745.19	702.98	669.18	641.66
55000	4873.83	2576.22	1813.69	1434.90	1209.60	1061.02	956.26	878.87	819.71	773.28	736.10	705.83
60000	5316.91	2810.42	1978.57	1565.35	1319.56	1157.47	1043.19	958.77	894.22	843.58	803.02	769.99
65000	5759.98	3044.63	2143.45	1695.79	1429.52	1253.93	1130.12	1038.66	968.74	913.88	869.93	834.16
70000	6203.06	3278.83	2308.33	1826.24	1539.49	1350.39	1217.06	1118.56	1043.26	984.17	936.85	898.33
75000	6646.13	3513.03	2473.21	1956.68	1649.45	1446.84	1303.99	1198.46	1117.78	1054.47	1003.77	962.49
80000	7089.21	3747.23	2638.09	2087.13	1759.41	1543.30	1390.92	1278.35	1192.30	1124.77	1070.69	1026.66
85000	7532.28	3981.43	2802.97	2217.57	1869.38	1639.75	1477.85	1358.25	1266.82	1195.07	1137.60	1090.82
90000	7975.36	4215.63	2967.85	2348.02	1979.34	1736.21	1564.79	1438.15	1341.33	1265.36	1204.52	1154.99
95000	8418.44	4449.83	3132.73	2478.46	2089.30	1832.66	1651.72	1518.05	1415.85	1335.66	1271.44	1219.16
100000	8861.51	4684.04	3297.61	2608.91	2199.27	1929.12	1738.65	1597.94	1490.37	1405.96	1338.36	1283.32

MONTHLY 11.50%

PAYMENT REQUIRED TO AMORTIZE A LOAN

TERM AMOUNT	13 YEARS	14 YEARS	15 YEARS	16 YEARS	17 YEARS	18 YEARS	19 YEARS	20 YEARS	25 YEARS	30 YEARS	35 YEARS	40 YEARS
50	.62	.61	.59	.58	.56	.55	.55	.54	.51	.50	.49	.49
100	1.24	1.21	1.17	1.15	1.12	1.10	1.09	1.07	1.02	1.00	.98	.97
200	2.48	2.41	2.34	2.29	2.24	2.20	2.17	2.14	2.04	1.99	1.96	1.94
300	3.72	3.61	3.51	3.43	3.36	3.30	3.25	3.20	3.05	2.98	2.93	2.91
400	4.96	4.81	4.68	4.57	4.48	4.40	4.33	4.27	4.07	3.97	3.91	3.88
500	6.19	6.01	5.85	5.71	5.60	5.50	5.41	5.34	5.09	4.96	4.89	4.85
600	7.43	7.21	7.01	6.85	6.71	6.59	6.49	6.40	6.10	5.95	5.86	5.81
700	8.67	8.41	8.18	7.99	7.83	7.69	7.57	7.47	7.12	6.94	6.84	6.78
800	9.91	9.61	9.35	9.13	8.95	8.79	8.65	8.54	8.14	7.93	7.81	7.75
900	11.15	10.81	10.52	10.28	10.07	9.69	9.74	9.60	9.15	8.92	8.79	8.72
1000	12.38	12.01	11.69	11.42	11.19	10.99	10.82	10.67	10.17	9.91	9.77	9.69
2000	24.76	24.01	23.37	22.83	22.37	21.97	21.63	21.33	20.33	19.81	19.53	19.37
3000	37.14	36.01	35.05	34.24	33.55	32.95	32.44	32.00	30.50	29.71	29.29	29.05
4000	49.52	48.01	46.73	45.65	44.73	43.94	43.25	42.66	40.66	39.62	39.05	38.74
5000	61.90	60.01	58.41	57.06	55.91	54.92	54.07	53.33	50.83	49.52	48.81	48.42
6000	74.28	72.01	70.10	68.47	67.09	65.90	64.88	63.99	60.99	59.42	58.57	58.10
7000	86.66	84.01	81.78	79.89	78.27	76.89	75.69	74.66	71.16	69.33	68.33	67.78
8000	99.04	96.01	93.46	91.30	89.45	87.87	86.50	85.32	81.32	79.23	78.09	77.47
9000	111.42	108.01	105.14	102.71	100.63	98.85	97.31	95.98	91.49	89.13	87.85	87.15
10000	123.80	120.01	116.82	114.12	111.81	109.83	108.13	106.65	101.65	99.03	97.62	96.83
11000	136.18	132.01	128.51	125.53	123.00	120.82	118.94	117.31	111.82	108.94	107.38	106.52
12000	148.56	144.01	140.19	136.94	134.18	131.80	129.75	127.98	121.98	118.84	117.14	116.20
13000	160.93	156.01	151.87	148.36	145.36	142.78	140.56	138.64	132.15	128.74	126.90	125.88
14000	173.31	168.01	163.55	159.77	156.54	153.77	151.38	149.31	142.31	138.65	136.66	135.56
15000	185.69	180.01	175.23	171.18	167.72	164.75	162.19	159.97	152.48	148.55	146.42	145.25
16000	198.07	192.01	186.92	182.59	178.90	175.73	173.00	170.63	162.64	158.45	156.18	154.93
17000	210.45	204.01	198.60	194.00	190.08	186.72	183.81	181.30	172.80	168.35	165.94	164.61
18000	222.83	216.01	210.28	205.41	201.26	197.70	194.62	191.96	182.97	178.26	175.70	174.30
19000	235.21	228.02	221.96	216.83	212.44	208.68	205.44	202.63	193.13	188.16	185.47	183.98
20000	247.59	240.02	233.64	228.24	223.62	219.66	216.25	213.29	203.30	198.06	195.23	193.66
21000	259.97	252.02	245.32	239.65	234.81	230.65	227.06	223.96	213.46	207.97	204.99	203.34
22000	272.35	264.02	257.01	251.06	245.99	241.63	237.87	234.62	223.63	217.87	214.75	213.03
23000	284.73	276.02	268.69	262.47	257.17	252.61	248.69	245.28	233.79	227.77	224.51	222.71
24000	297.11	288.02	280.37	273.88	268.35	263.60	259.50	255.95	243.96	237.67	234.27	232.39
25000	309.48	300.02	292.05	285.30	279.53	274.58	270.31	266.61	254.12	247.58	244.03	242.08
26000	321.86	312.02	303.73	296.71	290.71	285.56	281.12	277.28	264.29	257.48	253.79	251.76
27000	334.24	324.02	315.42	308.12	301.89	296.54	291.93	287.94	274.45	267.38	263.55	261.44
28000	346.62	336.02	327.10	319.53	313.07	307.53	302.75	298.61	284.62	277.29	273.32	271.12
29000	359.00	348.02	338.78	330.94	324.25	318.51	313.56	309.27	294.78	287.19	283.08	280.81
30000	371.38	360.02	350.46	342.35	335.43	329.49	324.37	319.93	304.95	297.09	292.84	290.49
31000	383.76	372.02	362.14	353.77	346.61	340.48	335.18	330.60	315.11	307.00	302.60	300.17
32000	396.14	384.02	373.83	365.18	357.80	351.46	345.99	341.26	325.28	316.90	312.36	309.86
33000	408.52	396.02	385.51	376.59	368.98	362.44	356.81	351.93	335.44	326.80	322.12	319.54
34000	420.90	408.02	397.19	388.00	380.16	373.43	367.62	362.59	345.60	336.70	331.88	329.22
35000	433.28	420.02	408.87	399.41	391.34	384.41	378.43	373.26	355.77	346.61	341.64	338.90
36000	445.66	432.02	420.55	410.82	402.52	395.39	389.24	383.92	365.93	356.51	351.40	348.59
37000	458.03	444.03	432.24	422.24	413.70	406.37	400.06	394.58	376.10	366.41	361.16	358.27
38000	470.41	456.03	443.92	433.65	424.88	417.36	410.87	405.25	386.26	376.32	370.93	367.95
39000	482.79	468.03	455.60	445.06	436.06	428.34	421.68	415.91	396.43	386.22	380.69	377.63
40000	495.17	480.03	467.28	456.47	447.24	439.32	432.49	426.58	406.59	396.12	390.45	387.32
41000	507.55	492.03	478.96	467.88	458.42	450.31	443.30	437.24	416.76	406.02	400.21	397.00
42000	519.93	504.03	490.64	479.29	469.61	461.29	454.12	447.91	426.92	415.93	409.97	406.68
43000	532.31	516.03	502.33	490.71	480.79	472.27	464.93	458.57	437.09	425.83	419.73	416.37
44000	544.69	528.03	514.01	502.12	491.97	483.25	475.74	469.23	447.25	435.73	429.49	426.05
45000	557.07	540.03	525.69	513.53	503.15	494.24	486.55	479.90	457.42	445.64	439.25	435.73
46000	569.45	552.03	537.37	524.94	514.33	505.22	497.37	490.56	467.58	455.54	449.01	445.41
47000	581.83	564.03	549.05	536.35	525.51	516.20	508.18	501.23	477.75	465.44	458.78	455.10
48000	594.21	576.03	560.74	547.76	536.69	527.19	518.99	511.89	487.91	475.34	468.54	464.78
49000	606.58	588.03	572.42	559.18	547.87	538.17	529.80	522.56	498.07	485.25	478.30	474.46
50000	618.96	600.03	584.10	570.59	559.05	549.15	540.61	533.22	508.24	495.15	488.06	484.15
55000	680.86	660.04	642.51	627.65	614.96	604.07	594.67	586.54	559.06	544.67	536.86	532.56
60000	742.76	720.04	700.92	684.70	670.86	658.98	648.74	639.86	609.89	594.18	585.67	580.97
65000	804.65	780.04	759.33	741.76	726.77	713.90	702.80	693.18	660.71	643.69	634.47	629.39
70000	866.55	840.04	817.74	798.82	782.67	768.81	756.86	746.51	711.53	693.21	683.28	677.80
75000	928.44	900.05	876.15	855.88	838.58	823.73	810.92	799.83	762.36	742.72	732.09	726.22
80000	990.34	960.05	934.56	912.94	894.48	878.64	864.98	853.15	813.18	792.24	780.89	774.63
85000	1052.24	1020.05	992.97	970.00	950.39	933.56	919.04	906.47	864.00	841.75	829.70	823.04
90000	1114.13	1080.05	1051.38	1027.05	1006.29	988.47	973.10	959.79	914.83	891.27	878.50	871.46
95000	1176.03	1140.06	1109.79	1084.11	1062.20	1043.39	1027.16	1013.11	965.65	940.78	927.31	919.87
100000	1237.92	1200.06	1168.19	1141.17	1118.10	1098.30	1081.22	1066.43	1016.47	990.30	976.11	968.29

11.75%

MONTHLY

PAYMENT REQUIRED TO AMORTIZE A LOAN

TERM AMOUNT	1 YEAR	2 YEARS	3 YEARS	4 YEARS	5 YEARS	6 YEARS	7 YEARS	8 YEARS	9 YEARS	10 YEARS	11 YEARS	12 YEARS
50	4.44	2.35	1.66	1.32	1.11	.98	.88	.81	.76	.72	.68	.65
100	8.88	4.70	3.31	2.63	2.22	1.95	1.76	1.62	1.51	1.43	1.36	1.30
200	17.75	9.40	6.62	5.25	4.43	3.89	3.51	3.23	3.01	2.85	2.71	2.60
300	26.62	14.09	9.93	7.87	6.64	5.83	5.26	4.84	4.52	4.27	4.06	3.90
400	35.50	18.79	13.24	10.49	8.85	7.77	7.01	6.45	6.02	5.69	5.42	5.20
500	44.37	23.48	16.55	13.11	11.06	9.72	8.76	8.06	7.53	7.11	6.77	6.50
600	53.24	28.18	19.86	15.73	13.28	11.66	10.52	9.67	9.03	8.53	8.12	7.79
700	62.12	32.87	23.17	18.35	15.49	13.60	12.27	11.29	10.54	9.95	9.48	9.09
800	70.99	37.57	26.48	20.97	17.70	15.54	14.02	12.90	12.04	11.37	10.83	10.39
900	79.86	42.27	29.79	23.60	19.91	17.48	15.77	14.51	13.54	12.79	12.18	11.69
1000	88.74	46.96	33.10	26.22	22.12	19.43	17.52	16.12	15.05	14.21	13.54	12.99
2000	177.47	93.92	66.20	52.43	44.24	38.85	35.04	32.24	30.09	28.41	27.07	25.97
3000	266.20	140.88	99.29	78.64	66.36	58.27	52.56	48.35	45.14	42.61	40.60	38.95
4000	354.93	187.83	132.39	104.85	88.48	77.69	70.08	64.47	60.18	56.82	54.13	51.94
5000	443.66	234.79	165.48	131.06	110.60	97.11	87.60	80.58	75.22	71.02	67.66	64.92
6000	532.40	281.75	198.58	157.27	132.71	116.53	105.12	96.70	90.27	85.22	81.19	77.90
7000	621.13	328.70	231.67	183.48	154.83	135.95	122.64	112.82	105.31	99.43	94.72	90.89
8000	709.86	375.66	264.77	209.70	176.95	155.37	140.16	128.93	120.35	113.63	108.25	103.87
9000	798.59	422.62	297.86	235.91	199.07	174.79	157.68	145.05	135.40	127.83	121.78	116.85
10000	887.32	469.57	330.96	262.12	221.19	194.21	175.20	161.16	150.44	142.03	135.31	129.84
11000	976.06	516.53	364.05	288.33	243.31	213.63	192.72	177.28	165.48	156.24	148.84	142.82
12000	1064.79	563.49	397.15	314.54	265.42	233.05	210.24	193.39	180.53	170.44	162.37	155.80
13000	1153.52	610.44	430.24	340.75	287.54	252.47	227.76	209.51	195.57	184.64	175.90	168.79
14000	1242.25	657.40	463.34	366.96	309.66	271.89	245.28	225.63	210.62	198.85	189.43	181.77
15000	1330.98	704.36	496.43	393.17	331.78	291.31	262.79	241.74	225.66	213.05	202.96	194.75
16000	1419.72	751.31	529.53	419.39	353.90	310.73	280.31	257.86	240.70	227.25	216.49	207.74
17000	1508.45	798.27	562.62	445.60	376.02	330.15	297.83	273.97	255.75	241.46	230.02	220.72
18000	1597.18	845.23	595.72	471.81	398.13	349.57	315.35	290.09	270.79	255.66	243.55	233.70
19000	1685.91	892.18	628.81	498.02	420.25	368.99	332.87	306.21	285.83	269.86	257.08	246.69
20000	1774.64	939.14	661.91	524.23	442.37	388.41	350.39	322.32	300.88	284.06	270.61	259.67
21000	1863.37	986.10	695.00	550.44	464.49	407.83	367.91	338.44	315.92	298.27	284.14	272.65
22000	1952.11	1033.05	728.10	576.65	486.61	427.25	385.43	354.55	330.96	312.47	297.67	285.64
23000	2040.84	1080.01	761.19	602.86	508.73	446.67	402.95	370.67	346.01	326.67	311.20	298.62
24000	2129.57	1126.97	794.29	629.08	530.84	466.10	420.47	386.78	361.05	340.88	324.73	311.60
25000	2218.30	1173.93	827.38	655.29	552.96	485.52	437.99	402.90	376.10	355.08	338.26	324.59
26000	2307.03	1220.88	860.48	681.50	575.08	504.94	455.51	419.02	391.14	369.28	351.79	337.57
27000	2395.77	1267.84	893.57	707.71	597.20	524.36	473.03	435.13	406.18	383.48	365.32	350.55
28000	2484.50	1314.80	926.67	733.92	619.32	543.78	490.55	451.25	421.23	397.69	378.85	363.54
29000	2573.23	1361.75	959.76	760.13	641.44	563.20	508.07	467.36	436.27	411.89	392.38	376.52
30000	2661.96	1408.71	992.86	786.34	663.55	582.62	525.58	483.48	451.31	426.09	405.91	389.50
31000	2750.69	1455.67	1025.95	812.55	685.67	602.04	543.10	499.59	466.36	440.30	419.44	402.49
32000	2839.43	1502.62	1059.05	838.77	707.79	621.46	560.62	515.71	481.40	454.50	432.97	415.47
33000	2928.16	1549.58	1092.14	864.98	729.91	640.88	578.14	531.83	496.44	468.70	446.50	428.45
34000	3016.89	1596.54	1125.24	891.19	752.03	660.30	595.66	547.94	511.49	482.91	460.03	441.44
35000	3105.62	1643.49	1158.33	917.40	774.15	679.72	613.18	564.06	526.53	497.11	473.57	454.42
36000	3194.35	1690.45	1191.43	943.61	796.26	699.14	630.70	580.17	541.57	511.31	487.10	467.40
37000	3283.08	1737.41	1224.52	969.82	818.38	718.56	648.22	596.29	556.62	525.51	500.63	480.39
38000	3371.82	1784.36	1257.62	996.03	840.50	737.98	665.74	612.41	571.66	539.72	514.16	493.37
39000	3460.55	1831.32	1290.71	1022.24	862.62	757.40	683.26	628.52	586.71	553.92	527.69	506.35
40000	3549.28	1878.28	1323.81	1048.46	884.74	776.82	700.78	644.64	601.75	568.12	541.22	519.34
41000	3638.01	1925.23	1356.90	1074.67	906.86	796.24	718.30	660.75	616.79	582.33	554.75	532.32
42000	3726.74	1972.19	1390.00	1100.88	928.97	815.66	735.82	676.87	631.84	596.53	568.28	545.30
43000	3815.48	2019.15	1423.09	1127.09	951.09	835.08	753.34	692.98	646.88	610.73	581.81	558.28
44000	3904.21	2066.10	1456.19	1153.30	973.21	854.50	770.85	709.10	661.92	624.93	595.34	571.27
45000	3992.94	2113.06	1489.28	1179.51	995.33	873.92	788.37	725.22	676.97	639.14	608.87	584.25
46000	4081.67	2160.02	1522.38	1205.72	1017.45	893.34	805.89	741.33	692.01	653.34	622.40	597.23
47000	4170.40	2206.98	1555.47	1231.93	1039.57	912.77	823.41	757.45	707.05	667.54	635.93	610.22
48000	4259.14	2253.93	1588.57	1258.15	1061.68	932.19	840.93	773.56	722.10	681.75	649.46	623.20
49000	4347.87	2300.89	1621.66	1284.36	1083.80	951.61	858.45	789.68	737.14	695.95	662.99	636.18
50000	4436.60	2347.85	1654.76	1310.57	1105.92	971.03	875.97	805.79	752.19	710.15	676.52	649.17
55000	4880.26	2582.63	1820.23	1441.62	1216.51	1068.13	963.57	886.37	827.40	781.17	744.17	714.08
60000	5323.92	2817.41	1985.71	1572.68	1327.10	1165.23	1051.16	966.95	902.62	852.18	811.82	779.00
65000	5767.58	3052.20	2151.18	1703.74	1437.70	1262.33	1138.76	1047.53	977.84	923.20	879.47	843.92
70000	6211.24	3286.98	2316.66	1834.79	1548.29	1359.44	1226.36	1128.11	1053.06	994.21	947.13	908.83
75000	6654.90	3521.77	2482.13	1965.85	1658.88	1456.54	1313.95	1208.69	1128.28	1065.23	1014.78	973.75
80000	7098.56	3756.55	2647.61	2096.91	1769.47	1553.64	1401.55	1289.27	1203.49	1136.24	1082.43	1038.67
85000	7542.21	3991.33	2813.08	2227.96	1880.06	1650.74	1489.15	1369.85	1278.71	1207.26	1150.08	1103.58
90000	7985.87	4226.12	2978.56	2359.02	1990.65	1747.84	1576.74	1450.43	1353.93	1278.27	1217.73	1168.50
95000	8429.53	4460.90	3144.03	2490.07	2101.25	1844.95	1664.34	1531.01	1429.15	1349.28	1285.38	1233.41
100000	8873.19	4695.69	3309.51	2621.13	2211.84	1942.05	1751.94	1611.58	1504.37	1420.30	1353.03	1298.33

MONTHLY 11.75%

PAYMENT REQUIRED TO AMORTIZE A LOAN

TERM AMOUNT	13 YEARS	14 YEARS	15 YEARS	16 YEARS	17 YEARS	18 YEARS	19 YEARS	20 YEARS	25 YEARS	30 YEARS	35 YEARS	40 YEARS
50	.63	.61	.60	.58	.57	.56	.55	.55	.52	.51	.50	.50
100	1.26	1.22	1.19	1.16	1.14	1.12	1.10	1.09	1.04	1.01	1.00	.99
200	2.51	2.44	2.37	2.32	2.27	2.24	2.20	2.17	2.07	2.02	2.00	1.98
300	3.76	3.65	3.56	3.48	3.41	3.35	3.30	3.26	3.11	3.03	2.99	2.97
400	5.02	4.87	4.74	4.63	4.54	4.47	4.40	4.34	4.14	4.04	3.99	3.96
500	6.27	6.08	5.93	5.79	5.68	5.58	5.50	5.42	5.18	5.05	4.98	4.95
600	7.52	7.30	7.11	6.95	6.81	6.70	6.59	6.51	6.21	6.06	5.98	5.94
700	8.78	8.51	8.29	8.11	7.95	7.81	7.69	7.59	7.25	7.07	6.98	6.92
800	10.03	9.73	9.48	9.26	9.08	8.93	8.79	8.67	8.28	8.08	7.97	7.91
900	11.28	10.95	10.66	10.42	10.22	10.04	9.89	9.76	9.32	9.09	8.97	8.90
1000	12.54	12.16	11.85	11.58	11.35	11.16	10.99	10.84	10.35	10.10	9.96	9.89
2000	25.07	24.32	23.69	23.15	22.70	22.31	21.97	21.68	20.70	20.19	19.92	19.77
3000	37.60	36.48	35.53	34.73	34.04	33.46	32.95	32.52	31.05	30.29	29.88	29.66
4000	50.13	48.63	47.37	46.30	45.39	44.61	43.94	43.35	41.40	40.38	39.84	39.54
5000	62.67	60.79	59.21	57.87	56.74	55.76	54.92	54.19	51.74	50.48	49.79	49.42
6000	75.20	72.95	71.05	69.45	68.08	66.91	65.90	65.03	62.09	60.57	59.75	59.31
7000	87.73	85.10	82.89	81.02	79.43	78.06	76.88	75.86	72.44	70.66	69.71	69.19
8000	100.26	97.26	94.74	92.60	90.77	89.21	87.87	86.70	82.79	80.76	79.67	79.07
9000	112.80	109.42	106.58	104.17	102.12	100.36	98.85	97.54	93.14	90.85	89.63	88.96
10000	125.33	121.57	118.42	115.74	113.47	111.51	109.83	108.38	103.48	100.95	99.58	98.84
11000	137.86	133.73	130.26	127.32	124.81	122.66	120.81	119.21	113.83	111.04	109.54	108.73
12000	150.39	145.89	142.10	138.89	136.16	133.81	131.80	130.05	124.18	121.13	119.50	118.61
13000	162.93	158.05	153.94	150.47	147.50	144.96	142.78	140.89	134.53	131.23	129.46	128.49
14000	175.46	170.20	165.78	162.04	158.85	156.12	153.76	151.72	144.88	141.32	139.42	138.38
15000	187.99	182.36	177.62	173.61	170.20	167.27	164.74	162.56	155.22	151.42	149.37	148.26
16000	200.52	194.52	189.47	185.19	181.54	178.42	175.73	173.40	165.57	161.51	159.33	158.14
17000	213.06	206.67	201.31	196.76	192.89	189.57	186.71	184.24	175.92	171.60	169.29	168.03
18000	225.59	218.83	213.15	208.34	204.23	200.72	197.69	195.07	186.27	181.70	179.25	177.91
19000	238.12	230.99	224.99	219.91	215.58	211.87	208.67	205.91	196.62	191.79	189.21	187.79
20000	250.65	243.14	236.83	231.48	226.93	223.02	219.66	216.75	206.96	201.89	199.16	197.68
21000	263.19	255.30	248.67	243.06	238.27	234.17	230.64	227.58	217.31	211.98	209.12	207.56
22000	275.72	267.46	260.51	254.63	249.62	245.32	241.62	238.42	227.66	222.08	219.08	217.45
23000	288.25	279.62	272.36	266.21	260.96	256.47	252.60	249.26	238.01	232.17	229.04	227.33
24000	300.78	291.77	284.20	277.78	272.31	267.62	263.59	260.09	248.36	242.26	239.00	237.21
25000	313.32	303.93	296.04	289.35	283.66	278.77	274.57	270.93	258.70	252.36	248.95	247.10
26000	325.85	316.09	307.88	300.93	295.00	289.92	285.55	281.77	269.05	262.45	258.91	256.98
27000	338.38	328.24	319.72	312.50	306.35	301.07	296.53	292.61	279.40	272.55	268.87	266.86
28000	350.91	340.40	331.56	324.08	317.69	312.23	307.52	303.44	289.75	282.64	278.83	276.75
29000	363.45	352.56	343.40	335.65	329.04	323.38	318.50	314.28	300.10	292.73	288.79	286.63
30000	375.98	364.71	355.24	347.22	340.39	334.53	329.48	325.12	310.44	302.83	298.74	296.51
31000	388.51	376.87	367.09	358.80	351.73	345.68	340.46	335.95	320.79	312.92	308.70	306.40
32000	401.04	389.03	378.93	370.37	363.08	356.83	351.45	346.79	331.14	323.02	318.66	316.28
33000	413.58	401.18	390.77	381.95	374.43	367.98	362.43	357.63	341.49	333.11	328.62	326.17
34000	426.11	413.34	402.61	393.52	385.77	379.13	373.41	368.47	351.84	343.20	338.57	336.05
35000	438.64	425.50	414.45	405.09	397.12	390.28	384.39	379.30	362.18	353.30	348.53	345.93
36000	451.17	437.66	426.29	416.67	408.46	401.43	395.38	390.14	372.53	363.39	358.49	355.82
37000	463.71	449.81	438.13	428.24	419.81	412.58	406.36	400.98	382.88	373.49	368.45	365.70
38000	476.24	461.97	449.97	439.82	431.16	423.73	417.34	411.81	393.23	383.58	378.41	375.58
39000	488.77	474.13	461.82	451.39	442.50	434.88	428.32	422.65	403.58	393.67	388.36	385.47
40000	501.30	486.28	473.66	462.96	453.85	446.03	439.31	433.49	413.92	403.77	398.32	395.35
41000	513.84	498.44	485.50	474.54	465.19	457.18	450.29	444.32	424.27	413.86	408.28	405.23
42000	526.37	510.60	497.34	486.11	476.54	468.34	461.27	455.16	434.62	423.96	418.24	415.12
43000	538.90	522.75	509.18	497.69	487.89	479.49	472.25	466.00	444.97	434.05	428.20	425.00
44000	551.43	534.91	521.02	509.26	499.23	490.64	483.24	476.84	455.32	444.15	438.15	434.89
45000	563.97	547.07	532.86	520.83	510.58	501.79	494.22	487.67	465.66	454.24	448.11	444.77
46000	576.50	559.23	544.71	532.41	521.92	512.94	505.20	498.51	476.01	464.33	458.07	454.65
47000	589.03	571.38	556.55	543.98	533.27	524.09	516.18	509.35	486.36	474.43	468.03	464.54
48000	601.56	583.54	568.39	555.56	544.62	535.24	527.17	520.18	496.71	484.52	477.99	474.42
49000	614.10	595.70	580.23	567.13	555.96	546.39	538.15	531.02	507.06	494.62	487.94	484.30
50000	626.63	607.85	592.07	578.70	567.31	557.54	549.13	541.86	517.40	504.71	497.90	494.19
55000	689.29	668.64	651.28	636.57	624.04	613.29	604.04	596.04	569.14	555.18	547.69	543.61
60000	751.95	729.42	710.48	694.44	680.77	669.05	658.96	650.23	620.88	605.65	597.48	593.02
65000	814.62	790.21	769.69	752.31	737.50	724.80	713.87	704.41	672.62	656.12	647.27	642.44
70000	877.28	850.99	828.90	810.18	794.23	780.56	768.78	758.60	724.36	706.59	697.06	691.86
75000	939.94	911.78	888.10	868.05	850.96	836.31	823.69	812.79	776.10	757.06	746.85	741.28
80000	1002.60	972.56	947.31	925.92	907.69	892.06	878.61	866.97	827.84	807.53	796.64	790.70
85000	1065.27	1033.35	1006.52	983.79	964.42	947.82	933.52	921.16	879.58	858.00	846.43	840.11
90000	1127.93	1094.13	1065.72	1041.66	1021.15	1003.57	988.43	975.34	931.32	908.47	896.22	889.53
95000	1190.59	1154.92	1124.93	1099.53	1077.88	1059.32	1043.34	1029.53	983.06	958.94	946.01	938.95
100000	1253.25	1215.70	1184.14	1157.40	1134.61	1115.08	1098.26	1083.71	1034.80	1009.41	995.80	988.37

12.00%
MONTHLY
PAYMENT REQUIRED TO AMORTIZE A LOAN

TERM AMOUNT	1 YEAR	2 YEARS	3 YEARS	4 YEARS	5 YEARS	6 YEARS	7 YEARS	8 YEARS	9 YEARS	10 YEARS	11 YEARS	12 YEARS
50	4.45	2.36	1.67	1.32	1.12	.98	.89	.82	.76	.72	.69	.66
100	8.89	4.71	3.33	2.64	2.23	1.96	1.77	1.63	1.52	1.44	1.37	1.32
200	17.77	9.42	6.65	5.27	4.45	3.92	3.54	3.26	3.04	2.87	2.74	2.63
300	26.66	14.13	9.97	7.91	6.68	5.87	5.30	4.88	4.56	4.31	4.11	3.95
400	35.54	18.83	13.29	10.54	8.90	7.83	7.07	6.51	6.08	5.74	5.48	5.26
500	44.43	23.54	16.61	13.17	11.13	9.78	8.83	8.13	7.60	7.18	6.84	6.57
600	53.31	28.25	19.93	15.81	13.35	11.74	10.60	9.76	9.12	8.61	8.21	7.89
700	62.20	32.96	23.26	18.44	15.58	13.69	12.36	11.38	10.63	10.05	9.58	9.20
800	71.08	37.66	26.58	21.07	17.80	15.65	14.13	13.01	12.15	11.48	10.95	10.51
900	79.97	42.37	29.90	23.71	20.03	17.60	15.89	14.63	13.67	12.92	12.32	11.83
1000	88.85	47.08	33.22	26.34	22.25	19.56	17.66	16.26	15.19	14.35	13.68	13.14
2000	177.70	94.15	66.43	52.67	44.49	39.11	35.31	32.51	30.37	28.70	27.36	26.27
3000	266.55	141.23	99.65	79.01	66.74	58.66	52.96	48.76	45.56	43.05	41.04	39.41
4000	355.40	188.30	132.86	105.34	88.98	78.21	70.62	65.02	60.74	57.39	54.72	52.54
5000	444.25	235.37	166.08	131.67	111.23	97.76	88.27	81.27	75.93	71.74	68.39	65.68
6000	533.10	282.45	199.29	158.01	133.47	117.31	105.92	97.52	91.11	86.09	82.07	78.81
7000	621.95	329.52	232.51	184.34	155.72	136.86	123.57	113.77	106.29	100.43	95.75	91.94
8000	710.80	376.59	265.72	210.68	177.96	156.41	141.23	130.03	121.48	114.78	109.43	105.08
9000	799.64	423.67	298.93	237.01	200.21	175.96	158.88	146.28	136.66	129.13	123.11	118.21
10000	888.49	470.74	332.15	263.34	222.45	195.51	176.53	162.53	151.85	143.48	136.78	131.35
11000	977.34	517.81	365.36	289.68	244.69	215.06	194.19	178.79	167.03	157.82	150.46	144.48
12000	1066.19	564.89	398.58	316.01	266.94	234.61	211.84	195.04	182.22	172.17	164.14	157.62
13000	1155.04	611.96	431.79	342.34	289.18	254.16	229.49	211.29	197.40	186.52	177.82	170.75
14000	1243.89	659.03	465.01	368.68	311.43	273.71	247.14	227.54	212.58	200.86	191.50	183.88
15000	1332.74	706.11	498.22	395.01	333.67	293.26	264.80	243.80	227.77	215.21	205.17	197.02
16000	1421.59	753.18	531.43	421.35	355.92	312.81	282.45	260.05	242.95	229.56	218.85	210.15
17000	1510.43	800.25	564.65	447.68	378.16	332.36	300.10	276.30	258.14	243.91	232.53	223.29
18000	1599.28	847.33	597.86	474.01	400.41	351.91	317.75	292.56	273.32	258.25	246.21	236.42
19000	1688.13	894.40	631.08	500.35	422.65	371.46	335.41	308.81	288.51	272.60	259.88	249.55
20000	1776.98	941.47	664.29	526.68	444.89	391.01	353.06	325.06	303.69	286.95	273.56	262.69
21000	1865.83	988.55	697.51	553.02	467.14	410.56	370.71	341.31	318.87	301.29	287.24	275.82
22000	1954.68	1035.62	730.72	579.35	489.38	430.11	388.37	357.57	334.06	315.64	300.92	288.96
23000	2043.53	1082.69	763.93	605.68	511.63	449.66	406.02	373.82	349.24	329.99	314.60	302.09
24000	2132.38	1129.77	797.15	632.02	533.87	469.21	423.67	390.07	364.43	344.34	328.27	315.23
25000	2221.22	1176.84	830.36	658.35	556.12	488.76	441.32	406.33	379.61	358.68	341.95	328.36
26000	2310.07	1223.92	863.58	684.68	578.36	508.31	458.98	422.58	394.80	373.03	355.63	341.49
27000	2398.92	1270.99	896.79	711.02	600.61	527.86	476.63	438.83	409.98	387.38	369.31	354.63
28000	2487.77	1318.06	930.01	737.35	622.85	547.41	494.28	455.08	425.16	401.72	382.99	367.76
29000	2576.62	1365.14	963.22	763.69	645.09	566.96	511.93	471.34	440.35	416.07	396.66	380.90
30000	2665.47	1412.21	996.43	790.02	667.34	586.51	529.59	487.59	455.53	430.42	410.34	394.03
31000	2754.32	1459.28	1029.65	816.35	689.58	606.06	547.24	503.84	470.72	444.76	424.02	407.16
32000	2843.17	1506.36	1062.86	842.69	711.83	625.61	564.89	520.10	485.90	459.11	437.70	420.30
33000	2932.02	1553.43	1096.08	869.02	734.07	645.16	582.55	536.35	501.08	473.46	451.38	433.43
34000	3020.86	1600.50	1129.29	895.36	756.32	664.71	600.20	552.60	516.27	487.81	465.05	446.57
35000	3109.71	1647.58	1162.51	921.69	778.56	684.26	617.85	568.85	531.45	502.15	478.73	459.70
36000	3198.56	1694.65	1195.72	948.02	800.81	703.81	635.50	585.11	546.64	516.50	492.41	472.84
37000	3287.41	1741.72	1228.93	974.36	823.05	723.36	653.16	601.36	561.82	530.85	506.09	485.97
38000	3376.26	1788.80	1262.15	1000.69	845.29	742.91	670.81	617.61	577.01	545.19	519.76	499.10
39000	3465.11	1835.87	1295.36	1027.02	867.54	762.46	688.46	633.87	592.19	559.54	533.44	512.24
40000	3553.96	1882.94	1328.58	1053.36	889.78	782.01	706.11	650.12	607.37	573.89	547.12	525.37
41000	3642.81	1930.02	1361.79	1079.69	912.03	801.56	723.77	666.37	622.56	588.24	560.80	538.51
42000	3731.65	1977.09	1395.01	1106.03	934.27	821.11	741.42	682.62	637.74	602.58	574.48	551.64
43000	3820.50	2024.16	1428.22	1132.36	956.52	840.66	759.07	698.88	652.93	616.93	588.15	564.78
44000	3909.35	2071.24	1461.43	1158.69	978.76	860.21	776.73	715.13	668.11	631.28	601.83	577.91
45000	3998.20	2118.31	1494.65	1185.03	1001.01	879.76	794.38	731.38	683.30	645.62	615.51	591.04
46000	4087.05	2165.38	1527.86	1211.36	1023.25	899.31	812.03	747.64	698.48	659.97	629.19	604.18
47000	4175.90	2212.46	1561.08	1237.70	1045.49	918.86	829.68	763.89	713.66	674.32	642.87	617.31
48000	4264.75	2259.53	1594.29	1264.03	1067.74	938.41	847.34	780.14	728.85	688.67	656.54	630.45
49000	4353.60	2306.61	1627.51	1290.36	1089.98	957.96	864.99	796.39	744.03	703.01	670.22	643.58
50000	4442.44	2353.68	1660.72	1316.70	1112.23	977.51	882.64	812.65	759.22	717.36	683.90	656.71
55000	4886.69	2589.05	1826.79	1448.37	1223.45	1075.27	970.91	893.91	835.14	789.10	752.29	722.39
60000	5330.93	2824.41	1992.86	1580.04	1334.67	1173.02	1059.17	975.18	911.06	860.83	820.68	788.06
65000	5775.18	3059.78	2158.94	1711.70	1445.89	1270.77	1147.43	1056.44	986.98	932.57	889.07	853.73
70000	6219.42	3295.15	2325.01	1843.37	1557.12	1368.52	1235.70	1137.70	1062.90	1004.30	957.46	919.40
75000	6663.66	3530.52	2491.08	1975.04	1668.34	1466.27	1323.96	1218.97	1138.82	1076.04	1025.85	985.07
80000	7107.91	3765.88	2657.15	2106.71	1779.56	1564.02	1412.22	1300.23	1214.74	1147.77	1094.24	1050.74
85000	7552.15	4001.25	2823.22	2238.38	1890.78	1661.77	1500.49	1381.50	1290.66	1219.51	1162.62	1116.41
90000	7996.40	4236.62	2989.29	2370.05	2002.01	1759.52	1588.75	1462.76	1366.59	1291.24	1231.01	1182.08
95000	8440.64	4471.98	3155.36	2501.72	2113.23	1857.27	1677.01	1544.02	1442.51	1362.98	1299.40	1247.75
100000	8884.88	4707.35	3321.44	2633.39	2224.45	1955.02	1765.28	1625.29	1518.43	1434.71	1367.79	1313.42

MONTHLY

PAYMENT REQUIRED TO AMORTIZE A LOAN

12.00%

TERM AMOUNT	13 YEARS	14 YEARS	15 YEARS	16 YEARS	17 YEARS	18 YEARS	19 YEARS	20 YEARS	25 YEARS	30 YEARS	35 YEARS	40 YEARS
50	.64	.62	.61	.59	.58	.57	.56	.56	.53	.52	.51	.51
100	1.27	1.24	1.21	1.18	1.16	1.14	1.12	1.11	1.06	1.03	1.02	1.01
200	2.54	2.47	2.41	2.35	2.31	2.27	2.24	2.21	2.11	2.06	2.04	2.02
300	3.81	3.70	3.61	3.53	3.46	3.40	3.35	3.31	3.16	3.09	3.05	3.03
400	5.08	4.93	4.81	4.70	4.61	4.53	4.47	4.41	4.22	4.12	4.07	4.04
500	6.35	6.16	6.01	5.87	5.76	5.66	5.58	5.51	5.27	5.15	5.08	5.05
600	7.62	7.39	7.21	7.05	6.91	6.80	6.70	6.61	6.32	6.18	6.10	6.06
700	8.89	8.63	8.41	8.22	8.06	7.93	7.81	7.71	7.38	7.21	7.11	7.06
800	10.15	9.86	9.61	9.39	9.21	9.06	8.93	8.81	8.43	8.23	8.13	8.07
900	11.42	11.09	10.81	10.57	10.37	10.19	10.04	9.91	9.48	9.26	9.14	9.08
1000	12.69	12.32	12.01	11.74	11.52	11.32	11.16	11.02	10.54	10.29	10.16	10.09
2000	25.38	24.63	24.01	23.48	23.03	22.64	22.31	22.03	21.07	20.58	20.32	20.17
3000	38.06	36.95	36.01	35.22	34.54	33.96	33.47	33.04	31.60	30.86	30.47	30.26
4000	50.75	49.26	48.01	46.95	46.05	45.28	44.62	44.05	42.13	41.15	40.63	40.34
5000	63.44	61.58	60.01	58.69	57.57	56.60	55.77	55.06	52.67	51.44	50.78	50.43
6000	76.12	73.89	72.02	70.43	69.08	67.92	66.93	66.07	63.20	61.72	60.94	60.51
7000	88.81	86.21	84.02	82.17	80.59	79.24	78.08	77.08	73.73	72.01	71.09	70.60
8000	101.50	98.52	96.02	93.90	92.10	90.56	89.24	88.09	84.26	82.29	81.25	80.68
9000	114.18	110.83	108.02	105.64	103.61	101.88	100.39	99.10	94.80	92.58	91.40	90.77
10000	126.87	123.15	120.02	117.38	115.13	113.20	111.54	110.11	105.33	102.87	101.56	100.85
11000	139.56	135.46	132.02	129.11	126.64	124.52	122.70	121.12	115.86	113.15	111.72	110.94
12000	152.24	147.78	144.03	140.85	138.15	135.84	133.85	132.14	126.39	123.44	121.87	121.02
13000	164.93	160.09	156.03	152.59	149.66	147.16	145.01	143.15	136.92	133.72	132.03	131.11
14000	177.62	172.41	168.03	164.33	161.18	158.48	156.16	154.16	147.46	144.01	142.18	141.19
15000	190.30	184.72	180.03	176.06	172.69	169.80	167.31	165.17	157.99	154.30	152.34	151.28
16000	202.99	197.03	192.03	187.80	184.20	181.12	178.47	176.18	168.52	164.58	162.49	161.36
17000	215.68	209.35	204.03	199.54	195.71	192.44	189.62	187.19	179.05	174.87	172.65	171.45
18000	228.36	221.66	216.04	211.28	207.22	203.76	200.77	198.20	189.59	185.16	182.80	181.53
19000	241.05	233.98	228.04	223.01	218.74	215.08	211.93	209.21	200.12	195.44	192.96	191.62
20000	253.74	246.29	240.04	234.75	230.25	226.40	223.08	220.22	210.65	205.73	203.11	201.70
21000	266.42	258.61	252.04	246.49	241.76	237.71	234.24	231.23	221.18	216.01	213.27	211.79
22000	279.11	270.92	264.04	258.22	253.27	249.03	245.39	242.24	231.71	226.30	223.43	221.87
23000	291.80	283.23	276.04	269.96	264.78	260.35	256.54	253.25	242.25	236.59	233.58	231.96
24000	304.48	295.55	288.05	281.70	276.30	271.67	267.70	264.27	252.78	246.87	243.74	242.04
25000	317.17	307.86	300.05	293.44	287.81	282.99	278.85	275.28	263.31	257.16	253.89	252.13
26000	329.86	320.18	312.05	305.17	299.32	294.31	290.01	286.29	273.84	267.44	264.05	262.21
27000	342.54	332.49	324.05	316.91	310.83	305.63	301.16	297.30	284.38	277.73	274.20	272.30
28000	355.23	344.81	336.05	328.65	322.35	316.95	312.31	308.31	294.91	288.02	284.36	282.38
29000	367.92	357.12	348.05	340.39	333.86	328.27	323.47	319.32	305.44	298.30	294.51	292.47
30000	380.60	369.43	360.06	352.12	345.37	339.59	334.62	330.33	315.97	308.59	304.67	302.55
31000	393.29	381.75	372.06	363.86	356.88	350.91	345.77	341.34	326.50	318.87	314.83	312.64
32000	405.98	394.06	384.06	375.60	368.39	362.23	356.93	352.35	337.04	329.16	324.98	322.72
33000	418.66	406.38	396.06	387.33	379.91	373.55	368.08	363.36	347.57	339.45	335.14	332.81
34000	431.35	418.69	408.06	399.07	391.42	384.87	379.24	374.37	358.10	349.73	345.29	342.89
35000	444.04	431.01	420.06	410.81	402.93	396.19	390.39	385.39	368.63	360.02	355.45	352.98
36000	456.72	443.32	432.07	422.55	414.44	407.51	401.54	396.40	379.17	370.31	365.60	363.06
37000	469.41	455.63	444.07	434.28	425.95	418.83	412.70	407.41	389.70	380.59	375.76	373.15
38000	482.10	467.95	456.07	446.02	437.47	430.15	423.85	418.42	400.23	390.88	385.91	383.23
39000	494.78	480.26	468.07	457.76	448.98	441.47	435.01	429.43	410.76	401.16	396.07	393.32
40000	507.47	492.58	480.07	469.50	460.49	452.79	446.16	440.44	421.29	411.45	406.22	403.40
41000	520.16	504.89	492.07	481.23	472.00	464.10	457.31	451.45	431.83	421.74	416.38	413.49
42000	532.84	517.21	504.08	492.97	483.52	475.42	468.47	462.46	442.36	432.02	426.54	423.57
43000	545.53	529.52	516.08	504.71	495.03	486.74	479.62	473.47	452.89	442.31	436.69	433.66
44000	558.22	541.83	528.08	516.44	506.54	498.06	490.77	484.48	463.42	452.59	446.85	443.74
45000	570.90	554.15	540.08	528.18	518.05	509.38	501.93	495.49	473.96	462.88	457.00	453.83
46000	583.59	566.46	552.08	539.92	529.56	520.70	513.08	506.50	484.49	473.17	467.16	463.91
47000	596.28	578.78	564.08	551.66	541.08	532.02	524.24	517.52	495.02	483.45	477.31	474.00
48000	608.96	591.09	576.09	563.39	552.59	543.34	535.39	528.53	505.55	493.74	487.47	484.08
49000	621.65	603.41	588.09	575.13	564.10	554.66	546.54	539.54	516.08	504.03	497.62	494.17
50000	634.34	615.72	600.09	586.87	575.61	565.98	557.70	550.55	526.62	514.31	507.78	504.25
55000	697.77	677.29	660.10	645.55	633.17	622.58	613.47	605.60	579.28	565.74	558.56	554.68
60000	761.20	738.86	720.11	704.24	690.73	679.18	669.24	660.66	631.94	617.17	609.33	605.10
65000	824.64	800.43	780.11	762.93	748.30	735.77	725.01	715.71	684.60	668.60	660.11	655.53
70000	888.07	862.01	840.12	821.61	805.86	792.37	780.77	770.77	737.26	720.03	710.89	705.95
75000	951.50	923.58	900.13	880.30	863.42	848.97	836.54	825.82	789.92	771.46	761.67	756.38
80000	1014.94	985.15	960.14	938.99	920.98	905.57	892.31	880.87	842.58	822.90	812.44	806.80
85000	1078.37	1046.72	1020.15	997.67	978.54	962.16	948.08	935.93	895.25	874.33	863.22	857.23
90000	1141.80	1108.29	1080.16	1056.36	1036.10	1018.76	1003.85	990.98	947.91	925.76	914.00	907.65
95000	1205.24	1169.86	1140.16	1115.04	1093.66	1075.36	1059.62	1046.04	1000.57	977.19	964.78	958.08
100000	1268.67	1231.43	1200.17	1173.73	1151.22	1131.96	1115.39	1101.09	1053.23	1028.62	1015.55	1008.50

12.25% MONTHLY

PAYMENT REQUIRED TO AMORTIZE A LOAN

TERM AMOUNT	1 YEAR	2 YEARS	3 YEARS	4 YEARS	5 YEARS	6 YEARS	7 YEARS	8 YEARS	9 YEARS	10 YEARS	11 YEARS	12 YEARS
50	4.45	2.36	1.67	1.33	1.12	.99	.89	.82	.77	.73	.70	.67
100	8.90	4.72	3.34	2.65	2.24	1.97	1.78	1.64	1.54	1.45	1.39	1.33
200	17.80	9.44	6.67	5.30	4.48	3.94	3.56	3.28	3.07	2.90	2.77	2.66
300	26.69	14.16	10.01	7.94	6.72	5.91	5.34	4.92	4.60	4.35	4.15	3.99
400	35.59	18.88	13.34	10.59	8.95	7.88	7.12	6.56	6.14	5.80	5.54	5.32
500	44.49	23.60	16.67	13.23	11.19	9.85	8.90	8.20	7.67	7.25	6.92	6.65
600	53.38	28.32	20.01	15.88	13.43	11.81	10.68	9.84	9.20	8.70	8.30	7.98
700	62.28	33.04	23.34	18.52	15.66	13.78	12.46	11.48	10.73	10.15	9.68	9.31
800	71.18	37.76	26.67	21.17	17.90	15.75	14.23	13.12	12.27	11.60	11.07	10.63
900	80.07	42.48	30.01	23.82	20.14	17.72	16.01	14.76	13.80	13.05	12.45	11.96
1000	88.97	47.20	33.34	26.46	22.38	19.69	17.79	16.40	15.33	14.50	13.83	13.29
2000	177.94	94.39	66.67	52.92	44.75	39.37	35.58	32.79	30.66	28.99	27.66	26.58
3000	266.90	141.58	100.01	79.38	67.12	59.05	53.37	49.18	45.98	43.48	41.48	39.86
4000	355.87	188.77	133.34	105.83	89.49	78.73	71.15	65.57	61.31	57.97	55.31	53.15
5000	444.83	235.96	166.67	132.29	111.86	98.41	88.94	81.96	76.63	72.46	69.14	66.43
6000	533.80	283.15	200.01	158.75	134.23	118.09	106.73	98.35	91.96	86.96	82.96	79.72
7000	622.77	330.34	233.34	185.20	156.60	137.77	124.51	114.74	107.28	101.45	96.79	93.01
8000	711.73	377.53	266.68	211.66	178.97	157.45	142.30	131.13	122.61	115.94	110.62	106.29
9000	800.70	424.72	300.01	238.12	201.34	177.13	160.09	147.52	137.93	130.43	124.44	119.58
10000	889.66	471.91	333.34	264.57	223.71	196.81	177.87	163.91	153.26	144.92	138.27	132.86
11000	978.63	519.10	366.68	291.03	246.09	216.49	195.66	180.30	168.59	159.42	152.09	146.15
12000	1067.59	566.29	400.01	317.49	268.46	236.17	213.45	196.69	183.91	173.91	165.92	159.44
13000	1156.56	613.48	433.34	343.94	290.83	255.85	231.23	213.08	199.24	188.40	179.75	172.72
14000	1245.53	660.67	466.68	370.40	313.20	275.53	249.02	229.47	214.56	202.89	193.57	186.01
15000	1334.49	707.86	500.01	396.86	335.57	295.21	266.81	245.86	229.89	217.38	207.40	199.29
16000	1423.46	755.05	533.35	423.31	357.94	314.89	284.59	262.25	245.21	231.88	221.23	212.58
17000	1512.42	802.24	566.68	449.77	380.31	334.57	302.38	278.64	260.54	246.37	235.05	225.87
18000	1601.39	849.43	600.01	476.23	402.68	354.25	320.17	295.03	275.86	260.86	248.88	239.15
19000	1690.35	896.62	633.35	502.68	425.05	373.93	337.95	311.42	291.19	275.35	262.70	252.44
20000	1779.32	943.81	666.68	529.14	447.42	393.61	355.74	327.82	306.52	289.84	276.53	265.72
21000	1868.29	991.00	700.02	555.60	469.80	413.29	373.53	344.21	321.84	304.34	290.36	279.01
22000	1957.25	1038.19	733.35	582.05	492.17	432.97	391.31	360.60	337.17	318.83	304.18	292.30
23000	2046.22	1085.38	766.68	608.51	514.54	452.66	409.10	376.99	352.49	333.32	318.01	305.58
24000	2135.18	1132.57	800.02	634.97	536.91	472.34	426.89	393.38	367.82	347.81	331.84	318.87
25000	2224.15	1179.76	833.35	661.42	559.28	492.02	444.67	409.77	383.14	362.30	345.66	332.15
26000	2313.12	1226.95	866.68	687.88	581.65	511.70	462.46	426.16	398.47	376.80	359.49	345.44
27000	2402.08	1274.14	900.02	714.34	604.02	531.38	480.25	442.55	413.79	391.29	373.31	358.73
28000	2491.05	1321.33	933.35	740.79	626.39	551.06	498.03	458.94	429.12	405.78	387.14	372.01
29000	2580.01	1368.52	966.69	767.25	648.76	570.74	515.82	475.33	444.45	420.27	400.97	385.30
30000	2668.98	1415.71	1000.02	793.71	671.13	590.42	533.61	491.72	459.77	434.76	414.79	398.58
31000	2757.94	1462.90	1033.35	820.16	693.51	610.10	551.39	508.11	475.10	449.26	428.62	411.87
32000	2846.91	1510.09	1066.69	846.62	715.88	629.78	569.18	524.50	490.42	463.75	442.45	425.16
33000	2935.88	1557.29	1100.02	873.08	738.25	649.46	586.97	540.89	505.75	478.24	456.27	438.44
34000	3024.84	1604.48	1133.36	899.53	760.62	669.14	604.75	557.28	521.07	492.73	470.10	451.73
35000	3113.81	1651.67	1166.69	925.99	782.99	688.82	622.54	573.67	536.40	507.22	483.92	465.01
36000	3202.77	1698.86	1200.02	952.45	805.36	708.50	640.33	590.06	551.72	521.72	497.75	478.30
37000	3291.74	1746.05	1233.36	978.90	827.73	728.18	658.11	606.45	567.05	536.21	511.58	491.59
38000	3380.70	1793.24	1266.69	1005.36	850.10	747.86	675.90	622.84	582.38	550.70	525.40	504.87
39000	3469.67	1840.43	1300.02	1031.82	872.47	767.54	693.69	639.24	597.70	565.19	539.23	518.16
40000	3558.64	1887.62	1333.36	1058.28	894.84	787.22	711.47	655.63	613.03	579.68	553.06	531.44
41000	3647.60	1934.81	1366.69	1084.73	917.22	806.90	729.26	672.02	628.35	594.18	566.88	544.73
42000	3736.57	1982.00	1400.03	1111.19	939.59	826.58	747.05	688.41	643.68	608.67	580.71	558.02
43000	3825.53	2029.19	1433.36	1137.65	961.96	846.26	764.83	704.80	659.00	623.16	594.53	571.30
44000	3914.50	2076.38	1466.69	1164.10	984.33	865.94	782.62	721.19	674.33	637.65	608.36	584.59
45000	4003.47	2123.57	1500.03	1190.56	1006.70	885.62	800.41	737.58	689.65	652.14	622.19	597.87
46000	4092.43	2170.76	1533.36	1217.02	1029.07	905.31	818.19	753.97	704.98	666.64	636.01	611.16
47000	4181.40	2217.95	1566.70	1243.47	1051.44	924.99	835.98	770.36	720.31	681.13	649.84	624.45
48000	4270.36	2265.14	1600.03	1269.93	1073.81	944.67	853.77	786.75	735.63	695.62	663.67	637.73
49000	4359.33	2312.33	1633.36	1296.39	1096.18	964.35	871.55	803.14	750.96	710.11	677.49	651.02
50000	4448.29	2359.52	1666.70	1322.84	1118.55	984.03	889.34	819.53	766.28	724.60	691.32	664.30
55000	4893.12	2595.47	1833.37	1455.13	1230.41	1082.43	978.27	901.48	842.91	797.06	760.45	730.73
60000	5337.95	2831.42	2000.04	1587.41	1342.26	1180.83	1067.21	983.44	919.54	869.52	829.58	797.16
65000	5782.78	3067.37	2166.70	1719.69	1454.12	1279.23	1156.14	1065.39	996.17	941.98	898.71	863.59
70000	6227.61	3303.33	2333.37	1851.98	1565.97	1377.64	1245.07	1147.34	1072.79	1014.44	967.84	930.02
75000	6672.44	3539.28	2500.04	1984.26	1677.83	1476.04	1334.01	1229.29	1149.42	1086.90	1036.97	996.45
80000	7117.27	3775.23	2666.71	2116.55	1789.68	1574.44	1422.94	1311.25	1226.05	1159.36	1106.11	1062.88
85000	7562.10	4011.18	2833.38	2248.83	1901.54	1672.84	1511.88	1393.20	1302.68	1231.82	1175.24	1129.31
90000	8006.93	4247.13	3000.05	2381.11	2013.39	1771.24	1600.81	1475.15	1379.30	1304.28	1244.37	1195.74
95000	8451.75	4483.08	3166.72	2513.40	2125.25	1869.65	1689.74	1557.10	1455.93	1376.74	1313.50	1262.17
100000	8896.58	4719.04	3333.39	2645.68	2237.10	1968.05	1778.68	1639.06	1532.56	1449.20	1382.63	1328.60

MONTHLY 12.25%
PAYMENT REQUIRED TO AMORTIZE A LOAN

TERM AMOUNT	13 YEARS	14 YEARS	15 YEARS	16 YEARS	17 YEARS	18 YEARS	19 YEARS	20 YEARS	25 YEARS	30 YEARS	35 YEARS	40 YEARS
50	.65	.63	.61	.60	.59	.58	.57	.56	.54	.53	.52	.52
100	1.29	1.25	1.22	1.20	1.17	1.15	1.14	1.12	1.08	1.05	1.04	1.03
200	2.57	2.50	2.44	2.39	2.34	2.30	2.27	2.24	2.15	2.10	2.08	2.06
300	3.86	3.75	3.65	3.58	3.51	3.45	3.40	3.36	3.22	3.15	3.11	3.09
400	5.14	4.99	4.87	4.77	4.68	4.60	4.54	4.48	4.29	4.20	4.15	4.12
500	6.43	6.24	6.09	5.96	5.84	5.75	5.67	5.60	5.36	5.24	5.18	5.15
600	7.71	7.49	7.30	7.15	7.01	6.90	6.80	6.72	6.44	6.29	6.22	6.18
700	8.99	8.74	8.52	8.34	8.18	8.05	7.93	7.83	7.51	7.34	7.25	7.21
800	10.28	9.98	9.74	9.53	9.35	9.20	9.07	8.95	8.58	8.39	8.29	8.23
900	11.56	11.23	10.95	10.72	10.52	10.35	10.20	10.07	9.65	9.44	9.32	9.26
1000	12.85	12.48	12.17	11.91	11.68	11.49	11.33	11.19	10.72	10.48	10.36	10.29
2000	25.69	24.95	24.33	23.81	23.36	22.98	22.66	22.38	21.44	20.96	20.71	20.58
3000	38.53	37.42	36.49	35.71	35.04	34.47	33.98	33.56	32.16	31.44	31.07	30.87
4000	51.37	49.90	48.66	47.61	46.72	45.96	45.31	44.75	42.87	41.92	41.42	41.15
5000	64.21	62.37	60.82	59.51	58.40	57.45	56.64	55.93	53.59	52.40	51.77	51.44
6000	77.06	74.84	72.98	71.41	70.08	68.94	67.96	67.12	64.31	62.88	62.13	61.73
7000	89.90	87.31	85.15	83.32	81.76	80.43	79.29	78.30	75.03	73.36	72.48	72.01
8000	102.74	99.79	97.31	95.22	93.44	91.92	90.61	89.49	85.74	83.84	82.83	82.30
9000	115.58	112.26	109.47	107.12	105.12	103.41	101.94	100.68	96.46	94.32	93.19	92.59
10000	128.42	124.73	121.63	119.02	116.80	114.90	113.27	111.86	107.18	104.79	103.54	102.87
11000	141.26	137.20	133.80	130.92	128.48	126.39	124.59	123.05	117.90	115.27	113.90	113.16
12000	154.11	149.68	145.96	142.82	140.16	137.88	135.92	134.23	128.61	125.75	124.25	123.45
13000	166.95	162.15	158.12	154.72	151.83	149.37	147.25	145.42	139.33	136.23	134.60	133.73
14000	179.79	174.62	170.29	166.63	163.51	160.85	158.57	156.60	150.05	146.71	144.96	144.02
15000	192.63	187.09	182.45	178.53	175.19	172.34	169.90	167.79	160.77	157.19	155.31	154.31
16000	205.47	199.57	194.61	190.43	186.87	183.83	181.22	178.98	171.48	167.67	165.66	164.59
17000	218.31	212.04	206.78	202.33	198.55	195.32	192.55	190.16	182.20	178.15	176.02	174.88
18000	231.16	224.51	218.94	214.23	210.23	206.81	203.88	201.35	192.92	188.63	186.37	185.17
19000	244.00	236.98	231.10	226.13	221.91	218.30	215.20	212.53	203.64	199.11	196.73	195.46
20000	256.84	249.46	243.26	238.04	233.59	229.79	226.53	223.72	214.35	209.58	207.08	205.74
21000	269.68	261.93	255.43	249.94	245.27	241.28	237.86	234.90	225.07	220.06	217.43	216.03
22000	282.52	274.40	267.59	261.84	256.95	252.77	249.18	246.09	235.79	230.54	227.79	226.32
23000	295.36	286.87	279.75	273.74	268.63	264.26	260.51	257.27	246.51	241.02	238.14	236.60
24000	308.21	299.35	291.92	285.64	280.31	275.75	271.83	268.46	257.22	251.50	248.49	246.89
25000	321.05	311.82	304.08	297.54	291.99	287.24	283.16	279.65	267.94	261.98	258.85	257.18
26000	333.89	324.29	316.24	309.44	303.66	298.73	294.49	290.83	278.66	272.46	269.20	267.46
27000	346.73	336.76	328.41	321.35	315.34	310.22	305.81	302.02	289.38	282.94	279.56	277.75
28000	359.57	349.24	340.57	333.25	327.02	321.70	317.14	313.20	300.09	293.42	289.91	288.04
29000	372.42	361.71	352.73	345.15	338.70	333.19	328.46	324.39	310.81	303.89	300.26	298.32
30000	385.26	374.18	364.89	357.05	350.38	344.68	339.79	335.57	321.53	314.37	310.62	308.61
31000	398.10	386.65	377.06	368.95	362.06	356.17	351.12	346.76	332.25	324.85	320.97	318.90
32000	410.94	399.13	389.22	380.85	373.74	367.66	362.44	357.95	342.96	335.33	331.32	329.18
33000	423.78	411.60	401.38	392.75	385.42	379.15	373.77	369.13	353.68	345.81	341.68	339.47
34000	436.62	424.07	413.55	404.66	397.10	390.64	385.10	380.32	364.40	356.29	352.03	349.76
35000	449.47	436.54	425.71	416.56	408.78	402.13	396.42	391.50	375.12	366.77	362.38	360.05
36000	462.31	449.02	437.87	428.46	420.46	413.62	407.75	402.69	385.83	377.25	372.74	370.33
37000	475.15	461.49	450.04	440.36	432.14	425.11	419.07	413.87	396.55	387.73	383.09	380.62
38000	487.99	473.96	462.20	452.26	443.82	436.60	430.40	425.06	407.27	398.21	393.45	390.91
39000	500.83	486.43	474.36	464.16	455.49	448.09	441.73	436.25	417.99	408.68	403.80	401.19
40000	513.67	498.91	486.52	476.07	467.17	459.58	453.05	447.43	428.70	419.16	414.15	411.48
41000	526.52	511.38	498.69	487.97	478.85	471.07	464.38	458.62	439.42	429.64	424.51	421.77
42000	539.36	523.85	510.85	499.87	490.53	482.55	475.71	469.80	450.14	440.12	434.86	432.05
43000	552.20	536.32	523.01	511.77	502.21	494.04	487.03	480.99	460.85	450.60	445.21	442.34
44000	565.04	548.80	535.18	523.67	513.89	505.53	498.36	492.17	471.57	461.08	455.57	452.63
45000	577.88	561.27	547.34	535.57	525.57	517.02	509.68	503.36	482.29	471.56	465.92	462.91
46000	590.72	573.74	559.50	547.47	537.25	528.51	521.01	514.54	493.01	482.04	476.28	473.20
47000	603.57	586.21	571.67	559.38	548.93	540.00	532.34	525.73	503.72	492.52	486.63	483.49
48000	616.41	598.69	583.83	571.28	560.61	551.49	543.66	536.92	514.44	503.00	496.98	493.77
49000	629.25	611.16	595.99	583.18	572.29	562.98	554.99	548.10	525.16	513.47	507.34	504.06
50000	642.09	623.63	608.15	595.08	583.97	574.47	566.31	559.29	535.88	523.95	517.69	514.35
55000	706.30	685.99	668.97	654.59	642.36	631.91	622.95	615.22	589.46	576.35	569.46	565.78
60000	770.51	748.36	729.78	714.10	700.76	689.36	679.58	671.14	643.05	628.74	621.23	617.22
65000	834.72	810.72	790.60	773.60	759.15	746.81	736.21	727.07	696.64	681.14	673.00	668.65
70000	898.93	873.08	851.41	833.11	817.55	804.25	792.84	783.00	750.23	733.53	724.76	720.09
75000	963.13	935.45	912.23	892.62	875.95	861.70	849.47	838.93	803.81	785.93	776.53	771.52
80000	1027.34	997.81	973.04	952.13	934.34	919.15	906.10	894.86	857.40	838.32	828.30	822.95
85000	1091.55	1060.17	1033.86	1011.63	992.74	976.59	962.73	950.78	910.99	890.72	880.07	874.39
90000	1155.76	1122.53	1094.67	1071.14	1051.14	1034.04	1019.36	1006.71	964.57	943.11	931.84	925.82
95000	1219.97	1184.90	1155.49	1130.65	1109.53	1091.49	1075.99	1062.64	1018.16	995.51	983.61	977.26
100000	1284.18	1247.26	1216.30	1190.16	1167.93	1148.93	1132.62	1118.57	1071.75	1047.90	1035.38	1028.69

12.50%

MONTHLY

PAYMENT REQUIRED TO AMORTIZE A LOAN

TERM AMOUNT	1 YEAR	2 YEARS	3 YEARS	4 YEARS	5 YEARS	6 YEARS	7 YEARS	8 YEARS	9 YEARS	10 YEARS	11 YEARS	12 YEARS
50	4.46	2.37	1.68	1.33	1.13	1.00	.90	.83	.78	.74	.70	.68
100	8.91	4.74	3.35	2.66	2.25	1.99	1.80	1.66	1.55	1.47	1.40	1.35
200	17.82	9.47	6.70	5.32	4.50	3.97	3.59	3.31	3.10	2.93	2.80	2.69
300	26.73	14.20	10.04	7.98	6.75	5.95	5.38	4.96	4.65	4.40	4.20	4.04
400	35.64	18.93	13.39	10.64	9.00	7.93	7.17	6.62	6.19	5.86	5.60	5.38
500	44.55	23.66	16.73	13.29	11.25	9.91	8.97	8.27	7.74	7.32	6.99	6.72
600	53.45	28.39	20.08	15.95	13.50	11.89	10.76	9.92	9.29	8.79	8.39	8.07
700	62.36	33.12	23.42	18.61	15.75	13.87	12.55	11.58	10.83	10.25	9.79	9.41
800	71.27	37.85	26.77	21.27	18.00	15.85	14.34	13.23	12.38	11.72	11.19	10.76
900	80.18	42.58	30.11	23.93	20.25	17.84	16.13	14.88	13.93	13.18	12.58	12.10
1000	89.09	47.31	33.46	26.58	22.50	19.82	17.93	16.53	15.47	14.64	13.98	13.44
2000	178.17	94.62	66.91	53.16	45.00	39.63	35.85	33.06	30.94	29.28	27.96	26.88
3000	267.25	141.93	100.37	79.74	67.50	59.44	53.77	49.59	46.41	43.92	41.93	40.32
4000	356.34	189.23	133.82	106.32	90.00	79.25	71.69	66.12	61.88	58.56	55.91	53.76
5000	445.42	236.54	167.27	132.90	112.49	99.06	89.61	82.65	77.34	73.19	69.88	67.20
6000	534.50	283.85	200.73	159.48	134.99	118.87	107.53	99.18	92.81	87.83	83.86	80.64
7000	623.59	331.16	234.18	186.06	157.49	138.68	125.45	115.71	108.28	102.47	97.83	94.08
8000	712.67	378.46	267.63	212.64	179.99	158.49	143.37	132.24	123.75	117.11	111.81	107.51
9000	801.75	425.77	301.09	239.22	202.49	178.31	161.30	148.76	139.21	131.74	125.78	120.95
10000	890.83	473.08	334.54	265.80	224.98	198.12	179.22	165.29	154.68	146.38	139.76	134.39
11000	979.92	520.39	367.99	292.38	247.48	217.93	197.14	181.82	170.15	161.02	153.73	147.83
12000	1069.00	567.69	401.45	318.96	269.98	237.74	215.06	198.35	185.62	175.66	167.71	161.27
13000	1158.08	615.00	434.90	345.54	292.48	257.55	232.98	214.88	201.08	190.29	181.69	174.71
14000	1247.17	662.31	468.36	372.12	314.98	277.36	250.90	231.41	216.55	204.93	195.66	188.15
15000	1336.25	709.61	501.81	398.70	337.47	297.17	268.82	247.94	232.02	219.57	209.64	201.58
16000	1425.33	756.92	535.26	425.28	359.97	316.98	286.74	264.47	247.49	234.21	223.61	215.02
17000	1514.41	804.23	568.72	451.86	382.47	336.80	304.67	280.99	262.95	248.84	237.59	228.46
18000	1603.50	851.54	602.17	478.44	404.97	356.61	322.59	297.52	278.42	263.48	251.56	241.90
19000	1692.58	898.84	635.62	505.02	427.47	376.42	340.51	314.05	293.89	278.12	265.54	255.34
20000	1781.66	946.15	669.08	531.60	449.96	396.23	358.43	330.58	309.36	292.76	279.51	268.78
21000	1870.75	993.46	702.53	558.18	472.46	416.04	376.35	347.11	324.82	307.39	293.49	282.22
22000	1959.83	1040.77	735.98	584.76	494.96	435.85	394.27	363.64	340.29	322.03	307.46	295.65
23000	2048.91	1088.07	769.44	611.34	517.46	455.66	412.19	380.17	355.76	336.67	321.44	309.09
24000	2137.99	1135.38	802.89	637.92	539.96	475.47	430.11	396.70	371.23	351.31	335.42	322.53
25000	2227.08	1182.69	836.35	664.50	562.45	495.28	448.04	413.23	386.69	365.95	349.39	335.97
26000	2316.16	1230.00	869.80	691.08	584.95	515.10	465.96	429.75	402.16	380.58	363.37	349.41
27000	2405.24	1277.30	903.25	717.66	607.45	534.91	483.88	446.28	417.63	395.22	377.34	362.85
28000	2494.33	1324.61	936.71	744.24	629.95	554.72	501.80	462.81	433.10	409.86	391.32	376.29
29000	2583.41	1371.92	970.16	770.82	652.45	574.53	519.72	479.34	448.56	424.50	405.29	389.72
30000	2672.49	1419.22	1003.61	797.40	674.94	594.34	537.64	495.87	464.03	439.13	419.27	403.16
31000	2761.57	1466.53	1037.07	823.98	697.44	614.15	555.56	512.40	479.50	453.77	433.24	416.60
32000	2850.66	1513.84	1070.52	850.56	719.94	633.96	573.48	528.93	494.97	468.41	447.22	430.04
33000	2939.74	1561.15	1103.97	877.14	742.44	653.77	591.41	545.46	510.43	483.05	461.19	443.48
34000	3028.82	1608.45	1137.43	903.72	764.93	673.59	609.33	561.98	525.90	497.68	475.17	456.92
35000	3117.91	1655.76	1170.88	930.30	787.43	693.40	627.25	578.51	541.37	512.32	489.15	470.36
36000	3206.99	1703.07	1204.34	956.88	809.93	713.21	645.17	595.04	556.84	526.96	503.12	483.79
37000	3296.07	1750.38	1237.79	983.46	832.43	733.02	663.09	611.57	572.30	541.60	517.10	497.23
38000	3385.15	1797.68	1271.24	1010.04	854.93	752.83	681.01	628.10	587.77	556.23	531.07	510.67
39000	3474.24	1844.99	1304.70	1036.63	877.42	772.64	698.93	644.63	603.24	570.87	545.05	524.11
40000	3563.32	1892.30	1338.15	1063.20	899.92	792.45	716.85	661.16	618.71	585.51	559.02	537.55
41000	3652.40	1939.60	1371.60	1089.78	922.42	812.26	734.78	677.69	634.17	600.15	573.00	550.99
42000	3741.49	1986.91	1405.06	1116.36	944.92	832.07	752.70	694.21	649.64	614.78	586.97	564.43
43000	3830.57	2034.22	1438.51	1142.94	967.42	851.89	770.62	710.74	665.11	629.42	600.95	577.86
44000	3919.65	2081.53	1471.96	1169.52	989.91	871.70	788.54	727.27	680.58	644.06	614.92	591.30
45000	4008.73	2128.83	1505.42	1196.10	1012.41	891.51	806.46	743.80	696.04	658.70	628.90	604.74
46000	4097.82	2176.14	1538.87	1222.68	1034.91	911.32	824.38	760.33	711.51	673.34	642.87	618.18
47000	4186.90	2223.45	1572.33	1249.26	1057.41	931.13	842.30	776.86	726.98	687.97	656.85	631.62
48000	4275.98	2270.76	1605.78	1275.84	1079.91	950.94	860.22	793.39	742.45	702.61	670.83	645.06
49000	4365.07	2318.06	1639.23	1302.42	1102.40	970.75	878.15	809.92	757.91	717.25	684.80	658.50
50000	4454.15	2365.37	1672.69	1329.00	1124.90	990.56	896.07	826.45	773.38	731.89	698.78	671.93
55000	4899.56	2601.91	1839.95	1461.90	1237.39	1089.62	985.67	909.09	850.72	805.07	768.65	739.13
60000	5344.98	2838.44	2007.22	1594.80	1349.88	1188.68	1075.28	991.73	928.06	878.26	838.53	806.32
65000	5790.39	3074.98	2174.49	1727.70	1462.37	1287.73	1164.89	1074.38	1005.40	951.45	908.41	873.51
70000	6235.81	3311.52	2341.76	1860.60	1574.86	1386.79	1254.49	1157.02	1082.73	1024.64	978.29	940.71
75000	6681.22	3548.05	2509.03	1993.50	1687.35	1485.84	1344.10	1239.67	1160.07	1097.83	1048.16	1007.90
80000	7126.63	3784.59	2676.30	2126.40	1799.84	1584.90	1433.70	1322.31	1237.41	1171.01	1118.04	1075.09
85000	7572.05	4021.13	2843.56	2259.30	1912.33	1683.96	1523.31	1404.95	1314.75	1244.20	1187.92	1142.28
90000	8017.46	4257.66	3010.83	2392.20	2024.82	1783.01	1612.92	1487.60	1392.08	1317.39	1257.79	1209.48
95000	8462.88	4494.20	3178.10	2525.10	2137.31	1882.07	1702.52	1570.24	1469.42	1390.58	1327.67	1276.67
100000	8908.29	4730.74	3345.37	2658.00	2249.80	1981.12	1792.13	1652.89	1546.76	1463.77	1397.55	1343.86

MONTHLY   12.50%

PAYMENT REQUIRED TO AMORTIZE A LOAN

TERM AMOUNT	13 YEARS	14 YEARS	15 YEARS	16 YEARS	17 YEARS	18 YEARS	19 YEARS	20 YEARS	25 YEARS	30 YEARS	35 YEARS	40 YEARS
50	.65	.64	.62	.61	.60	.59	.58	.57	.55	.54	.53	.53
100	1.30	1.27	1.24	1.21	1.19	1.17	1.15	1.14	1.10	1.07	1.06	1.05
200	2.60	2.53	2.47	2.42	2.37	2.34	2.30	2.28	2.19	2.14	2.12	2.10
300	3.90	3.79	3.70	3.63	3.56	3.50	3.45	3.41	3.28	3.21	3.17	3.15
400	5.20	5.06	4.94	4.83	4.74	4.67	4.60	4.55	4.37	4.27	4.23	4.20
500	6.50	6.32	6.17	6.04	5.93	5.84	5.75	5.69	5.46	5.34	5.28	5.25
600	7.80	7.58	7.40	7.25	7.11	7.00	6.90	6.82	6.55	6.41	6.34	6.30
700	9.10	8.85	8.63	8.45	8.30	8.17	8.05	7.96	7.64	7.48	7.39	7.35
800	10.40	10.11	9.87	9.66	9.48	9.33	9.20	9.09	8.73	8.54	8.45	8.40
900	11.70	11.37	11.10	10.87	10.67	10.50	10.35	10.23	9.82	9.61	9.50	9.45
1000	13.00	12.64	12.33	12.07	11.85	11.67	11.50	11.37	10.91	10.68	10.56	10.49
2000	26.00	25.27	24.66	24.14	23.70	23.33	23.00	22.73	21.81	21.35	21.11	20.98
3000	39.00	37.90	36.98	36.21	35.55	34.99	34.50	34.09	32.72	32.02	31.66	31.47
4000	52.00	50.53	49.31	48.27	47.39	46.65	46.00	45.45	43.62	42.70	42.22	41.96
5000	64.99	63.16	61.63	60.34	59.24	58.31	57.50	56.81	54.52	53.37	52.77	52.45
6000	77.99	75.80	73.96	72.41	71.09	69.97	69.00	68.17	65.43	64.04	63.32	62.94
7000	90.99	88.43	86.28	84.47	82.94	81.63	80.50	79.53	76.33	74.71	73.87	73.43
8000	103.99	101.06	98.61	96.54	94.78	93.29	92.00	90.90	87.23	85.39	84.43	83.92
9000	116.98	113.69	110.93	108.61	106.63	104.95	103.50	102.26	98.14	96.06	94.98	94.41
10000	129.98	126.32	123.26	120.67	118.48	116.61	115.00	113.62	109.04	106.73	105.53	104.90
11000	142.98	138.95	135.58	132.74	130.32	128.27	126.50	124.98	119.94	117.40	116.08	115.39
12000	155.98	151.59	147.91	144.81	142.17	139.93	138.00	136.34	130.85	128.08	126.64	125.88
13000	168.97	164.22	160.23	156.87	154.02	151.59	149.50	147.70	141.75	138.75	137.19	136.36
14000	181.97	176.85	172.56	168.94	165.87	163.25	161.00	159.06	152.65	149.42	147.74	146.85
15000	194.97	189.48	184.88	181.01	177.71	174.91	172.50	170.43	163.56	160.09	158.29	157.34
16000	207.97	202.11	197.21	193.07	189.56	186.57	184.00	181.79	174.46	170.77	168.85	167.83
17000	220.97	214.74	209.53	205.14	201.41	198.23	195.50	193.15	185.37	181.44	179.40	178.32
18000	233.96	227.38	221.86	217.21	213.26	209.89	207.00	204.51	196.27	192.11	189.95	188.81
19000	246.96	240.01	234.18	229.27	225.10	221.55	218.50	215.87	207.17	202.78	200.50	199.30
20000	259.96	252.64	246.51	241.34	236.95	233.21	230.00	227.23	218.08	213.46	211.06	209.79
21000	272.96	265.27	258.83	253.41	248.80	244.87	241.49	238.59	228.98	224.13	221.61	220.28
22000	285.95	277.90	271.16	265.47	260.64	256.53	252.99	249.96	239.88	234.80	232.16	230.77
23000	298.95	290.53	283.49	277.54	272.49	268.19	264.49	261.32	250.79	245.47	242.71	241.26
24000	311.95	303.17	295.81	289.61	284.34	279.85	275.99	272.68	261.69	256.15	253.27	251.75
25000	324.95	315.80	308.14	301.67	296.19	291.51	287.49	284.04	272.59	266.82	263.82	262.23
26000	337.94	328.43	320.46	313.74	308.03	303.17	298.99	295.40	283.50	277.49	274.37	272.72
27000	350.94	341.06	332.79	325.81	319.88	314.83	310.49	306.76	294.40	288.16	284.92	283.21
28000	363.94	353.69	345.11	337.87	331.73	326.49	321.99	318.12	305.30	298.84	295.48	293.70
29000	376.94	366.32	357.44	349.94	343.58	338.15	333.49	329.49	316.21	309.51	306.03	304.19
30000	389.93	378.96	369.76	362.01	355.42	349.81	344.99	340.85	327.11	320.18	316.58	314.68
31000	402.93	391.59	382.09	374.07	367.27	361.47	356.49	352.21	338.01	330.85	327.13	325.17
32000	415.93	404.22	394.41	386.14	379.12	373.13	367.99	363.57	348.92	341.53	337.69	335.66
33000	428.93	416.85	406.74	398.21	390.96	384.79	379.49	374.93	359.82	352.20	348.24	346.15
34000	441.93	429.48	419.06	410.27	402.81	396.45	390.99	386.29	370.73	362.87	358.79	356.64
35000	454.92	442.11	431.39	422.34	414.66	408.11	402.49	397.65	381.63	373.55	369.34	367.13
36000	467.92	454.75	443.71	434.41	426.51	419.77	413.99	409.02	392.53	384.22	379.90	377.62
37000	480.92	467.38	456.04	446.47	438.35	431.43	425.49	420.38	403.44	394.89	390.45	388.11
38000	493.92	480.01	468.36	458.54	450.20	443.09	436.99	431.74	414.34	405.56	401.00	398.59
39000	506.91	492.64	480.69	470.61	462.05	454.75	448.49	443.10	425.24	416.24	411.55	409.08
40000	519.91	505.27	493.01	482.67	473.90	466.41	459.99	454.46	436.15	426.91	422.11	419.57
41000	532.91	517.90	505.34	494.74	485.74	478.07	471.48	465.82	447.05	437.58	432.66	430.06
42000	545.91	530.54	517.66	506.81	497.59	489.73	482.98	477.18	457.95	448.25	443.21	440.55
43000	558.90	543.17	529.99	518.87	509.44	501.39	494.48	488.55	468.86	458.93	453.76	451.04
44000	571.90	555.80	542.31	530.94	521.28	513.05	505.98	499.91	479.76	469.60	464.32	461.53
45000	584.90	568.43	554.64	543.01	533.13	524.71	517.48	511.27	490.66	480.27	474.87	472.02
46000	597.90	581.06	566.97	555.07	544.98	536.37	528.98	522.63	501.57	490.94	485.42	482.51
47000	610.90	593.69	579.29	567.14	556.83	548.03	540.48	533.99	512.47	501.62	495.97	493.00
48000	623.89	606.33	591.62	579.21	568.67	559.69	551.98	545.35	523.37	512.29	506.53	503.49
49000	636.89	618.96	603.94	591.27	580.52	571.35	563.48	556.71	534.28	522.96	517.08	513.98
50000	649.89	631.59	616.27	603.34	592.37	583.01	574.98	568.08	545.18	533.63	527.63	524.46
55000	714.88	694.75	677.89	663.67	651.60	641.31	632.48	624.88	599.70	587.00	580.39	576.91
60000	779.86	757.91	739.52	724.01	710.84	699.61	689.98	681.69	654.22	640.36	633.16	629.36
65000	844.85	821.06	801.14	784.34	770.08	757.91	747.47	738.50	708.74	693.72	685.92	681.80
70000	909.84	884.22	862.77	844.67	829.31	816.21	804.97	795.30	763.25	747.09	738.68	734.25
75000	974.83	947.38	924.40	905.01	888.55	874.51	862.47	852.11	817.77	800.45	791.45	786.69
80000	1039.82	1010.54	986.02	965.34	947.79	932.81	919.97	908.92	872.29	853.81	844.21	839.14
85000	1104.81	1073.70	1047.65	1025.67	1007.02	991.11	977.46	965.72	926.81	907.17	896.97	891.59
90000	1169.79	1136.86	1109.27	1086.01	1066.26	1049.41	1034.96	1022.53	981.32	960.54	949.73	944.03
95000	1234.78	1200.01	1170.90	1146.34	1125.49	1107.71	1092.46	1079.34	1035.84	1013.90	1002.50	996.48
100000	1299.77	1263.17	1232.53	1206.67	1184.73	1166.01	1149.96	1136.15	1090.36	1067.26	1055.26	1048.92

12.75%
MONTHLY
PAYMENT REQUIRED TO AMORTIZE A LOAN

TERM / AMOUNT	1 YEAR	2 YEARS	3 YEARS	4 YEARS	5 YEARS	6 YEARS	7 YEARS	8 YEARS	9 YEARS	10 YEARS	11 YEARS	12 YEARS
50	4.47	2.38	1.68	1.34	1.14	1.00	.91	.84	.79	.74	.71	.68
100	8.93	4.75	3.36	2.68	2.27	2.00	1.81	1.67	1.57	1.48	1.42	1.36
200	17.85	9.49	6.72	5.35	4.53	3.99	3.62	3.34	3.13	2.96	2.83	2.72
300	26.77	14.23	10.08	8.02	6.79	5.99	5.42	5.01	4.69	4.44	4.24	4.08
400	35.69	18.97	13.43	10.69	9.06	7.98	7.23	6.67	6.25	5.92	5.66	5.44
500	44.61	23.72	16.79	13.36	11.32	9.98	9.03	8.34	7.81	7.40	7.07	6.80
600	53.53	28.46	20.15	16.03	13.58	11.97	10.84	10.01	9.37	8.88	8.48	8.16
700	62.45	33.20	23.51	18.70	15.84	13.96	12.64	11.67	10.93	10.35	9.89	9.52
800	71.37	37.94	26.86	21.37	18.11	15.96	14.45	13.34	12.49	11.83	11.31	10.88
900	80.29	42.69	30.22	24.04	20.37	17.95	16.26	15.01	14.05	13.31	12.72	12.24
1000	89.21	47.43	33.58	26.71	22.63	19.95	18.06	16.67	15.62	14.79	14.13	13.60
2000	178.41	94.85	67.15	53.41	45.26	39.89	36.12	33.34	31.23	29.57	28.26	27.19
3000	267.61	142.28	100.73	80.12	67.88	59.83	54.17	50.01	46.84	44.36	42.38	40.78
4000	356.81	189.70	134.30	106.82	90.51	79.77	72.23	66.68	62.45	59.14	56.51	54.37
5000	446.01	237.13	167.87	133.52	113.13	99.72	90.29	83.34	78.06	73.92	70.63	67.97
6000	535.21	284.55	201.45	160.23	135.76	119.66	108.34	100.01	93.67	88.71	84.76	81.56
7000	624.41	331.98	235.02	186.93	158.38	139.60	126.40	116.68	109.28	103.49	98.88	95.15
8000	713.61	379.40	268.59	213.63	181.01	159.54	144.46	133.35	124.89	118.28	113.01	108.74
9000	802.81	426.83	302.17	240.34	203.63	179.49	162.51	150.01	140.50	133.06	127.13	122.33
10000	892.01	474.25	335.74	267.04	226.26	199.43	180.57	166.68	156.11	147.84	141.26	135.93
11000	981.21	521.67	369.32	293.74	248.88	219.37	198.62	183.35	171.72	162.63	155.38	149.52
12000	1070.41	569.10	402.89	320.45	271.51	239.31	216.68	200.02	187.33	177.41	169.51	163.11
13000	1159.61	616.52	436.46	347.15	294.13	259.26	234.74	216.69	202.94	192.20	183.63	176.70
14000	1248.81	663.95	470.04	373.86	316.76	279.20	252.79	233.35	218.55	206.98	197.76	190.29
15000	1338.01	711.37	503.61	400.56	339.38	299.14	270.85	250.02	234.16	221.76	211.89	203.89
16000	1427.21	758.80	537.18	427.26	362.01	319.08	288.91	266.69	249.77	236.55	226.01	217.48
17000	1516.41	806.22	570.76	453.97	384.64	339.03	306.96	283.36	265.38	251.33	240.14	231.07
18000	1605.61	853.65	604.33	480.67	407.26	358.97	325.02	300.02	280.99	266.12	254.26	244.66
19000	1694.81	901.07	637.90	507.37	429.89	378.91	343.08	316.69	296.60	280.90	268.39	258.25
20000	1784.01	948.49	671.48	534.08	452.51	398.85	361.13	333.36	312.21	295.68	282.51	271.85
21000	1873.21	995.92	705.05	560.78	475.14	418.80	379.19	350.03	327.82	310.47	296.64	285.44
22000	1962.41	1043.34	738.63	587.48	497.76	438.74	397.24	366.69	343.43	325.25	310.76	299.03
23000	2051.61	1090.77	772.20	614.19	520.39	458.68	415.30	383.36	359.04	340.04	324.89	312.62
24000	2140.81	1138.19	805.77	640.89	543.01	478.62	433.36	400.03	374.65	354.82	339.01	326.21
25000	2230.01	1185.62	839.35	667.59	565.64	498.57	451.41	416.70	390.26	369.60	353.14	339.81
26000	2319.21	1233.04	872.92	694.30	588.26	518.51	469.47	433.37	405.87	384.39	367.26	353.40
27000	2408.41	1280.47	906.49	721.00	610.89	538.45	487.53	450.03	421.48	399.17	381.39	366.99
28000	2497.61	1327.89	940.07	747.71	633.51	558.39	505.58	466.70	437.09	413.96	395.52	380.58
29000	2586.81	1375.31	973.64	774.41	656.14	578.33	523.64	483.37	452.70	428.74	409.64	394.17
30000	2676.01	1422.74	1007.21	801.11	678.76	598.28	541.69	500.04	468.31	443.52	423.77	407.77
31000	2765.21	1470.16	1040.79	827.82	701.39	618.22	559.75	516.70	483.92	458.31	437.89	421.36
32000	2854.41	1517.59	1074.36	854.52	724.01	638.16	577.81	533.37	499.53	473.09	452.02	434.95
33000	2943.61	1565.01	1107.94	881.22	746.64	658.10	595.86	550.04	515.14	487.88	466.14	448.54
34000	3032.81	1612.44	1141.51	907.93	769.27	678.05	613.92	566.71	530.75	502.66	480.27	462.13
35000	3122.01	1659.86	1175.08	934.63	791.89	697.99	631.98	583.38	546.36	517.44	494.39	475.73
36000	3211.21	1707.29	1208.66	961.33	814.52	717.93	650.03	600.04	561.97	532.23	508.52	489.32
37000	3300.41	1754.71	1242.23	988.04	837.14	737.87	668.09	616.71	577.58	547.01	522.64	502.91
38000	3389.61	1802.14	1275.80	1014.74	859.77	757.82	686.15	633.38	593.19	561.80	536.77	516.50
39000	3478.81	1849.56	1309.38	1041.44	882.39	777.76	704.20	650.05	608.80	576.58	550.89	530.09
40000	3568.01	1896.98	1342.95	1068.15	905.02	797.70	722.26	666.71	624.41	591.36	565.02	543.69
41000	3657.21	1944.41	1376.53	1094.85	927.64	817.64	740.31	683.38	640.02	606.15	579.15	557.28
42000	3746.41	1991.83	1410.10	1121.56	950.27	837.59	758.37	700.05	655.63	620.93	593.27	570.87
43000	3835.61	2039.26	1443.67	1148.26	972.89	857.53	776.43	716.72	671.24	635.72	607.40	584.46
44000	3924.81	2086.68	1477.25	1174.96	995.52	877.47	794.48	733.38	686.86	650.50	621.52	598.05
45000	4014.01	2134.11	1510.82	1201.67	1018.14	897.41	812.54	750.05	702.47	665.28	635.65	611.65
46000	4103.21	2181.53	1544.39	1228.37	1040.77	917.36	830.60	766.72	718.08	680.07	649.77	625.24
47000	4192.41	2228.96	1577.97	1255.07	1063.39	937.30	848.65	783.39	733.69	694.85	663.90	638.83
48000	4281.61	2276.38	1611.54	1281.78	1086.02	957.24	866.71	800.06	749.30	709.64	678.02	652.42
49000	4370.81	2323.80	1645.11	1308.48	1108.64	977.18	884.76	816.72	764.91	724.42	692.15	666.01
50000	4460.01	2371.23	1678.69	1335.18	1131.27	997.13	902.82	833.39	780.52	739.20	706.27	679.61
55000	4906.01	2608.35	1846.56	1468.70	1244.40	1096.84	993.10	916.73	858.57	813.12	776.90	747.57
60000	5352.01	2845.47	2014.42	1602.22	1357.52	1196.55	1083.38	1000.07	936.62	887.04	847.53	815.53
65000	5798.01	3082.60	2182.29	1735.74	1470.65	1296.26	1173.67	1083.41	1014.67	960.96	918.15	883.49
70000	6244.01	3319.72	2350.16	1869.26	1583.78	1395.97	1263.95	1166.75	1092.72	1034.88	988.78	951.45
75000	6690.01	3556.84	2518.03	2002.77	1696.90	1495.69	1354.23	1250.08	1170.77	1108.80	1059.41	1019.41
80000	7136.01	3793.96	2685.90	2136.29	1810.03	1595.40	1444.51	1333.42	1248.82	1182.72	1130.04	1087.37
85000	7582.01	4031.09	2853.77	2269.81	1923.16	1695.11	1534.79	1416.76	1326.87	1256.64	1200.66	1155.33
90000	8028.01	4268.21	3021.63	2403.33	2036.28	1794.82	1625.07	1500.10	1404.93	1330.56	1271.29	1223.29
95000	8474.01	4505.33	3189.50	2536.85	2149.41	1894.53	1715.36	1583.44	1482.98	1404.48	1341.92	1291.25
100000	8920.01	4742.45	3357.37	2670.36	2262.54	1994.25	1805.64	1666.78	1561.03	1478.40	1412.54	1359.21

MONTHLY 12.75%

PAYMENT REQUIRED TO AMORTIZE A LOAN

TERM AMOUNT	13 YEARS	14 YEARS	15 YEARS	16 YEARS	17 YEARS	18 YEARS	19 YEARS	20 YEARS	25 YEARS	30 YEARS	35 YEARS	40 YEARS
50	.66	.64	.63	.62	.61	.60	.59	.58	.56	.55	.54	.54
100	1.32	1.28	1.25	1.23	1.21	1.19	1.17	1.16	1.11	1.09	1.08	1.07
200	2.64	2.56	2.50	2.45	2.41	2.37	2.34	2.31	2.22	2.18	2.16	2.14
300	3.95	3.84	3.75	3.67	3.61	3.55	3.51	3.47	3.33	3.27	3.23	3.21
400	5.27	5.12	5.00	4.90	4.81	4.74	4.67	4.62	4.44	4.35	4.31	4.28
500	6.58	6.40	6.25	6.12	6.01	5.92	5.84	5.77	5.55	5.44	5.38	5.35
600	7.90	7.68	7.50	7.34	7.21	7.10	7.01	6.93	6.66	6.53	6.46	6.42
700	9.21	8.96	8.75	8.57	8.42	8.29	8.18	8.08	7.77	7.61	7.53	7.49
800	10.53	10.24	10.00	9.79	9.62	9.47	9.34	9.24	8.88	8.70	8.61	8.56
900	11.84	11.52	11.24	11.01	10.82	10.65	10.51	10.39	9.99	9.79	9.68	9.63
1000	13.16	12.80	12.49	12.24	12.02	11.84	11.68	11.54	11.10	10.87	10.76	10.70
2000	26.31	25.59	24.98	24.47	24.04	23.67	23.35	23.08	22.19	21.74	21.51	21.39
3000	39.47	38.38	37.47	36.70	36.05	35.50	35.03	34.62	33.28	32.61	32.26	32.08
4000	52.62	51.17	49.96	48.94	48.07	47.33	46.70	46.16	44.37	43.47	43.01	42.77
5000	65.78	63.96	62.45	61.17	60.09	59.16	58.37	57.70	55.46	54.34	53.76	53.46
6000	78.93	76.76	74.94	73.40	72.10	71.00	70.05	69.23	66.55	65.21	64.52	64.16
7000	92.09	89.55	87.42	85.63	84.12	82.83	81.72	80.77	77.64	76.07	75.27	74.85
8000	105.24	102.34	99.91	97.87	96.13	94.66	93.40	92.31	88.73	86.94	86.02	85.54
9000	118.40	115.13	112.40	110.10	108.15	106.49	105.07	103.85	99.82	97.81	96.77	96.23
10000	131.55	127.92	124.89	122.33	120.17	118.32	116.74	115.39	110.91	108.67	107.52	106.92
11000	144.70	140.71	137.38	134.57	132.18	130.15	128.42	126.92	122.00	119.54	118.28	117.62
12000	157.86	153.51	149.87	146.80	144.20	141.99	140.09	138.46	133.09	130.41	129.03	128.31
13000	171.01	166.30	162.35	159.03	156.22	153.82	151.76	150.00	144.18	141.28	139.78	139.00
14000	184.17	179.09	174.84	171.26	168.23	165.65	163.44	161.54	155.27	152.14	150.53	149.69
15000	197.32	191.88	187.33	183.50	180.25	177.48	175.11	173.08	166.36	163.01	161.28	160.38
16000	210.48	204.67	199.82	195.73	192.26	189.31	186.79	184.61	177.45	173.88	172.04	171.08
17000	223.63	217.46	212.31	207.96	204.28	201.14	198.46	196.15	188.54	184.74	182.79	181.77
18000	236.79	230.26	224.80	220.20	216.30	212.98	210.13	207.69	199.63	195.61	193.54	192.46
19000	249.94	243.05	237.28	232.43	228.31	224.81	221.81	219.23	210.72	206.48	204.29	203.15
20000	263.09	255.84	249.77	244.66	240.33	236.64	233.48	230.77	221.82	217.34	215.04	213.84
21000	276.25	268.63	262.26	256.89	252.35	248.47	245.15	242.31	232.91	228.21	225.04	224.54
22000	289.40	281.42	274.75	269.13	264.36	260.30	256.83	253.84	244.00	239.08	236.55	235.23
23000	302.56	294.21	287.24	281.36	276.38	272.13	268.50	265.38	255.09	249.94	247.30	245.92
24000	315.71	307.01	299.73	293.59	288.39	283.97	280.18	276.92	266.18	260.81	258.05	256.61
25000	328.87	319.80	312.21	305.83	300.41	295.80	291.85	288.46	277.27	271.68	268.80	267.30
26000	342.02	332.59	324.70	318.06	312.43	307.63	303.52	300.00	288.36	282.55	279.56	278.00
27000	355.18	345.38	337.19	330.29	324.44	319.46	315.20	311.53	299.45	293.41	290.31	288.69
28000	368.33	358.17	349.68	342.52	336.46	331.29	326.87	323.07	310.54	304.28	301.06	299.38
29000	381.48	370.96	362.17	354.76	348.48	343.12	338.54	334.61	321.63	315.15	311.81	310.07
30000	394.64	383.76	374.66	366.99	360.49	354.96	350.22	346.15	332.72	326.01	322.56	320.76
31000	407.79	396.55	387.14	379.22	372.51	366.79	361.89	357.69	343.81	336.88	333.32	331.46
32000	420.95	409.34	399.63	391.46	384.52	378.62	373.57	369.22	354.90	347.75	344.07	342.15
33000	434.10	422.13	412.12	403.69	396.54	390.45	385.24	380.76	365.99	358.61	354.82	352.84
34000	447.26	434.92	424.61	415.92	408.56	402.28	396.91	392.30	377.08	369.48	365.57	363.53
35000	460.41	447.72	437.10	428.15	420.57	414.11	408.59	403.84	388.17	380.35	376.32	374.22
36000	473.57	460.51	449.59	440.39	432.59	425.95	420.26	415.38	399.26	391.21	387.08	384.92
37000	486.72	473.30	462.07	452.62	444.61	437.78	431.93	426.92	410.35	402.08	397.83	395.61
38000	499.87	486.09	474.56	464.85	456.62	449.61	443.61	438.45	421.44	412.95	408.58	406.30
39000	513.03	498.88	487.05	477.09	468.64	461.44	455.28	449.99	432.54	423.82	419.33	416.99
40000	526.18	511.67	499.54	489.32	480.65	473.27	466.96	461.53	443.63	434.68	430.08	427.68
41000	539.34	524.47	512.03	501.55	492.67	485.10	478.63	473.07	454.72	445.55	440.84	438.38
42000	552.49	537.26	524.52	513.78	504.69	496.94	490.30	484.61	465.81	456.42	451.59	449.07
43000	565.65	550.05	537.00	526.02	516.70	508.77	501.98	496.14	476.90	467.28	462.34	459.76
44000	578.80	562.84	549.49	538.25	528.72	520.60	513.65	507.68	487.99	478.15	473.09	470.45
45000	591.96	575.63	561.98	550.48	540.74	532.43	525.32	519.22	499.08	489.02	483.84	481.14
46000	605.11	588.42	574.47	562.72	552.75	544.26	537.00	530.76	510.17	499.88	494.60	491.84
47000	618.26	601.22	586.96	574.95	564.77	556.09	548.67	542.30	521.26	510.75	505.35	502.53
48000	631.42	614.01	599.45	587.18	576.78	567.93	560.35	553.83	532.35	521.62	516.10	513.22
49000	644.57	626.80	611.94	599.41	588.80	579.76	572.02	565.37	543.44	532.48	526.85	523.91
50000	657.73	639.59	624.42	611.65	600.82	591.59	583.69	576.91	554.53	543.35	537.60	534.60
55000	723.50	703.55	686.87	672.81	660.90	650.75	642.06	634.60	609.98	597.69	591.36	588.06
60000	789.27	767.51	749.31	733.97	720.98	709.91	700.43	692.29	665.44	652.02	645.12	641.52
65000	855.04	831.47	811.75	795.14	781.06	769.07	758.80	749.98	720.89	706.36	698.88	694.98
70000	920.82	895.43	874.19	856.30	841.14	828.22	817.17	807.67	776.34	760.69	752.64	748.44
75000	986.59	959.38	936.63	917.47	901.22	887.38	875.54	865.36	831.79	815.02	806.40	801.90
80000	1052.36	1023.34	999.07	978.63	961.30	946.54	933.91	923.05	887.25	869.36	860.16	855.36
85000	1118.13	1087.30	1061.52	1039.80	1021.39	1005.70	992.28	980.74	942.70	923.69	913.92	908.82
90000	1183.91	1151.26	1123.96	1100.96	1081.47	1064.86	1050.64	1038.44	998.15	978.03	967.68	962.28
95000	1249.68	1215.22	1186.40	1162.12	1141.55	1124.02	1109.01	1096.13	1053.60	1032.36	1021.44	1015.74
100000	1315.45	1279.18	1248.84	1223.29	1201.63	1183.17	1167.38	1153.82	1109.06	1086.70	1075.20	1069.20

13.00%   MONTHLY

PAYMENT REQUIRED TO AMORTIZE A LOAN

TERM AMOUNT	1 YEAR	2 YEARS	3 YEARS	4 YEARS	5 YEARS	6 YEARS	7 YEARS	8 YEARS	9 YEARS	10 YEARS	11 YEARS	12 YEARS
50	4.47	2.38	1.69	1.35	1.14	1.01	.91	.85	.79	.75	.72	.69
100	8.94	4.76	3.37	2.69	2.28	2.01	1.82	1.69	1.58	1.50	1.43	1.38
200	17.87	9.51	6.74	5.37	4.56	4.02	3.64	3.37	3.16	2.99	2.86	2.75
300	26.80	14.27	10.11	8.05	6.83	6.03	5.46	5.05	4.73	4.48	4.29	4.13
400	35.73	19.02	13.48	10.74	9.11	8.03	7.28	6.73	6.31	5.98	5.72	5.50
500	44.66	23.78	16.85	13.42	11.38	10.04	9.10	8.41	7.88	7.47	7.14	6.88
600	53.60	28.53	20.22	16.10	13.66	12.05	10.92	10.09	9.46	8.96	8.57	8.25
700	62.53	33.28	23.59	18.78	15.93	14.06	12.74	11.77	11.03	10.46	10.00	9.63
800	71.46	38.04	26.96	21.47	18.21	16.06	14.56	13.45	12.61	11.95	11.43	11.00
900	80.39	42.79	30.33	24.15	20.48	18.07	16.38	15.13	14.18	13.44	12.85	12.38
1000	89.32	47.55	33.70	26.83	22.76	20.08	18.20	16.81	15.76	14.94	14.28	13.75
2000	178.64	95.09	67.39	53.66	45.51	40.15	36.39	33.62	31.51	29.87	28.56	27.50
3000	267.96	142.63	101.09	80.49	68.26	60.23	54.58	50.43	47.27	44.80	42.83	41.24
4000	357.27	190.17	134.78	107.31	91.02	80.30	72.77	67.23	63.02	59.73	57.11	54.99
5000	446.59	237.71	168.47	134.14	113.77	100.38	90.96	84.04	78.77	74.66	71.39	68.74
6000	535.91	285.26	202.17	160.97	136.52	120.45	109.16	100.85	94.53	89.59	85.66	82.48
7000	625.23	332.80	235.86	187.80	159.28	140.52	127.35	117.66	110.28	104.52	99.94	96.23
8000	714.54	380.34	269.56	214.62	182.03	160.60	145.54	134.46	126.03	119.45	114.21	109.98
9000	803.86	427.88	303.25	241.45	204.78	180.67	163.73	151.27	141.79	134.38	128.49	123.72
10000	893.18	475.42	336.94	268.28	227.54	200.75	181.92	168.08	157.54	149.32	142.77	137.47
11000	982.50	522.97	370.64	295.11	250.29	220.82	200.12	184.88	173.29	164.25	157.04	151.21
12000	1071.81	570.51	404.33	321.93	273.04	240.89	218.31	201.69	189.05	179.18	171.32	164.96
13000	1161.13	618.05	438.03	348.76	295.79	260.97	236.50	218.50	204.80	194.11	185.59	178.71
14000	1250.45	665.59	471.72	375.59	318.55	281.04	254.69	235.31	220.56	209.04	199.87	192.45
15000	1339.76	713.13	505.41	402.42	341.30	301.12	272.88	252.11	236.31	223.97	214.15	206.20
16000	1429.08	760.67	539.11	429.24	364.05	321.19	291.08	268.92	252.06	238.90	228.42	219.95
17000	1518.40	808.22	572.80	456.07	386.81	341.26	309.27	285.73	267.82	253.83	242.70	233.69
18000	1607.72	855.76	606.50	482.90	409.56	361.34	327.46	302.54	283.57	268.76	256.97	247.44
19000	1697.03	903.30	640.19	509.73	432.31	381.41	345.65	319.34	299.32	283.70	271.25	261.18
20000	1786.35	950.84	673.88	536.55	455.07	401.49	363.84	336.15	315.08	298.63	285.53	274.93
21000	1875.67	998.38	707.58	563.38	477.82	421.56	382.04	352.96	330.83	313.56	299.80	288.68
22000	1964.99	1045.93	741.27	590.21	500.57	441.64	400.23	369.76	346.58	328.49	314.08	302.42
23000	2054.30	1093.47	774.97	617.04	523.33	461.71	418.42	386.57	362.34	343.42	328.36	316.17
24000	2143.62	1141.01	808.66	643.86	546.08	481.78	436.61	403.38	378.09	358.35	342.63	329.92
25000	2232.94	1188.55	842.35	670.69	568.83	501.86	454.80	420.19	393.84	373.28	356.91	343.66
26000	2322.25	1236.09	876.05	697.52	591.58	521.93	473.00	436.99	409.60	388.21	371.18	357.41
27000	2411.57	1283.63	909.74	724.35	614.34	542.01	491.19	453.80	425.35	403.14	385.46	371.15
28000	2500.89	1331.18	943.44	751.17	637.09	562.08	509.38	470.61	441.11	418.08	399.74	384.90
29000	2590.21	1378.72	977.13	778.00	659.84	582.15	527.57	487.42	456.86	433.01	414.01	398.65
30000	2679.52	1426.26	1010.82	804.83	682.60	602.23	545.76	504.22	472.61	447.94	428.29	412.39
31000	2768.84	1473.80	1044.52	831.66	705.35	622.30	563.96	521.03	488.37	462.87	442.56	426.14
32000	2858.16	1521.34	1078.21	858.48	728.10	642.38	582.15	537.84	504.12	477.80	456.84	439.89
33000	2947.48	1568.89	1111.91	885.31	750.86	662.45	600.34	554.64	519.87	492.73	471.12	453.63
34000	3036.79	1616.43	1145.60	912.14	773.61	682.52	618.53	571.45	535.63	507.66	485.39	467.38
35000	3126.11	1663.97	1179.29	938.97	796.36	702.60	636.72	588.26	551.38	522.59	499.67	481.12
36000	3215.43	1711.51	1212.99	965.79	819.12	722.67	654.92	605.07	567.13	537.52	513.94	494.87
37000	3304.74	1759.05	1246.68	992.62	841.87	742.75	673.11	621.87	582.89	552.45	528.22	508.62
38000	3394.06	1806.59	1280.38	1019.45	864.62	762.82	691.30	638.68	598.64	567.39	542.50	522.36
39000	3483.38	1854.14	1314.07	1046.28	887.37	782.90	709.49	655.49	614.39	582.32	556.77	536.11
40000	3572.70	1901.68	1347.76	1073.10	910.13	802.97	727.68	672.30	630.15	597.25	571.05	549.86
41000	3662.01	1949.22	1381.46	1099.93	932.88	823.04	745.88	689.10	645.90	612.18	585.33	563.60
42000	3751.33	1996.76	1415.15	1126.76	955.63	843.12	764.07	705.91	661.66	627.11	599.60	577.35
43000	3840.65	2044.30	1448.84	1153.59	978.39	863.19	782.26	722.72	677.41	642.04	613.88	591.09
44000	3929.97	2091.85	1482.54	1180.41	1001.14	883.27	800.45	739.52	693.16	656.97	628.15	604.84
45000	4019.28	2139.39	1516.23	1207.24	1023.89	903.34	818.64	756.33	708.92	671.90	642.43	618.59
46000	4108.60	2186.93	1549.93	1234.07	1046.65	923.41	836.84	773.14	724.67	686.83	656.71	632.33
47000	4197.92	2234.47	1583.62	1260.90	1069.40	943.49	855.03	789.95	740.42	701.77	670.98	646.08
48000	4287.23	2282.01	1617.31	1287.72	1092.15	963.56	873.22	806.75	756.18	716.70	685.26	659.83
49000	4376.55	2329.55	1651.01	1314.55	1114.91	983.64	891.41	823.56	771.93	731.63	699.53	673.57
50000	4465.87	2377.10	1684.70	1341.38	1137.66	1003.71	909.60	840.37	787.68	746.56	713.81	687.32
55000	4912.46	2614.81	1853.17	1475.52	1251.42	1104.08	1000.56	924.40	866.45	821.21	785.19	756.05
60000	5359.04	2852.51	2021.64	1609.65	1365.19	1204.45	1091.52	1008.44	945.22	895.87	856.57	824.78
65000	5805.63	3090.22	2190.11	1743.79	1478.95	1304.82	1182.48	1092.48	1023.99	970.52	927.95	893.51
70000	6252.21	3327.93	2358.58	1877.93	1592.72	1405.19	1273.44	1176.51	1102.76	1045.18	999.33	962.24
75000	6698.80	3565.64	2527.05	2012.07	1706.49	1505.56	1364.40	1260.55	1181.52	1119.84	1070.71	1030.97
80000	7145.39	3803.35	2695.52	2146.20	1820.25	1605.93	1455.36	1344.59	1260.29	1194.49	1142.09	1099.71
85000	7591.97	4041.06	2863.99	2280.34	1934.02	1706.30	1546.32	1428.62	1339.06	1269.15	1213.47	1168.44
90000	8038.56	4278.77	3032.46	2414.48	2047.78	1806.67	1637.28	1512.66	1417.83	1343.80	1284.85	1237.17
95000	8485.15	4516.48	3200.93	2548.62	2161.55	1907.05	1728.24	1596.69	1496.60	1418.46	1356.24	1305.90
100000	8931.73	4754.19	3369.40	2682.75	2275.31	2007.42	1819.20	1680.73	1575.36	1493.11	1427.62	1374.63

MONTHLY

13.00%

PAYMENT REQUIRED TO AMORTIZE A LOAN

TERM AMOUNT	13 YEARS	14 YEARS	15 YEARS	16 YEARS	17 YEARS	18 YEARS	19 YEARS	20 YEARS	25 YEARS	30 YEARS	35 YEARS	40 YEARS
50	.67	.65	.64	.62	.61	.61	.60	.59	.57	.56	.55	.55
100	1.34	1.30	1.27	1.24	1.22	1.21	1.19	1.18	1.13	1.11	1.10	1.09
200	2.67	2.60	2.54	2.48	2.44	2.41	2.37	2.35	2.26	2.22	2.20	2.18
300	4.00	3.89	3.80	3.72	3.66	3.61	3.56	3.52	3.39	3.32	3.29	3.27
400	5.33	5.19	5.07	4.96	4.88	4.81	4.74	4.69	4.52	4.43	4.39	4.36
500	6.66	6.48	6.33	6.20	6.10	6.01	5.93	5.86	5.64	5.54	5.48	5.45
600	7.99	7.78	7.60	7.44	7.32	7.21	7.11	7.03	6.77	6.64	6.58	6.54
700	9.32	9.07	8.86	8.68	8.54	8.41	8.30	8.21	7.90	7.75	7.67	7.63
800	10.65	10.37	10.13	9.92	9.75	9.61	9.48	9.38	9.03	8.85	8.77	8.72
900	11.99	11.66	11.39	11.16	10.97	10.81	10.67	10.55	10.16	9.96	9.86	9.81
1000	13.32	12.96	12.66	12.40	12.19	12.01	11.85	11.72	11.28	11.07	10.96	10.90
2000	26.63	25.91	25.31	24.80	24.38	24.01	23.70	23.44	22.56	22.13	21.91	21.80
3000	39.94	38.86	37.96	37.20	36.56	36.02	35.55	35.15	33.84	33.19	32.86	32.69
4000	53.25	51.82	50.61	49.60	48.75	48.02	47.40	46.87	45.12	44.25	43.81	43.59
5000	66.57	64.77	63.27	62.00	60.94	60.03	59.25	58.58	56.40	55.31	54.76	54.48
6000	79.88	77.72	75.92	74.40	73.12	72.03	71.10	70.30	67.68	66.38	65.72	65.38
7000	93.19	90.67	88.57	86.80	85.31	84.04	82.95	82.02	78.95	77.44	76.67	76.27
8000	106.50	103.63	101.22	99.20	97.49	96.04	94.80	93.73	90.23	88.50	87.62	87.17
9000	119.81	116.58	113.88	111.60	109.68	108.04	106.65	105.45	101.51	99.56	98.57	98.06
10000	133.13	129.53	126.53	124.00	121.87	120.05	118.49	117.16	112.79	110.62	109.52	108.96
11000	146.44	142.48	139.18	136.40	134.05	132.05	130.34	128.88	124.07	121.69	120.48	119.85
12000	159.75	155.44	151.83	148.80	146.24	144.06	142.19	140.59	135.35	132.75	131.43	130.75
13000	173.06	168.39	164.49	161.20	158.42	156.06	154.04	152.31	146.62	143.81	142.38	141.64
14000	186.37	181.34	177.14	173.60	170.61	168.07	165.89	164.03	157.90	154.87	153.33	152.54
15000	199.69	194.29	189.79	186.00	182.80	180.07	177.74	175.74	169.18	165.93	164.28	163.43
16000	213.00	207.25	202.44	198.40	194.98	192.07	189.59	187.46	180.46	177.00	175.24	174.33
17000	226.31	220.20	215.10	210.80	207.17	204.08	201.44	199.17	191.74	188.06	186.19	185.22
18000	239.62	233.15	227.75	223.20	219.36	216.08	213.29	210.89	203.02	199.12	197.14	196.12
19000	252.93	246.11	240.40	235.60	231.54	228.09	225.14	222.60	214.29	210.18	208.09	207.01
20000	266.25	259.06	253.05	248.00	243.73	240.09	236.98	234.32	225.57	221.24	219.04	217.91
21000	279.56	272.01	265.71	260.40	255.91	252.10	248.83	246.04	236.85	232.31	230.00	228.80
22000	292.87	284.96	278.36	272.80	268.10	264.10	260.68	257.75	248.13	243.37	240.95	239.70
23000	306.18	297.92	291.01	285.20	280.29	276.10	272.53	269.47	259.41	254.43	251.90	250.59
24000	319.50	310.87	303.66	297.60	292.47	288.11	284.38	281.18	270.69	265.49	262.85	261.49
25000	332.81	323.82	316.32	310.00	304.66	300.11	296.23	292.90	281.96	276.55	273.80	272.38
26000	346.12	336.77	328.97	322.40	316.84	312.12	308.08	304.61	293.24	287.62	284.76	283.28
27000	359.43	349.73	341.62	334.80	329.03	324.12	319.93	316.33	304.52	298.68	295.71	294.17
28000	372.74	362.68	354.27	347.20	341.22	336.13	331.78	328.05	315.80	309.74	306.66	305.07
29000	386.06	375.63	366.93	359.60	353.40	348.13	343.63	339.76	327.08	320.80	317.61	315.96
30000	399.37	388.58	379.58	372.00	365.59	360.13	355.47	351.48	338.36	331.86	328.56	326.86
31000	412.68	401.54	392.23	384.40	377.78	372.14	367.32	363.19	349.63	342.93	339.51	337.75
32000	425.99	414.49	404.88	396.80	389.96	384.14	379.17	374.91	360.91	353.99	350.47	348.65
33000	439.30	427.44	417.53	409.20	402.15	396.15	391.02	386.62	372.19	365.05	361.42	359.54
34000	452.62	440.39	430.19	421.60	414.33	408.15	402.87	398.34	383.47	376.11	372.37	370.44
35000	465.93	453.35	442.84	434.00	426.52	420.16	414.72	410.06	394.75	387.17	383.32	381.33
36000	479.24	466.30	455.49	446.40	438.71	432.16	426.57	421.77	406.03	398.24	394.27	392.23
37000	492.55	479.25	468.14	458.80	450.89	444.17	438.42	433.49	417.30	409.30	405.23	403.13
38000	505.86	492.21	480.80	471.20	463.08	456.17	450.27	445.20	428.58	420.36	416.18	414.02
39000	519.18	505.16	493.45	483.60	475.26	468.17	462.12	456.92	439.86	431.42	427.13	424.92
40000	532.49	518.11	506.10	496.00	487.45	480.18	473.96	468.64	451.14	442.48	438.08	435.81
41000	545.80	531.06	518.75	508.40	499.64	492.18	485.81	480.35	462.42	453.55	449.03	446.71
42000	559.11	544.02	531.41	520.80	511.82	504.19	497.66	492.07	473.70	464.61	459.99	457.60
43000	572.43	556.97	544.06	533.20	524.01	516.19	509.51	503.78	484.97	475.67	470.94	468.50
44000	585.74	569.92	556.71	545.60	536.20	528.20	521.36	515.50	496.25	486.73	481.89	479.39
45000	599.05	582.87	569.36	558.00	548.38	540.20	533.21	527.21	507.53	497.79	492.84	490.29
46000	612.36	595.83	582.02	570.40	560.57	552.20	545.06	538.93	518.81	508.86	503.79	501.18
47000	625.67	608.78	594.67	582.80	572.75	564.21	556.91	550.65	530.09	519.92	514.75	512.08
48000	638.99	621.73	607.32	595.20	584.94	576.21	568.76	562.36	541.37	530.98	525.70	522.97
49000	652.30	634.68	619.97	607.60	597.13	588.22	580.61	574.08	552.64	542.04	536.65	533.87
50000	665.61	647.64	632.63	620.00	609.31	600.22	592.45	585.79	563.92	553.10	547.60	544.76
55000	732.17	712.40	695.89	682.00	670.24	660.24	651.70	644.37	620.31	608.41	602.36	599.24
60000	798.73	777.16	759.15	744.00	731.17	720.26	710.94	702.95	676.71	663.72	657.12	653.71
65000	865.29	841.93	822.41	806.00	792.10	780.29	770.19	761.53	733.10	719.03	711.88	708.19
70000	931.85	906.69	885.67	868.00	853.04	840.31	829.43	820.11	789.49	774.34	766.64	762.66
75000	998.41	971.45	948.94	930.00	913.97	900.33	888.68	878.69	845.88	829.65	821.40	817.14
80000	1064.97	1036.22	1012.20	992.00	974.90	960.35	947.92	937.27	902.27	884.96	876.16	871.62
85000	1131.53	1100.98	1075.46	1053.99	1035.83	1020.37	1007.17	995.84	958.67	940.27	930.92	926.09
90000	1198.09	1165.74	1138.72	1115.99	1096.76	1080.39	1066.41	1054.42	1015.06	995.58	985.68	980.57
95000	1264.65	1230.51	1201.99	1177.99	1157.69	1140.42	1125.66	1113.00	1071.45	1050.89	1040.44	1035.04
100000	1331.22	1295.27	1265.25	1239.99	1218.62	1200.44	1184.90	1171.58	1127.84	1106.20	1095.20	1089.52